*"There is a place within a woman*
*No man has ever known.*
*A place touched only by God*
*and a few brave souls*
*with healing hands*
*and prayerful hearts*
*who dare to journey with her.*
*They weep with her*
*and rock her gently*
*leading her back to herself . . ."*

—*Kathleen*

# FORBIDDEN GRIEF

## The Unspoken Pain of Abortion

# FORBIDDEN GRIEF

## The Unspoken Pain of Abortion

Theresa Burke, Ph.D.
with David C. Reardon, Ph.D.

Foreword by
Dr. Laura Schlessinger

**Acorn Books**
Springfield, IL

**Forbidden Grief: The Unspoken Pain of Abortion**

Published by Acorn Books, P.O. Box 7348, Springfield, IL 62791-7348.
Cover Photography by Robert Ervin Photography

Portions of this book have been adapted from these previous works by the authors:
    Theresa Karminski Burke, Ph.D. "A Daughter's Grief and a Family's Burden," *The Post-Abortion Review* 5(2):1-3 (1997).
    Theresa Karminski Burke, Ph.D. "When the Doll Breaks," *The Post-Abortion Review* 6(1):1-2 (1998).
    Theresa Karminski Burke, Ph.D. & David C. Reardon, Ph.D. "Abortion Trauma and Child Abuse," *The Post-Abortion Review* 6(1):3-4 (1998).
    David C. Reardon, Ph.D. "Psychological Reactions Reported After Abortion," *The Post-Abortion Review* 2(3):4-8 (1994).

**Publisher's Cataloging-in-Publication Data**
Theresa Karminski Burke, Ph.D. and David C. Reardon, Ph.D.
Forbidden grief: the unspoken pain of abortion / Theresa Karminski Burke and David C. Reardon
            p.      cm.
            Includes bibliographical references and index.
            ISBN 0-9648957-8-1 (hardcover)
            1. Abortion—United States.
            2. Abortion—United States—Psychological aspects.
            3. Abortion—Complications.
            4. Abortion—Counseling.
            I. Title.
            HQ767.5  2001        363.4'6
            Library of Congress Control Number: 2001135181

*Dedicated to the memory of my beloved father,*
*Stanley J. Karminski,*
*who taught me how a woman should be treated,*
*with respect, dignity, and the highest esteem,*
*made authentic through his gentle love.*

# CONTENTS

ACKNOWLEDGMENTS                                                          xi

FOREWORD                    Dr. Laura Schlessinger                       xii

INTRODUCTION                                                             xv

CHAPTER ONE                 Gina's Story                                 23

CHAPTER TWO                 Hiding the Truth                             31

CHAPTER THREE               Forbidding the Grief                        49

CHAPTER FOUR                A Time to Grieve, A Time to Heal            63

CHAPTER FIVE                Maternal Confusion                          69

CHAPTER SIX                 Mind Games: The Use and Misuse of          81
                            Defense Mechanisms

CHAPTER SEVEN               Connections to the Past                     93

CHAPTER EIGHT               Abortion as a Traumatic Experience         105

CHAPTER NINE                Memories Unleashed                         121

CHAPTER TEN                 Reenacting Trauma                          133

CHAPTER ELEVEN              Repeat Abortions                           145

CHAPTER TWELVE              Sexual Abuse and Abortion                  157

CHAPTER THIRTEEN            Something Inside Has Died: Booze,          167
                            Drugs, Sex, and Suicide

CHAPTER FOURTEEN            Broken Babies                              179

CHAPTER FIFTEEN      *What's Eating You? Abortion And Eating Disorders*      **187**

CHAPTER SIXTEEN      *Paradise Lost: Abortion and Ruined Relationships*      **201**

CHAPTER SEVENTEEN      *No Choice, Hard Choice, Wrong Choice*      **221**

CHAPTER EIGHTEEN      *The Labor of Grief and Birth of Freedom*      **245**

APPENDIX A      *The Politics of Trauma*      **267**

APPENDIX B      *The Complexity and Distortions of Post-Abortion Research*      **277**

APPENDIX C      *The Elliot Institute Survey: Psychological Reactions Reported After Abortion*      **287**

APPENDIX D      *Resources*      **301**

BIBLIOGRAPHY      **307**

NOTES      **311**

INDEX      **325**

# ACKNOWLEDGMENTS

To my best friend and husband, Kevin—words could never adequately express my deepest appreciation for the gift that you have been in my life. This book would never be a reality without your loving support and the nurturing of my spirit. To my children, Kevin, Katie, Aleena, Steven, and Stanley—thank you for the humor and fun you bring, helping me to balance my work with a sense of joy.

To my mother, Margie Karminski—for your strength, love and nurturance, cultivating my life out of selfless love. And my wonderful sisters—Katie D'Annunzio, for your unending help with computer problems, taxes, and the countless other details that needed attention, and Maggie Neves. My brothers Jack and Stan and my grandmother Bobchi—for your simplicity and positive outlook.

I would like to thank Dr. David Reardon for his contributions to this work as an editor, publisher and researcher. His tireless passion for this subject and dedication to the field through his work at the Elliot Institute have always been an inspiration to me, both professionally and personally. Dr. Reardon has served as a personal advisor who shares his expertise freely and openly. He has been a trusted mentor who has fostered immeasurable encouragement to rewrite and rewrite, while providing enthusiasm and vision. He helped synthesize a mountain of material into a readable flow through his superb editing and organizational skills—for this, I am profoundly appreciative.

Thanks to my special friends who have provided immense encouragement and companionship: Barbara Cullen, Gerri Simboli, Mary Beth Arechabala, Lucy Hoy, Rosemary and Danny Heim, Mary Alice and Joe Schonberger, Julie Schomp, Kari Curtin, Donna Huttenlock, Donna Augustine, Rose Rossi, Lisa Ann McGeady, Uncle John Walsh, Chuck and June Piola and Paul and Judie Brown. In gratitude to Linda Milligan and Cheryl Karminski for assistance with typing, and especially to Mitch Harbison, Judy Rogers, Amy Sobie, Kim Emmert, Michael Tirpak, and Anita Kuhn for their many hours of proofreading. My thanks to Bob Ervin, Mark Romesser, Linda Ulrich, and Chris Camp for their extraordinary help with the cover.

And most important, I am grateful to those who have entrusted themselves to me while sharing their deepest and most complex emotions. Your brutal honesty, grief, and pain have inspired me to venture into the innermost chambers of the damaged human spirit with the quest to discover a profound eternal transformation. Each and every one of you is an incredible person—courageous, strong, and passionate, full of hope and love. You have been relentlessly earnest in your search for healing.

With profound gratitude, I treasure you—for allowing me the great privilege to accompany you on the journey to find life, liberation and truth. I appreciate the many who have contributed their personal diaries, letters, and intimate revelations. And special appreciation goes to the many group members who have exposed their souls in Rachel's Vineyard—for your sisterhood, friendship, and love.

# FOREWORD
## Dr. Laura Schlessinger

L et me see . . . didn't I read some feminist psychologist's report stating that there were no emotional or psychological side-effects of abortion? Wait, no, that wasn't it—it was that the only women who grieved or suffered post-abortion trauma already had serious emotional problems. The study's conclusion was that only disturbed women had abortion angst. Normal, well-adjusted women, it was suggested, just sailed along without grief or pain.

That's not the message I've heard from women who have called into my radio program over the last quarter-century. Women, young and old, have called me about their guilt, hurt, regret and anger over exercising a "reproductive right" that was supposed to be liberating. They have mourned over "a bunch of cells"; they have grieved over a "procedure"; they have felt shame over a "constitutional right"; they have agonized over their "women's rights"; and they have felt remorse and regret over a "women's health issue."

In other words, millions of women have suffered over their decisions to have abortions. But the politically correct feminist climate in America does not allow such revelations to go unpunished. Women who dissent from the feminist pro-abortion position are castigated as having a pre-existing mental condition or falling victim to radical religiosity. The "sisterhood" has no sympathy for the painful truth that abortion is a tragic, traumatic act that leaves lifelong scars on women's lives, some of which are not apparent for quite a long while.

*Forbidden Grief* is a strong, thoughtful, and compassionate revelation that eliminating a life within the womb diminishes the value of life for all humanity and impacts the life of the woman in ways she cannot anticipate.

I've had women call my radio program who feel as though they aren't entitled to happiness because ten or 15 years ago, they had an abortion to "get out of a jam." Other women have expressed being afraid to let their children out of their sight, because they are fearful that something awful will happen to their child as cosmic payback for the child they terminated. Many women have believed that they were irretrievably bad and unworthy of love from the wonderful men in their lives who didn't know their dark secret. Some women have told me about their nightmares and flashbacks, which are sometimes so severe that they find it difficult to relax or get any pleasure out of life.

All of these women regret their abortions. The women's movement has not only abandoned these women who regret their "choice," it disdains and dismisses them—and in so doing, insults them again.

One woman was brave enough to come on my program to ask me about admitting to her adolescent daughters that she had had an abortion before her marriage to their dad. I worried aloud about the impact of that information on her young daughters' feelings about her, as well as about some permission that they might give themselves to be sexually active, with the abortion fall-back. I asked her why she wanted to involve them in her personal struggles.

"Because I am repenting," she said. "I know that taking responsibility and having remorse aren't enough. I want to repair what I've done. I know I can't go back and change history, but I want to take that pain, my hurt, and teach young girls that what they are being 'sold' is a travesty. It isn't just a 'procedure.' It's not just an 'event.' It's a life-altering action. I want to save them from pain and their babies from death."

We later had a follow-up conversation, and I learned that, as I had anticipated, her girls were at first stunned and angry. But after having time to process their mother's revelation, they told her they were very proud that she was trying to save not only babies, but also the psyches of the young women who know not what they'll reap emotionally.

I was proud of her, too.

And I am personally and professionally grateful for *Forbidden Grief* because I now have a specific resource to recommend to women suffering from the very human, decent reaction to abortion—grief—and a way to help them heal.

**Laura C. Schlessinger, Ph.D.**
Internationally syndicated talk show host and author

*The Ten Commandments* (HarperCollins)
*Stupid Things Women Do to Mess Up Their Lives* (HarperCollins)

# INTRODUCTION

As a young graduate student, I was assigned to lead a weekly support group for women with eating disorders. It was there that I first observed how abortion is a *forbidden grief*.

It all began with Debbie. She cautiously and fearfully confided to the group that she was having flashbacks to an abortion that had happened several years earlier. She was also having recurring nightmares involving a baby.

These intrusive memories were bad enough. Her anxiety was made worse, however, by her ex-husband. He would phone and leave messages on her answering machine, calling her a "murderer," describing the abortion in vivid and horrifying detail. Debbie found this extremely disturbing not only for herself but for her three children, who would often hear the incoming message.

After these phone calls Debbie would become quite agitated. On numerous occasions she became suicidal and engaged in borderline cutting behaviors. She repeatedly cut her wrists with a razor blade and often ended up in the emergency room of the local hospital.

Debbie had always struggled with weight issues, but her eating disorder became full-blown after the abortion. She was severely anorexic. Her story sparked a series of confessions within the group.

Beth Ann said she knew how Debbie felt because she, too, had undergone an abortion. "It would kill me if someone kept reminding me about it. It's something I try to forget about. Your husband is a horrible man," Beth Ann said with contempt.

Diane immediately jumped in with an irritated hiss. "---- him! We have a right to control our bodies and decide if we want their ------ interfering with our bodies. To hell with him!"

The other women were silent.

"Diane, you seem quite angry," I observed. "Has anyone hurt you like that?"

Diane dismissed the idea with explicit certainty. "Nobody hurts me!" she stated. "Especially men! That's why I had my abortion, so the ------ couldn't screw with me and mess up my life. And you know what? It was the best thing I ever did. Taking control of your life is nothing to feel guilty over and ---- anyone who tries to tell me to feel otherwise. ---- them all!"

At that moment, Judith, obviously very upset, got up and left the room.

As Judith closed the door, Sarah, normally quiet and reserved, politely asked Diane to watch her mouth. She told her that her relentless use of the f-word was probably offensive to some and it showed a lack of class.

Diane quickly retorted, "---- you, ya prude! You guys are all a bunch of ------ prigs."

I began to feel quite inadequate and wondered how to proceed with the meeting, which at that moment felt like a battleship rapidly sinking in the sea as a volley of torpedoes struck its hull.

Week after week we had discussed very emotional issues: mothers, fathers, problem relationships, family dynamics, dependency, divorce, self-esteem, stress, assertiveness, sexual conflicts, lesbianism, depression, and a gamut of other anxiety-producing issues. But never had I seen a subject create such severe hostility, fear, and pain among the members of our group. The meeting was becoming as volatile as an erupting volcano as the group members began to vent their toxic feelings through verbal attacks on each other. I just wanted the meeting to end. I couldn't wait to get home.

Suddenly, Lasheera, who usually just sat back and observed the others, chimed in. "Calm down! Everybody chill!" The white around her dark eyes flashed out from a black complexion like shimmering rays of light, signaling a cease-fire. "Do you like my new sweater?" she asked with sincere curiosity.

We ended the meeting early that night.

When I got home, I called Judith, who had walked out of the meeting, to make sure she was okay. Judith said she was sorry for leaving so abruptly, but then added, "I hate the subject of abortion and wish that we could focus on eating disorders instead."

I asked her if she, too, had experienced an abortion. After a prolonged silence, she murmured, "It was a long time ago. I really don't want to talk about it."

The events of that evening weighed on my mind for the entire week. Our group discussion had not even remotely helped any of these women to address their tremendous anxiety about their past abortions. We had only scratched the surface.

Six out of the eight women in our group had undergone abortions. The other two had been sexually molested as children. The common denominator in their histories was a traumatic event, abortion or sexual molestation, which some were not even able to verbalize.

If their feelings about their abortions were that powerful, I wanted to know more about them. Unexpressed emotions are key issues in the treatment of eating disorders. Because women with eating disorders are overwhelmingly concerned with image and pleasing others, they often deny and repress their real feelings. This is accomplished by binding their emotions and anxieties up in ritual behaviors. Their eating disorders are a battle over food, which is really a surrogate enemy, a symbol of negative feelings like grief, tension, anger, frustration, boredom, and fear. In this sense, an eating disorder can serve to distract a person from other problems that he or she cannot confront. I knew it was quite reasonable to suspect that abortion trauma could be disguised through eating disorders. As Sarah later explained:

> I am never hungry when I binge . . . I eat because I am full. Full of anger, hurt, sadness, and loneliness. I throw up because that is the way I empty myself of those feelings.

Getting in touch with such feelings is fundamental to recovery. However, this can be a tricky process because any discussion of these unwanted emotions generates tremendous resistance, denial, and fear.

The issue of abortion was clearly a threatening topic for our group. Those who could speak about it could only do so by angrily blaming others. In subsequent discussions, all six women indicated that their abortions were perhaps the most difficult decisions they had ever made. At the same time, however, they denied that their abortions had any significant effect on their lives. This "no big deal" claim, however, was in striking contrast to the intense emotions and avoidance behavior that I had observed. Clearly, a lot of unexplored and unresolved feelings were being denied, repressed, or suppressed.

Unfortunately, however, I was not permitted at that time to delve more deeply into my group's obvious difficulties with past abortions. When I shared my assessment with my supervisor, a psychiatrist, he became irritated and defensive. He emphatically told me that I had no business prying into people's abortions. I pointed out that it was Debbie who had raised the issue because of her flashbacks. He insisted that Debbie's flashbacks were a psychotic reaction caused by a medication she was taking. I questioned this and pointed out that her abortion had been a very traumatic experience and her flashbacks sounded more like post-traumatic stress disorder. When I suggested it might be helpful for her to talk about it, the psychiatrist looked me straight in the eye and said, "This is a support group for eating disorders . . . not abortion." He firmly instructed me not to bring up the subject again.

Despite the discouraging comments of my supervisor, this experience sparked my interest in treating post-abortion grief and trauma. In the years since, I have worked with well over two thousand women who have struggled with post-abortion issues and have taught scores of therapists around the country how to treat post-abortion issues.

At the time I began this work, there were very few resources available to help therapists, much less the general public, understand the painful and confusing processes of grief which may follow an abortion. As a result, many women and men suffer in silence, in complete numbness, or with the frightening and bewildering feeling that they are going crazy. Grief following an abortion can be extremely complicated and can be experienced on all levels of the personality. For many women, the source of their distress may go unrecognized, unspoken, and unnamed.

The symptoms I and others have observed vary widely between individuals. The bulk of this book will examine many of these symptoms in greater detail. Despite the diversity of emotional and behavioral reactions, however, these symptoms are all rooted in the experience of abortion. For many, it is primarily an issue of unresolved grief. For many other women, it is a traumatic event which has disordered their coping skills and distorted their lives and behavior in dramatic and even bizarre ways.

As I look back at this incident with my group, I can now see how this cast of characters is representative of our society at large. They show us why our culture is woefully unprepared to voice, accept, or even respect post-abortion grief. All of the characters in this mini-drama represent reasons why post-abortion healing is made more difficult than it needs to be.

First, there was Debbie. She bravely tried to share her feelings, but quickly saw that this just upset everyone. She ended up apologizing and feeling guilty because she had disrupted the group's harmony. Sadly, she learned the lesson that friends, families, and therapists often teach those who try to share their emotions about a past abortion: "You're making us uncomfortable. Just stop thinking about it and get on with your life." Society doesn't want to hear about it.

Second, there was Judith. She felt compelled to run away from the discussion. The abortion issue simply struck too close to a secret pain that she didn't want to think or talk about. The problem with this approach was that it required her to expend great amounts of energy trying not to think about it. Despite her efforts to avoid the topic, her pent-up emotions were distorting other aspects of her life.

Third, there was Diane. She was the polar opposite of the withdrawn Judith. She was filled with such rage toward anyone and everyone who had hurt her that she could only feel disgust for those who did not share her rage. Diane's anger was so consuming that she had no time to offer sympathy to others who were also hurting. She barely had time to notice Debbie's personal grief because the mention of abortion had triggered in her an overpowering need to vent her own feelings of anger and blame.

Fourth, there was Lasheera, who graciously and skillfully changed the subject to something quite superficial—her new sweater. She represents those who seek peace through distraction. A temporary calm was restored, but fundamental issues were left unresolved to raise their heads again some other day. Denial was given another opportunity to reestablish itself.

Fifth, there was Debbie's ex-husband. He was unforgiving and emotionally abusive. His condemning and vicious remarks, coupled with her own grief, drove Debbie to despair and suicidal behaviors. Rather than helping her to heal, he fixated on reminding Debbie what a "bad" person she was. He reinforced her fear that she would never be understood or forgiven by others.

Sixth, there was my supervisor. He represents thousands of professional therapists who will compassionately listen to any personal problem—except abortion. Such therapists are always sure that the problem must really be something else, even if the woman insists that the abortion *is* the problem. Their view is that abortion helps women, period.

Seventh, there was me. I wanted to help, but I didn't know how. My heart was in the right place, but the issues were complex, my experience was limited, and I was denied any support from the "powers that be."

These seven characters offer a rough sketch of our society at large. We are either (1) struggling with this forbidden grief, (2) reinforcing the social rules that forbid expression of this grief, or (3) trying to create a more open and healing environment for those women and men who do struggle with post-abortion issues.

If you fit into any of these three categories, this book is for you.

Whatever your political or moral beliefs about abortion, I hope that you can approach this book with an open mind and a compassionate heart. Try to appreciate the diversity of post-abortion responses. Every woman is different. Abortion touches a person's life on many levels. It impacts one's views of oneself in medical, political, religious, philosophical, social, and familial ways. Because it affects one's life in so many dimensions, it is a very complex experience. This is why it is exceptionally difficult for people to understand, process, and reconcile this experience with who they are and who they want to be.

If you're an advocate of abortion rights, it may be painful to hear how abortion has scarred and injured some women. You may feel the impulse to reject the truth of these cases out of fear that such information could threaten the legal status of abortion or inappropriately discourage women from making the "right choice" to abort. I ask you, however, to set aside your political and ideological goals, at least for the moment. Read about the real experiences of the women in this book. Don't reject their experiences simply because they do not fit your vision of women who are liberated and empowered by abortion.

Abortion is not a panacea. The fact that it has caused so much division and anxiety in our country's political life clearly suggests that it can also cause internal divisions and anxiety in an individual's life. How can it  possibly be a perfect solution for *all* women in *all* situations?

Many—perhaps even most—women choose abortion not according to their conscience, but in violation of their conscience. Various studies have found that 65 to 70 percent of women seeking abortions have a negative moral view of abortion.[1] This evidence is supported by a national random poll conducted by the *Los Angeles Times,* which found that 74 percent of those admitting a past abortion stated that while they believed women should be able to choose for themselves, they personally believed that abortion "is morally wrong."[2]

Many of the women I have treated knowingly violated their conscience or betrayed their maternal desires because of the pressures they faced. Those pressures were many: abandonment by their partner, poverty, homelessness, violence, lack of education, unemployment, emotional problems, incest, rape, and fetal abnormalities, to name just a few. Many women felt they had "no choice" but to submit to an unwanted abortion.

Some of these women faced immediate feelings of regret and grief. Others stoically denied their feelings for years or even decades, until finally they could no longer avoid the need to understand what they did in the context of who they want to be.

At the other end of the spectrum, I have also counseled women who, at the time of their abortions, had no moral qualms about their choice. It was an easy decision, in accord with all of their beliefs. But even this was no guarantee of future satisfaction with their choice. These women sought me out because some later event in their lives suddenly raised unexpected feelings of confusion or grief.

Are all women emotionally hurt by abortion?  Is it only a matter of time before their abortions come back to haunt them? Many critics of abortion believe so, but that is a broad generalization that can never be proved or disproved. All I can say with certainty is that many women and men are severely hurt, emotionally and psychologically, by their experience with abortion.

This problem is made even more tragic by the fact that so many have no one to turn to who can help them work through their grief. Many feel isolated and totally alone in their feelings. They are trapped in the mistaken belief that no one can understand their feelings.

One of the reasons I wrote this book is simply to validate the experience of these millions of women and men. My hope is that *Forbidden Grief* will provide both insight into post-abortion reactions and an explanation of the symptoms that may develop when mourning is inhibited and feelings are repressed.

All the cases described in this book are true. While each woman's recovery is not described, all of these women experienced elimination or significant reduction of the problems for which they sought counseling. This was accomplished because I understood the complexities of their abortion experience and provided them with a non-judgmental environment in which they could explore their experience, and because I honored their need to grieve and to understand what they experienced. Their healing is evidence that their post-abortion problems were properly diagnosed, which is also an indication that their presenting problems were truly related to their abortions.

To preserve patient confidentiality, all the names of my clients and their family members have been changed.

# CHAPTER ONE

# GINA'S STORY

"I was hoping you could help my daughter. She needs counseling. Somebody objective. God certainly knows I'm not." Mr. Davis's voice trailed off as if in regretful thought.

"What's the problem?" I asked, shifting the telephone receiver to my shoulder so I could jot down a few notes.

"Well," he stammered, "my daughter, Gina, is dating this guy. He's verbally and physically abusive. He's ruining her life."

Mr. Davis sounded desperate. In his voice I could detect anger and hurt but worst of all helplessness. "I can't just sit back and watch my daughter ruin her life. This guy already has another kid he can't support. I don't know what she sees in him. My Gina—she's a great girl."

His tone changed to a hushed whisper. "I love her so much but I'm losing her." He was silent for a moment, then his voice cracked, "Please, can you do something? Can you help her see what a creep he is? Gina won't listen to me anymore."

I informed Mr. Davis that I couldn't break them up, but I could help Gina examine her relationship and sort out her feelings about this man. Then I asked Mr. Davis if anything else had happened between Gina and her boyfriend.

The question itself was a threat. Mr. Davis hesitated. Finally he answered, "Well, there is something, but it should really come from her. I think she should be the one to tell you. After all, it's her life, and I don't want her to think I was talking behind her back."

"Did your daughter have an abortion?" I asked in a matter-of-fact tone. The word was said. Abortion. There was silence, as is almost always the case. I had a telephone listing for "The Center for Post-Abortion Healing," yet still people would often struggle to explain why they were calling.

I met his daughter that night. Gina was 19, with long blond hair and sad blue eyes. "My dad made me have it," she explained. "He told me I couldn't live with them if I didn't. He knew it might make me hate him, but he was willing to take that risk. I'd get over it, he said. I was not raised to believe in abortion. In high school I even wrote a paper on it." Her eyes welled with tears, shining like brilliant sapphires.

For three years Gina had never told anyone about the abortion; within a few moments, the memory surfaced like a tidal wave of grief. The surges of the experience came crashing against the fortress of my therapeutic composure as I attempted to steady her for the next gush of emotion.

Gina's story came out between distressing sobs and gasps for air. "I came home from college on a Friday to tell them about the pregnancy and what we were planning to do. . . . My dad hit the roof. He wanted to know what he ever did to deserve this. Dad took my boyfriend into the kitchen to have a man-to-man talk. They would not let me in. Dad tried to pressure him to convince me that abortion was the best thing."

With much difficulty, she continued. "Two days later I was up on a table, my feet in stirrups. . . . I cried the whole way there. . . . My mom took me. . . . I kept telling her I did not want this. . . . 'Please, no! Don't make me do this, don't make me do this. . . .' I said it the whole way there. . . . No one listened. When a counselor asked me if I was sure, I shrugged my shoulders. . . . I could hardly speak. They did it. . . . They killed my baby."

Overcome with heartache, Gina began to moan. Bent over, holding her womb, she couldn't believe she had actually had an abortion. After a long, tearful pause, she continued, "Just as quickly as it had happened, everyone seemed to forget about it. My parents never talked about it. They were furious when they found out that I was still seeing Joe. They never let up on their negative comments about him. Things were not so good between Joe and me either. We were always fighting. I was so depressed and did not know how to handle my feelings. I was too ashamed to talk about the abortion with my friends, and my parents made me promise not to tell anyone."

As her story unraveled, I saw many signals of complicated mourning. Anger and hurt filled Gina's heart. There was grief, too— tremendous grief—over a dead baby who would never be there to offer joy and hope. Anything related to babies made her cry: baby showers, diaper commercials, even children. Everything triggered relentless heartache. There was a wound in her soul that would not stop bleeding.

Though Gina's family had been nominally Christian, religious faith did not hinder their desire for an abortion. Her parents had believed that by insisting on abortion they would save her from a life of poverty and tribulation with a man they did not believe could love or support their precious daughter. Joe already had a child whom he was not supporting. They feared for her future with such a man.

Now the future was here. Her self-esteem crumbled, depression was a constant companion, and her parents watched sadly as a negative transformation robbed them of the daughter they knew.

Gina joined our support group and also came for individual therapy. Once in treatment for post-abortion trauma, she became able to express some of her feelings. She was enraged at her parents for not being able to accept her pregnancy. They just wanted to get rid of the problem. She also felt angry at Joe for not protecting her and the baby. But since it was *her own parents* who wanted the abortion, Joe put the blame back on Gina.

Gina had been in deep psychic pain. Caught between loyalties— toward her parents, Joe, and her unborn child—Gina was immobilized and unable to process her own feelings about the event. In a developmental sense she was stuck. She had not been given permission to grow up, have a baby, and become a mother. Her desire for independence and adulthood had been frustrated by her unsuccessful attempt to break her emotional reliance on her parents, who had always been so vital in her life. When she aborted her child, her embryonic womanhood had been aborted too. The result of the abortion was that she had become emotionally immobilized and uncertain. The loss of her child was an unprecedented assault on her sense of identity. Because she could not carry out the role of a protective mother, she felt an extraordinary sense of failure. In a state of severe depression, Gina was incapable of making decisions, powerless to assert herself, and unable to love.

Despite Joe's abusive behavior, Gina clung to him. His mistreatment confirmed her low self-esteem and sense of powerlessness. Moreover, she knew her parents hated him. By forcing her parents to accept Joe, she was unconsciously lashing back—echoing the way they had forced her to accept an unwanted abortion. This dynamic gave her a sense of control, yet Gina was trapped in a vicious cycle in which she was punishing both herself and her father.

Perhaps most important, Joe signified her connection to their aborted baby. Gina feared that giving him up would destroy the only bond remaining to the child she still needed to grieve.

Once Gina was in treatment for post-abortion trauma, she was able to express these feelings. It was important for both her sake and that of her family that her parents enter into the therapy process with her. She needed them to validate her loss and accept their responsibility for contributing to her emotional devastation. Without this recognition, their relationship could never be fully healed.

In entering into this family counseling situation, I knew both parents would attempt to justify and defend their actions as they struggled with their daughter's experience. This resistance or inability to confront and admit emotional or spiritual pain is called denial. In this phase of treatment, denial is a powerful temptation.

Gina's mom came first. She listened to her daughter and expressed sorrow. I watched a pained expression come over the woman's face, which persisted along with the inevitable excuses: "I know you are hurting, but we thought we were doing the best thing. . . . I realize this is hard, but you must get on with your life. . . . You wanted the baby, but how would you ever pay for it? How would you finish school?"

"But, but, but. . . ." The list goes on and on like dirty laundry—never ending, never finished. Each exception robbed Gina of the gift of fully acknowledging her loss. The suspended feelings were then buried, becoming depression, anxiety, and self-punishment.

Gina needed permission to grieve. Her parents had deprived her of the genuine compassion and acceptance she needed from them. They had not accepted the pregnancy, and now they could not even accept her grief. She felt utterly rejected by them.

## FATHER KNOWS BEST?

Gina's father had no idea what she had sacrificed in order to please him. The night before our meeting, he called me.

"My stomach has been upset all week since I heard about this meeting," he said. "I want to do what is best for Gina."

Then his tone became more formal and forceful: "I just want you to know that this is NOT a moral issue to me. Gina had to have that abortion! I still think we made the right decision. If I had it to do again, I would choose the same thing. I know this is not what she wants to hear. Should I lie about it to make her feel better? Is that what I should do? Tell her I made a mistake? I cannot do that!"

With renewed determination, I explained, "Mr. Davis, I know you love your daughter very much. I know that she loves you or she never would have consented to have an abortion. But the fact remains that your daughter lost something. What she lost was a child. Her baby—your grandchild. Gina thinks about it every day. She cries about it every night. The event is far from over for her. You need to hear how the abortion has affected her."

Mr. Davis did not respond. With conviction, I continued, "When someone dies, the worst thing another can say is 'it was for the best; it's better this way.' This does nothing to comfort and console; it only makes the person angry because you are not appreciating his loss or grief. Worse for Gina is that you don't recognize the life that she is missing. Gina misses her baby, a child you have not been able to acknowledge."

Eventually, Mr. Davis agreed that he would try to listen and that maybe he had something to learn. I really couldn't hope for more than that.

"Men are not prone to emotional mushiness," he reminded me. He honestly wished he could feel sorrow and compassion over the baby, but he could not. Nevertheless, he would listen if it would help his daughter.

## LISTENING AND TAKING RESPONSIBILITY

When Mr. Davis came in the next morning, he opened with a surprising statement. "I had no right to make that choice," he said. After wrestling with various points in our conversation all night, he admitted that for the first time he realized that abortion was not Gina's choice.

The session began and it was very intense. Gina expressed her anger, hurt, and feelings of rejection. She also shared her grief about the aborted baby.

Mr. Davis began to face some things for the first time. He was finally able to consider the baby and to separate Joe from the pregnancy. Abortion was a way to scrape out any symptom of his daughter's sexual activity and "heroically" free her from the consequences of her own actions. He began to realize that his daughter was a woman now, one he should not have tried to control. He needed to trust Gina to be capable of making her own decisions without the threat of abandonment.

As these interpretations became clear to Mr. Davis, denial could no longer sustain its powerful grip. Suddenly, grief came upon him. He stared in disbelief, as if a light had abruptly cast shocking rays into a blackened room.

His voice broke with anguish. "Oh, my baby, my sweet baby, my Gina," he cried. "I am so sorry. I was so wrong." He pressed his face against her cheek, and the tears finally came. His tears mingled with Gina's as they both wept. Gina put her arms around him. They embraced tightly as her father gently stroked her long hair. All the anger, the bitterness, the pent-up emotions, the grief, gave way. They sobbed in each other's arms. He begged for her forgiveness. Between tears and tissues, he told Gina she would have been an incredible mother. In one beautiful moment, her motherhood had been validated, and Gina cried with relief.

In a subsequent joint session with her parents, Gina took personal responsibility for having allowed the abortion to occur and asked her parents to do the same. This time, her parents listened without defending or rationalizing what had happened.

Therapy helped Gina's parents to understand the grave mistake they had made in forcing Gina to choose between them and her baby. I encouraged them not to make her choose again between them and Joe. In bitterness and grief, Gina might permit another type of abortion: a termination of her role as their daughter.

By acknowledging Gina's grief, and sharing it with her, Mr. and Mrs. Davis restored their relationship with their daughter. Gina's loving and happy personality was eventually able to bloom once more. She could continue forward in her journey toward becoming a confident and capable adult. With the support of therapeutic intervention, she found that she was able to identify her own needs—like the desire to break up with Joe—and to attain her own goals.

## A Family That Mirrors Society

Gina's story illustrates how complex abortion, and the decision to abort, truly is. It involves issues of family relationships, self-identity, morality, and psychological and physical well-being.

When Gina's parents were pushing for the abortion, they honestly believed that the abortion would benefit her life. They could not have imagined the psychological toll it would exact upon either their daughter or their family. Even after Gina began having her emotional problems, they could not understand or empathize with her trauma.

The same is true of most families who pressure or encourage their loved ones to abort. It is all too easy to imagine that abortion is a "quick fix" that will "turn back the clock" and allow a woman's life to go back and be the same as it was before. But this is a very superficial view. Once a woman is pregnant, the choice is not simply between (1) having a baby and (2) not having a baby. The choice is between (1) having a baby and (2) having the experience of an abortion. Both are life-changing experiences. Both have significant psychological consequences, either contributing to or hindering a person's mental health.

Defenders of abortion have often tried to sidestep the question of abortion's psychological risks by arguing that having an "unwanted" baby is even more "traumatic" than having an abortion. This argument, however, is always raised in the context of dismissing evidence regarding post-abortion trauma. It is never accompanied by research citations showing that women who give birth suffer more psychological injury than women who have abortions, because no such studies exist. Instead, this argument is an unsupported assertion that is really an attempt to shift attention away from the real issue at hand: the fact that abortion does have significant psychological consequences. While it is fitting to compare the psychological experiences of having a child and having an abortion, very little research has been done to make this comparison. All we have at present are people's assertions.

In addition, even if it were proven that giving birth to an "unwanted child" is more psychologically damaging than experiencing a traumatic abortion, this does not change the fact that women and their families should still be told the mental health risks of abortion. For many women, abortion is the most deeply traumatic and emotionally painful experience of their lives. They have a right to know that this is a possibility. But in practice, women and the friends and family members advising them are not being given an accurate picture of the possible negative effects of abortion and their risk of suffering from these effects.

Everyone knows, at least to some degree, what the burdens of being a parent involve. This is public knowledge. It is also public knowledge (supported by all the scientific research on this subject) that most women will quickly come to love and treasure an unplanned child. They and their family members will relish the many pleasures and benefits that offset the corresponding burdens of parenthood and the disruptions of personal goals.

In my opinion, the "trauma" of unexpectedly becoming a parent is generally self-healing within a very short period of time. In addition, it is clear that there is an abundance of social resources that can be offered by family, friends, and government to help new parents raise their children. This social support is crucial to being able to adjust to parenthood.

Unfortunately, none of this is true with regard to abortion. In my clinical experience, I have seen that the emotional pain related to an abortion is (1) likely to be prolonged, and (2) likely to create negative distortions in a person's life that are not readily understood or accepted by themselves or others. Moreover, the general public has very little understanding of the post-abortion experience. This is why there are very few resources available to help women and men struggling with the psychological or physical consequences of abortion.

At the very least, the scales of the balance are tipped. There is social awareness of the need to support parents who are raising their children, but there is very little social awareness of the need to support women and men on their journey to emotional healing after an abortion.

The ignorance and denial exhibited in the story of the Davis family is typical of our society as a whole. Just as this ignorance and denial about the consequences of abortion were an obstacle in the way of Gina's recovery, they are also obstacles in the way of the healing and recovery of millions of women and men. If, as a society, we want to contribute to the mental health of women and men, we must be willing to take a more critical look at the many complex ways that abortion can affect their lives.

It is equally tragic that the widespread ignorance and denial regarding abortion's consequences contribute to the problem of women being coerced into unwanted abortions. When families, boyfriends, spouses, counselors, and health care workers mistakenly believe that most women can have an abortion and then "just forget about it," it is far more likely that they will mislead, manipulate, and pressure women into submitting to unwanted abortions for "the good of everyone." This is especially important, since up to 53 percent of women who experience significant post-abortion problems subsequently state that they felt pressured by other people to choose abortion.[1]

In the next two chapters, I will try to examine why there is so much ignorance and denial regarding post-abortion issues. In the subsequent chapters, I will look more specifically at the range of emotional consequences that I have treated in my own counseling work.

# CHAPTER TWO

# HIDING THE TRUTH

Patty's dried tears had left streaks of black mascara beneath her hazel eyes. Fleeting, nervous smiles of relief danced awkwardly across her downcast face, alternating with expressions of sorrow. Patty had waited thirteen years to have another person validate the anguish she suffered after an abortion. At long last she was in a room full of women and men who were divulging kindred stories of agonizing heartache. Reflecting on her own silent struggle, Patty shared her experience:

> I thought that if I had an abortion everything would be over with and my life would go back to normal. That's what everyone at the clinic promised. But now I know that after an abortion your life is way different.
>
> My abortion didn't end my pain . . . it began it. For the longest time I thought I must be completely nuts. When I tried to confide in friends about my anguish, they shook their heads with disapproving looks. It made me feel so alone, so weird. Sometimes I felt like I was going crazy.

Patty had believed the myth that abortion is nothing more than the removal of a "blob of tissue." Indeed, some abortion clinic counselors tell women that abortion is about equivalent in terms of pain and risks to having a tooth pulled. If this were true, Patty concluded, then she must be crazy to feel the way she did.

Her sense of feeling "crazy" and "weird" was intensified by the fact that none of her friends were able to accept her emotions as valid and legitimate. Their "disapproving looks" convinced her that she had to bury her "crazy" emotions deeper and deeper. Sadly, burying negative emotions to please others simply prolonged her suffering.

Patty's experience is typical of millions. Most women seeking abortions do not anticipate or understand the potential severity of the psychological problems they may later face. The false expectation that abortion can simply "turn back the clock" leaves women totally unprepared for what may follow.

The tragedy of this false expectation was well described by one woman's "letter to the editor," in which she wrote:

> I am angry. I am angry at Gloria Steinem and every woman who ever had an abortion and didn't tell me about this kind of pain. There is a conspiracy among the sisterhood not to tell each other about guilt and self-hatred and terror. Having an abortion is not like having a wart removed or your nails done or your hair cut, and anyone who tells you [otherwise] is a liar or worse.[1]

As a society, we don't understand abortion. We debate it. We pass laws about it. We argue about it as a moral and political issue. But we don't understand it as a life-changing experience. In that latter regard, grief after an abortion is neither expected nor permitted in our society.

This is a great national tragedy and a central concept of this book, so I will repeat it. *Grief after abortion is neither expected nor permitted in our society.*

In this chapter we will briefly look at how casual assumptions, bad science, and abortion politics have contributed to the false notion that abortion has few, if any, psychological risks. In the next chapter, we will examine why the women who do experience severe emotional problems after an abortion are often condemned to suffer in silence, without the support of friends, family, or even professional therapists. Then, in the following chapters, I will describe specific types of post-abortion problems I have treated in my clinical practice to illustrate why this problem is so important to individuals, families, and our nation.

## "Everyone Knows Abortion is Safe"

Because abortion is legal, it is presumed to be safe. Indeed, it is commonly identified as a woman's "right." This right, or privilege, is supposed to liberate women from the burden of unwanted pregnancies. It is supposed to provide them with relief, not grief.

Indeed, while more than one in three women will immediately experience feelings of grief, loss, or depression after abortion, the majority of abortion patients report feelings of relief.[2] This is because most women feel a tremendous amount of tension before their abortions. They are nervous about the abortion itself. They may wonder whether or not they are making the right choice. They may feel pressured by circumstances or people that make the pregnancy a problem in their lives.

Immediately after the abortion, the finality of that moment invites a release of these tensions. It's over with. It's done. It's time to put it all behind you and go on with your life. For most women, all the tensions associated with the pregnancy and their fear of having an abortion recede, at least temporarily.

At the same time that abortion relieves this stress, however, it can also plant the seeds for future stress. As will be discussed at length in later chapters, unresolved memories and feelings about the abortion can become sources of pressure that may erupt years later in unexpected ways.

In part, this is because abortion touches on three central issues of a woman's self-concept: her sexuality, her morality, and her maternal identity. It also involves the loss of a child, or at least the loss of an opportunity to have a child. In either case, this loss must be confronted, processed, and grieved in order for the woman to resolve her experience.

Few women sort through all of these issues before their abortions. Instead, during this period of crisis when their futures appear threatened or uncertain, there is a tendency to rush to "get it over with," so most women simply put these other these issues "on hold." This is why immediate feelings of relief are no guarantee that problems will not surface later. Unresolved emotions will demand one's attention sooner or later, often through the development of subsequent emotional or behavioral disturbances.

This view is supported by the observations of Dr. Julius Fogel, who is both a psychiatrist and an obstetrician and who has personally performed over 20,000 abortions. Though a long-time advocate of abortion, Dr. Fogel insists:

> Every woman—whatever her age, background or sexuality—has a trauma at destroying a pregnancy. A level of humanness is touched. This is a part of her own life. When she destroys a pregnancy, she is destroying herself. There is no way it can be innocuous. One is dealing with the life force. It is totally beside the point whether or not you think a life is there. You cannot deny that something is being created and that this creation is physically happening. . . . Often the trauma may sink into the unconscious and never surface in the woman's lifetime. But it is not as harmless and casual an event as many in the pro-abortion crowd insist. A psychological price is paid. It may be alienation; it may be a pushing away from human warmth, perhaps a hardening of the maternal instinct. Something happens on the deeper levels of a woman's consciousness when she destroys a pregnancy. I know that as a psychiatrist.[3]

The tendency of people to think that abortion is "no big deal" is largely unchallenged because (1) immediate negative reactions tend to be dismissed as temporary and passing, and (2) most negative emotions are delayed.

When loved ones inquire how a woman is feeling immediately after an abortion, any expression of relief is quickly interpreted as meaning that she will be "fine" with it forever, which is not necessarily true. On the other hand, if the woman expresses distress, it is likely the abortion clinic staff and even her family and friends will dismiss it as just a temporary mood that will soon go away. This is what everyone hoped and expected. They anticipated that the abortion would "turn back the clock" so her life could go on as it was before. Because this is what they hope and want to believe has occurred, everyone will be quick to find reasons to conclude that their expectations were fulfilled.

In general, once a woman has made the pronouncement "I'm fine," even her most intimate friends will often not ask about the abortion again for fear of arousing bad feelings. No one wants to go below the surface because no one knows how to deal with what may lie underneath.

As we will see in the next chapter, once a woman's loved ones are assured that she is okay after an abortion, they may not allow her the opportunity to express any subsequent doubts and regrets. If she herself tries to discuss these delayed negative feelings, those around her will become uncomfortable. The message she will hear, explicitly or implicitly, is, "Don't stir up the past. Focus on the future." This was the experience of Helen:

> The only one who ever asked me how I was after my abortion was my boyfriend. He asked me if I was okay on our way back from the clinic. I felt sick to my stomach the whole way home. I wanted to cry but I felt so numb. I told my boyfriend I was okay and he said, "That's my girl." He dropped me off and went to play pool. I was so angry at him for leaving me there by myself. I did not want to be alone. Later, if I ever started to cry about it, my boyfriend would tell me not to think about it. If I did, he called me a "downer." He even accused me of trying to get attention. Soon after that we broke up and there was no one else who knew. My abortion was the only thing I could ever think about—not because I wanted to, but I honestly could not get the experience out of my head. I swallowed my grief at that point. I felt I had to be strong or no one would want me.

The predominant social experience with abortion, then, is largely based on the immediate reports of women who have told their loved ones, "I'm fine. I'm glad it's over with. I don't really want to talk about it." Unfortunately, such superficial statements reinforce the social perception that abortion is "no big deal." Friends and relatives often pass this expectation along to other women considering abortion with reassurances like, "Judy had an abortion. It was no big deal. She's fine."

In reality, abortion is a deeply private and complex experience. For most women, their feelings and memories about an abortion simply do not lend themselves to casual conversation. Women who will enthusiastically compare pregnancy and delivery stories over tea would never dream of talking about their feelings and memories related to past abortions. One of my clients, Beverly, described her inability to reveal her pain in a diary entry:

> I am trying to learn to live with this and how to put on a show for the world. Sometimes, I feel like I won't be able to keep this show going for much longer. On the outside it seems like life has gone on like normal, but on the inside I feel like I am falling apart. It is even harder to pretend that I am enjoying myself when all I want to do is be alone and cry until I can cry no more, but even then the tears never seem to stop.

For Sharon, when she discovered the depth of her loss in the recovery room, she also discovered a secret connection to other post-abortive women.

> When it was over, I was led into the "recovery room." I ended up sitting next to

the same women I had been with when we were all still pregnant. Nobody was happy. A great heaviness hung over all of us. As we talked, between the tears, I made the remark that I was about 12 weeks pregnant. The woman next to me looked at me and said, "You were. . . ." That's when it really hit me. My baby was gone . . . forever. On my way out I had to walk through the recovery room of brand new "patients" who were no longer pregnant. My eyes met one of them and I gave her a salute. She returned the gesture. We never spoke. We didn't have to. We were now sisters in a secret sad society of women who had done something we didn't want to do, but saw no other way out. Like brave soldiers on the front lines of the battlefield, we never had a "choice."

Through her abortion, Sharon had entered into a "sisterhood of denial" where post-abortive women support each other with no more than looks of understanding. Looks of empathy are safe. Words, especially the "a-word," are difficult, inadequate, even dangerous if they release more pain than either woman can bear.

As a general rule, women simply don't talk about their abortions as readily as they talk about their other pregnancies. The only exception to this rule of social etiquette is when abortion experiences are casually discussed in a group of vocal pro-choice feminists. But even in this case, the rules of the discussion are very strict. The recounting of one's experience must be masked by nonchalance. Dwelling on one's doubts, grief, or guilt is simply not appropriate. Such conversations provide informal group therapy with the goal of reinforcing each other's past decisions.

## ABORTION CLINIC BIAS

The expectation that abortion has no significant emotional consequences is strongly reinforced at most abortion clinics. Ignoring all evidence to the contrary, most abortion counselors will tell women that psychological reactions to abortion are rare or even non-existent. As in Patty's case, some counselors even tell women that an abortion is no more painful or risky than having a tooth pulled, a ludicrous comparison.

In a retrospective survey of 252 women who experienced post-abortion problems, 66 percent said their counselors were very "biased" toward choosing abortion. This is especially important since 40 to 60 percent described themselves as uncertain of their decision prior to counseling. Of all the women surveyed, 44 percent were actively hoping to find some option other than abortion during their counseling sessions. Only 5 percent reported that they were encouraged to ask questions, while 52 to 71 percent felt their questions were sidestepped, trivialized, or inadequately answered. In all, over 90 percent said they were not given enough information to make an informed decision. These omissions are especially relevant since 83 percent said that it was very likely that they would have chosen differently if they had not been so strongly encouraged to abort by others, including their abortion counselor.[4]

Research also shows that a person involved in a crisis is especially vulnerable to being influenced, for good or ill, by a third party. This reliance on others, especially on an authority figure who appears capable of providing an escape from the crisis, is called heightened psychological accessibility.[5] Women considering abortion are especially vulnerable to directive counseling that encourages them to ignore their doubts. Wendy was one such victim:

> During the group counseling session prior to my abortion, I questioned my choice to have an abortion. I said I didn't want to abort but my boyfriend did. I was struggling because I couldn't afford to raise a child on my own. The counselor quickly told me that meant I wanted to have an abortion. She told me it was not right to have a child if you don't have money. I figured she probably knew what should be done because she was a counselor. I was too emotional and scared to think for myself. A week after I had my abortion, I wondered how she could possibly have let me do it, when I had expressed so many times that I wanted my baby.

Another client, Missy, felt manipulated by the fear that having a baby would trap her into a life she did not want. Her counselor never told her that having an *abortion* might also trap her into a life she did not want.

> Before I had my abortion, the counselor could see that I was anxious about what I was about to do. I was thinking about leaving when she told me you can never give a baby back and that my life would never be the same with a child in it. Her words seemed to give me the reassurance I needed and confirmed my decision to terminate the pregnancy, and yet when I look back at those crucial moments before it all happened, all I can think of is why didn't I leave? I know I would have been open to another option if anyone had been positive about the pregnancy. But there was no support like that. Everyone told me abortion was the best solution.

When abortion counselors introduce their own biases into the counseling situation, or try to "sell" women on the option of abortion as the "best solution" despite the woman's own moral or maternal reservations, the results can be tragic. Michelle wrote the following entry in her diary:

> My counselor told me that after a few months I would start feeling better. It has been two years now and things are not getting any better. I feel like I am losing my mind. I don't know what could be worse than this. Living with myself has been a hell. I thought I made the right choice, but hurting so much makes it feel like the wrong choice. I can't stand the pain . . . I just want it to end. Nobody told me I would not be able to live with myself for this. Everyone told me it was the best thing to do. Everyone told me I would be just fine. Well, I'm not fine! My life can and will never be the same. It is a life filled with guilt, shame, a feeling of worthlessness, and unfillable emptiness. I can't bear this pain much longer. I

thought about suicide again. It's scary to have these thoughts, but it seems like the only way to end the pain.

Michelle's diary frankly shares the depth of her misery, regret, and grief. She was totally unprepared for such an onslaught of negative emotions. Fortunately, counseling and grief work enabled Michelle, Wendy, and Missy to move beyond their negative and condemning thoughts.

Research conducted at abortion clinics has also found that the majority of women seeking abortion have little or no prior knowledge about the abortion procedure, its risks, or fetal development.[6] For most women, as for Nadine, the counseling they receive at the clinic is the only information they will receive.

> I was so naive. I had no idea what an abortion actually was. They made it all sound so safe, so easy, so simple. They promised an abortion would take care of my problem and I'd be back to my old self and I could continue with whatever I wanted in my life. The counselor even said, "If you were my daughter, I'd be telling you the same thing. It's the right thing to do."
>
> Everyone assured me not to worry, that there was nothing to be afraid of. The counseling I received was like, yes, you can do this; yes, it's safe; and don't worry, you won't have any problems.
>
> I have been emotionally tortured by this experience for the past 24 years. It's made my life a pit of depression and anxiety.

Most abortion clinic counselors promote the false expectation that there are few, if any, psychological risks to abortion, despite overwhelming evidence to the contrary. The reasons for this vary among individuals and the clinics in which they are trained.

Some abortion counselors have a financial bias. They are "in the business" of selling abortions.[7] Others are paternalistic, honestly believing that abortion is the best solution to every problem pregnancy and that it is their duty to guide women to make the "right" choice.[8] Still others have a psychological need to see other women choose abortion, as they once did, thus seeking affirmation of a choice that still troubles them on some deeper level.[9] When they give emotional pep-talks to their clients, such counselors are also giving impassioned pep-talks to themselves.

One of my clients, Rita, spent four years working as a counselor in an abortion clinic before she mustered the courage to deal with her own abortion loss.

> I was completely driven to help other women obtain abortions. I was totally invested in keeping abortion safe and legal. I never recognized how pushy and one-sided my counseling was until I became pregnant and wanted a child. Everyone around me was so critical of my own pregnancy. I realized then that I had been the same way toward every pregnant woman who entered our clinic. It's almost like we needed them to abort so that we could feel better about our own abortions. I was too busy justifying what I had done to be aware

that I carried any grief about it.

Perhaps most worrisome of all, some abortion providers see abortion as a tool for social engineering. Whether they seek to use it to reduce welfare rolls, eliminate the "unfit," or save the world from overpopulation, these social engineers see every abortion as a step toward some "greater good." To the elitist social engineers of our society, misinformation, deception, and a "little" guilt among the women and men who choose abortion is a small price to pay for achieving this "greater good."[10]

## OUT OF SIGHT, OUT OF MIND

While there are reasons for deliberate deception, most counselors probably do care about the women they serve. Even if they have been poorly trained or misled by their employers regarding the true risks of abortion, most would not deliberately mislead women if they knew how much it could hurt them. Of course, they have seen many women crying in the recovery room. But the counselors assume they will get over it.

This bias in perception can arise from the abortion counselor's need to believe that her work is truly benefitting the women she serves. No one who provides abortions wants to believe the horror stories of women recounted in this book. They truly want to help women. It is difficult to accept that at least some of the women they have counseled have been very ill-served by abortion.

The expectations of abortion counselors are also colored by their own very limited experience with women who have had post-abortion problems. Most women who are emotionally injured by abortion don't return to the abortion clinic.[11] The more intense a woman's negative feelings after her abortion, the more averse she will be to being anywhere near the abortion clinic or its counselors, because they are emotionally connected to her grief and guilt.

One example of this I have seen in my own practice was with Amanda. She was twenty-one, industrious, bright, and very pretty. Two days after her abortion, Amanda overdosed on a nearly lethal combination of sleeping pills and alcohol. I met with her and her friends after her release from the hospital. Amanda was having difficulty speaking due to the unrelenting stream of tears and choking grief. Her bewildered friends took turns telling me what had happened. Day after day we struggled to devise a plan for her continued safety. Her friends were wonderful about offering support and reassurance to get her through this critical time. But when it came time to go back to the abortion clinic for her two-week check-up, Amanda refused go. She felt she could not handle going back to the "scene of the crime." The appointment came and went. No one from the clinic called to ask how she was doing. No one at the clinic knew she had attempted suicide.

Ruthann was another example. A few days after her abortion, she tried to hang herself in her clothes closet. Fortunately, the screws that held the rod in place tore out from the wall under the weight of her body. She then devised another plan to asphyxiate herself by running her car engine with the garage door shut. This suicide attempt failed, too. Curiously, Ruthann did return to the clinic for her two-week post-operative check-up, where she was presented with a questionnaire. Although feeling extremely suicidal, she gave "positive" responses to all the questions. As she later told me, "I just wanted to have my exam and get out of that place!" Consequently, no one at the clinic ever knew that the woman rushing through their questionnaire reporting how well she was doing had in fact become actively suicidal because of her abortion.

The simple truth is that most women suffering from post-abortion trauma simply don't want to see anyone or anything related to their abortions. If they can summon the courage to seek counseling, they are far likely to turn elsewhere, to a therapist, pastor, general practitioner, or friend. From this perspective, abortion clinic counselors who say, "We see very few problems," are being honest. But the fact that they are in a poor position to see the problems doesn't mean that the problems don't exist.

At this point, readers may rightly question whether my own perspective is equally slanted in the opposite direction. After all, my experience with women who have had abortions is biased primarily toward women who have had post-abortion problems, rather than women who have benefitted from abortion. Therefore, it is quite likely that I would tend to overestimate the extent of post-abortion problems by instinctively projecting my clinical experience onto the whole population.

There is certainly merit to that argument. Everyone's perspective is colored by his or her own limited experiences. On the other hand, the point of this book is not to argue that all, or even most, women have the type of emotional problems described herein. My goal is simply to show that a wide variety of emotional problems can result from abortion. These problems are generally ignored by both society and health care professionals, to the detriment of millions of women. I believe that any reasonable examination of the evidence, both statistical and clinical, will prove this to be true. The best I can do in striving for a "perfectly" balanced perspective is to try to remain open to any evidence abortion proponents may bring forward to document the emotional benefits of abortion. But even if such evidence is forthcoming, it cannot erase the fact that many women are severely traumatized by abortion. This leaves us with two questions: How can we help them, and what should we do to protect others from the same negative experiences?

## EXCEPTIONS TO THE RULE

Despite the generalizations above, it is important to note that some abortion clinic counselors do try to prepare women for the emotional reality of abortion. For example, Charlotte Taft was a counselor and director of a Dallas abortion clinic for 14 years. Instead of steering clients away from the tough issues surrounding abortion, Taft explored them with her clients. She attempted to help women confront the loss of their children before their abortions. In some cases, she even asked women to write good-bye notes to their children. During counseling, many of her clients chose not to abort, and she respected their decisions.[12]

Taft's approach, however, was harshly criticized by many abortion proponents. Planned Parenthood, for example, stopped making referrals to Taft's clinic. In defending that decision, the president of Planned Parenthood of Dallas and Northeast Texas took strong "exception to statements [made by Ms. Taft] about the pro-choice community not being completely honest with women," and issued a report stating, "there exists no evidence of significant emotional sequelae post-abortion." In response to this, Dr. William West, an abortionist at Taft's clinic, noted that in Planned Parenthood's own supporting literature, citations demonstrated that there were "marked, severe, or persistent" psychological problems in at least 10 percent of women, in short-term follow-up studies alone. Noting that even a 10 percent rate translated into over 160,000 cases per year in the United States alone, West charged that if Planned Parenthood "was not being dishonest with women . . . I can only regard it as delusion or ignorance."[13]

Sadly, while more abortion clinic counselors are recognizing the need for post-abortion counseling, they still struggle with telling patients that this need exists. For example, Sheila Kriefels, the head counselor at San Jose's Planned Parenthood abortion clinic, told a reporter that they had a post-abortion counseling program, but that it was only offered to women who initiated a request for it. The program was not advertised or disclosed in pre-abortion counseling. It was virtually a secret. Few people on their staff even knew about the post-abortion counseling program.

Kriefels admitted the program was not promoted for political reasons. Offering post-abortion counseling is a tacit admission that abortion can hurt women, she conceded to the reporter, and "we don't want to give ammunition to the other side."[14]

## Promoting False Expectations

A few abortion counselors, like Charlotte Taft, may challenge women to explore their decision and their preparedness to live with the consequences of an abortion. But since the early seventies, the prevailing view of abortion counselors has been that their function is to be *facilitators*. Most assume that by the time the woman enters the clinic her decision is already well thought out and final. As counselors, then, their job is to reduce the woman's stress and avoid raising doubts about what is already a settled decision. They often see their roles as companions, handholders, and cheerleaders for women who are about to undergo what is inevitably an emotionally draining and physically ugly experience.

As facilitators rather than counselors, they tend to avoid probing any emotional or moral conflicts the woman may have not yet resolved. When patients ask questions about abortion's risks or the stages of fetal development, abortion counselors are afraid that too much candor will arouse anxiety and doubts. They tend toward answers that will evade, dismiss, or minimize the patient's concerns. This approach has been taught as the norm since the early 1970s.[15]

As a result, most women undergoing abortion will be explicitly told either (1) that there are no psychological risks to abortion, or (2) that significant emotional problems are extremely rare. They are typically reassured that most women experience tremendous relief after abortion. Some counselors may admit that a few women may have some sadness or "the blues" for a little while, but they insist that this will go away quickly. At least some counselors will even suggest that these temporary "blues" occur only because the woman's body undergoes a hormonal shift from a pregnant to a non-pregnant state. Sandy shares what happened to her:

> The private counselor I talked to before I had my abortion told me that I might be a little sad or agitated for about a month after my abortion. I shouldn't worry because this was just my hormones getting back to their normal levels. She said that I might think about my abortion once in a while for the first year, but then it would become a distant memory. When things weren't back to normal after a month I thought there was something wrong with me. I tried going back to the counselor, but she didn't want to talk about my abortion at all. She insisted that it was something else bothering me. When a year passed and I still thought about my abortion every day, I thought I must be really crazy. It seemed like my life should be going on like normal, but in reality it was quickly falling into a million pieces, and I didn't know if I would ever be able to put all the pieces back together. I tried so hard to put on a front for everyone that I knew because I thought if they saw what was really going on inside of me that they would have me committed to a mental institution. I thought I was the only person who had this kind of reaction to their abortion.

Abortion advocates justify such deliberate efforts to conceal the full range of emotional risks by citing a study published by Brenda Major that evaluated women just before their abortions and then again three weeks later. In this study, the researchers found that women who expected to cope poorly after their abortions did indeed report more emotional problems than women who expected to cope well.[16] Since its publication, this study has been used to justify withholding potentially upsetting information from women on the grounds that exposing women to "unnecessary" information about potential risks will strengthen their anxiety and thereby increase their risk of subsequent emotional problems.

There are many problems with this theory. First, it violates the patients' fundamental right to full disclosure of risks. It treats women like little children who are too fragile and naive to hear the truth and weigh it for themselves. Instead, abortion counselors either (1) paternalistically decide what women need to know and what they don't need to know, or (2) give women only the information that will most likely encourage them to proceed with an abortion.

Second, when properly interpreted, Major's study actually shows that women with low coping expectations are predictably at higher risk of suffering negative reactions soon after the abortion. It is very likely that these women have lower expectations of coping well precisely because they are very conscious of internal conflicts over their abortion decision. In many cases, these women are submitting to unwanted abortions in violation of their maternal desires or moral conscience. Many feel forced to give up their wish to have their babies because they "have no choice" but to abort. No wonder they expect to feel grief, loss, regret, and guilt. For such women, these are realistic expectations. At best, dismissing this reality with false assurances may help to reduce short-term anxiety, but only at the high price of exacerbating long-term reactions. If women later discover that they were deceived, they may experience, in addition to the "normal" post-abortion reactions, a deep-rooted inability to trust themselves or others, especially health care workers. Lorrie describes her difficulties:

> For years I had a difficult time making any kind of decision. I couldn't trust my own judgement. I found it difficult to trust doctors, counselors, and even boyfriends who would make any kind of recommendations to me. I became paranoid of doing the "wrong thing." At the time I did not understand why choices were so difficult for me to make, but I am certain now that it is because of my abortion—and the feeling in my gut that I had made such a horrible choice because I had allowed others to lead me. This problem has affected my entire life.

The third problem with the theory that women should be "protected" from upsetting information is that even if screening of information *could* reduce feelings of grief, loss, regret, and guilt in the first few weeks after an abortion, there is no evidence to support the belief that this will produce any long-term benefits. Instead, it is quite likely simply to delay and aggravate negative reactions. For example, Jane had an abortion when she was three months pregnant at the age of 19. As her life went on, she thought little about the procedure until she attended nursing school. During one of her classes she learned about fetal development and saw her first ultrasound. Jane was utterly traumatized when she was confronted with this information—the reality that the clinic had intentionally withheld.

> I remember raising many questions before my abortion. All my questions were brushed aside as "nothing to worry about." I asked how far my baby had developed. The counselor pressed her pencil on a paper, making a micro-dot. "That's what the 'product of conception' looks like," she said. I was 12 weeks along in my pregnancy—this was such a lie! As I learned the truth in nursing school, I can't tell you how betrayed I felt! The new information also made me completely sick. I almost dropped out of nursing school because of my grief. Thinking about that little baby . . . and how . . . how in God's name I could have destroyed it.

Jane is an example of the dangers inherent in efforts to paternalistically shield women from the truth. What assurance is there that the truth will always remain hidden? Who will be there for these women when they see the images of a developing human fetus on a television documentary, or on the cover of a news magazine? When they are pregnant with a child they are carrying to term and go to look at a poster on prenatal development at their doctor's office, who will be there to explain why the child they aborted was any less human than the child in their womb?

The fourth problem with concealing anxiety-provoking truths about abortion is that inadequate, inaccurate, or biased counseling is statistically linked to more frequent and severe negative psychological problems following the abortion.[17] Women who discover, too late, that their expectations were wrong are more likely to feel exploited and angry, both at themselves and the people involved in their abortions.

Finally, if low expectations are a risk factor for more negative reactions, the proper solution is not to withhold information and encourage falsely optimistic expectations. The ethical obligation of health care workers is to screen for this risk factor, provide additional counseling, and, if it becomes clear that the woman's low expectations arise from the fact that abortion violates her own needs or desires, to assist her in resolving the problems surrounding the pregnancy so she no longer feels "forced" into an unwanted abortion.

Clearly, in failing to correct the false expectation that abortion is without psychological risks, abortion clinics are exposing women to the risk of making ignorant, tragic, and irreversible decisions. Women like Rayna:

> Everything I read on abortion before I experienced it told me that 99.9 percent of women who have abortions do not suffer from depression or regret afterwards. In fact, the information told me that I could expect to feel relieved just as all these other women did at not being pregnant anymore! Where did they get that from? I will never be the same again! My entire life has changed, and I just want to know that there are other women who go through this trauma and feel like me.

## DISTORTIONS OF KOOP'S LETTER

Research on the psychological aftereffects of abortion has been extremely difficult and highly politicized. Appendix A describes some of the difficulties involved in post-abortion research and examines some of the most blatant examples of how the conclusions of researchers have been twisted for political reasons.

Distorted reviews of the literature are actually the rule rather than the exception. For example, in 1989, Surgeon General C. Everett Koop attempted to clarify this state of uncertainty in a letter to President Reagan, in which he reported that after a one-year review of the scientific literature on abortion, it was his conclusion that all of the existing research was "flawed methodologically." While acknowledging that some women do experience physical and psychological complications following abortion, Koop properly concluded that "scientific studies do not provide conclusive data about the health effects of abortion on women." Therefore, he said, it was impossible to accurately measure the frequency or severity of these complications. Koop concluded his letter with a recommendation for a five-year study on abortion, at a price tag of 10 to 100 million dollars.[18]

Abortion advocates immediately interpreted Koop's letter as meaning that *no* health risks to abortion could be found. Indeed, abortion proponents blocked Koop's recommendation for a federally funded study by claiming that since abortion was already known to be safe, the study would be a waste of tax dollars.

Distortions of Koop's conclusions continue to surface even to this day. For example, in a letter to the editor of *The Wall Street Journal*, Planned Parenthood's Gloria Feldt complained about a guest editorial that discussed abortion-related injuries. Feldt claimed that the question of abortion risks was "fully researched" by Koop and his staff and that it was "concluded that abortion does not pose a health risk to women."[19]

For his part, Koop has consistently refuted this distortion of his conclusions and has stated, "I know that there are short- and long-term adverse effects of abortion psychologically on women . . . there is no doubt in my mind that problems exist."[20] Koop has repeatedly and correctly asserted that the existing research was (and still is) too flawed to document with any accuracy the true extent or frequency of both the risks and the perceived benefits, if any, of abortion.

Despite these clarifications, whenever the issue of abortion safety is raised in the press, abortion proponents like Feldt will routinely make misleading statements to the effect that "Since even Surgeon General Koop couldn't find any risks to abortion, there must not be any. There is no scientific basis to this anti-choice propaganda. Abortion is safe."

The impact such misleading statements have in perpetuating false expectations regarding the safety of abortion cannot be underestimated. Not only do they mislead those who make public policy, they mislead women and families who are faced with problem pregnancies. They lead them to believe that the "experts" and government officials have determined that abortion is "safe." It is most particularly tragic when young women who do not want to have an abortion, knowing that it will emotionally devastate them, are convinced by loved ones to set aside their fears because the "experts" have proven that there are no psychological risks to abortion.

## APPROACHING THE TRUTH

For all the reasons described in Appendix B, no one knows how widespread the post-abortion problems described in this book really are. Anyone who claims that he does is, at best, offering an informed guess.

We do, however, have a reasonable profile of that group of women who do report experiencing post-abortion problems. Appendix C in this book includes the summary statistics of an Elliot Institute survey of 260 women who, on average, had their first abortions 10.6 years prior to being surveyed. The women who volunteered to answer this survey were either seeking counseling for post-abortion emotional problems, had received post-abortion counseling, or had a history of abortion and were seeking help at a crisis pregnancy center to carry a subsequent pregnancy to term. The findings in this study appear to be representative of *the group of women who experience negative emotional reactions to abortion*. But it would be inappropriate to project the percentages reported in this study on the entire population of women who have had abortions, of whom very little is known.

Perhaps the biggest challenge we face concerns women who conceal their abortions. We simply have no way of knowing what the post-abortion experience is of women who, when approached by researchers, will deny having had an abortion. Through a variety of means, researchers have found that approximately 50 percent of women who have had an abortion will conceal that fact from interviewers.[21] Demographic comparisons of women who refuse to be interviewed about a past abortion are more likely to match the profile of women who report the greatest post-abortion distress.[22] Breanne offers some insight into this problem:

> Most of us who are suffering after our abortions are too ashamed to admit it. The feeling is that you just want to forget about the whole horrible thing. If anyone ever mentioned abortion I became frozen. Either I would leave the room or keep quiet. I didn't want anyone to know what I had done. If I was questioned about abortion, I didn't want to talk about it because I was afraid I might start into one of my uncontrollable crying fits. Those were moments I reserved for my bedroom where no one else could see the tears.

The only available approach to the problem of women concealing their past abortions is to look at record-based studies. Record-based studies do not rely on surveys of women, but instead on looking directly at their medical records. Unfortunately, there are only four such studies.

The first of these is a study using government records in Finland. Because all health care costs, including abortion, are covered by the Finnish government, the results of this study could not be distorted by women concealing a past abortion. Unfortunately, the study was limited by both the time frame and the post-abortion "symptoms" that were studied. Specifically, the researchers only looked at all cases of suicide that had occurred during a seven-year period. They then examined the medical records and linked the death certificates to records for giving birth or having an abortion in a one-year period prior to the suicide. Their finding was that women who had had an abortion were three times more likely to commit suicide within a year of their abortions than women in the general population, and *more than six times* more likely to commit suicide than women who carried their pregnancies to term.[23]

The second study linked medicaid claim records for 173,279 low-income women in California to death records. In this case, the researchers found that the death rates among aborting women remained elevated for at least eight years. Compared to women who delivered, those who aborted were 154 percent more likely to die from suicide and 82 percent more likely die from accidents (which may be related to suicidal behavior). The higher suicide rates were most pronounced in the first four years following the pregnancy outcome.[24]

The third record-based study used government records in Denmark, which, like Finland, has government-funded health care. In this study, the records of women who carried their pregnancies to term or who aborted were examined for admissions to psychiatric hospitals during a three-month period following the abortion or delivery. The researchers found that "at all parities, women who obtained abortions are at higher risk for admission to psychiatric hospitals than are women who delivered." The admission rate into psychiatric hospitals during the first three months post-event was 18.4 per 10,000 for aborting women, 12.0 for delivering women, and 7.5 for all Danish women. Even more troublesome are the findings concerning women who lacked the support of a spouse at the time of abortion or delivery because of divorce, separation, or widowhood. The rate of psychiatric admission was 63.8 per 10,000 for women who aborted versus 16.9 for similar women who carried to term.[25]

The significantly higher rates of psychiatric admissions after abortion are particularly noteworthy given the fact that the researchers in this study limited their report to only the first three months following the abortion or birth. While three months is adequate to identify virtually all cases of post-partum depression following birth, it is quite likely that the *bulk* of psychiatric admissions following abortion occur *after* three months. In other words, the researchers were comparing virtually all post-partum psychiatric hospitalizations to what is likely only the earliest phase of post-abortion reactions.

This shortcoming was addressed by the fourth record-based study, which also examined psychiatric admissions over a period of four years following the pregnancy outcome. In this study, aborting women had a significantly higher relative risk of subsequent psychiatric admission compared to delivering women across all age groups. After controlling for prior psychiatric history, age, and number of pregnancies, the relative rate of admission among aborting women ranged from a high of 4.26 times higher than delivering women at 90 days after the pregnancy event to a low of 1.67 times higher in the fourth year. In other words, while the risk of being hospitalized for psychiatric problems steadily declined, even four years later it remained 67 percent higher. Aborting women were especially more likely to be admitted for adjustment reactions, depressive psychosis, and neurotic and bipolar disorders.[26]

These record-based studies were limited in the scope of reactions studied (suicide and psychiatric hospitalization), the length of follow-up (three months to eight years), and by incomplete obstetric histories (many women in the childbirth groups used for comparison actually had a history of abortion prior to the study period examined). Despite these limitations, these are the best-designed studies published to date, and they clearly show that abortion can cause or exacerbate severe psychological problems, at least for some women.

The extent of less severe problems is hinted at by a major national poll of 3,583 people that was conducted in 1989 by the *Los Angeles Times*. In that survey, pollsters found that 56 percent of women admitting to a past abortion reported a sense of guilt, and 26 percent regretted choosing abortion. Among men admitting involvement in a past abortion, the negative responses were even more pronounced. Two-thirds reported feelings of guilt, and over one-third said they regretted the choice to abort.[27]   As with all abortion surveys, the number of people admitting a past abortion in this survey was far below the national average. Only 8 percent of women and 7 percent of men admitted having a past abortion experience. This suggests that at least two out of three people surveyed who had a past abortion concealed it from the pollsters. Also, as previously mentioned, it is probable that the rate of guilt and regret among the "concealers" is higher than that reported by the "revealers."[28]

But even if we apply the 56 percent guilt rate and 26 percent regret rate to the general population, this is clearly suggestive of a widespread problem. What other medical procedure has such a high dissatisfaction rate? No one wants to undergo surgery, but would one in four heart attack patients regret their decision to undergo heart bypass surgery? Probably not. I suspect this high rate of regret is unique to abortion and is indicative of the psychological conflict that continues to haunt women and men for years after their abortions.

Similarly, do 56 percent of patients report feelings of guilt persisting for years after any other surgery? No. Such widespread feelings of guilt following abortion are clearly indicative of the fact that most women and men who have experienced abortion are neither psychologically nor emotionally at peace with their experience.

Approximately 60 million women and men have lost one or more unborn children to a legal abortion. Even if only 34 million (56 percent) are still feeling guilt and only 16 million (26 percent) regret their choice, this represents a multitude of negative feelings that we, as a nation, are keeping bottled up.

In the next chapter, we will look at why these millions of people are being denied a healing environment where they can safely explore, understand, and release these negative feelings.

## CHAPTER THREE

# FORBIDDING THE GRIEF

The sixty seconds of silence seemed far longer. Dianna stared at me, or perhaps through me to thoughts or memories that were entirely her own. From this strained silence, I already knew the answer to my question. But Dianna needed to voice her answer in her own way. This is why I sat silently, prepared to wait twenty minutes, if necessary, for her to speak first.

Dianna was in her mid-forties, formally and impeccably dressed. This was our first meeting. In our initial telephone conversation she complained of anxiety, periodic bouts of depression, and difficulty in relationships as evidenced by three divorces. She stated that she had failed to make progress with her former therapist and wanted to interview me to see if we had the proper rapport.

Everything proceeded normally during my initial intake questions until I asked, "Have you ever had a pregnancy loss? Miscarriage, abortion, or a stillbirth?"

Another thirty seconds passed before Dianna began to speak in a slow, careful cadence that rapidly became a repeated demand. "Why did you ask me that? I've been to seven therapists over the last ten years. None of them have ever asked me that. Why did you? What made you ask that?"

I could see that my question had aroused a momentary paranoia. Dianna was afraid that I could see too far into her secrets, especially without her permission. I tried to assuage her confusion and fear by calmly explaining that this was simply a routine question I asked all of my clients. Pregnancy loss could be associated with a number of unresolved emotions, I explained. In my experience, many individuals had made tremendous progress once they received support in working through unresolved grief, guilt, or anger related to prior pregnancy losses.

After another brief silence, Dianna's breath slowly escaped and her body sagged into a slump. Her tears began to flow as she told me of her abortion nearly thirty years earlier.

With one simple question, I had opened the door that Dianna had been afraid to touch. I had given her permission to express her grief about an experience in her life that her ex-husbands, family, friends, and *seven previous therapists* were either too ignorant or too afraid to allow her to share.

Once she received permission to grieve, Dianna made rapid progress in the weeks that followed. Her entire demeanor was transformed. The last time I saw her, she said her goodbye with a smile and a toss of her hand. She had finally rediscovered the sense of freedom and hope that had eluded her for decades.

## Normal Grief

Grief is a natural and necessary response to loss. It is a readjusting of one's outlook and emotions which must occur after every loss, large or small. If the loss is large, such as the death of one's entire family, the grief can be prolonged and disabling. If the loss is minor, such as a ten-dollar bet on the football pool, the grief will generally be small and fleeting—*if* the person who experiences this small loss is emotionally balanced, mature, and experienced in dealing with that type of grief. If these conditions are not met, even a small loss can be experienced as devastating. For example, consider the weeping and raging child who did not win the game of Candy Land. Or remember back to the days or even months of moping and depression when your first love (or infatuation) rejected you, or worse, didn't even notice you. Even when your head said "get over it," it took a long time for your heart to follow.

Through such experiences, we learn how to grieve. Some people can handle grief well. Others cannot. In addition, the ability to grieve can vary dramatically from situation to situation.

Grief is more than a single emotion. It can include feelings of loss, confusion, loneliness, anger, despair, and more. Grief can be overpowering. It can penetrate and darken every corner of one's life. It cannot be turned off and on at will. It does not automatically come to an end of its own accord.

Working through grief requires confronting one's loss, admitting the loss, grieving the loss, learning to live with the loss, and working through the grief to find a renewed sense of meaning or purpose beyond the loss. Each of these processes must be successfully completed in order to resolve one's grief. This is what therapists call "grief work." It is called "work" because it can be a laborious process that takes time and effort. It consumes enormous amounts of physical, emotional and spiritual energy. In order to work through your feelings in a healthy manner, you must actively address them.

Healthy persons learn to respect grief as one of life's most powerful teachers. Through the experience of grief, people can learn much about themselves, others, and the great truths about the purpose and meaning of life.

After an experience with grief, some people will become motivated to help alleviate the suffering of others because of their own new-found insight and compassion. When the grief is associated with the experience of death, it can bring about a reevaluation of priorities. In these and other ways, grieving can lead to a time of personal growth and renewal.

## DISENFRANCHISED GRIEF

When a person experiences a secret sorrow that cannot be shared or confronted, this is called "disenfranchised grief." The term "disenfranchised" means to be denied the freedom or license to do something. In this case, it means being denied permission to openly display one's grief. This makes it far more difficult to complete the grief process, and may not only prolong one's grief but also make it worse. Such "impacted" grief can even become integrated into one's personality and touch every aspect of one's life.

There are many reasons, both internal and external, why people may not feel free to grieve. For example, a sexually abused child may be afraid to expose the abuse because of the threat of severe retribution if she tells anyone about it. The child may also be afraid that if she does tell others, she won't be believed. Or even if she knows she would be believed, she may still fear that others will think she is "bad" or "dirty" for allowing it to happen. Alternatively, the child may simply believe that what she has experienced is normal. Everyone's life is like hers. She should simply learn to accept it. Such confusion, combined with feelings of fear, shame, and guilt, can make it very difficult to grieve the loss of one's sexual innocence—even decades later when the abuse has long since ceased.

In later chapters, we will look at how this "forbidding of grief" can prolong and worsen the emotional consequences of abortion. But first, in the remainder of this chapter, we will look at some of the internal and external forces that conspire to forbid the expression of abortion-related grief.

## INTERNAL OBSTACLES TO WORKING THROUGH GRIEF

One of my clients, Karen, described why she did not talk about her abortion in this way:

> I think the reason women do not talk about their abortions is because it was probably the hardest time in their life. I thought if I could suppress my feelings, they would go away. I also think women feel they are not allowed to be upset about the abortion. We have no right to get upset because we did it to ourselves. I am the one who made the decision to abort. I have to suffer.

The obstacles Karen described are very common among both women and men. First, there is the natural tendency to repress or run away from negative feelings. For many people, denial can be maintained for quite a long time. Even when women and men know they have unresolved feelings about an abortion, they will typically face a major approach-avoidance conflict. This means that while they want to be free from their unresolved feelings, at the same time they also know that confronting these feelings will be upsetting and painful. Expressing their feelings is both desirable and undesirable. As a result, they may vacillate between approach and avoidance behaviors. For many, it is like putting off a needed heart surgery until after a nearly fatal heart attack. Delay appears to be a friend, when in fact it can contribute to ever-worsening health.

Second, Karen described the common belief of women that they have no right to grieve over their past abortions. This expectation is often instilled or reinforced at the abortion clinic, where women who cry in the recovery room are often asked, "What are you crying for? Isn't this what you wanted?" Through such questions, abortion counselors are trying to refocus the woman's attention on "the good" that is supposed to follow from her decision to abort. The unintended message, however, is, "You have no right to cry. You knew what you were doing."

Third, Karen's comments reflect the popular view that each of us should learn to bear our pain alone. Perhaps this reflects a bit of the American pioneer spirit, which puts so much emphasis on the ideal of each of us being independent. According to this ideal, a strong person should be able to deal with life's problems without complaining—especially when one's disappointments are the result of one's own choices. In their efforts to be strong, many women and men suffer in silence. But as a result, they suffer much longer than is necessary because they deprive themselves of the comfort and support that can help them heal faster.

A fourth obstacle to healing, for some women, is the unrecognized desire to "make up" for their abortion by hanging onto their grief and guilt. Some women and men mistakenly believe that the only way they can honor the memory of their aborted child is to keep the flames of pain and guilt burning in their hearts.

This is not a healthy or productive mindset. Unfortunately, however, it is rather common. That is why one goal in post-abortion counseling is to help women and men to see how they can honor the memory of their aborted children with positive thoughts—focusing on the day they will be with them in heaven, for example. Post-abortion healing does not mean learning how to *forget* one's past or one's child. Instead, completing the grief process after an abortion means learning how to *understand* one's past, including one's good and bad choices, and how to *remember* one's child in positive ways that renew hope rather than feed despair.

## The Fear of Telling One's Story

I remember Pamela, a 47-year-old legal secretary who joined one of our support groups for post-abortion healing. Pamela described her decision to finally deal with her abortion as *coming out of the closet.* The others in the group nodded with understanding, keenly aware of the risk at which their presence at such a meeting placed them.

When 29-year-old Audrey entered the room on the first night of a post-abortion retreat, she saw an old friend from high school. Even though her former classmate had also had an abortion, Audrey could not bear the fact that someone else knew she was there. She withdrew from the group and informed me she could not possibly stay because of her embarrassment. After I provided several moments of nurturing reassurance, Audrey decided it was more herself than her old classmate whom she couldn't bear to face.

Recovery depends on one's willingness to tell his or her story and transform the pain. This involves dealing honestly with what really happened and recognizing one's feelings about the abortion and its meaning in her life—not necessarily what she wants the meaning to be, but what the meaning truly *was* in her life.

Becoming aware of the ways abortion affected her is crucial if the woman is to work through her feelings to find resolution and peace. As Kimberly explained:

> I was afraid to think about my abortion because I wanted to keep it "numb." I thought if I talked about it, all these emotions would emerge and I would actually realize what I had done. I thought this would make me feel worse than originally. Now I know these feelings need to be dealt with so that I can let them loose.

## The Social Obstacles

Telling one's story contributes to healing. But if there is no one willing to listen, has the story really been told? No.

We are social beings. The willingness, or unwillingness, of others to *listen* to our grief experiences will make the path toward healing either easier or more difficult.

Successful grieving, particularly of major losses, involves a social component. Grief that is shared is easier to bear because it is not borne alone.

This is why all cultures have funeral rites. While the support of family and loved ones is clearly very important, even the kind words and support of virtual strangers can ease one's pain. Why? Because when other people acknowledge our grief, they are also acknowledging the legitimacy of our loss. They are validating our feelings. When we know that others understand and empathize with our loss, we no longer feel alone. When we feel that the burden of our grief is shared by others, we no longer feel powerless beneath its weight. The compassionate presence of others who have survived similar losses strengthens us for the grief work that we must now confront.

In addition, we need to know that others care not only about us, but about the loved ones whom we have lost. By sharing our grief, even a little, others show that they remember and love our lost loved ones, if only a little. This honors both our feelings and the memory of our loved ones.

But how do we, as a society, treat the loss involved in an abortion?

Abortion is generally perceived as a woman's choice, something she wanted. Something that was supposed to bring relief, not grief. As described in the previous chapter, the general public does not *expect* grief, or at least not serious grief, to follow an abortion. Most people simply do not view it as a grief experience that can be equivalent to the loss of a spouse or a parent. Indeed, many assume that it is a big fat zero of an experience—a non-event. The truth, however, is that most women and men experience very real conflicts about abortion. Although they may have consented to the procedure, they hate what they went through.

More often than not, women and men who want to talk about grief over their past abortion will soon feel boxed into a corner. They are afraid to talk to friends and family members who are religious or pro-life because they are terribly afraid of being judged. But if they try to share their pain with pro-choice friends, they will typically hear responses like, "Just forget about it. It was your best choice at the time. It wasn't really a baby yet. You can have another baby some day."

These statements are meant to offer reassurance. But what those grieving an abortion hear is the subtext: "It was nothing. It's over and there's nothing you can do to change it. Why let yourself think about it? Just forget it. It's not worth talking about." They come away feeling that their grief is irrational, unimportant, or even abnormal. As a result, many will try even harder to bury their pain.

But this buried pain is their problem! They *want* to expose it, work through it, and get beyond it. But they need the support of their loved ones to do this. If a woman is in emotional pain, conversation-stopping platitudes are not the answer. The answer is to let her grieve. Furtive and evasive conversation can only amplify her sense of abandonment.

In abortion, something is lost. Whether one calls it the loss of a child or just the loss of an "opportunity" to have a child, the loss is real. It has to be grieved and released. If friends and loved ones deny this grief, the grief process will actually be prolonged.

## "Spare Us the Details"

As a society, we know how to debate about abortion as a political issue but we don't know how to talk about it on an intimate and personal level. If we are confronted with another person's grief over a past abortion, most of us tend to mumble, shift about awkwardly, and look for ways to change the topic.

There is no social norm for dealing with an abortion. There are no Hallmark cards for friends who have had an abortion, declaring either sympathy or congratulations. We don't send flowers. We don't have any ceremonies, either joyous or mournful. We have no social customs or rules of etiquette governing acknowledgment of an abortion. Instead, we all try to ignore it.

In the first few days following an abortion, a woman may, if she is lucky, have friends and family members who are truly understanding, sympathetic, and willing to listen. In most cases, however, this opportunity is short-lived. Subsequent attempts by the woman to "dredge up the past" are likely to be discouraged. Too many details, too many regrets, too much pain simply makes everyone uncomfortable. Sharon describes her experience with friends this way:

> Friends who appeared to know what was best for me at the time of my unplanned pregnancy now appear afraid and unsure of the person the abortion has made me. If I bring up the subject, they avoid me like the plague.

When Tina initially confided in her sister about her post-abortion pain, her sister assured her that she had done the best thing. Tina explained to me that her sister's response unintentionally silenced her. She felt unable to express herself any further.

> If you regret an abortion, nobody wants to hear about it. After all, there's nothing anyone can do to fix the problem. So you have to tell yourself what happened was good—and everyone around you tells you the same thing. After that, I knew I would never bring up the subject again.

After the birth of her second child, Kathy could no longer contain her grief or her secret. She needed to talk to someone, so she told her mother. Unfortunately, her mother did not know how to help her except by encouraging silence and avoidance. Twelve years after the abortion, Kathy contemplated the event and the meaning it had for her. This excerpt is from a letter she wrote to her mother.

> Dear Mom,
>
> I'm sorry I never told you the truth about my abortion for so long. I told you I was having minor surgery—female problems. Remember? And what really kills me the most is that you and Daddy came to see me that night in the hospital. You brought me a sandwich in case I was hungry. I was so scared—scared you'd find out what really happened that day. Man, was I hurting inside.

And there you two were standing at the foot of my bed extending your love and concern. Mom, didn't you notice I couldn't even look you in the eyes? And over the years the times I turned from you whenever the abortion issue was raised?

I can still see your face the moment I finally told you. Eight years later. You were reading the newspaper and I was holding my newborn. I just blurted it out, trembling from head to toe. You never looked up at me, but I saw the tightness in your throat. I guess I expected you to jump all over me with the "How could you?" But you sat quietly and gently spoke to me. Just as long as I kept my shameful secret, you were willing to keep it too. You wanted to bring it quickly to an end. To get my confession over with and forget about it. But for one split second—just one split second—I felt free. Oh how I wish you had been able to talk about it . . . to cry with me, to help me get through that horrible time. You knew it all . . . but we never talked. I was so desperately alone.

The silence and isolation that typically surround the abortion experience leaves women and men with no place to process their grief. They have no strategy to deal with their feelings about the event. If this has been your experience, or the experience of someone you love, you are not alone.

## UNEASY PRAGMATISTS

One of the reasons we don't want to talk about the grief of those who have had abortions is that we, as a society, are deeply troubled by the abortion issue. While the majority believe that abortion should be legally available in some circumstances, most are also morally troubled by it. According to one major poll, 77 percent of the public believes abortion is the taking of a human life, with 49 percent equating it with murder. Only 16 percent claim to believe that abortion is only "a surgical procedure for removing human tissue." Even one-third of those who describe themselves as most strongly pro-choice still admit to believing that abortion is the taking of a human life.[1]

These findings suggest that most Americans put their own moral beliefs about abortion "on hold" for the sake of respecting a "woman's right to choose." This represents a pragmatic choice. As a society, we have chosen to tolerate the deaths of unborn children for the purpose of improving the lives of women.

This moral compromise is disturbed, however, when women speak about their broken hearts after an abortion. They make their listeners uncomfortable and confused. When confronted with a woman's grief over a past abortion, the uneasy pragmatist may have thoughts such as, "But it was your choice. I stood by you. I still want what's best for you. Do you want me to say you did the wrong thing or the right thing? If I say it was wrong, won't I make you feel worse? If it was wrong, was I wrong not to tell you then? If it hasn't made your life better, was I wrong to agree that it was for the best?"

Grief over a past abortion forces us to look not only at the pain of an individual, but at the angst of our society. It is a deeply complex and troubling issue. Most of us don't want to look too deeply. It's easier to change the topic.

## POLITICAL FEAR

I described above some of the emotional obstacles that make it difficult for people to listen to and comfort those who are suffering from post-abortion grief. This situation is complicated even further by the politics of abortion.

Pro-choice advocates are often hesitant to recognize the reality of post-abortion grief because they fear this means they have to recognize the death of a baby, which may somehow undermine the political argument for legal abortion. Kayla described how politics stood in the way of her finding help in this way:

> I contacted the clinic where I had the abortion. They did not know of any support groups to help me deal with my suicidal feelings. So I called the head of the Abortion Rights Action Group. She told me that my drive to get a post-abortion group started was not necessary, and actually went so far as to imply that it might even have a very negative impact on the whole abortion situation in general! She then went on asking me how I would have handled my situation if I had decided to keep my baby and how I would be feeling now. Without any prompting or indication of any spiritual motivation in my inquiry, she also vehemently stated how violently opposed the organization was to any form of "religion" being brought into this kind of support structure.
>
> What I want to know is what right does this tired old woman have to fight for abortion rights for women and then prescribe to them ways in which they may or may not deal with the aftermath of their hard-won victory?

Sadly, abortion proponents and many professional counselors are unwilling to acknowledge the true nature of the grieving person's dilemma, which means their advice to women and men is useless, if not outright damaging. For example, on a website sponsored by a Planned Parenthood affiliate in Illinois, women are encouraged to deal with intrusive thoughts about their abortions by deliberately practicing stuffing techniques:

> You can say or yell "stop" whenever you have disturbing thoughts. . . . If you find yourself fantasizing too often about what the child might have been like, you should substitute another fantasy: a baby crying because you had no time to give it . . . a picture of yourself feeling angry, resentful or stressed by children you weren't ready to have.

Rather than offering comfort to the woman who is feeling the loss of her child, they encourage her to simply reinforce the "rightness" of her decision. In essence, they are telling women that the grief related to abortion can best be assuaged by constantly reminding themselves how horrible life would be if their babies were here with them today.

Would you tell someone grieving at a funeral to try and picture how awful his life would be if his loved one had survived? This advice is counterproductive in that, if it is followed, it will actually inhibit and prolong the grieving process.

When Gretta had severe emotional problems the day after her abortion, she called the clinic, hoping they would offer her help or at least refer her to someone who could.

> I was extremely distraught. I almost committed suicide. When my best friend discovered what had happened, we first tried to call the clinic I had been to. A nurse called back; she was the one who had "counseled" me before my abortion. After I told her my state of despair, she proceeded to give me a lecture on using birth control. I threw the phone across the room. I was terribly sad and upset, but not so much I couldn't see her response as inexcusable.

This inability, or unwillingness, of abortion counselors to come to grips with the reality of women's pain and grief after an abortion reminds me of a telephone call from a woman named Noreen, who had heard that I ran groups for abortion recovery.

"Are you pro-choice or pro-life?" she asked in a rather determined manner. I hesitated for a minute, thinking it a bit peculiar that this was the first point of conversation. Noreen persisted. "I need to know if you are pro-choice or pro-life."

"I am a therapist," I replied. "I help women deal with their feelings. After an abortion a woman has many emotions that are difficult to talk about. I help her explore her feelings about her decision and identify how the abortion is affecting her."

There was silence on the other end of the phone.

"Is there something I can help you with?" I asked.

Noreen replied with some hesitation, "Well, we have some women who need some help . . . but we can't send them to you if you are going to make them feel guilty."

Noreen was a counselor at an abortion clinic. She epitomized the conflict of so many women: the fear that recognizing what an abortion took away will actually make the problem worse. She was cautious, as she should have been. Dealing with the reality of post-abortion aftermath is no simple undertaking. There is great fear about fully exploring one's feelings. Noreen was apprehensive about authorizing such an awareness. However, my training as a mental health professional emphasizes support of human emotion and transformation of self-defeating thought processes and behaviors. If a woman is grieving over the death of her baby, the best thing I can do is acknowledge the reality of that experience with her.

Even if an individual wanted the abortion, there can still be a deep and aching wound. I explained this to Noreen. "I can assure you that I am not responsible for how a woman feels after her abortion. If a woman feels guilt, I help her resolve it. If she feels grief, I give her permission to express it."

Noreen persisted. "I still need to know if you are pro-choice or pro-life," she stated flatly. I remained silent for a moment, sad that personal ideology could prevent us from having a dialogue and dismayed that Noreen's own doctrine had the power to deny someone the help she requested.

Clearly, she wanted to respond to the frequent complaints of distress she heard and saw. But she was afraid to send women to someone who might acknowledge their loss. She wanted to see them helped only in a way that would reinforce the belief that abortion was the right choice. But the grief process cannot be completed by denying one's loss or by minimizing its significance. For many women, it is clear in their own minds that their abortions were not the destruction of tissue but the destruction of their children. Yet Noreen was afraid to refer them to a counselor who would allow them to embrace this loss under those terms.

I wondered if someone like Noreen could understand the work I did as a therapist. Could she understand the distressing experience of accompanying a woman twice my age as she uncontrollably laments the loss of her child in an illegal abortion? Could she understand the flood of emotions that are released in a post-abortion support group? Could she understand the effort involved in being awakened in the middle of the night to leave my husband and family to help a woman contemplating suicide because of an abortion? No. To Noreen, protecting her ideology was more important than helping women who might regret their choices.

I understand why Noreen and millions like her might withdraw from witnessing such expressions of grief. Helping someone work through such grief can be difficult to stomach. It is horrible. But just as battered or sexually abused women can find the freedom to move on with their lives and stop reenacting the traumas of their past once they acknowledge and begin to deal with their experiences honestly, so it is with women and men who have been emotionally hurt by past abortions. I could not possibly do this work if I did not see the incredible liberation and strength restored in those who engage in the healing process after abortion. It is a most painful labor, but it eventually gives birth to authentic integrity and self-awareness—things often lost in the aftermath of a traumatic abortion.

Again Noreen asked the question, this time impatiently. "Are you pro-choice or pro-life? I need to know."

"Noreen," I answered, "I have seen that abortion hurts women. Not all women, but many women. The individuals I have come to know in my work with post-abortion recovery are women whom I truly love and respect. I have tremendous compassion for women and the dire circumstances which lead them to abort. Women do not come to me if they do not need healing because of their choice. They do not seek my services if they are happy with their decision. My job is to help those who are not happy grieve their loss so that they can move forward. I would not be an effective therapist if I told them what happened to them was good and that they should be willing to do it again if necessary, even if everything inside them is screaming with repulsion and humiliation."

Noreen was silent. I sensed that my remarks hadn't surprised her, and felt that on a deeper level she knew there could be no other answer. Abortion counselors have seen glimmers of the truth. Many women experience intense reactions immediately after their abortions. Some begin to experience extreme reactions even *during* their abortions. If abortion clinic workers haven't recognized these things as the onset of grief, surely they must notice the blank, dull, emotionless faces of some women, going through the motions, trying so hard *not* to feel.

Unfortunately, Noreen ended our conversation because she was unable to accept her patients' grief on their own terms. Politics and ideology stood in the way of referring them to a therapist who could not promise to treat them in a way that would advance a "pro-choice" philosophy. She could not accept that I would allow my patients to regret their abortions, or even to believe that they were a terrible choice. Perhaps she honestly believed that the only way women could find healing was by finally learning how to believe that their abortions were "for the best." But the path to healing is not found in hiding one's emotions or in convincing oneself that a mistaken choice was good. Healing should not be held hostage to "pro-choice" sentiments.

## THE NEGLECT OF PROFESSIONAL THERAPISTS

The interaction between therapists and women who have experienced abortion is obstructed by unspoken secrets, fears, and political biases. It should be no surprise that because of their own psychological needs, many counselors simply don't want to delve into the subject of abortion. If they do, some prefer to quickly reassure clients that they did the best thing and thereby close off any further expressions of grief. This occurs because many counselors have neglected to identify their own fears and anxieties that might be aroused by such conversations.

Many therapists have been involved in an abortion themselves. Others have encouraged clients to abort or have given their therapeutic "blessing" to the abortion option for clients considering abortion.

This is often done out of ignorance of the research that shows that women with prior psychological problems fare poorly after an abortion.[2] There is no evidence that abortion ever improves or alleviates psychological problems. The research indicates that it is more likely to make a woman's emotional problems more complicated. While some therapists may simply be ignorant of these undisputed findings, others simply ignore or disbelieve them for their own psychological or political reasons.

Once a counselor has encouraged or approved of an abortion for Patient A, he may become "invested" in defending abortion. If he subsequently allows Patient B to delve into her post-abortion grief and associated pathologies, then the counselor may be forced to question his advice to Patient A. He may be instinctively wary of witnessing an intense post-abortion reaction because it may provoke the his own sense of guilt in having given Patient A bad advice.

Julianne described her experience with her therapist this way:

> After my abortion, I could not stop crying. I went to see the therapist who had encouraged me to have the abortion. I cried the whole time there. She sat across from me with a blank look on her face. She said nothing. During this session she was removed and distant—emotionally cold and withdrawn.
>
> As I was leaving her office, she came up to me and said, "I don't usually touch my patients, but you look like you need a hug." She then proceeded to embrace my shoulders and offer a squeeze. I felt like I was being embraced by an evil presence. I shuddered at her touch. How dare she even come near me! A hug! I was sickened at the thought of such a trite expression—after having encouraged me to kill my own child!
>
> Never a word of support for my motherhood! Not an alternative plan, or a resource to help me. She knew I didn't want another abortion. She told me to have a ------ abortion because I would not be able to handle another baby.
>
> Then she offered me a hug!
>
> God, I miss my baby. That's who I wanted to hug . . . my baby who is gone, whom I will never hold or cuddle.

If the therapist has personally had an abortion, a client's confession of grief is quite likely to run into either a wall of denial or another quagmire of unsettled issues. According to another of my clients, Hanna:

> I thought I had put my own experiences behind me. I was totally unprepared for the onset of emotions evoked by hearing one of my clients talk about her abortion. There are times when I feel as though I have opened a Pandora's box and my life will never be normal again. Memories I did not know existed have been surfacing at the most inopportune times. My sleeping hours are plagued by graphic nightmares. I vacillate between feeling finally in control and fully out of control. As a professional counselor, I struggle to find a bridge that will allow me to merge my professional expertise with my personal trauma. "Physician, heal thyself!" I do know that the time to reconcile this is now and that it is no accident. I have arrived at this particular fork in the road.

Fortunately, Hanna recognized her own symptoms that screamed for attention and decided to seek help. She was willing to deal with the trauma that she had for many years successfully pushed away but had never truly worked through.

## MISSED OPPORTUNITIES

There were many trained professionals in Kasey's life who had the opportunity to help, but they either misunderstood her, cut her off, or ignored her.

> I remember my teacher pulling me aside and telling me that she thought I was a little flaky. A week later she told me that she had looked at my charts and medical history, which had been forwarded to the school. She saw that I had had an abortion. I will never forget my feeling at that moment. I was completely horrified and mortified.
>
> At the same time, however, I felt a strange relief that my secret was out. I felt like the woman was showing concern for me, and I was relieved that someone recognized the source of my pain. I broke into tears and told her how awful it had been. I told her everything I had been going through. I had been exposed—stripped naked—and then left alone to deal with my shame.
>
> Then, after telling her everything, she firmly told me to pull myself together. . . and that was the end of it. That nearly drove me over the edge.

Kasey wanted a mother-figure to give her compassion and support. Her teacher's discovery of her abortion, although frightening at first, had also been a moment of hope. Sadly, she instead simply heard, "Pull yourself together." At that point Kasey felt completely abandoned, and her trauma got the best of her. She was unable to work through it because there was no one who would help. Eventually she had a nervous breakdown.

During her hospitalization Kasey informed numerous doctors and therapists that her problems began after the abortion. Despite her explanations, no one would consider abortion as a counseling issue. Everyone thoroughly dismissed her abortion as irrelevant.

> They treated me with drugs: tranquilizers, antidepressants and anxiety medication. That's how they handled my grief and pain. They turned me into a zombie.

For six years Kasey was treated with medications and viewed herself as a "mental case." But after doing extensive grief work related to her abortion, she made a full recovery.

Unfortunately, Kasey's pain was unnecessarily prolonged because the people around her, and especially counselors and mental health workers, were unable or unwilling to assist her in dealing with her abortion as a traumatic grief experience. How long will other women and men be denied the permission to grieve their past abortions?

# CHAPTER FOUR

# A TIME TO GRIEVE, A TIME TO HEAL

Maura entered therapy for depression and anxiety. At 32 years of age, she had battled cancer for four years.

Her eyes, swollen from tears, seemed permanently reddened by the profound ache of her grief and loss. The chemotherapy and radiation treatments had taken quite a toll. The smooth surface of her bald head shimmered under the lamp adjacent to her chair. Through the translucent skin that covered her skull, I could detect veins and arteries that protruded from her glossy dome. Above her somber eyes lay a vacant space where her brows had once perched above her lids. Her visage appeared like that of an alien creature. I struggled to get beyond the exterior and relate to her as a friend . . . as a woman.

"What were you like before cancer?" I asked. Maura seemed excited and anxious to share her memories. I learned that she had been a vibrant and active girl who needed little coaxing to get up in front of people and entertain them with jokes, stories, and songs. Before the chemotherapy, long curly locks of black hair had cascaded down her back. She had been popular, and many men had tried to win her heart. Now a caricature of her former self, Maura sat before me and struggled with fears of pain and death.

In therapy her life continued to unravel before me, like an interesting tapestry with brilliant colors followed by shades of somber black and deep hues of blue. Maura recalled turning good men away and engaging in naughty escapades with bad ones. She seemed puzzled by this pattern and anxious to gain self-insight.

She mentioned an abortion, then quickly moved on to the next event. I did not miss her keen surveillance of my response, or the fact that her eyes brimmed once again with tears. My heart filled with sympathy and I acknowledged how difficult such a decision must have been.

"What was the abortion like for you?" I asked.

A barricade of defenses tumbled down as Maura burst into tears. She did not have the luxury of being able to run away from this pain anymore. Her illness had stripped her of any denial or defenses that would normally put the incident out of her mind. Maura told me that I was the first and only one of many therapists to ever ask her that question. She was tremendously relieved finally to have an opportunity to talk about it.

After the abortion the familiar shame and secrecy experienced by many others like her had victimized Maura. She had always managed to avoid lifting the lid of this Pandora's box. But now, faced with the threat of death, Maura could no longer keep it shut. Its contents fueled excessive fears, which had become so dreadful that she slept in her parents' room every night. She bore a hellish fear of being alone in the hour of her passing. Maura was terrified of judgment.

I placed my hand on her shoulder and assured her that she would not be alone. Together we would explore the hidden fabric of her life and bring her secret to the light. With reverence, we gently went back to the abortion, and Maura began to express some of her long-repressed feelings of anger, shame, abandonment, guilt, and despair.

## I DON'T DESERVE TO LIVE

That night, Maura confessed the abortion to her mother. She blurted out the entire sequence of events, which had occurred over a decade earlier, as if they had just happened. Her mother felt devastated that her daughter had gone through this pain alone for so many years, and they wept together.

Maura utterly believed that God had given her cancer because of the abortion. She was certain that cancer was her due punishment.

"God does not work that way," her mother tried to reassure her, but all the guarantees meant nothing to Maura.

"I don't deserve to live," she said. "Why should I live when my baby did not?"

Maura demonstrated a type of survivor guilt. She believed that she had done wrong, and despite promises that God understood and could forgive her, she felt despair, grief and hopelessness about a life she didn't feel she deserved to live.

Certainly forgiveness is at the cornerstone of all Judeo-Christian religions. Despite the fact that the Old Testament patriarchs repeatedly fell into grave errors, the Torah speaks of God's unending love for his chosen people. The message of God's mercy is the very heart of the life and teachings of Jesus and the foundation of all Christian religions. Even the Eastern religions emphasize the need for inner harmony. In a broad sense, all religions teach that the goal of our spiritual journey is to reconcile our pasts and find peace. But Maura's sense of guilt and shame were stronger than any notion of God's mercy and compassion. Her lack of inner tranquillity after the abortion was still quite evident.

The connection between stress and many diseases, such as heart attacks and cancer, has been well-documented. While cancer is not a punishment sent from God, we cannot underestimate the role that stress and some of the acting-out behaviors that followed Maura's abortion played in disrupting her immune system.

After the abortion, Maura began to drink heavily. Her diet was poor at best. Between alcohol and "life in the fast lane," her body began to break down. Most significant in this case, however, was that when Maura first discovered a lesion (which turned out to be cancerous), she waited nearly a year before she consulted a doctor. This clearly revealed a lack of self-care, which can be traced directly to low self-esteem, and quite possibly, to an unconscious desire for punishment.

Maura also believed that if she *had* given birth to a baby, she would have changed her lifestyle. She would have been forced to take better care of herself because her child would have needed her.

While focusing too much on such ideas could drive someone crazy, these thoughts were very real to Maura. She tortured herself by obsessing about different things she might have done to prevent the cancer from pillaging her life. Since we could not undo the past, we focused on healing the present. For Maura to move toward death peacefully, reconciliation was imperative.

## An Angel Named "Joey"

Maura had identified her loss. Now she could begin the grief work she had never been able to face.

The following month, Maura attended a Rachel's Vineyard Retreat for healing after abortion. She was grateful for the experience of meeting others who shared similar feelings of grief. A sisterhood developed among all the participants as they set aside the tedious ideologies of choice, reproductive freedom, and stoicism for a weekend of soul-sharing, devoid of pretense and disguise.

Maura invited her family to attend a memorial service during which she honored her aborted child. Her family did not have the opportunity to support her during the crisis of pregnancy because Maura had kept it a guarded secret. However, she wanted them present as she sought to reconcile the abortion. She was tired of secrets and had neither the time nor the energy to spend on them.

Such memorial services are always emotionally overwhelming. The beauty of Maura's family gathering with her in grief was something I will never forget. Her five siblings attended the ceremony and wept together with their sister. Her mother and father also accompanied her and shared in her pain at the loss of their grandchild. Finally, Maura's isolation was shattered. She was not alone any longer.

That weekend, Maura reconciled her abortion with her Creator and herself. She named her baby "Joey" and imagined him as a little angel who was now coming to offer her peace and forgiveness.

After the retreat, she no longer felt compelled to sleep with her parents. When she embraced in spirit and love the memory of her little child, she laid to rest a tremendous amount of anxiety.

When I went to visit Maura after she had surgery for yet another tumor, the doctor told me she had only a few weeks to live. Her tumors were growing with a vengeance, and only frequent doses of morphine could alleviate her suffering.

Maura had fought a long and brave fight against cancer. But the knowledge that God loved and forgave her, and that in death she would be united in spirit with her sweet baby Joey, with whom she longed to be reconnected, pacified her fears of death.

The beauty of this reconciliation came back to me when I attended her funeral. At the casket I looked lovingly down at Maura. She looked so beautiful and peaceful. Her hair had grown almost two inches since the cancer treatments had ended. I combed my fingers through her hair and gently touched her cheek. Her lips were sealed tightly, never to speak of the mystery of passing. I felt a great love for Maura. We had surpassed the confines of a therapeutic relationship as her spirit began to soar toward an imminent death.

As I sobbed at Maura's coffin, I remembered holding her hand as she wept at the memorial for her child lost through an abortion. The peace that followed that expression of grief and her ability to share that grief with her family and have it validated with honor and respect was inspiring.

I bent down to kiss her forehead as a frail attempt to convey my final farewell. Although my heart ached with pangs of grief over such a beautiful life cut short, my faith gave me the hope that she was reunited with her son and joyfully welcomed by a merciful God who loved her. Despite this conviction, I experienced pain.

While in line to extend my condolences, I felt like an intimate member of Maura's family, although I had only known them a few months. The tight and unreserved embraces I received conveyed an unspoken sense of the sacred journey on which I had accompanied their daughter and sister. We would all miss Maura.

Bereavement counseling has taught me not to feel ashamed of my grief. I used to be the type of person who ran from funerals. When I saw someone cry, it triggered my own mourning and fears about losing someone I loved. I was afraid to make my nose red with crying or cause my mascara to smear. I wanted to look neat and pretty and in control. Yet there is something quite liberating about allowing yourself to feel and express the sadness instead of swallowing it and pushing it back down into your gut.

Grief can be healing. It signals our living and feeling in connection with others. It represents our vulnerability, our humanity. When we remember and mourn our losses, we free our souls to move beyond the pain. This is the purpose of funerals. As difficult as they are, they provide a public expression of our grief, a way to say goodbye while surrounded by friends and loved ones, and a place to remember with dignity our lasting connections to one another.

Women who undergo abortions are never permitted this social connection. Abortion is a death. For many, it is as dramatic and poignant as any situation where a mother suffers the loss of a child born years ago. What hurts so much when a baby dies is the awareness of the life unlived, the lost potential, the existence cut short. There is always a profound ache of grief when death takes someone young from the world. That pang is greatly intensified in a person who feels that the death could have been prevented or who feels responsible for that untimely death.

Maura lived her life running from the grief and guilt she carried in her heart. She actually believed that she did not deserve to live. By grieving her loss, naming her baby, making it real and claiming her pain, she discovered strength and hope. This process enabled her to resolve her guilt and be at peace with what had happened to her. She called Joey her little angel. By acknowledging his life, Maura became connected to peace, love, and ultimately, her Creator.

# CHAPTER FIVE

# MATERNAL CONFUSION

Clarissa was 19 when she became pregnant. Mike, a 21-year-old college student, was her high-school sweetheart, whom she had been dating for four years. They often talked of marriage and an exciting future together. But when she told him that she was pregnant, he became agitated and nervous and he wondered how they would manage.

At the time, Clarissa was living with her older sister Jane, who suggested that Clarissa have an abortion. Jane herself had undergone an abortion at the age of 18. She reassured Clarissa that abortion was no big deal—she would be fine and life would go on. Jane also insisted that Clarissa would have to move out if she decided to have the baby.

Although abortion was in direct opposition to her instinct and reason, Clarissa followed her sister's directives and had the abortion. Because her boyfriend had acted so unsure about having a baby, Clarissa hoped that her decision would please him. After all, she loved him very much and figured they could have another child someday in the future.

When she entered the clinic, she was crying and upset. Apparently, none of the clinic's staff observed or cared that Clarissa was deeply distressed and ambivalent, even though such symptoms are well known risk factors that clearly predict subsequent psychological problems. The only counseling Clarissa received was about birth control. No effort was made to help her to sort out her true feelings. Furthermore, no time was given to help Mike adjust to the idea of becoming a father.

Immediately after the abortion, Clarissa knew she had made a terrible mistake. She grieved heavily. When she cried to Jane about her feelings, her sister responded coldly, "Oh, well, too bad. I guess you made a mistake."

Mike was deeply distressed because he genuinely loved Clarissa. He was remorseful that his fears had prompted her to abort the pregnancy so swiftly. He knew how much she was hurting, yet nothing he did or said could console her. Clarissa missed her baby with all her heart. She had frequent thoughts of suicide as a way to be reunited with her child again. Her only other hope was to become pregnant again. Another child might serve to "replace" the child she had lost.

Although Clarissa wanted desperately to become pregnant again, she felt she did not have the "right" to have a baby. Additionally, she felt as though she did not deserve to "coddle and coo" little babies. While other women were drawn to them like magnets and would eagerly fuss over a new baby, Clarissa felt she had to watch from afar. She exiled herself to a lonely world where the endearing expressions of an infant's face were inaccessible and forbidden pleasures. As time passed, Clarissa realized she had become cruelly altered. She was angry. She felt alone, violated, and betrayed.

Several months later, when a woman at work announced her pregnancy, Clarissa instantly became jealous and irritated. Perhaps this was exactly how her own sister felt when Clarissa disclosed her pregnancy. Her sister had been denied her child. Why should Jane have offered Clarissa support when she became pregnant?

Clarissa's experience is an example of how an abortion can become interwoven with issues concerning maternal identity. In this chapter we will explore how abortion can affect a woman's perception of her own maternal nature and that of others.

## "I Hate Pregnant Women"

After an abortion, many women develop an aversion toward pregnant women because they are visible reminders of what they have lost. This was Clarissa's experience, and perhaps the experience of her sister Jane as well. Kathleen described her struggle in this way:

> Whenever I see a pregnant woman, I panic. They make me so sad. I think, how come they can have their baby and I couldn't? I know this sounds bizarre, but I start to feel jealous and angry. I know abortion was my choice, but it was because I had to . . . not because I wanted to. What gives pregnant women the right to have a baby when I couldn't? I hate pregnant women. I hate to see them.

Another client, Gwen, had been able to repress her post-abortion grief until a woman she worked with became pregnant. Up to that point, she had been able to avoid the sight of pregnant women. But afterwards, her "forced" proximity to this pregnant woman became so unbearable she felt she simply had to quit a job she loved.

> When I found out my co-worker was pregnant, I was overcome with anxiety and fear. I didn't want to even look at her. I knew I couldn't take watching her belly growing each day with a baby. Hearing everyone come up to her to give congratulations was more than I could bear. I knew I had to leave that job because of her pregnancy—and I did after three weeks of torturous anxiety and guilt.
>
> I just couldn't take it. I didn't want to be around to hear about a nursery being decorated, maternity clothes, and just witnessing the whole thing. It filled me with panic—my heart felt like it could beat out of my chest. I always had a knot in my stomach and sickness in my heart. I liked that job, but I could not put myself through watching her for the next nine months, so I quit.

In their hurt and despair, some women will jealously "claw" at the pregnant women around them who remind them of their loss. They despise those who would dare to enjoy what they cannot. A sad example of this was voiced by Mirna:

> I am a top sales supervisor for a leading pharmaceutical company. My job was my life. It had to be. I aborted three pregnancies so that I could compete in the business world. Now I've gone as far as I can go. When I tried to have children, I couldn't . . . I guess it was too late. It wasn't until then that I began to grieve what I had lost.
>
> Facing the emptiness of my life . . . with this supposedly brilliant career, I felt unhappy, unfulfilled, insecure and bitter. For years I was mean and angry because I had never dealt with my losses. I took my anger out on women working under me who had kids. I literally made their lives hell. Since I couldn't juggle multiple roles, I didn't want anyone else to . . . at least not without misery.

## "WHO WANTS A BABY ANYWAY?"

Carol felt smothered and panicky every time she saw a baby. She avoided baby showers, kiddy birthday parties, and any events which featured toddlers. She explained:

> I don't know why . . . but I'm not comfortable around kids. They make me nervous. I guess I don't have the patience for them. Kids give me a funny feeling in the pit of my stomach.

This queasiness around children did not develop until after her abortion. Carol used to love children and recalls babysitting jobs as a teenager as something she enjoyed. At an earlier time, before the abortion, Carol even had ambitions of becoming a teacher.

Peggy also avoided anything to do with babies and children. She despised children and had a particular hatred and cynicism toward pregnant women. When she saw a co-worker after the woman had given birth, she exclaimed, "Every mother I know must have had a lobotomy after giving birth. Did you get yours when the kid came out?"

Peggy, too, did not have these negative attitudes prior to her abortion. An unconscious need to justify her own abortion had turned into an irrational projection that having children made you stupid. Who in her right mind would want kids? Peggy not only disowned her natural desire for children, she also developed a loathing of youngsters and motherhood to bolster her defense against the loss she experienced through abortion.

Maryelle was also disturbed by pregnant women and their children.

> I have worked in a supermarket for eight years. Since my abortion, every time I see a pregnant woman coming into the checkout line, I feel like I've got to shake off a disgusting feeling. I look away and try not to notice her belly. It's weird. First I feel disgusted by her. Then I feel sorry for her. If she has kids with her, they are always annoying little brats. I have absolutely no patience. Then I feel really sad. When I start to feel sad, I think about how irritating those little kids are.

Maryelle's defense against her own feelings of grief and sadness was to focus on how miserable mothers with children must really be. Her reaction was straight out of Aesop's fable of the fox and the grapes. Unable to reach the beautiful bunch of grapes, the fox walked off, complaining that they must certainly have been "sour grapes" and that he was better off without them.

## "I Need a Baby So Bad"

Shortly after their abortions, as many as one out of four women report that they experience the desire for a "replacement baby." Nearly half of these will become pregnant within a year of their abortions (see Appendix C). According to Hannah:

> After my abortion, I wanted to get pregnant in the worst way. I wanted a baby so bad. I would go through the stores and look at baby clothes, cribs, and strollers—imagining which ones I would buy. I envisioned ripping a hole in my boyfriend's condom with my teeth so that we could conceive another child.

For some women, becoming pregnant is not only a way to "replace" the child lost to abortion but also a way to reclaim their former selves. According to Alicia:

> My abortion made me very unstable as a person. Soon afterwards, I became pregnant again. I loved being pregnant! I felt so beautiful and very feminine. I felt like I was carrying diamonds and gold in my womb.

Because they are so anxious to become pregnant, many post-abortive women are predisposed to feel guilt and anxiety if they do not succeed in becoming pregnant right away. Kim's concerns about her fertility were directly related to her traumatic experience with abortion.

> After my abortion I was fearful that I might not get another chance. I got married shortly after and tried to get pregnant right away. It didn't happen immediately and I was a complete wreck. I felt guilty and sad and anxious. I was worried all the time. My husband tried to reassure me and constantly told me to calm down. I was a frantic mess. I probably spent hundreds of dollars taking pregnancy tests. I was obsessed with becoming pregnant.

Kim's experience is also an example of the fact that for many women the preoccupation with becoming pregnant is a useful distraction from their unresolved grief. By focusing their worries and hopes on becoming pregnant, the post-abortion pain is pushed into the background.

There are two problems with this strategy. First, at best it only delays the inevitable. Even if the woman successfully becomes pregnant, she will soon discover her newborn child cannot "replace" the child who was lost. Indeed, as we will see in examples throughout this book, watching her "replacement" child grow may even prompt unpredictable attacks of post-abortion grief for the child who cannot share the family's experiences. Sooner or later the postponed grief work will still demand her attention.

The second risk with this strategy is that if the woman faces any setbacks in becoming pregnant, her anxiety level is likely to grow exponentially, as in Kim's case. This heightened anxiety can actually make it more difficult to become pregnant, thereby increasing her anxiety level even more. It can become a vicious cycle.

It is very common for women who have had abortions to experience doubts about their ability to have children in the future. This fear can be centered upon either actual physical consequences of abortion or on an irrational fear that God will punish them for their abortion by denying them any other children. Jackie shared her ordeal:

> When my husband and I were trying for our first one, it was taking longer than we thought. I thought for sure I was being punished. Even before I married, I was always afraid that I would never be able to get pregnant. Believe me, I really thought I had earned that punishment. I felt so much guilt. I thought I didn't deserve children. I had already been given two chances. I aborted them both.

Even if there is no desire for a "replacement baby" or any anxiety about future fertility, it is common for women to suddenly face unresolved abortion issues during a subsequent pregnancy. According to Meredith:

> When I finally decided to have a baby, my abortion began to bother me. I had some difficulties with bleeding and premature labor. I was fearful that I would never be able to have children. Emotionally I was a wreck. I stayed in bed for nearly six months of the pregnancy. I was afraid to do anything that might hurt the baby. I was so anxious and fearful, and underneath that was a ton of guilt. I cried all the time. I couldn't talk about it though—I just reacted by trying as hard as I could to bring the baby into the world safely. I got sick of people telling me to "calm down" and "relax." They had no idea about my abortion. I realize that's why I was so upset all the time.

## A COMFORT, NOT A CURE

I want to stress that while having a baby is not a cure for post-abortion problems, a child may provide the woman with an intimate relationship, as well as an opportunity to develop and express her loving and maternal nature. The only caveat is that neither women nor their loved ones should imagine that everything can be fixed just by having another child.

Nora, for example, sought therapy for depressive thoughts and feelings after a botched abortion. She had to return to the clinic to "finish the job." She complained of grief, insomnia, loss of appetite, and flashbacks to the abortion. She couldn't concentrate and remained preoccupied with thoughts of the baby she could have had.

In my evaluation, it was clear that Nora was suffering from symptoms of trauma: intense grief, bitter regret, guilt, depression, anger, helplessness, self-condemnation, pain in sexual relations, hatred of the doctor responsible, and fear and distrust of doctors in general. She also suffered from an obsessive anxiety over her reproductive health.

Nora was obsessed with a desire to get pregnant. To her, achieving this goal was the only way to alleviate the fear that the abortion had permanently damaged her reproductive capacity. At the same time, this goal of becoming pregnant had become the channel for her tremendous anxiety.

A gynecological exam revealed possible pelvic inflammatory disease (PID), which is strongly correlated to a history of abortion. Her physician advised her to follow through with treatment and antibiotics. But because of her abortion, Nora had developed a persistent distrust and fear of doctors. For this reason, she did not follow the medication plan. She became suicidal, tormented by feelings of hopelessness, abandonment, and fears of punishment by God.

After months of trying to get pregnant, Nora finally conceived. Although unmarried, she was intent on having the baby to prove to herself that the abortion had not damaged her. Throughout her pregnancy, she bargained with God not to punish her with a defective child. "If God does give me a baby with a problem, I will understand," she said. "That is really what I deserve."

Nora delivered a beautiful, healthy child. This event helped her to resolve and move beyond the trauma of her abortion. Since the birth occurred after she had already worked through most of the other issues related to her abortion in our counseling sessions, giving birth helped bring final closure to her abortion grief. If she had not already confronted her unresolved abortion issues, however, it is likely that the abortion would have continued to haunt the birth and mothering of her newborn.

Post-abortion recovery can free a woman to move beyond her secret fears and inadequacies and to find new ways to express the restored integrity of her maternal nature. According to Carol, "After doing grief work with my abortion, now I actually can't get enough of babies. I love to look at them, hold them, and kiss them."

Reclaiming a maternal identity, however, is not dependent on actually having or raising other children. For example, Laura had suppressed any desire for children for over twenty years after her abortion. It was not until she underwent the hormonal changes of menopause that she began to grieve the loss of both her child and her maternal identity. Part of her resolution of this grief came with being able to care for other people's children through teaching.

> It's ironic to me at the age of 46, that at this particular time of my life I'm realizing my damaged identity as a woman who could have mothered. It is just beginning to heal. For many years I just couldn't or wouldn't allow myself to seriously consider having a baby. In the last few years, however, I've started teaching young children. It's been a real joy and challenge—with some residual longing for the children I never had. I think I am finally beginning to resolve this poor maternal image. I really love the children I teach. I can at last realize that I could have been a good mother. I never realized this because of the blight of the negative impact abortion left on me for so many years. It took a long time to heal.

## "Unworthy" to Become Pregnant

It is sad to listen to clients like Connie who, because of the guilt they carry over a past abortion, have deliberately deprived themselves of the wonderful opportunity to have other children.

> I've had two abortions. I chose not to have children after that. I asked myself, "How could one so horrible as me have children?" It has made me extremely sad when I see mothers with their children, knowing at this stage of my life I will never have a "second chance." I'm deeply saddened at the pain that I've caused my family and most of all at the pain and sorrow that I carry within my own self.

Another client echoed the same feeling this way:

> I used to have fantasies about being pregnant and having a baby. Because of my three abortions, I didn't feel "worthy" of being pregnant. Because my husband couldn't mourn with me over the children we lost, I couldn't bear the thought of having a baby with him. I never had children . . . mostly because of my anger and guilt.

Such cases are examples of how a past abortion can sometimes dictate the future course of a woman's life. It can take control over fundamental choices, ruling out the fulfillment of desires the woman no longer feels she deserves.

One of the goals in therapy, of course, is to overthrow this tyrant. While decisions about the future should be *informed* by past experience, they should not be *ruled* by past traumas. One of the most important milestones in recovering from any trauma, whether it is related to abortion or not, is feeling free to choose according to one's reasonable assessments as opposed to one's irrational fears.

## Arrested Mothers

If a woman's first pregnancy ended in an abortion, she may associate later pregnancies with the agitation and buried psychic trauma of the first pregnancy. As a result, the births of later, wanted children can be times of anxiety, stress, and depression.

> After the birth of my three children, I was overcome with grief, pain, and sadness at the thought of my abortion. I would hold their beautiful tiny bodies and stare into their eyes, the sweetest angelic faces. I would become so overwhelmed with guilt and grief I would just cry and cry. These overpowering feelings happened after each birth. It made me feel like a horrible mother.

The process of becoming a parent is a major formative life experience. It shapes us emotionally and psychologically. But our ability to parent is also shaped by all our other experiences as a child, an adolescent, and an adult. If all goes well, a woman will develop a competent and nurturing "mother-self" that integrates both her childhood and adult experiences.

Even prior to having children, young women will naturally begin to develop important aspects of this maternal nature during their teenage years and early twenties. An abortion at this time can arrest or even reverse this maternal development. It can give rise to deeply rooted ambivalence and self-doubt regarding one's ability to be a mother. Claire described her experience in this way:

> After my abortion I felt like I was unworthy of motherhood. For years I told myself I didn't want to ever have children. When I finally had a baby, I was afraid to touch him. I felt like I might hurt him or something. I couldn't wait to get back to work. I always considered myself a bad mother. I was extremely sensitive to any criticism over my mothering. After I finally dealt with my abortion and allowed myself to grieve the loss, I was able to reclaim my broken maternity. I realize now that I was afraid to get close to my children. I was cold and emotionally withdrawn.
>
> Since the retreat I went on for post-abortion healing, I have rediscovered my whole self and I know now that I am a good mother. I know that I truly do love my children. Because of my emotional pain, I couldn't show it. Healing my abortion has freed me to be a much better mother. I thank God every day for the gift of my children.

Unresolved issues about a past abortion can literally suck the joy out of expecting a newborn child. It can result in more anxiety during labor, and thereby increased difficulty in labor, which may contribute to a higher incidence of complications during delivery. It can also disrupt maternal bonding with the newborn child. Mel described her pregnancy as "horrible."

> I kept feeling like something bad was going to happen to the baby. I worried all the time. I had dreams that someone was trying to get us and hurt us. After my baby was born, I suffered a major post-partum depression. Aside from the hormonal flux, I was in deep grief over my previous abortion . . . but it was nothing I understood at the time. I didn't know how to allow myself to acknowledge what I had done, but all the symptoms were there. My depression made it hard for me to bond with the baby. I was a failure at breast feeding and

comforting her. That was the most painful time in my life. I felt so inadequate—like I would not be able to protect her and love her.

If mother-child bonding is blocked, arrested, or distorted by past trauma, this may affect the mother-child relationship for many years, even for a lifetime. Michelle sought counseling, at least in part, because all of her efforts to develop a good relationship with her daughter seemed fruitless.

I feel like such a bad mother. When I get angry at my daughter, I become cold and withdrawn. When she is hurt, I find it difficult to comfort her. I feel so guilty when I hurt her. Sometimes I feel scared of her. My life is no better because of that abortion. It makes me hate myself. It made my brain screwed up or something. . . . I can't even deal with my own kid now. I wonder what she would ever think if she knew what I've done. I know she would hate me. I couldn't bear it if she ever found out.

Abortion damaged Michelle's image of herself as a mother. She had a guilt-ridden concept of herself that made it difficult for her to love. If she could not love herself, how could she love her daughter? Because Michelle believed her daughter would end up hating her, she distanced herself from any opportunities to give or receive love.

While every woman's experience of abortion and reaction to it is unique, when these various patterns arise again and again, it is clear that they are not rare or isolated problems. Cinda's description of her pregnancies echoes many of the themes already discussed.

After my abortion, my pregnancies have been times of fear and anxiety. I kept expecting that God was going to punish me with a retarded child because I had an abortion. I was always depressed and worried. When my daughter was born, I felt like I didn't deserve to be a mother. I was so badly depressed. My sadness and anger made me not want to be around her. I felt like a failure.

## CONFUSED MOTHERS

Clearly, unresolved issues over a past abortion can distort relationships with later children. In some cases, post-abortion trauma can drive some women to become hovering, overprotective mothers. In other cases, post-abortion issues can simply rob women of the joys of being a mother, leaving only the labor and drudgery of motherhood and making parenthood feel like a curse. Below are just a few examples of how abortion can confuse a woman's role as a mother.

### The "Perfect" Mother

After my son was born, I was filled with wonder that this perfect child had been produced in my body. The awe that he was given to us to nurture and love was mixed with the feeling that I didn't want to mess up his life because of my own shortcomings. Because of my abortion, I always had a sense of my own unworthiness. I could not trust my ability to do the right thing because of what I had done. My ability to raise a child was always in question.

Because of these inner doubts, Monica was an anxious, overprotective, and doting mother. Her efforts to become a "perfect" mother were an attempt to compensate for her underlying feelings of inadequacy and shame. She expended tremendous energy in an effort to prove to everyone that she was a good mom. She assisted at school functions as a homeroom mother, party coordinator, and extravagant refreshment provider. She earned a reputation for creating the best displays of picturesque goodies and crafts at the school fair. In her constant search for approval and praise, she felt devastated if anyone gave the slightest hint of displeasure or indifference about some "motherly" thing she had done.

Because of her abortion, Monica felt her efforts were never good enough. She felt like a bad person and an incompetent mother no matter how many good things she did. She was obsessed with trying to vindicate herself. There was no sense of joy or fun connected with all her motherly activities. Instead, every undertaking was conscientiously handled as an obligation, a duty, a redemptive act.

As long as Monica avoided dealing with her unresolved feelings regarding her abortion, none of her maternal efforts were able to restore her self-esteem. Each little act of mothering was like a tiny band-aid placed over a gaping wound. It was instantly soaked with blood, obviously useless, and discarded as worthless. Her wound was simply too big to patch up with isolated acts of good mothering. So she remained self-critical, self-deprecating, and discontented.

Fortunately, Monica sought post-abortion counseling that could address the real source of her wounded spirit. Subsequently, her acts of mothering were no longer ineffective efforts to alleviate guilt, but acts of love that bore fruit which she could at last enjoy. Plus, she was finally free to say "no" to unwanted commitments.

## The Spoiler

Some people abort their children because they feel they can't give them "the best of everything." When a later child is born, these parents may feel obligated by their past choice to give their "planned" child everything money can buy. Elizabeth, for example, was quite aware that she was spoiling her child, but she felt she had no choice.

I felt so guilty after my abortion. When I finally had a child, I know I spoiled her. I bought her whatever she wanted, whenever she wanted. I was afraid to discipline my child. I was afraid to do anything "mean," and that she wouldn't like me because I already felt like a bad mother.

Dana's guilt over a past abortion made her feel horrified at the thought of setting limits. She compensated for these feelings by gratifying every whim and desire of her two children.

> I never had any control with my children. I was afraid to upset them or cause a fight. My kids got anything they ever asked for because I was afraid to say no. I feared they would get angry with me. I needed them to love me because that made me feel like a better mom. At first this seemed to work, but as time went on, I realized I had created so many problems. My two children are self-absorbed, disrespectful, angry, demanding, and defiant.

Dana's husband, who had also been involved in the abortion, shared a similar feeling of helplessness. He claimed that he was a "hostage to their demands," but was unable to take control of the situation. Like Dana, he felt a need to lavish his children with every material item to make up for his feelings of inadequacy, failure, and wounded fatherhood.

## The Protector

Some mothers compensate for their loss of self-esteem and maternal integrity by being overprotective of their children. Often this overprotectiveness is rooted in an irrational fear that God will punish them for their abortions by taking away their later children, whom they feel they don't deserve. In Sandi's case, these feelings haunted her whenever her children were out of sight.

> After my abortion I felt like the world was a dangerous place. The people I thought I could trust hurt me so bad. I didn't trust anyone . . . especially with my kids. I had a paranoia about something bad happening to my children. I distrusted them with anyone but myself. My husband told me I smothered them. I was fearful something bad would happen to them. I was afraid to let them do anything.

Yvonne's fears overwhelmed her whenever she took her children out in public.

> Whenever we were in a shopping mall, library, or playground, I was scared to death that someone would steal my children or hurt them in some way. I never let them out of my sight. I was constantly on the alert. . . . It was exhausting! Even allowing them to play at a neighbor's house was out of the question unless I went with them. I felt I had to protect them from anyone around who might be out to get them.

Janet describes the burden of trying to be a protective mother.

> Every time my child got a bump or a bruise, I felt like it was my fault. I always felt guilty and frustrated. I also believed others were always judging me, and so I became very isolated. I withdrew from playgroups and other social functions because I couldn't stand comparing myself to other mothers. It was so hard for me to relax. I never felt confident in the job I was doing. Friends and family members told me I was "overprotective."

*The Abuser*

After an abortion, some women will have difficulty bonding with their later children. If one is unworthy to be a mother, why try at all? Under such circumstances, subsequent planned children can become an irksome burden, a constant reminder of how unfit the woman sees herself to be.

Jennifer, for example, never thought about her abortion until she stared into the eyes of her newborn baby twelve years later. From that moment on, self-loathing and doubt filled her. Jennifer berated herself constantly with unmerciful questions: "What kind of mother am I? How could I have killed my own child?"

As soon as she rejected herself as a fit mother, Jennifer also rejected her baby. She was unable to bond with him because she felt incapable of nurturing and loving him. She felt constantly irritated and had difficulty tolerating any outside friction. Jennifer's anger at herself made her respond impatiently and with rage toward her son. She admitted being abusive to him. This in turn supported her image of herself as a horrible person and perpetuated her sense of guilt and shame. The more guilt and shame she felt, the more unworthy she felt to be a parent. These negative feelings about herself reinforced her rejection of her son, whose very presence reminded her of her failings. The vicious cycle was established. Fortunately, post-abortion counseling helped Jennifer to break free of the cycle, to experience forgiveness, and to begin building a positive relationship with her son.

Unfortunately, Jennifer's situation is not unique. Numerous studies have identified an association between abortion and subsequent rejection and abuse of later *planned* and *"wanted"* children.[1] We will return to this issue in a later chapter.

# CHAPTER SIX

# MIND GAMES
# The Use and Misuse of Defense Mechanisms

"Buried emotions are like rejected people; they make us pay a high price for having rejected them."

—Rev. John Powell

There once was a woman who discovered a corroded pipe in her basement. To hide the ugly sight, she built a wall around it. Once the wall was painted, papered, and decorated, she was relieved to know that neither she nor anyone else would ever have to look at that corroded pipe again.

For a time, she was content. But then she noticed a wet spot in the carpet. No matter how thoroughly she dried it, it soon returned even worse than before. Soon she was constantly cleaning and drying the carpet. All the effort was making her exhausted and stressed. Whenever she fell behind, the carpet began to mildew. In one corner of the basement, the floorboards began to rot. She blamed the problem on the high water table, or perhaps heavy rains.

Occasionally she would think of the corroded pipe behind the wall. Perhaps it was the cause of her problems. But quickly she turned her mind away from that possibility, for she had invested so much in building and decorating the wall that she was very afraid to pull it down. It was easier, and less messy, she told herself, to just keep cleaning up the carpet. Once the rainy season had passed, perhaps the problem would go away.

After many months, the worn-out woman burst into rage and tore the wall down. There was the rotted pipe, steadily weeping water down its length. She collapsed into tears. Even when she could cry no more, she simply sat staring at the leaking pipe. It appeared to be beyond repair. She did not know how anything could fix it. Her despair was complete. Her house could never be made beautiful again. She simply waited for the strength to cry some more.

In this analogy to post-abortion reactions, we see that hiding unresolved internal conflicts is like hiding a corroded pipe. The problem is still there. Like water from a leaky pipe, negative emotions inevitably seep out into other areas of one's life. If the root problem is not addressed, these problems begin to multiply. They drain away energy from other duties of life. They demand notice. And even when they are finally faced, they can appear to be an unsolvable, impossible burden if they are confronted without the support and love of others.

We can stretch this analogy a bit further. Every home with leaks will experience different patterns of water damage because each home has different low spots. Similarly, every person has differences in personality, temperament, and life experiences, so unresolved stress will be displayed in ways unique to each individual. Some will try to hide their problems through drinking or drug abuse. Others may become workaholics or obsessed with becoming the perfect parent. Still others may become angry and violent, become suicidal, or develop eating disorders. These are just a few of many ways that unresolved grief can cause damage to the foundation of a person's life.

## APPROACH? OR AVOID?

An important concept to remember in trying to understand post-abortion reactions is the concept of approach-avoidance conflicts. A common example of such conflicts, often used in freshman psychology classes, is the case of a man who wants honey but is afraid of bees. This hypothetical man takes two steps forward, then three back, then four forward and two back, as his desire and fear each battle for supremacy.

Sometimes an approach-avoidance conflict is consciously understood. For example, the man above is fully aware of both his desire for honey and his fear of being stung. In other cases, the approach-avoidance issues can be partially or totally hidden or suppressed. This is especially common after traumatic experiences.

By definition, a trauma is an overwhelming experience that is simply "too much" for a person to handle or understand. The ordinary response to a trauma is to banish the experience from one's mind—to run away from it, hide it, or repress it. It is natural for trauma victims to try to forget and put their horrible experience behind them forever.

In conflict with this avoidance reaction, however, is the equally powerful human need to understand our experiences and find meaning in them. Thus, while a person may consciously choose to avoid thinking about the traumatic experience, his or her subconscious insists on calling attention to the trauma. The subconscious knows that an unresolved trauma is unfinished business. In order to be conquered, the horror of the traumatic event must be exposed, proclaimed, and understood. This tension between the need to hide a trauma and the need to expose it is at the heart of many of the psychological symptoms resulting from abortion.

More simply put, women who suffer from post-abortion problems want to avoid and deny those problems while at the same time seeking resolution and peace of heart. These two needs are working at cross purposes. Avoidance behavior, conscious or unconscious, can sabotage a woman's desire to confront and resolve her problems. Conversely, avoidance behavior will be disrupted and challenged by the subconscious release of unexpected emotions or behaviors that are designed to draw attention to the unresolved problems.

The distortions of women's attitudes toward pregnancy, pregnant women, and their children, described in the previous chapter, reflect this push-and-pull battle between the need to avoid and the need to resolve an abortion experience. For example, avoiding pregnant women may be a way to avoid confronting one's own negative feelings about a past abortion. But every time this effort fails, irrational feelings of abhorrence, fear, or simply an unnameable discomfort are aroused, forcing the woman to wonder, "What's wrong with me? Why does this bother me so much?" Conversely, it is very common for women to make the decision to participate in a post-abortion healing program, but at the last minute to be overcome with an overwhelming fear of "exposing the past." This is an example of how avoidance behavior can complicate and delay recovery.

In the chapters that follow, we will see many examples of this approach-avoidance conflict. Many of the symptoms of post-abortion psychological problems can best be understood by seeing how the behavior or emotion is being employed, consciously or unconsciously, to either hide the unresolved issues or to expose them.

## DEFENSE MECHANISMS AND COPING SKILLS

The term "defense mechanism" refers to any of several ways in which the human mind attempts to avoid or hide anxiety-provoking truths. The military term "defense" is used because a mind that is using defense mechanisms is fighting an internal conflict. It is striving to protect what the person wants to believe from being overthrown by what is really true.

Defense mechanisms all serve, in one way or another, to sustain denial—the denial of one's unwanted emotions or the denial of one's flaws, mistakes, or responsibilities. Some defense mechanisms concentrate on containing the unwanted emotions. Others provide a means to release pent-up emotions in ways that disguise their true meaning or source, thereby preserving deniability.

While the use of defense mechanisms is always a sign of unresolved emotional conflicts, the mechanisms are not inherently bad. For example, if a child witnesses the slaughter of his family by enemy soldiers, his mind may repress the horrible image of their deaths. Even the memory of how they died may be blocked off from his conscious mind. This "grace of forgetfulness" gives the child time to reattach with other people and to restore some sense of self-confidence and emotional well-being. Because of this positive role that defense mechanisms can play, many therapists prefer to describe them as "coping mechanisms," or even more positively as "coping skills."

Defense mechanisms may provide time for healing, but like a crutch, they are not meant to be permanent. At some point, probably as an adult, a child who has blocked out memories of his family's murder is likely to face emotional conflicts surrounding issues related to death, security, the military, and so forth, which are connected to his unresolved trauma. At that point, with the support, love and understanding of others, his peace of mind can only be regained by a willingness to surrender the crutch of repression, face the truth, and complete the grief process.

Defense mechanisms are to the mind what safety features are to a car. For example, when a collision causes a car's air bag to inflate, this protects the driver. But if the air bag is not deflated and put back into place, the car won't work properly. Similarly, if the driver's side mirror is bumped, it is designed to fold back instead of breaking off. This good design protects the mirror, but it also leaves it in the wrong position. If the driver doesn't put the mirror back in its right place, he won't be able to see traffic properly and may make wrong or even dangerous decisions.

The same principle is true with psychological defense mechanisms. They have temporary value. They can save us from "losing our minds" by confronting too much all at once, without the support of others. But when we rely too much on these defense mechanisms (or "coping skills"), especially when we keep them in place as permanent "fixes" to our problems, the mechanisms themselves become part of the problem.

If the walls we erect to defend ourselves are never taken down, they become no different than the walls of a prison. They deprive us of the freedom to explore the fullness of our own potential and the richness of relationships with others. As long as we hide some truth about ourselves, we cannot know who we really are. As long as we withhold ourselves from others, we cannot experience their embrace of who we are.

The following is a list of some of the most common defense mechanisms. You will recognize these in stories throughout this book, and perhaps in your own life and in the behavior of your family and friends.

*Suppression*

When unacceptable thoughts and feelings are *consciously* pushed out of one's mind, this is called suppression. In surveys of women who have had abortions, one of the most common responses to the question, "How have you dealt with your abortion?" is "I just don't let myself think about it."

For example, in the weeks following her abortion, Carla was severely depressed and obsessed with constant thoughts about what had happened. Overcome with grief, she would find herself crying at the most inappropriate times throughout the day. But as her graduation from school approached and she was confronted with her final exams, she forced herself to suppress all her thoughts and feelings about her abortion. "I just put it out of my mind," she said. "I had to, or I would not have been able to answer any questions." By exercising her mind's powers of suppression, she was able to adapt to the specific need of that moment, passing her exams. Fortunately, Carla subsequently completed the grieving process.

## Repression

Repression is a form of selective amnesia. It is the complete blocking out of an intolerable memory, thought, or emotion from the conscious mind. The mind pushes these objectionable experiences or emotions down into the unconscious, as far away from one's immediate awareness as possible, and acts as if the unacceptable subject or feeling does not exist.

The victim of a traumatic car accident, for example, may not remember a period of time both before and after the accident. In the case of Lorraine's traumatic abortions, she could not remember important facts concerning any of the three abortions she underwent. She even had great difficulty recalling the names of her boyfriends, although she considered her relationship with each one to have been "serious." Lorraine could not even remember how she felt after each of these men had abandoned her.

Repression may also manifest itself by a lack of awareness of the meaning of obvious behavior, by confusion or an inability to understand objective, scientific facts, or simply by keeping any item or concept away from consciousness. For example, after her abortion Madeline reacted angrily and jealously toward women who had children. Although her envy and temper were evident to everyone around her, Madeline was completely unaware of her feelings. Only in the course of subsequent counseling did she become aware of her own behavior and feelings.

Repression is a powerful and costly defense mechanism. It requires a great deal of emotional and mental energy to patrol the mind and repress unconscious truths. In some cases, the repression can be so complete that the person is not even aware that there is a missing memory. This is often the case with memories of traumatic events that occurred in childhood.

Women undergoing abortion routinely employ repression. One of my clients, Diane, could not remember a single detail about her abortion. Although she knew that the event took place, it was as if every other memory about it had been completely erased from her mind. The abortion memory was a vague perception, an impression, that resided not in her mind but in her body. Diane trembled and got violent butterflies in her stomach whenever she attempted to think about the abortion. If she persisted, her body went on full alert and she would be overcome with nausea, forcing her to attend to her physical needs rather than her emotional ones. Her attacks of nausea were like the sudden outbursts of a vigilant watchdog patrolling the edge of her consciousness, ready to repel any effort to approach her forbidden memory.

### Rationalization

Rationalization is used to cover up mistakes, misjudgments, and failures. It is an attempt to fabricate reasonable arguments to justify behavior that is called into question by others or oneself. Fundamentally, rationalization is the way the mind distorts reality in order to protect one's self-esteem. It will typically involve a distortion of facts, events, or experiences and may also employ the use of false logic. Through rationalization, the mind attempts to construct explanations for behavior so that it appears to be logical or socially approved. A strong ego can accept failure, mistakes, and misjudgments, but a weak ego would rather distort the truth than admit it.

For example, Virginia had demanded that her 18-year-old daughter have an abortion. In the weeks following the abortion, her daughter was acutely grief-stricken and frequently suicidal. When she heard that I had counseled her daughter, Virginia called my office. She was angry at me for acknowledging her daughter's distress, insisting that she was "simply going through some teenage adjustment problems." Virginia argued that the abortion was a good choice—lots of women had them and were simply fine. She went on to explain how she had found the absolute best doctor to perform the abortion and that her daughter had received excellent medical care. Virginia was certain that her daughter would have been unhappy with a child. Now, because of the abortion, her daughter would be able to finish college and have a fantastic job.

Because Virginia had vehemently argued and pushed for the abortion, she could not tolerate the idea that her daughter had been hurt in any way by the experience, much less that she had made a mistake in pushing for the abortion. Every fact to the contrary was dismissed through rationalization. Her daughter's present grief and misery were viewed as temporary and insignificant compared to the wonderful, but unrealized, future that Virginia hoped to obtain for her daughter through the abortion. By clinging to her rationalizations, Virginia was able to deny any responsibility for her daughter's emotional problems.

## Reaction formation

When the conscious mind takes a position that is the polar opposite of one's true feelings, this is called reaction formation. A textbook example is the story of a coed who discovers that the sorority she has joined is disappointing, at best. In her effort to cope with her unhappiness, she tries to force herself to enjoy it and brag about it and soon becomes the sorority's most ardent advocate. Her public behavior completely misrepresents her inner feelings. Another classic example is that of the shell-shocked soldier who is deeply terrified by the prospect of returning to battle, but who has consciously or unconsciously chosen to hide and defeat his fear by acting in a bold, reckless, fearless-warrior fashion.

In the case of abortion, reaction formation is evident in the cases of women who suddenly become ardent pro-choice activists even though their own abortion experiences were deeply disturbing. Unacceptable feelings are repressed and completely opposite feelings are asserted.

Another example is described by many women who feel emotionally abandoned by the fathers of their aborted children but continue to shower these men with loving behavior. Janet, for instance, was overcome with resentment, anger, grief, and jealousy following her abortion. Yet she continued in the relationship, maintained an active sex life, and even scribbled love notes and cooked romantic dinners for her partner. She often spoke of their future together, but underneath this devoted facade lay profound rage and murderous hatred.

Reaction formation can also play a role in a woman's decision to abort a wanted pregnancy in violation of her own conscience and maternal desires. When a man's response to a pregnancy is rejection, it is sometimes easier for the woman to displace her disappointment and anger at him toward her unborn child. This may occur because she does not have the emotional stamina to confront or blame the male. While on a fundamental level she loves her child and wants to bring him into the world, the anger and frustration resulting from her partner's rejection are more easily directed at her pregnancy and child than at her partner, to whom she feels a prior, and even higher, commitment.

## Introjection

Introjection is the absorbing of another person's values or opinions in place of one's own. This is a very common defense mechanism employed by women who seek to avoid conflict. Rather than explore their own feelings and beliefs, women attempt to mirror the feelings and beliefs of those around them, such as their boyfriends, parents, or abortion counselors.

Yvonne, for example, repressed her own objections to abortion in order to please her husband. He was focused on having a better home, an education, a brilliant career, and some "fun" before they would even consider having a child. She adopted his opinions as her own, and under their influence, aborted their first two children. Because these were not truly her own values, however, they cost her much loss and grief, and Yvonne eventually rejected them.

## Undoing

Undoing refers to activities designed to reverse or nullify a previous action that resulted in feelings of guilt. In undoing, Freud pictured the ego as trying to "blow away" not only the consequences of an event, but also the fact that the event itself ever took place. Replacement pregnancies are a commonly employed form of undoing among women who have had abortions. In the Elliot Institute survey in Appendix C, approximately 29 percent of the women surveyed reported attempting to conceive a replacement pregnancy, of whom around 45 percent succeeded within the first year following their abortions. Undoing may also be exhibited in the compulsion to be a "perfect mother" to subsequent children, as described in the previous chapter.

Another example of undoing is illustrated by women who try to make up for their guilt by laboring long hours in the service of some social cause or charity. In Diane's case, for example, volunteering became an obsessive chore that she felt she "owed" to society to atone for her abortion. No matter how much good she did, it never seemed enough to erase her sense of guilt. This sense of incomplete atonement compelled her to wear herself out by volunteering for an endless number of causes.

While charitable work is good and normally quite gratifying, it is never an adequate substitute for grief work. Only after one's grief work is complete can one's charitable works be fully satisfying.

## Projection

Projection is when an individual refuses to recognize a flaw or objectionable behavior in himself but is quick to see, or even to imagine, this behavior in others. This tendency often explains why people often become most upset by that behavior in others which is most similar to their own. For example, an intolerant person may become incensed at any real or imagined intolerance on the part of others toward his own behavior or beliefs, while at the same time denying that he himself is intolerant. Similarly, a fundamentally dishonest person may become incensed whenever he feels cheated or misled, while boldly proclaiming his own honesty.

One of the most common symptoms of projection that occurs among post-abortive women and men is a great anger or fear of abortion opponents. Some individuals cannot admit their own hostility and so ascribe it to others though delusions of persecution. Post-abortive women often project their own feelings of self-rejection onto politicians, pro-life activists, or religious figures or institutions whom they see as hateful, hypocritical, and rejecting. The message that these parties reject abortion as a moral choice but still have compassion for those who have had abortions, is unheard, disbelieved, or scorned. On a conscious or unconscious level, many post-abortive women need an outside "enemy" on whom they can project their own unresolved feelings of self-rejection.

## Provocative Behavior

When a woman denies her own emotions or needs, she may sometimes try to provoke displays of her own emotion in other people. This defense mechanism provides a means of expressing one's emotions through a surrogate—the person provoked—while concealing one's own emotional needs.

In this vein, post-abortive women and men who are filled with unexpressed anger may attempt to provoke anger in others. If they are unable to give themselves pity, they may manipulate situations to extract pity from others. Those who are filled with unexpressed self-blame may say and do things to draw the blame of others.

After her abortion, Margie felt unlovable. To compensate for this deep-seated low self-esteem, she became alarmingly promiscuous. She dressed in an enticing fashion and attracted men through her charm and sexually inviting postures. Through her promiscuity, Margie provoked expressions of love and acceptance from a long string of willing men. Purchased for the price of sex, their admiration was a substitute for the feelings of affection she was unable to express to herself.

## Displacement

Displacement is the process of releasing negative, pent-up feelings on people who are considered less dangerous than those who initially provoked the emotion. A textbook example of displacement is the case of a child who ridicules and hits his brother when he is actually angry at his mother.

In the case of abortion, a woman who is angry at her boyfriend may develop a general anger and hostility toward all men. Or a woman who is angry at herself may blow up at a concerned friend who asks if her abortion is bothering her.

## Conversion

When the mind and body interact to convert emotional pain into physical pain, this is called conversion. Physicians will often refer to these problems as "psychosomatic disorders." Some of the most common psychosomatic problems in women who have had abortions revolve around stomach cramping and symptoms related to the reproductive system.[1] Conversion or psychosomatic illnesses may help explain why women with a history of abortion are more likely to report more general health problems than are women without a pregnancy loss.[2]

After her abortion, Heather began to experience headaches, dizziness, exhaustion, fatigue, and nausea. She traveled from doctor to doctor seeking a diagnosis and relief from these various ailments. She kept insisting that "something was *dreadfully wrong*," even through numerous physicians and expensive tests had revealed normal results. She was certain she had cancer or some rare disease, or even a brain tumor.

Through conversion, it was easier for Heather to experience fear, sadness, and grief over her perceived health problems than to deal with her abortion. Furthermore, her health-related problems gave her much needed attention and sympathy at a time when she was feeling very demoralized and alone. Fortunately, Heather eventually entered post-abortion counseling and all of her physical complaints disappeared.

## Withdrawal

People who fear rejection or failure will frequently resort to withdrawal. By withdrawing, the person is trying to avoid uncomfortable feelings and psychological pain. Unfortunately, this coping style invariably leads to intense feelings of loneliness and isolation.

Withdrawal after an abortion can be manifested by many behaviors. One of the most common is the use of alcohol or drugs. Silence is another means by which a post-abortive woman or man may curtail his or her communication with others. Running away from responsibilities and problems is still another form of withdrawal.

## Regression

Regression is returning to early childhood behavior when faced with a new trauma. Thumb-sucking and violent temper tantrums are two examples. Another form of severe regression was demonstrated by Laura. Every time she was confronted with painful memories surrounding her abortion, she would curl into the fetal position and freeze.

## Deflection

Deflection is a pattern of changing a subject that has the potential to cause discomfort or anxiety. Anger and sometimes joking are the most common methods of deflecting people away from difficult subjects.

## Denial

Denial is a broad, catch-all term that is commonly used to refer to any one or more of the defense mechanisms more specifically described above. Most people do not confine themselves to the use of a single defense mechanism. Suppression, repression, rationalization, projection, and other specific mechanisms can come into play at different times.

For example, Phyllis was a married woman who had an abortion but told her family and friends that she had simply miscarried. After a time, this lie took on a reality of its own that she half-believed herself. Her conscious defense mechanism was transformed into an unconscious one. In such a case, denial is a useful term for describing a pattern of behavior involving more than one specific defense mechanism.

In other cases, the term "denial" is useful for noting that some defense mechanism is obviously being employed, even when it is not immediately clear which one. For example, Kristin came to me for counseling regarding frequent panic attacks. Verbally, Kristin thoroughly denied that her abortion had ever bothered her. Yet it became obvious as she told her story that discussion of her abortion was provoking enormous anxiety. This was evidenced by her sweaty palms, rapid breathing, trembling voice, and fingers that twirled impatiently around long strands of hair, which she feverishly chewed on. At this initial stage of our interview, it was not clear whether she had suppressed or repressed her feelings, but it was obvious, despite her denial to the contrary, that her abortion was not a settled or insignificant issue.

Another good illustration of how multiple defense mechanisms contribute to denial can be seen in the case of Rebecca. Just three hours after her abortion, Rebecca insisted on returning to the preschool where she worked. She acted as if nothing significant had happened. Her behavior was no different than if she had just returned from buying a new party dress at the mall (reaction formation). As she ran and jumped with the toddlers, a co-worker saw broad rivulets of blood running down Rebecca's leg and urged her to sit down and rest. She had just been through surgery, after all. But Rebecca shrugged her shoulders, dismissing her friend's concerns. "I'm fine," she said. "I feel great!" Rebecca's cavalier attitude (deflection) about her heavy bleeding was a sign of how she was not yet ready to think about the reality of all that had happened (repression). Her bleeding, like her feelings of loss and grief, had to be completely denied.

## PITFALLS

The defense mechanisms described above operate to prevent or disguise the experience of painful emotions. But they always exact a price. In many cases, they can create more problems in our lives than they solve. They can also hurt the people around us whom we love. Here are just a few of the pitfalls inherent to defense mechanisms.

First, defense mechanisms consume a great deal of emotional and physical energy. Prolonged use of defensive coping mechanisms may even weaken our immune systems, making us more vulnerable to heart disease, cancer, and other stress-induced illnesses.

Second, defense mechanisms can distort our perception of reality. When we do not see or understand ourselves and others clearly, we are doomed to fail repeatedly in dealing with our problems in a productive way.

Third, these defenses do not just filter out painful emotions. Unfortunately, they serve as defenses against *all* emotions. They deaden the range of all of our emotional responses. The more we use defensive mechanisms to protect ourselves from painful feelings, the more we are cutting ourselves off from experiencing the gratifying, heartwarming, joyous, and cheerful feelings that make life meaningful.

Fourth, these defenses can themselves give rise to major mental health problems. These can include suicidal behavior, substance abuse, eating disorders, repeated abortions, traumatic reenactments, and the repetition of disturbing relationships and events, to name just a few of the myriad of symptoms described throughout this book.

Finally, defense mechanisms simply do not cleanse us of our negative experiences. They protect us from unwanted emotions, but they do not eliminate our painful memories and feelings. These problems are concealed, not resolved. As more and more pain is accumulated and hidden away, we will suffer from anxiety, nervousness, agitation, and irritability. We may become emotionally toxic and unpredictable. Whenever the defenses falter, we experience a roller coaster of emotional explosions. It is impossible to fix a leaky pipe until you first acknowledge that it is leaking. The same is true of unwanted emotions. If we deny that they exist, we deny ourselves the chance to deal with them. We deny ourselves an opportunity to heal. Defense mechanisms are not a cure; they are only a series of delaying tactics.

# CHAPTER SEVEN

# CONNECTIONS TO THE PAST

During the first six years after her abortion, Caitlyn's defense mechanisms were firmly in place. She seldom thought about it and was not conscious of any grief or guilt. Then, without any warning, her defenses collapsed in an unexpected way.

> I remember taking my dog to the veterinarian. I got her when she was a puppy and I was really attached to her. Her name was Vagabond. Well, she ended up getting real sick and the vet recommended I have her put to sleep because she was suffering so much.
>
> As he began to schedule the arrangements, I realized I just couldn't do it. I told the vet that I had a hard time allowing something to be killed. As I spoke those words, the memory of my abortion came back like an overpowering nausea. My thought was literally, "Well, you killed your baby; why can't you let your dog die?"
>
> I thought I would throw up right there on the spot. My legs started shaking. I couldn't catch my breath. My abortion had never bothered me until that very moment. I felt so much guilt. My brother ended up taking the dog to the vet for me. I guess I realized I couldn't go through that pain again.
>
> When she was gone, I missed Vaggs, but even more I missed my baby—who should never have died. I kept thinking that I should have a six-year-old there with me! It was really horrible.
>
> My friends thought I was ridiculous because I cried all the time, for almost a year. I would burst into tears at work during the most inappropriate times. I just couldn't hold back my pain. The worst part was that my friends would say, "Why don't you just get another dog?" This would make me cry even harder because it wasn't even the stupid dog I was missing . . . it was my baby. Of course I couldn't tell anyone that!

This is an example of how buried emotions may suddenly burst past the defense mechanisms set up by one's mind. Caitlyn's defense mechanisms had been firmly rooted for years. But when her veterinarian asked her to allow him to put her dog to sleep, this became a powerful mental "connector" to the time she had authorized the death of her unborn child. In this case, the connector was so strong, and the accusation from Caitlyn's unconscious was so unexpected and mockingly vicious, it triggered the complete collapse of her defense mechanisms. Her repressed emotions seized control of her conscious mind and could no longer be ignored. In the absence of adequate support and understanding, however, it was a long time before those feelings of guilt and grief could finally be resolved.

## CONNECTIONS, CONNECTIONS, EVERYWHERE CONNECTIONS

Simply put, while defense mechanisms try to keep unwanted emotions out of the conscious mind, these unwanted feelings are constantly alert for opportunities to breach the defenses and gain attention for themselves. One of their chief means of doing this is through "connectors."

Any person, place, event, or time in the present that even remotely resembles the unwanted memories related to the suppressed emotions can serve as the connector between the present and the past. When a connection is made, the suppressed emotions will surface. In most cases, they will be quickly pushed away by the mind's defense mechanisms. In addition, the mind is well aware of the unwanted emotions' form of attack and will consciously or unconsciously avoid connectors. In chapter five, for example, we saw how many women will avoid pregnant women or babies because these people are connectors to their unresolved feelings over a past abortion. In these examples, the connectors (children and pregnant women) are very hard to avoid completely.

Other connectors are more easily shunned. For example, the first place Sara ate after her abortion was Taco Bell. Thereafter, she developed an aversion to Mexican food. She knew she used to enjoy it, but she had lost her taste for it. It was only after she was in post-abortion counseling that she realized that Mexican food had become a connector to her abortion. Whenever she had seen tacos or burritos on a menu, her ever-alert defense mechanisms would warn her to avoid this troublesome connector by choosing something else.

In a post-abortion group counseling session, Sandra reported a similar insight into an irrational behavior of her own. For years, she had been irritated by the "arrogance" of any man whom she dated who would pay for their dinner with a credit card. If he clicked the card onto the table, she was especially repulsed. It was only after she had begun dealing with her post-abortion grief that Sandra realized that this was a connector to how her boyfriend had paid for the abortion—with the click of a credit card on the receptionist's counter. This visual and audible connector had resulted in an irrational judgment of men for many years, until Sandra finally exposed the connector for what it really was.

Some women will go to extraordinary lengths to avoid connectors to their abortions. Sherry, for example, took a 35-minute detour each day on her way to and from work in order to avoid passing the Women's Health Clinic where she had undergone her abortion.

> I just can't go near that place. It freaks me out. I'd rather drive a hundred miles than have to pass that place. I just can't do it. It makes me sick.

Sherry was conscious of why she was avoiding the clinic. Tina, on the other hand, developed a more general aversion—to music—which she did not understand.

> After my abortion, I had a distressing time going anywhere that played music . . . any kind of music. The only memory I had of my abortion was the songs playing in the background. Afterwards, when I heard music, I got sweaty, my heart raced and I felt frightened and upset. I always felt like something horrifying was going to happen.

One of Nancy's connectors was the weather. For a long time she could not understand why she would frequently experience days of deep sadness and depression. These days seemed to hit her for no apparent reason. Finally Nancy realized that her negative emotions were linked to misty, damp days similar to the day when she had her abortion.

> I remember the moistness in the air the day of my abortion. The earth drizzled with the rain . . . and my tears.

For many women, doctors, hospitals, and surgical equipment are powerful connectors. Rianna had a major post-abortion reaction when she went to visit a friend at a hospital.

> Since my abortion I always hated doctors, hospitals, and waiting rooms. I remember going into a hospital to visit my friend who had been in a car accident. She was okay, just looking for company. As I walked down the corridor I remember being overcome with grief, anxiety, and an unnamed panic. I couldn't control my crying.
>
> On the elevator I remember crying so hard that I could not see the number to push for the correct floor. I was so embarrassed that I could not stop crying. People were looking at me and I remember thinking that they must assume that someone I love just died, due to the way I was grieving. I felt so stupid! I never made it in to see my friend. I had to leave the hospital.
>
> It took me a while to figure out the source of my hysterics. On the way home I realized that the last time I had been in a hospital was the day of my abortion. And actually, if someone on the elevator thought that a death had occurred, they were right. It's just that it happened a long time ago, but I never felt the grief. To this day whenever I go to a hospital I feel a pervasive anxiety and sadness.

Post-abortive women frequently report that gynecological exams are tense and unnerving experiences because of the many strong connectors to their abortions. Wendy described her panic attack this way:

> I remember a particular incident when I was at the gynecologist for a routine exam and pap smear. The nurse pulled out the leg stirrups from underneath the exam table and instructed me to put my feet in them. I remember being in that position and staring at the block ceiling above. Suddenly, from out of the blue, I began to panic. Later I realized that it was the same kind of block ceiling I had stared at during my abortion. All I could say was, "I have to get up . . . I have to get up!" I started screaming, "I have to get out of here!" The doctor helped me to sit up and instructed me to place my head between my legs to stop the hyperventilation. I could barely catch my breath. The attendants were

very kind and gentle, and I slowly began to calm down. Then they offered me orange juice . . . yet another connector. It was the same beverage they gave me following my abortion . . . and to this day I can't stand orange juice.

People, like places and events, can also be connectors. Jeannette's traumatic abortion memories were unexpectedly triggered when she saw the father of her aborted child 14 years after her abortion.

I was working as a teller in a bank. I saw Paul go over to the counter for a transaction. My emotional state exploded. Floodgates of memories and emotions came crashing all around me. I began having panic attacks. I stopped sleeping. I'd just lie in bed half the night and cry.

Jeannette did not initially connect her panic attacks to the abortion. Shocked by her response, she struggled to make sense of why they happened.

The second time he came into the bank, he looked right at me. I don't think he recognized me. I began having physical symptoms of cramping and I almost passed out. I had to leave work. At that point I knew I needed help. I thought I was going crazy.

The cramping sensation Jeannette experienced was very real. The sight of Paul had triggered a buried psychic trauma which reemerged in the form of cramping, the same pain she had felt during her abortion. As she thought about Paul and their relationship, she remembered the abortion, but as if she were watching from a distance, or viewing a foreign film captioned with subtitles. Her grief over the abortion surfaced like a tidal wave, and she cried for days in utter agony.

For many, news stories about abortion arouse intense emotions: anger, fear, and defensiveness. In the Elliot Institute survey, over half of the women surveyed reported that their negative feelings about their abortion became more intense whenever they were exposed to information about fetal development in the media or any kind of news or commentary about abortion from either side of the issue. Rita explained:

I can't stand to watch television or flick through the channels. I am so afraid of coming across some abortion controversy in the news. When there is a story or political protest going on, I never watch TV. It drives me crazy that this issue is in the news. I just want to forget about it.

Whenever exposure to the topic of abortion activates deeply repressed memories and feelings, women and men who normally cope by avoidance are unable to engage the topic with even a remote degree of objectivity. They are more likely to become angry and accusatory.

Another common connector for post-abortive women and men is the mention of God, churches, and anything related to religion. This is because abortion is clearly an important moral issue. For those who are trying to avoid thinking about this issue, distancing themselves from religious beliefs or activities they were previously involved in may become necessary. For Shawn, churches and babies were both strong connectors to her abortion.

> After the abortion, I got panic attacks and negative feelings whenever I went into a church. I also had a difficult time seeing other women pregnant. I felt like a baby killer. I was afraid to hold babies.

The connection between abortion and religious beliefs can lead to avoidance and distancing behaviors. According to Kitty:

> I had been active in a gospel church choir on Sundays. After my abortion I could never step foot in a church again. I figured God hated me for what I had done, and I did not feel worthy. I reasoned that if I went to church I was a hypocrite.

## ANNIVERSARY REACTIONS

Anniversary dates are often connectors to past trauma. In the case of abortion, researchers have found that women are more likely to experience depression, suicidal ideation, nightmares, difficulty concentrating, abdominal pain, cramping, headaches, and increased relationship conflicts around the anniversary of the abortion or on the anticipated due date of the aborted child than at other times.[1] In addition to the anniversary dates, holidays such as Mother's Day or those associated with children (e.g. Christmas and Halloween) can serve as connectors that aggravate post-abortion symptoms. These times can become regular and predictable triggers of traumatic memories. In the case of Rosetta, she faced a double-whammy:

> My baby would have been born at Christmas. Now I hate Christmas. Holiday carols just kill me, and anything to do with Baby Jesus puts me over the edge. I feel excruciating sadness when I go past stores with baby clothing. I try to stay away from kids because they make me sad with thoughts about what I could have had. But Christmas is really the worst. It's a time for kids and I aborted mine, so I can never enjoy the season. Every year I have to suck it up.

Often the anniversary connection is not consciously recognized. It was only after she had begun working through her post-abortion experience that Bonnie came to understand her lack of interest in Mardi Gras.

> Every year I experienced depression. It was always at the time of Mardi Gras, in February. This is a time when things are supposed to be one big "party-all-the-time." But I could never get into it. I just wanted to crawl into bed and let it all go away. My husband would sometimes go to the festivities without me, and that would make me furious. I felt such alienation and depression! I never knew why. I had never allowed myself to figure a due date on the pregnancy that I aborted because "it wasn't meant to be." Doing all the arithmetic would have made it real. After going through an abortion retreat, I sat down one night and calculated the approximate birth date of my child, and sure enough, it was right there in the throes of the Carnival season. All those years, my body

knew that I was mourning, but I never connected the depression to the abortion. I had turned my attention away from the loss . . . all those years!

Another of my clients, Carol had spent several years in therapy trying to uncover the source of a draining depression that made her apathetic, unmotivated, and an underachiever at work. Unfortunately, her counselor assumed that forgotten childhood abuse was the origin of her helplessness and apparent amnesia. But her unconscious sent out clear clues, particularly on February 24—the anniversary date of her abortion—when Carol made the following entry in her diary:

> February 24 . . .
> Seems funny—like I know this day . . .
> So what's to remember about today?
> A clouded memory is the ritual of my unconscious
> telling me what I can remember now,
> and what I can leave alone,
> What is okay to get into,
> And when I must exit the scene.
> What cannot be endured
> and what must be erased.
> How could I forget this day?
> It is the day I had an abortion . . .
> Abortion . . . my pen trembles as I write the word.
> I have spent three years in therapy giving the same stupid answer.
> I can't remember, I think I forget.
> Let's talk about something different today.
> I don't remember being abused. Was I?
> Can everyone notice my pain is intolerable?
> Like the life of my child, I have obliterated the ache,
> By forgetting what happened.
> Like a dream, like a vapor, it all never was . . . was it?
> I am left with an uncertainty about who I am,
> Because I can't remember who I was
> or about the life that tried to come from me.
> And how I felt when it was destroyed.
> There are no feelings. Just blank space where other people
> write on the pages of my life
> about who they want me to be.

Something about the diary entry gave Carol the vague feeling that another loss was at the root of her melancholy. It had taken her 15 years to write down that word: "abortion." It took another four years for her to gain the strength to deal with it. It was at that point that she joined one of my support groups. Hearing the stories of other women helped to confirm the validity of her own reactions. Although Carol still had trouble recalling specifics about her own abortion, their stories were a bridge to releasing her own strong emotions and grief. Looking back, it amazed Carol that she had been able to block such a dramatic event from her memory so successfully.

While not strictly an anniversary reaction, many women discover that Mother's Day is a connector to unresolved abortion issues. For Rachel, buying a Mother's Day card was the trigger.

> I went to buy my mom a card for Mother's Day. I was reading the cards and I suddenly became irritated and anxious. I actually left the store because I felt as though I might burst into tears. I kept telling myself "I have to get out of here!" I figured it was probably my hormones or sugar levels, because I was about to have my period. Later that same week, I went back to the mall a second time to buy a card. I read some more "sappy" cards and felt myself getting upset again. I was so overwhelmed by my feelings! I ended up grabbing a card, without even thinking. It was so weird . . . I bought a card with a mother holding an infant baby. Later, when I read the card I started to cry so hard and I realized why I had been so upset. It was another Mother's Day that I would not be honored, because my own child had been aborted. This was such a painful realization. I cried for days and days. I never did give the card to my own mother, because I thought the card was really for me.

For some women, a different kind of calendar acts as their countdown to grief. Deirdre, for example, did not have any particular recollection of her abortion until her daughter turned 16. At that point Deirdre became agitated and anxious and began to smother her daughter with controlling overprotectiveness. She finally realized she was terrified that her daughter might get into a situation like the one she had found herself in at 16: pregnant and seeking an abortion.

Once Deirdre understood the reasons behind her anxiety, she began to experience grief and depression over her own abortion. She acknowledged her previously forgotten abortion as the greatest trauma of her life. Unfortunately, although Deirdre realized what bothered her and its connection to her 16-year-old daughter's sexual development, she could not explain her apprehension and fears to her daughter. She felt too ashamed to tell her about the abortion and its impact on her. Her own embarrassment, low self-esteem, and shame silenced any meaningful communication that she might have shared.

## MONTHLY REACTIONS

One of the strongest connectors for Natalie was her menstrual period. The sight of blood was symbolic of death and a pointed reminder of her barren womb. "Each day of my period reminds me of my abortion," she explained. "I can't stand the sight of it. I am filled with panic and then depression." Using birth control pills allowed Natalie to cut her period down to two days rather than five. She said she didn't think she would ever go off them, purely for the sake of minimizing her period.

Natalie's conscious reaction may be indicative of a more widespread *unconscious* reaction. A survey of Japanese women aged 20-44 compared the characteristics of menstruation among women with and without a history of induced abortion. Those who had experienced abortion reported a significantly higher incidence of cramps, swelling, and nervousness compared to women with no abortions. The authors of the study suggested that this difference might reflect a psychological reaction.[2]

A woman's capacity to reproduce is brought to her attention every month when she has her period. When her fertility has become associated with the traumatic memory of an abortion, she may become more prone to anxiety, pain, or nervousness during her menstrual flow. This finding suggests that more studies should be undertaken to look for a link between abortion and pre-menstrual syndrome (PMS). PMS is considered to be a modern-day epidemic. While many other factors may also be involved, it is quite possible that much of the emotional distress, tension, and stress associated with a woman's period might actually be related to psychic trauma arising from a history of abortion or sexual abuse.

> It's eleven years since my abortion. Trying to get pregnant has been one of the greatest heartaches for me. I continually think of the abortion and I feel enormous guilt. Each period pulls me into a depression and fear of being punished. I feel my husband would leave me if I ever shared this secret of my past. So I continue to carry on . . . all alone.

## THE BIRTH AND DEATH OF BABIES

The birth of her sister's baby was the trigger that released Tessie's delayed reaction to her abortion.

> The night my sister had a baby, I partied my brains out. I got stoned and drank all the time. Within a month of my nephew's birth, I got kicked out of school. I got in another school and was almost finished . . . till I disappeared one night with some cutthroat scum-bag. For two days I popped pills—uppers and downers—and drank and drank. I ended up almost comatose in the hospital. That was the weekend of my graduation. I was on a deep destructive streak. It was pure chaos. I totally hated myself and wished for death. By the end of the summer I got pregnant again. I knew I couldn't have another abortion so I decided to go it alone.

Tessie tried hard to numb her feelings through drugs and alcohol. She found an outlet for her grief by acting out self-destructive, suicidal, and masochistic behaviors. She punished herself through delinquency, promiscuity, and substance abuse. In the end she got pregnant with a replacement, or atonement, baby.

The birth of later children is often a trigger for post-abortion reactions. In the Elliot Institute survey, nearly half of the women surveyed stated that their negative feelings about their past abortion became worse when they gave birth to later children.

The sight, feel, and smell of a newborn child can overwhelm one's defense mechanisms with the realization that, "I aborted a child just like this beautiful baby. What have I done?" For Julie, this was expressed in her dreams.

> After the births of each of my living children, I experienced nightmares where I was frantically searching the bed for the "lost" baby. My fear was not for my new baby because I knew that one was safe. It was for the other one that I was searching—the one I would never find—the one that I was never told I might miss someday.

Kelly's denial of her feelings was roughly disturbed every time her husband suggested buying a baby gift for the wife of one of his friends.

> I've had two abortions. People having babies always trigger memories of my abortions. I remember my husband wanting me to buy gifts for friends who were "having babies." I used to get furious with him. I thought it was cruel of him to ask me to go out and buy presents for women having babies. I was so ticked-off because he had never acknowledged our baby.

For Brenda, rather than the birth of a child, it was the death of her niece from Sudden Infant Death Syndrome (SIDS) which became the triggering connector to her own unnamed loss.

> I didn't realize the events were related at the time—but I had never grieved the loss of my baby who was aborted. When my niece died, I took it so hard. You would have thought she was MY child. I quit my job. I cried all the time. It took me about a year to let go of the pain.

Since the pain of her own abortion was still being denied, Brenda's unconscious used the death of her niece as an occasion to release her own repressed grief. Grieving for her niece, at that time, was more acceptable to Brenda's conscious mind than grieving over her aborted baby, which would have involved questioning her own decision to have the abortion. Mourning a baby's death over which she had no control was easier than confronting her abortion.

## HANGING ON TO BABY

In the previous chapter, I described the approach-avoidance conflict of women and men who want to resolve (approach) unsettled feelings about a past abortion but who also want to avoid the painful expression of those feelings. There is another interesting two-sided aspect to the abortion experience that helps explain post-abortion trauma.

While memories of abortion bring pain, memories of being pregnant and of one's unborn child may be fondly and jealously guarded. In the latter case, connectors related to the "missing" child may not provoke avoidance behavior, but rather lead to approach behavior. By this I mean that women may save, nurture, and protect memories, feelings, relationships or objects that they associate with the "missing child." This behavior is analogous to how families who have lost a child will often keep the deceased child's bedroom intact, refusing to change or move anything for many years. The child's possessions, saved as if the child might return any day, are preserved as a shrine to memorialize the child.

In the case of an aborted child, however, it is not so easy to create a shrine of possessions to the child's memory. But there are parallels. For example, when attending her post-abortion support group, Jan suddenly had a realization. Reaching into her purse, she pulled out a receipt and spoke to the group.

> I've just realized that I've been carrying this around with me for eight years. It's the receipt from the abortion clinic. I've never paid much attention to it, but for all these years, every time I transferred my stuff from one purse to another, I never threw it away. Just now, I finally realized why. . . . It's the only thing I have that's a connection to my baby. It's the only thing I have that is evidence that he was once alive.

As if little light bulbs were turned on in the heads of the group, three other women fumbled around in their purses and pulled out their own abortion clinic receipts. What most people would consider a morbid bit of trash was to these women nothing less than a "birth certificate" substitute—or more, a physical connection to the children they never held.

For Cindy, the connector she hung onto was a pair of shoes.

> At the abortion clinic, I wore new house shoes that my mother had given me. They had blood on them from my walk from the bathroom to the bed [after the abortion]. After I returned home, I wrapped them in a towel and hid them under long dresses in the back of my closet. Every time I moved between dorm rooms and apartments after college, I moved them and hid them at the back of my new closet. After several years, I washed them but still couldn't look at them because I could still see the blood. Finally, it came to me that I could throw them away.[3]

Samantha remained connected to her aborted child by picketing outside abortion clinics. She was a pro-life activist, yet none of her friends ever knew about her abortion. Although she was aware that her abortion had always haunted her, she had never told anyone or gone through any process of grieving. Meanwhile, she was consumed by the compulsion to be present at every demonstration, regardless of other needs or family demands.

> I have been a protester outside abortion clinics for the past 16 years. I go faithfully, several times a week. My family has complained that I am obsessed with abortion, and I have to agree with them. I might be fighting a cold and it could be snowing out, and I will drag myself out of bed. I curse the whole thing, but don't feel like I have the choice to stay home. The whole abortion thing makes me so angry.

Samantha's grief was funneled into angry protests. By picketing out-side abortion clinics she was able to hold a memorial vigil for her dead child. Her unwavering loyalty and sacrifice to anti-abortion activities was motivated by years of repressed grief and guilt. After attending a retreat for post-abortion healing, Samantha did not feel the burning and unbridled drive for protests. While still opposed to abortion, she can now make freer choices about which activities she will undertake. She is no longer motivated by feelings of agitation and guilt.

## BABY SUBSTITUTES

As previously discussed in chapter five, babies and pregnant women can be connectors to a past abortion that elicit strong feelings of anger and disgust. For some post-abortive women, however, the reaction is exactly the opposite. In the Elliot Institute survey, roughly 20 to 30 per-cent of the women surveyed described themselves as becoming "exces-sively interested" in pregnant women or babies. Marta described her feelings this way:

> After my abortion I desperately wanted to be around babies. My abortion left me empty inside and yearning to hold a child. I ended up taking a job as a nanny in a family with newborn twins and a 3-year-old toddler. Both parents were professionals and were seldom home. I lavished those children with my time and attention, especially the babies. Sometimes I felt a lot of anger at the parents for being too busy to pay attention to their kids . . . but I savored the feeling that the children needed me.

Marta described a genuine love and affection for the children under her care. This satisfied her need to be a mother. At the same time, she was able to redirect her own feelings of grief and anger into her resent-ment of the working mother who was not the "good mother" Marta wanted to be. Marta was not confronted with her own grief until five years later when the twins were enrolled in pre-school. She felt as though they were being unfairly taken away from her. This was the event that triggered Marta's grieving for her own child.

Molly's interest in babies led her to start a daycare center in her home. She describes her craving:

> I have to say my love for babies did not develop for quite a long time. Five years after the last abortion I had my daughter. Not long after that it was pretty clear we were only going to be able to have one child. For a long time I thought it was a kind of punishment for having had the abortions. Of course I was thrilled with the child I was blessed to have, but I wanted more. My girlfriend's situation is exactly the same. As we get older, I think the true reality of what we have done and lived through hits home more and more. The simple joy of watching a mother nurse her child can bring me to tears. I do love children. There is something so pure and totally innocent about them, especially babies. I think it has to do with something we could not capture with our aborted

babies. To love all the ones we can now, while we have the chance, is somehow affirming.

## MAKING THE CONNECTION

Every thought, every emotion, is connected to other thoughts and emotions. It is part of our human nature. We can never escape these connections. Nor would we want to. They are fundamental to the nature of our memory, our intuition, and our wisdom. Without connections between our memories, our emotions, and our thoughts, we would not have any meaningful memories, emotions, or thoughts.

The problem is not connectors, but our lack of awareness of connectors to negative memories, emotions, or thoughts. Whenever these connectors trigger aversions or feed compulsions, their effect is to inhibit our free will. Connectors that are not understood end up distorting our ability to make rational choices. They can be likened to pinball bumpers that spring up unexpectedly in our lives and send us off in a different direction than we intended to go.

When connectors are related to negative emotions and experiences, they are there to call our attention to unresolved issues. If we do not want to be controlled by these connectors, if we want to be free to choose our own course without feelings of fear, anxiety, depression, and guilt, we must trace these connectors to their source, see them, acknowledge them, and understand them. By following these connectors to their source, we finally confront the truth, and in doing so, overcome our bondage to fear and past mistakes. By acknowledging the past and seeing it for what it is—the past—we are no longer bound by it, but are able to build on it.

The past is like a great cave. It's easy to be afraid of what might be lying in all those dark corners. But when we fearlessly explore it and understand its terrain, we can mine it for precious gems and nuggets of gold. Those memories of mistakes, those experiences of trauma, which we were once afraid to explore, can be mined for nuggets of wisdom and empathy that will serve us well in the future. By exploring these dark crannies, these disturbing connections, we will discover the resolve and resources to better serve both others and ourselves.

# CHAPTER EIGHT

# ABORTION AS A TRAUMATIC EXPERIENCE

Eleven months after her marriage, Lora thought her American dream had come true. She had a handsome husband, a home of her own, and now she was pregnant! She carefully planned how to tell her husband, John, the good news. She bought a tiny baby's bib, waited for a private moment together, and gently laid it upon his chest, offering him the gift of her child.

Instead of rejoicing, John cursed at her. He insisted they weren't ready. They couldn't afford a baby. She would have to have an abortion.

Lora was stunned. She had been raised in a traditional Catholic home. She had always believed that a child was the greatest gift a woman could give her husband. She didn't realize that her young husband, who had been abandoned by his mother and father as a child and raised by relatives, had his own unresolved fears about becoming a father. In many way he was immature and narcissistic. Many elements of their relationship suggested that he wanted Lora to fill the role of both a wife and the mother he never had. Perhaps the idea that a child, even his own child, might compete with him for her maternal affections was intolerable. In any case, no matter how much Lora pleaded with him, he would not relent. Abortion was the only option.

When Lora insisted that she would have the baby anyway, John threatened to leave her. For Lora, this was a grave threat. Divorce was unthinkable. She had been raised to believe that a couple must be willing to make any sacrifice to keep their marriage afloat. She turned to a friend, seeking support for her desire to keep her baby. But her friend encouraged the idea of abortion, telling Lora she had "had a couple of abortions and it wasn't that bad." Lacking support from any quarter, and torn between her love for her child and her duty to her husband, Lora gave in.

On June 15th, when she would otherwise have been busy planning to celebrate their first wedding anniversary three days later, Lora had an abortion. Immediately afterwards, she felt as if her life was over. Emotionally she felt as if she was falling apart. She no longer found pleasure in any of the activities she had previously enjoyed. She experienced her first major depression. She became sexually frigid. She began stealing supplies and cash from her employer.

Lora and John's relationship was poisoned by the abortion. She resented him. He felt rebuked by every sign of her sadness, anger, and depression. They became verbally and physically abusive with each other. He taunted her with a string of extramarital affairs.

During the next three years, they were separated twice. But there was a bond between them that neither wanted to break. After making mutual promises to reform their behavior, they moved into an apartment together.

Finally, Lora hoped, they could have the "replacement" baby she so desired. But then, as had happened several times before, John invited one of his buddies to come live with them. Lora saw the writing on the wall. Once again she would be burdened with another long-term house guest with whom her husband would spend his nights partying. It was as if he were afraid to let their own relationship become too close. Having a party buddy in the house was his way of keeping her at a safe emotional distance. Lora threw down the gauntlet. If John's friend Robbie moved in, she would move out.

As the deadline approached, Lora began complaining to friends and neighbors that John had been raping and abusing her, but she refused all their offers of shelter. Still hoping to conceive her replacement pregnancy, Lora continued to have consensual intercourse with John. She wouldn't leave him yet.

The timing for this conflict could not have been worse. John's friend, Robbie, was due to arrive on Father's Day, just two days after their fourth wedding anniversary and five days after the third anniversary of her abortion. Lora spent her wedding anniversary at her doctor's office with all the symptoms of a classic post-abortion anniversary reaction. Her hands were shaking and she was hyperventilating. She had cramping in her abdomen, feelings of anxiety, and difficulty concentrating.

Two days later, Robbie arrived. Lora moved many of her belongings out of the apartment but continued to sleep with John and declined another girlfriend's offer of shelter. On the third night after Robbie moved in, John came to bed at three in the morning after being out drinking with his friend. Shortly after that, Lora found herself in the kitchen experiencing flashbacks to her abortion. All the loss and anger she felt about the abortion and her chaotic relationship with John came to a head. She picked up a knife, walked into the bedroom and cut off her husband's penis. Before he or Robbie could react, she fled the house with it, pausing only long enough to grab up Robbie's portable Game Boy.

By this point, you almost certainly will have realized that Lora's real name is Lorena. She and her husband, John Wayne Bobbitt, were at the center of one of the world's most spectacular trials of the late twentieth century.

As you may recall, Lorena Bobbitt was acquitted of the crime of malicious wounding on the grounds that she suffered from temporary insanity arising from post-traumatic stress disorder (PTSD). The psychiatrists who offered expert testimony for both the defense and the prosecution agreed that Lorena had PTSD and was experiencing major depression at the time of the cutting incident. There was even substantial testimony in the trial regarding the coerced abortion, Lorena's subsequent psychological problems, and her flashbacks to the abortion prior to the cutting. But this connection was never fully explored in the trial, much less in the media coverage of the case. As a result, few people in the general public understand the underlying cause of Lorena's mental breakdown.

But post-abortion specialists, and many women who have suffered from abortion-related PTSD, immediately suspected a connection to a traumatic abortion as soon as the first stories about the attack were released. (These suspicions were later confirmed by subsequent reports.[1]) Indeed, Jane, one of my own post-abortion clients, came into my office shortly after this incident proclaiming, "Someone finally did it . . . I wish I had the nerve!"

Jane's comment reflected the experience of many women who have had their own fertility stolen from them by men who coerced them into unwanted abortions. It is not unusual for women to describe themselves as feeling "castrated" by an abortion. This experience was first reported by psychiatrist Theodor Reik in 1953.[2] In less severe cases, a woman may feel that her partner's support for abortion is a rejection of her sexuality.[3]

I have frequently seen this dynamic present in my own counseling practice. For example, Megan had become excessively preoccupied with thoughts of the man who had impregnated her. She experienced detailed fantasies and dreams of revenge, castration, and events that would heap misfortune and chaos upon his life. She wanted him to hurt in the same way she had been hurt. Her intense anger and fixation on him was a way to avoid her grief. It served as a means by which she desperately kept her relationship with her aborted child alive. Rage became a tool she used to survive endless moments of intolerable pain.

Megan did not act on her fantasy. But it takes no great leap of the imagination to see how a woman like Lorena Bobbitt, who felt sexually mutilated by her abortion, at least on a subconscious level, would in a moment of bitter passion focus her attack on an attempt to castrate her husband in return.

I am not suggesting that Lorena consciously made a decision to sexually mutilate her husband that night. But the known facts of the case, and the powerful symbols involved in the attack, lead directly to the conclusion that Lorena's abortion shaped not only the form of the attack (on John's sexuality) but also the timing of it (on approximately the third anniversary of the abortion.)

The fact that Lorena ran off with the penis still in her hand clearly supports the argument that she was not acting rationally that night. Her deranged behavior is further evident in the fact that she also grabbed up a child's toy when fleeing the house. On a rational level, the theft of a Game Boy after mutilating her husband is extremely odd. But highly symbolic acts are often disturbing. Indeed, the irrationality of this act underscores its symbolic importance.

One possible explanation is that she stole the video game as a means of punishing John (and his intrusive friend) for his preoccupation with toys and adolescent escapades. John's cherished toys and partying friend reflected his inability to assume the responsibilities of fatherhood and a mature marital relationship. He had deprived her of their child in order to protect his adolescent lifestyle from the responsibilities of fatherhood. Now, she was depriving him of his immature games and his sexual license.

Alternatively, as Lorena was fleeing the house and their doomed relationship, she may also have been reflexively grabbing up symbols of her aborted, *wanted* child whom she did not want to leave behind. In one hand she clutched a phallic symbol, the source of her aborted child's life. In the other hand she held a Game Boy, which even by its very name symbolized the missing little boy she so desperately wanted to take with her. On that night, perhaps, Lorena was not just running from the scene of horrible domestic violence; she was reclaiming and fleeing with her symbolic replacement child. But it was only that, symbolic.

John Wayne Bobbitt's reproductive organ was stitched back into place. As subsequent headlines revealed, John's sexual function and adolescent lifestyle were renewed. But there is no miraculous surgery to repair Lorena's loss.

In choosing to begin this chapter with the Bobbitts' story, I've taken a calculated risk. Though it was a highly publicized, dramatic story, most people did not recognize that Lorena's abortion was the underlying cause of her post-traumatic stress disorder (PTSD), which preceded her violent act. On the other hand, the Bobbitt case is also an extreme example. Most women who suffer from PTSD following abortion do not "snap" and become violent. Still, the Bobbitt story, along with many of the other women's stories recorded in this book, does illustrate that PTSD following abortion can result in bizarre behaviors. As we will see in the next few chapters, these irrational behaviors can only be understood in the context of reenacting the trauma of a past abortion.

## WHAT IS POST-TRAUMATIC STRESS DISORDER?

In the previous two chapters we discussed how defense mechanisms are used to avoid unwanted thoughts, memories, emotions, or truths. These defense mechanisms are waging a battle against all those forces—

one's unconscious mind, daily experiences, or the admonitions of one's friends or family—that seek to draw the conscious mind to face these unpleasant thoughts, memories, emotions, or truths.

Post-traumatic stress disorder is simply a special variation of this common mental conflict. Not everyone who uses defense mechanisms suffers from PTSD. Not everyone who has an abortion suffers from PTSD. Nor does everyone who has been exposed to a traumatic experience necessarily suffer from PTSD.

Fundamentally, PTSD is not a tangible thing, like a virus or a brain tumor. It is simply a label therapists use to describe a specific grouping of psychological symptoms. By classifying and grouping these symptoms, therapists are better able to communicate with each other about the types of emotional problems they are treating and about the types of treatment that are most effective. Knowing that symptom B is often found when symptom A is present also helps therapists explore underlying issues that a patient or client might not initially volunteer.

The American Psychiatric Association's definition of PTSD represents some of the most modern theory on the nature and effects of trauma. As described in Appendix A, however, the study of trauma has historically been marked by controversy and political maneuvering. Trauma victims and their advocates have been dismissed as exaggerators by those who either support social structures that perpetuate the causes of trauma or are simply embarrassed to confront the causes of trauma. This same pattern of denial continues to be played out with regard to abortion trauma. (See Appendix A for more on the controversy regarding abortion-related PTSD and chapters 2 and 3 regarding other examples of social and professional denial.)

As it is currently defined, PTSD can be described as a psychological disorder that results from a traumatic experience that overwhelms a person's normal defense mechanisms. The shock of this experience is so great that the person's defense mechanisms become disorganized and disconnected from reality, either temporarily or for a prolonged and indefinite period of time.

More precisely, the formal definition of PTSD involves two major elements and three types of symptoms. The first element, a traumatic event, can be any event in which one either witnesses or experiences "actual or threatened death or serious injury, or a threat to the physical integrity of oneself or others." If a person has "experienced, witnessed, or been confronted with" such a traumatic event and "the person's response involved intense fear, helplessness, or horror," he or she is considered eligible for a diagnosis of PTSD.[4]

Following this initial evaluation of circumstances, a clinical diagnosis of PTSD requires identification of symptoms in all three of the following broad categories: hyperarousal, intrusion, and constriction.

*Hyperarousal* is a characteristic of inappropriately and chronically aroused "fight or flight" defense mechanisms. In some way, the person is almost always on the alert for threats of danger. Symptoms of hyperarousal include exaggerated startle responses, anxiety attacks, difficulty falling or staying asleep, irritability, outbursts of anger or rage, aggressive behavior, difficulty concentrating, hyper-vigilance, or physiological reactions upon exposure to situations that symbolize or resemble an aspect of the traumatic experience. Connectors, such as those described in chapter seven, may often trigger symptoms of hyperarousal. For instance, when a post-abortive woman experiences anxiety, an elevated pulse, or sweating during a routine pelvic exam, this is an example of hyperarousal.

*Intrusion* is the reexperience or reliving of the traumatic event in one of many ways. In the case of abortion-related PTSD, intrusion can include recurrent and intrusive thoughts about the abortion or the aborted child, flashbacks in which the woman momentarily reexperiences an aspect of the abortion experience, nightmares about the abortion or child, or anniversary reactions of intense grief or depression on the due date of the aborted pregnancy or the anniversary date of the abortion. Repeat abortions and replacement pregnancies are two common ways in which women reenact elements of their abortion trauma. In many cases, some aspect of the trauma is recreated in disguised or symbolic ways. Risk-taking behavior, suicidal impulses, and obsessive-compulsive behaviors may arise from unconscious reenactment of elements related to the unresolved trauma.

*Constriction* is the numbing of one's emotions or the development of behavior patterns designed to avoid any sights, sounds, smells, or feelings associated with the trauma. It is often marked by feeling helpless or powerless to control or direct one's life. It involves an attempt to deny and avoid negative feelings and/or people, places, or things that aggravate the feelings associated with the trauma. In post-abortion trauma cases, constriction may include: an inability to recall the abortion experience or important parts of it; efforts to avoid activities or situations that may arouse recollections of the abortion; withdrawal from relationships, especially estrangement from those involved in the abortion decision; avoidance of children; efforts to avoid or deny thoughts or feelings about the abortion; a restricted range of loving or tender feelings; a sense of a foreshortened future (e.g., does not expect a career, marriage, or children, or a long life); diminished interest in previously enjoyed activities; drug or alcohol abuse; suicidal thoughts or acts; and other self-destructive tendencies.

It is common in cases of PTSD for the symptoms of *hyperarousal*, marked by high levels of emotion, to alternate with periods of pronounced *constriction*, the numbing of one's emotions. This alternating between states reflects a form of the approach-avoidance conflict discussed in chapter six. Through *constriction* one seeks to avoid thoughts and memories related to the trauma. By means of *intrusion*, the subconscious draws attention to some aspect of the traumatic experience, resulting in a period of *hyperarousal*. As a woman (or man) who suffers from PTSD oscillates through this approach-avoidance cycle, she may observe that she is constantly alternating between feeling emotionally numb and feeling emotionally overtaxed. It is very likely that the emotionally overtaxing periods will be triggered by thoughts or events that symbolically force her to relive aspects of the traumatic event.[5]

The three categories of PTSD symptoms are themselves symbolic of different aspects of the traumatic experience: "Hyperarousal reflects the persistent expectation of danger; intrusion reflects the indelible imprint of the traumatic moment; constriction reflects the numbing response of surrender."[6]

Victims of PTSD typically experience an initial state of numbness while psychologically trying to integrate the traumatic experience. Later symptoms, which may not appear for months or even years, include irritability, depression, an unreasoned sense of guilt for having survived while others did not, memory impairment or trouble concentrating, and difficulties relating emotionally to other people. Nightmares, flashbacks to the traumatic scene, and overreaction to noises or situations that remind one of the trauma are also common.[7]

## TRAUMATIC FEAR, HELPLESSNESS, OR HORROR

As Molly lay on the abortion clinic operating table, she fought a grave fear that something bad would happen to her. In part, this was due to the natural nervousness she felt at undergoing her first surgery of any kind. But she also feared that God would punish her for having an abortion, and this punishment might come in the form of an immediate injury or long-term reproductive damage.

> My abortion was a horrifying experience. I remember lying back on the table . . . unable to lay my head back because I wanted to see what was happening. My legs were shaking and I kept trying to close them together. The doctor appeared irritated and told me that he could not work if I did not keep my legs spread apart. I was terrified that something would go wrong. What if the doctor's instrument slipped? What if he cut my uterus and I ended up in the hospital? What if I could never have children? I tried to do as instructed, but I was terrified. I could not control my tears, shaking, and crying. For a few moments during the procedure, I wished for death. What if I died during the operation? I had fantasies about them taking my body out of the clinic to the morgue and my mother having to come identify me.
>
> When it was all over, I felt a horrible guilt. I was certain that God would punish me for what I had done. I felt I did not deserve to have a baby because

I had killed one. I was tormented by this fear for years, along with a disturbing fear that when and if I had kids, they would be retarded, handicapped, or would die from some terrible disease.

In Molly's case, the intense fear she felt at the time of the abortion was focused on the idea that she might die or be seriously injured herself. Later that anxiety was focused into fears of appalling things happening to any children she might have in the future. In Katrina's case, on the other hand, the same event—abortion—produced an emotional reaction focused on her horror at seeing her aborted child.

My doctor promised me that the procedure would be safe and private right in her office. The sooner it was done, the better, since the baby had no shape at this point . . . just a bunch of growing tissue. I wanted to believe that, in spite of knowing better myself. I posed no questions and neither did my fiance. The date was set for a Saturday.

That morning we drove there together in silence. I was taken in and prepared for the surgery. The doctor came in, but it wasn't my regular doctor. It was a man I'd never seen before. He was not introduced but went right to work. It hurt terribly; he was very rough and spoke harshly to me when I cried. The nurse held my hand and told me to just relax. The machine went off and I thought the procedure was over. They went over to the sink and were doing something. Then they came back and on went the machine again. It seemed to go on forever. Finally it was over.

They left the room, telling me to get dressed. In my curiosity, I went over to the sink to see what they were looking at. There were all the reassembled parts of my baby: arms, legs, torso and what must have been the head. They were tiny and perfect. In that instant I felt an incredible horror. This was my baby! Torn apart, in bloody pieces. The terror and agony of that moment is etched deeply into my soul. My doctor, the abortionist, the staff—all liars! Surely they could see what I could see. I hated them. But at the same time, I knew I was part of that lie because I knew I could never tell anyone. I left the office in a state of numb repulsion. I began to despise myself even more than them.

In many cases, especially when the woman feels she has no choice but to abort because of pressure from others or her circumstances, her overriding emotional response at the time may be a sense of helplessness. She feels unable to alter the course of events that are driving her inexorably toward an unwanted abortion. A particularly dramatic case is Jennifer, who had been incestuously raped by her father.

The doctor informed me that I was pregnant and asked me what I wanted. I had seen the "Silent Scream" in high school religion class and knew that abortion was murder. In spite of the pain and guilt I felt, knowing who the father of the baby was, it was far better to have a baby than the alternative—to kill it. I refused to have an abortion.

My father flew into an uncontrollable rage and demanded that I consent to the abortion, or that the doctor do it with or without my permission. The doctor refused because of my wishes. My father demanded that an abortionist be found—regardless of the cost.

Within one hour, this man arrived at the hospital, talked with my parents and decided to do the abortion, without speaking to me. I refused and tried to get off the examining table. He then asked three nurses to hold me while he strapped me to the bed and injected me with a muscle relaxant to keep me from struggling while he prepared to kill my baby. I continued to scream that I didn't want an abortion. He told me, "Shut up and quit that yelling!" Eventually, I was placed under general anesthesia and my child was brutally killed. . . .

I grieve every day for my daughter. I have struggled to forget the abuse and the abortion. I can do neither. All I think of is, "I should have done more, fought more, struggled more for the life of my child."[8]

Frequently, women report that shortly after their abortion began, they suddenly changed their minds and told the abortionist to stop. In many cases, the doctor told them it was too late to stop and continued despite their protests. Such experiences can reinforce a woman's sense of helplessness during an abortion. This can contribute, as in the case of Alexa, to subsequent survivor guilt.

I had convinced myself that having an abortion would be for the best. I was in a no-win situation and I had to take this route. In the waiting room, I was shaking but confident. I wouldn't allow any negative thoughts to enter my head.

When they called my name, I got up. As I went with them, I began trembling even harder. I knew I was going to have to be strong. I got up on the table as directed, and a feeling of disbelief came over me. Was I really doing this? When the doctor came in, I asked him some questions. I don't even remember what I asked, just that he ignored me and the nurse answered me, sort of covering for him. I began to feel that I didn't want to be there. I told them I wanted to leave, but again, I was ignored. A fear rose in my chest. I was truly frightened . . . what was I doing there? I grabbed the nurse's hand and held tightly as the procedure began. There was no way out. I was there and I didn't want to be. I wanted to leave but couldn't. My life was being sucked out of me. I was helpless. I began to beg them to let me leave. The nurse just held my hand more securely. Then the fear in me surged and I tried to throw myself off the table. I had to get out of that place. They held me down. I couldn't go, I couldn't breathe, I felt I was being suffocated. I screamed and they held me with reinforcements. I thought I was dying. Nothing mattered but to get off the table. I was becoming weaker, and then I don't remember anything. I don't know what happened . . . they just finished with me. When I woke up, I cried. I feel like I've been crying ever since.

## ABORTION AS AN EXPERIENCE OF VIOLENCE

Regardless of the reasons why they have chosen to abort, and even if they are morally comfortable with their decision, many women experience abortion as a violation of their "physical integrity," as it is termed in the definition of PTSD. In many cases, women have described their abortions as feeling like "surgical rape."[9] This analogy is not surprising when one considers the actual mechanics of abortion. The woman is prone on her back, legs spread, with a masked stranger plunging instruments into her sexual organs, painfully and literally sucking life out of her womb. Linda described her abortion as follows:

> I was fully awake, no pills given, or shots. I lay there with tears rolling down my face. The room was cool. My tears felt like fire on my face, cutting it, slice by slice, tear by tear. My hands were wet with sweat; my right hand squeezed the counselor's thin, cold hand as though squeezing the life out of her. My left hand lay fisted, clenched tightly on my vibrating stomach as the abortion oc-curred. It felt as though someone was raping me with a 15-Amp canister vacuum hose with no mercy as I lay there helpless, crying calmly, as if agree-ing to be raped.

This experience of abortion as a violation of a woman's physical integrity is likely to be even more pronounced in women with a history of being sexually abused or raped. In these instances, the abortion is a connector to these other traumas. This is why a history of sexual abuse is a risk factor for greater post-abortion psychiatric problems. Adding trauma on top of trauma is not healthy, even if the victim is freely con-senting to the abortion. As we will see in the next chapter, the intrusion aspect of trauma means that the victims are more likely to recreate trauma in their lives. Providing abortions to women with a history of sexual assault or abuse contributes, in many cases, to self-destructive tendencies. This is especially worrisome in light of recent studies that indicate that up to one-third of women have been the victims of rape or sexual abuse.[10]

According to one abortion clinic nurse, "Abortion is the narrowest edge between kindness and cruelty. Done as well as it can be done, it is still violence. . . . "[11] According to Missy:

> My abortion was extremely traumatic. The pain was excruciating. They kept telling me not to arch my back. I remember nurses coming in to hold me down. The machine sounded like a broken-down air conditioner. It was so loud. I felt helpless, trapped, violated. I fainted when I sat up after the abortion.

By its very nature, abortion requires a violation of a woman's body. Her cervix, which nature has designed to remain closed to protect the developing human fetus, must be forcibly opened. Then, her womb, which is designed to nurture life, must be penetrated, suctioned, and scraped. For many women, this experience is nothing less than their first intimate encounter with death.

> The pain of the abortion procedure was a physical manifestation of the taking of life from my body. It was an experience I will never forget. After it was over, I felt confused and shaken; then, sitting in the recovery room, I was overcome with enormous regret. I felt so overwhelmed by the emotion that I didn't even sit there for 40 seconds before I got up, dressed, and walked out, pretending as if nothing in my life had changed. But everything had.

For Rosemary, the sight of babies became the connector to the death experience of abortion.

> When I was on that table, for the first time ever in my life, I experienced death

in all its blackness and finality. Now I have what I call "lock on" syndrome. I zoom in on every single infant around me wherever I am and am reminded of the incredible pain and guilt and panic at the horror of my choice. I am having deep feelings of regret and self-hatred. I am having immense difficulty reconciling the life around me with the death and the irretrievable loss I feel inside.

To fully ponder the tragedy of aborting one's own child is frightening, overwhelming, and perhaps simply impossible. For Heather, this memory lingered at the edges of her conscience, keeping the pain of her loss intensely alive.

The pain of my abortion is so real. The thought of killing your own child can push you over the edge. It has taken me years to overcome this grief. Abortion destroyed not only my child, but myself. I wish people knew that the aborted baby never really goes away.

For Kari, the death of her child also involved a death of some part of herself.

A part of me died, and it took me nine-and-a-half years to identify what died. The part of me that died from my abortion was my son or daughter whom I'll never know. I repressed and denied this for so long that emotionally I started to die too. I started to lose interest in life. My husband didn't matter. My children didn't matter. I wanted to die, but I never knew why. I felt like I was a lost child who didn't want to find my way home. I was a tree in spring without a bud of life on any branch. My roots lost their ability to drink the water of life. I never quite knew what was wrong with me.

## Victims or Perpetrators?

It is extremely important to note that PTSD is not limited simply to "victims" as we normally think of the term. The perpetrators of violence can suffer from PTSD just as easily as their direct victims. Indeed, as Dr. Judith Lewis Herman has noted, "the risk of a post-traumatic disorder is highest of all when the survivor has been not only a passive witness but also an active participant in violent death or atrocity."[12] This is because the horror of what has happened is magnified by a sense of personal responsibility and self-blame.

In the case of abortion-related PTSD, women are generally more likely to see themselves as perpetrators than victims. From a third-person perspective, however, it has been my observation that in the vast majority of abortion cases there are elements of both free consent and lack of freedom. On one hand, most women know on some level what will truly happen and are responsible for choosing or consenting to an abortion. On the other hand, most also feel hemmed in by outside pressures, whether from individuals or their circumstances, that make them feel they have no choice but to concede to an abortion. In this respect, they share the characteristics of victims.

My boyfriend called the clinic and set up the abortion for two weeks later. I never told anyone else about my situation and still no one close to me knows what happened. I never wanted the abortion, my boyfriend did. The day of the abortion, the counselor asked me if I wanted my boyfriend to come in with me while she talked to me. I said yes, knowing that I could not tell her myself that the abortion was what I wanted. She asked me questions, and *he* answered them for me. I don't see how she could have missed the tears in my eyes and the lump in my throat. She must have sensed my reluctance, but it seemed like all she cared about was "selling the abortion." I admit that most of the blame lies with me for allowing my boyfriend to bully me into this. My motherly instinct to protect the baby was running strong within me, but I was scared. I felt like I was in a dream where I tried to scream but no sound would come out–I was petrified and paralyzed with fear. However, I do not feel the clinic should have allowed my boyfriend to set up the appointment and to answer for me.

As one woman put it, rather than choosing abortion, she "made the choice to be weak," to simply allow those around her to guide her into the "only thing" that could be done. In such cases, an abortion may lead women to experience all three of the responses that are marks of trauma: fear, helplessness, and horror.

It is quite likely that most women having abortions fall into this over-lapping category. Numerous studies have shown that most women see abortion as involving their participation in the destruction of a human life, specifically, their own child's life. Eleanor describes her experience:

I am in the abortion clinic with at least 100 women in the waiting room, sitting, standing—everywhere! To protect our identities, we were each given a number. So I waited for my number to be called. For hours there was dead silence. I felt like I was in a morgue. Frozen in fear, I hear my number being called. They check your name to match your number; then they take you to get ready for the procedure. "Everything will be fine," says the nurse, "it will be over in a few minutes." As I lay in terror, I hear a voice shriek through my head, "No Mommy! Nooooo!" I sit up in shock and terror. The nurse pushes me down saying, "It's okay; it's all over now!" The doctor leaves to go to the next patient. I grab the nurse in tears: "I heard my child's voice! I heard my child cry!" "Don't worry," says the nurse. "In time it will go away." Somehow I blocked that moment out until 12 years later in therapy I began to face my fears. Slowly I began to deal with all the problems in my life.

Seventy percent of women undergoing abortion believe abortion involves the killing of a human life, which violates their own moral standards.[13] Thirty to 60 percent were initially happy about being pregnant and enjoyed being pregnant.[14] As many as 60 to 80 percent would actually have preferred to give birth if only their circumstances had been better.[15] And between 30 and 55 percent report that they felt pressured to abort by others.[16]

These statistics underline two points in the above discussion. First, the majority of women having abortions recognize it as an event that involves the killing of an innocent life. Second, they participate in this violation of their consciences because they feel helpless to resist or change the circumstances that are "forcing" them to choose abortion. Lorri reflects on her experience:

> I regret that no one comforted me and offered a different solution to my situation. You see, that baby was in my womb. The bond was between my baby and me, and not even an abortion could break it. However, the love I feel for my baby is mixed with an incredible amount of guilt for taking his life; and I miss him so very much. I am left alone with the memory of the warmth of that little life within me, and the shame of allowing it to be killed.

For most women, abortion is, at best, "a type of murder" that is endured as an evil necessity only because it will "save her life."[17] The desperation that lies behind many abortion decisions has been well described in the analogy: "No woman wants an abortion as she wants an ice cream cone or a Porsche. She wants an abortion as an animal caught in a trap wants to gnaw off its own leg."[18]

## How Often Does Abortion Cause PTSD?

There are a wide variety of reactions to abortion. No woman will experience every symptom that has been reported. Some women experience clusters of symptoms; others may have a very dramatic and debilitating reaction; still others may appear to tolerate the procedure and its aftermath with little, if any, effect, at least during the period in which their reactions are studied.

When one listens to the intense pain, grief, and confusion women experience after an abortion that was supposed to make their lives better, it is easy to understand their need to withdraw and deny their experience. Without the understanding and support of loved ones, it is simply too much to bear on one's own. For many, the denial begins immediately. For example, Terry spent four hours in a subway coffee shop after her abortion.

> I was in a complete daze. I couldn't believe what I had actually done. I couldn't think about it. I sat and stared at people walking by. I felt as though I had left my own body.

For another client, Sonnie, the fear of confronting the source of her trauma resulted in years of confused denial.

> I was afraid to think about my abortion. I couldn't allow myself to think of my abortion as a loss. For years I did not even know what was wrong with me. I never identified the source of my anger and pain. I just knew I was hurting inside . . . real bad. I cut myself off from my feelings. I was always numb.

No woman is safe from these negative emotions. Even those who have spent years battling for abortion rights, and who have intellectually confronted all the issues surrounding the question of abortion, may suddenly find themselves ill-prepared to cope with the emotional impact of abortion.[19]  As previously quoted,  Dr. Julius Fogel, a psychiatrist and obstetrician who has performed more than 20,000 abortions, insists:

> Every woman—whatever her age, background or sexuality—has a trauma at destroying a pregnancy. A level of humanness is touched. This is a part of her own life. When she destroys a pregnancy, she is destroying herself. There is no way it can be innocuous. One is dealing with the life force. It is totally beside the point whether or not you think a life is there. You cannot deny that something is being created and that this creation is physically happening.[20]

As described in Appendix B, there are no clear answers as to how many women experience negative emotional reactions to an abortion. The diagnosis of abortion as producing a traumatic reaction is especially politicized, as described in Appendix A.

While many studies have looked at a wide variety of post-abortion reactions, very few have collected statistically validated data directly examining the PTSD model. Perhaps the most important of these studies was conducted by Catherine Barnard, who studied 80 women who had all undergone abortions at a Baltimore clinic three to five years earlier. Using standardized measures for PTSD, Barnard found that approximately one in five women (19 percent) met all the criteria for diagnosable post-traumatic stress disorder (PTSD). Approximately half had many, but not all, of the symptoms of PTSD, and 20 to 40 percent showed moderate to high levels of stress and avoidance behavior relative to their abortion experiences.[21]

Barnard's study would appear to have established a base-line estimate of around 20 percent for the incidence of PTSD following abortion in the general population. The actual rate of PTSD, however, may be significantly higher, since half of the women who were contacted refused to participate in the study. (Other research has shown that the women who refuse to participate in post-abortion follow-up studies are the most likely to match the characteristics of the women reporting the most problems.[22]  In other words, women who find their abortions a painful subject are least likely to participate in studies examining their pain.) Among women who actually seek out post-abortion counseling, as many as 73 percent may be diagnosed as suffering from PTSD using standardized tools for evaluation.[23]

## DELAYED PTSD REACTIONS

A person's immediate emotional response to a traumatic event does not solely determine whether or not that person will suffer the symptoms of PTSD. A considerable period of time may intervene between the trauma-causing event and the traumatic reaction. For example, imagine a new terrorist recruit who is instructed to throw a bomb over a wall. At the sound of the explosion, the young terrorist may actually feel powerful rather than helpless, courageous rather than fearful, jubilant rather than horrified. But if the young bomb thrower later walks around the wall and sees the bodies of his victims, his emotional response might be instantly changed. Though in his mind he knew what to expect, the horror of actually seeing the results of his act may overwhelm his intellectual justifications for doing what "had to be done." If he subsequently develops symptoms of hyperarousal, intrusion, and constriction, he has developed PTSD.

Similarly, for many women, the traumatic nature of their abortion is not fully released until some subsequent event triggers a fuller understanding of everything that has happened. In the case of abortion, PTSD symptoms can obviously be triggered by exposure to the ghastly image of a dismembered fetus. But a similar sense of horror can also be triggered by what are normally wonderful experiences. Any experience that arouses a sense of awe about the value of life can trigger the release of a traumatic reaction to a past abortion. From such a summit of awe, the memory of having been involved in an abortion may suddenly appear to be a terrible horror. This was Audrey's experience during the pregnancy and birth of her first child.

> Throughout my pregnancy I was anxious. The experience of having a baby brought on all the memories of my abortion and an enormous amount of guilt. I thought I would die after seeing my first ultrasound. I watched the screen amazed and mortified. Amazed to see my baby, the outline of her face, her hands, beating heart, spine and so forth. Mortified that this is not at all what I thought was being "evacuated" years before when I had an abortion.

For Robin, it was a visit home for her parents' anniversary and the sight of her nieces and nephews that released her traumatic reactions.

> I had my abortion at the age of nineteen. I was fine afterwards, and grateful to the clinic and staff who assisted me. I became pregnant again two years later and had another abortion. Later, I helped several of my friends get abortions because I was the "experienced" one. I used humor and sarcasm to deal with any feelings. I entered the airline business and traveled all over the country. Most people thought I had a glamorous life, and my freedom was the envy of many.
>
> Then one summer it all fell apart. I was invited home for an anniversary party that my brothers and sisters were having for my parents. I had not been home in 11 years. I felt terrified to go and thought of all the ways I could avoid the trip. I became depressed and started drinking a lot. A good friend asked me what I was afraid of . . . and I honestly could not tell her. Anyway, I forced myself to go home . . . and that's when everything fell apart. Returning home brought up some very painful memories regarding my abortions. When I saw my parents and all my nieces and nephews I had crazy thoughts . . . I wondered why I didn't have kids? I felt like my own children should have been there with us. I felt so much grief! I could not believe the amount of pain and anguish which flooded my heart. I found myself crying all the time, and drinking to

numb the pain, and wanting to sleep the days away. I stopped eating, and became very withdrawn. I honestly could not function, and I cursed the fact that I had ever come home. All I could think of was that I had to get away. But even after I left, the grief followed. There was no escaping my misery and it affected everything . . . my job, my friendships, my self-worth. The depression, the drinking, the crying spells . . . it went on for a long time before I sought help.

In the Elliot Institute survey discussed in Appendix C, over 60 percent of the women surveyed reported that there was a period of time during which they would not have reported any negative feelings about their abortion. They reported that the average time before they even recognized that they had negative reactions was slightly over five years. This delayed reaction to abortion is one of the major reasons why abortion trauma is so poorly understood by both society and mental health workers.

# CHAPTER NINE

# MEMORIES UNLEASHED

The doctor wouldn't stop, even though Lee Ann had changed her mind. She pleaded with him to stop the abortion, but he insisted it was too late. Years later, the abortion continued to haunt her at every turn.

> I feel like I am falling down a very deep hole, dark and damp, grungy and grimy. The sadness at work is unbearable. I want to grab that baby and place it inside of me. I feel drained, achy, violated and abused.
>
> I freak when my menstrual blood smears my thighs, hurling me back to the gurney and the abortion. The way I knew my baby was dead was by waking and seeing the blood on my thighs.
>
> I fall apart when I see pregnant women. I turn away when I see babies. I change lanes in the supermarket to avoid being close to them.
>
> The Saturdays (the day of the abortion) of my life hold funeral services for my baby and me. This must explain why I feel numb—my legs, my arms, my hands. Like my daughter they are appendages and like her they are dead.
>
> I think when I sleep more feelings surface. Without sleep, I stay numb. I feel angry and depressed. The tears freely form whenever I am alone . . . they come out from hiding, revealing thoughts I don't yet know I have. But my tears know . . . and they come. They visit at dark. I wonder if they will ever leave.
>
> I have terrible nightmares of throwing my baby down on the floor in the kitchen. In one dream, I chopped off my hair, a vital part of me. I also dreamt I slit my wrists . . . I have intense, uncontrollable anger and rage. I feel barren and I can't forgive myself.
>
> The world keeps the wound alive. I am alive, just half of me, half of *us*, maybe. I lay on the floor last night for three and a half hours crying, curled up like a fetus.[1]

Lee Ann's description of her experience reflects many layers of intrusive symptoms: flashbacks prompted by the sight of her menstrual blood, avoidance of pregnant women and babies, depressive symptoms on Saturdays (an anniversary-type reaction), nightmares, and even the reenactment of crying while curled up like a fetus.

In the previous chapter, we examined how PTSD provides a framework for understanding the interrelationship between the many symptoms of hyperarousal, constriction, and intrusion that may follow an abortion. Of these three categories, intrusion is the most obvious indicator of trauma and the most reliable demonstration that trauma has occured.[2] Intrusive symptoms can be expressed in a great number of ways, often in the form of disguised reenactment of some element of the trauma. We will examine some of these forms of reenactment in subsequent chapters. But first, let's look at some of the more obvious ways in which memories of an abortion demand attention through flashbacks, dreams, and obsessive behaviors.

## FLASHBACKS

When a flashback occurs, women may find themselves over-responding to sights, sounds, or smells that remind them of their abortion. Joan, for example, couldn't vacuum the rugs in her house because of acute panic attacks that paralyzed her. The sound of the vacuum reminded her of the suction aspiration machine used by her abortionist. That sound alone was enough to make her hands shake, her heart race, and her head become confused and dizzy.

In the Elliot Institute survey of post-abortive women, 63 percent reported experiencing flashbacks to their abortion. Although flashbacks usually last for only several minutes, many women develop "anticipatory anxiety," which means a sense of constant fear of the next attack. As a result of this fear, they may then begin to avoid situations where their anxiety may be triggered. For example, many women, like Joan, will refuse to vacuum and will insist on being out of their house when someone else does it.

Another common trigger for flashbacks is exposure to doctors, especially gynecologists. Suzanne, for example, could not get up the nerve to visit a gynecologist for eight years following her abortion. A yeast infection finally forced her to seek treatment. While on the exam table, she began to tremble and cry. She could feel the frenzied pounding of her heart against her breast.

> I remember being terrified out of my mind. I thought I was going to die. I was shaking and crying and I could hardly breathe. The doctor must have thought I was crazy. I told him I did not think I could go through with the exam and left his office. I wanted to kill myself. I felt completely berserk.

In the flashback to her abortion, Suzanne experienced panic and a flight response for her survival; she had to get off the table and leave the office. A similar experience was reported by Carol when she saw a suction aspiration machine several years after her abortion:

> Today I had to go see my oncologist because the radiologist found another "spot" on my cervix. . . . After the nurse left the room, I started looking around, checking things out. To my shock and complete loss of control, I saw, two feet from my left foot, a suction aspirator machine! I freaked out. I had a total flashback to the abortion experience. I began crying uncontrollably, got up, dressed, and ran into the hall, hyperventilating. . . . I wonder, will it ever end?[3]

As with Lee Ann, Evelyn's menstrual cycle was a regular monthly trigger for flashbacks to her abortion.

> I have a lot of flashbacks. I find myself staring into space and reliving my

abortion piece by piece. Every time my period comes around, I think I am pregnant. I feel paranoid. I feel back aches, extra tiredness, nausea. I go to the bathroom twenty times a day to check for spotting.

For Jill, one of her most powerful connectors was jelly. The sight of jelly reminded her of blood clots she passed after her abortion. Whenever she attempted to make a peanut butter and jelly sandwich for her daughter, she experienced anxiety, intrusive memories, and other traumatic symptoms.

For Lisa, the reexperience of her abortion was centered on her overwhelming sense of fear.

When I think about my abortion, only one word comes to mind: *fear*. When I think back to certain memories, I feel fear all through my body. My heart races and my stomach turns upside down. I play back the scenes over and over again. It's not something I can think too much about. Usually I just shut it off.

In addition to flashbacks accompanied by the psychological feelings of panic and terror, many people experience disturbing bodily sensations during a panic attack. These can include shortness of breath, dizziness, faintness, choking, chest pain, palpitations, trembling, sweating, nausea, diarrhea, headaches, tingling and numbing sensations, hot flashes or chills, and feelings of disembodiment.

Barbara's panic attacks began after an ectopic pregnancy. Because of the life-threatening dangers associated with such a pregnancy, doctors had to surgically remove the fallopian tube containing the embryo. This incident recreated her abortion experience. Intrusive thoughts, accompanied by overwhelming anxiety, paralyzed her with fear.

Having my feet up in stirrups, the smell of the hospital, the violation of instruments entering my body and taking a life from me . . . these things all came back to me, and I felt exactly like I was having an abortion. I cried and cried. I guess I was hysterical. The doctor had to give me a sedative. He became quite angry with me.

The fact that her life was at risk because of the ectopic pregnancy did not reduce Barbara's grief or fear. The smell of disinfectant, her feet up in stirrups, and gloved hands probing her with assorted metal devices created a vivid flashback to her original trauma. Years of repressed grief and pain surfaced like a tidal wave. Within moments, her panic attack became so severe the doctor had to sedate her. After the surgery, the anxiety and flashbacks continued. Fortunately, Barbara connected the panic to her abortion and was able to obtain the help she needed.

## DREAMS AND NIGHTMARES

When the conscious mind sleeps, the defense mechanisms in charge of repelling unwanted thoughts are relaxed. This is why intrusive thoughts related to a suppressed trauma often arise in the form of dreams or nightmares. Sometimes the dreams are clearly related to the abortion. For example, Olivia had a recurring dream where she was in the delivery room about to give birth.

I dream I am pushing a baby down through the birth canal. I am excited and nervous and eager to see the baby. There are doctors and nurses around me telling me when to push, holding my hand and helping with the delivery. Finally I deliver a baby and it comes out dead! To my horror, all the attendants act happy—as if it is normal to deliver a dead baby—like nothing is wrong. I start to scream and cry and they all just look at me like I'm crazy. I always wake up from this dream crying so hard I can hardly catch my breath. It takes me hours to calm down.

Rebecca's recurring dream echoes similar elements, but with an emphasis on her fear that her family would discover her secret abortion.

I keep having dreams that I am in the hospital. I just had an abortion and suddenly my parents and brothers and sisters all come into the room with balloons and flowers. Each of them is carrying a baby in their arms. They are smiling and happy and saying congratulations. I start screaming at everyone, telling them to get the hell out of my room. I always wake up hysterical. They didn't know I had an abortion . . . and here they were all coming in to congratulate me as if I had given birth to a baby.

For Helaine, her repetitive nightmare underscored her deep sense of horror, shame, and helplessness.

Three years after my second abortion I started having nightmares in which I saw myself in a baby parts cemetery and holding a dead baby in my arms and crying for the ones I lost. I was seeing myself naked in this cemetery—much like a holocaust image—holding a dead baby and trying to bring him back to life.

Many dreams are less obviously related to the abortion. For example, Vivian's dream reflected many aspects of her abortion dilemma in symbolic form.

My dreams are very frightening. In one frequent dream I am out at the store and I'm buying baby clothes, toys and diapers. My cart is full of stuff and I spend hours shopping, trying to find just the right things. This part of the dream feels like it goes on forever. Finally, when I get to the checkout counter, the cashier calls the police. They surround me, grab my arms and handcuff them behind my back. There are people all around looking at me. They accuse me of stealing. They tell me harshly, "You can't take those things!" I wake up screaming. It all feels so real.

Vivian had her abortion out of desperation because she felt helpless to provide for her child by herself. In her dream she spends hours gathering up provisions, only to lose them. Her self-condemnation is reflected in how she is accused of a crime and exposed to humiliation and punishment. The police in her dream symbolize the judgment of her own conscience. After waking from this dream, Vivian would cry for hours, feeling victimized, powerless and alone.

Pam had an abortion at the age of 18. Immediately following the procedure, she began to have disturbing and intrusive nightmares about dismembered babies and thoughts regarding her responsibility toward them. It came as no surprise to me to learn that after her abortion Pam had sought a job in the trauma unit of a world-renowned children's hospital. On a day-to-day basis, children come into the emergency room with horrific injuries, burns, and mutilations. Pam's dedication to her stressful profession reflected her need to "put the babies back together." Through her vocation, Pam was able to channel her energies into a form that helped address the pain of her psychic trauma.

Often, the nightmares employ symbols of death and fertility, and are marked with failed rescue attempts and feelings of helplessness and fear. Ellen's recurrent nightmare began six years after her abortion. The dream was so disturbing she became afraid to go to bed at night.

> The dream usually had a little girl crying for Mommy. I hear her crying out to me. I can't get to her and I have a panicky sense that she is in danger. On some nights I see a tiny helpless rabbit. I reach out to the struggling form and then it vanishes into a sinking lagoon tinged red with blood. Sometimes I try to call out—but nothing comes out of my mouth. It's like I'm trying to scream but nothing comes out. Then the little thing plunges down and comes up again with an urgent gasp for air. With each step I take forward, I go backwards as blood swirls around, like waves coming in and out against the shore. I keep trying to save the rabbit . . . as I reach out there is only sand, a scarlet sand, slipping between my fingers.

Ellen began to fear the dark. As night approached, she would numb herself with alcohol or drugs. If she could "knock herself out," she wouldn't have to worry about having nightmares. As Ellen described the dream to me, it was clear that she was completely unnerved by it. Tears painted streaks of mascara down her cheeks. She believed that the nightmares were related to her abortion. She sat quiet and reflective, then began to cry, "I wish I had never done it. I will never forgive myself. Sometimes I could kill myself for that. I will never be able to forgive myself."

Ellen's disturbing dreams involved a horrific reexperience of her feelings of helplessness associated with her abortion. Fortunately, she responded to this prompting of her subconscious and sought the help she needed to work through her traumatic symptoms and her impacted grief.

Periods of insomnia are a common problem among women with a history of abortion. In the Elliot Institute survey, 45 percent of the women surveyed reported bouts of insomnia that were strongly associated with reports of nightmares. Some women will go to great extremes to avoid the nightmares that come with sleep. For example, when Cecilia began suffering from bad dreams after her abortion, she tried to put off sleep with a spectacular nightlife. She went on lots of dates and escapades in bars and would linger until last call. Often she would bed down with the first available man—anyone to avoid being alone at night.

Before the abortion Cecilia had been able to maintain a steady job and had been careful about entering into sexual relationships. After the abortion her world fell apart and her nightmares paralleled the horror of Freddy Krueger movies. Through promiscuity and staying awake to the point of exhaustion, she attempted to avoid her dreams. This lifestyle took a physical toll on Cecilia and exposed her to numerous risks, which perhaps also reflected an unconscious means of self-punishment.

## HALLUCINATIONS

Many dreams involve what women experience as a "visitation" from the spirit of their aborted child. In most cases, the visiting spirit is seen as benign or forgiving, but in the Elliot Institute survey, about one-fourth of the women who reported such visitations described the mood as "vengeful."

In some cases, these visitations may spill over into daytime fantasies and hallucinations. For example, Kathryn experienced hallucinations of little baby angels floating around in her backyard after her abortion. She felt they had come looking for some sort of satisfaction or appeasement, so she spent day after day tending the yard in an attempt to create a "heavenly garden" for her celestial phantoms. Kathryn would even flood her porch until the water cascaded off the edge like a fountain. Her seemingly bizarre rituals were a requiem, a memorial service to appease the baby angels.

Naturally, her obsessive preoccupation and reenactment were quite misunderstood. Kathryn was eventually committed to a local state hospital and labeled a schizophrenic. For three years she was in and out of psychiatric clinics and psychiatrists' offices and spent hours with different therapists—without improvement. However, once in treatment for abortion trauma, Kathryn began to improve and quickly regained normal functioning.

Other women have also reported hallucinations of their dead children, especially during states of severe depression. Jenna, for example, felt robbed even of life's simple pleasures by visions of her phantom child.

> Whenever I was enjoying something . . . like a colorful sunset, or the beauty of the ocean, I would see what I believe to be the face of my aborted child . . . up in the clouds or in the waves of the ocean. I would break down with grief and

feel an incredible pain and sense of loss. It became hard to enjoy anything because the child was always there . . . always reminding me . . . always popping up all over the place.

In many cases, the hallucinations are strictly auditory. Ginny didn't begin to hear voices until she became pregnant again five years after her abortion.

I would wake up because I heard a child crying, "Mommy, mommy." I would sit up in bed and the voices would continue. I would cry for hours because I knew who was calling me. I knew it was my aborted child.

In some cases, post-partum psychosis may be linked with previous abortion trauma. Such was the case with Fran, who had two abortions before giving birth to a beautiful, healthy boy. Her nightmare began within hours of giving birth. While still in the hospital, Fran began to hear voices instructing her to kill her newborn baby. The voices were taunting and relentless . . . "You killed the others; why don't you get rid of him? He's better off without you."

In reaction to these hateful voices, Fran was afraid to touch her infant, terrified to look at him, and unable to nurse. Fran's sister volunteered to take care of the baby until her psychosis subsided. Fran was fortunate to have the support of her family. Nonetheless, her traumatic experience caused an incredible shattering of her self-image as a mother and nurturer and destroyed the normal bonding process with her infant.

While these accounts may appear bizarre, many of my clients have been prompted by such incidents to seek the help they need to process their hidden grief and guilt. After they dealt with the trauma of their abortions, these unusual visual and auditory hallucinations have disappeared.

## Trauma and Memory

PTSD is, at its core, an emotional conflict with past memories. As a result, memories of a traumatic event can be either intensely clear or completely repressed. In many cases, certain memories are clear and others are inaccessible.

Roseanne remembered each particular detail of her abortion with fastidious recall. She continually played back the dialogue of everything said and done during her abortion experience. Like a record with a bad scratch, Roseanne's mind continually went over and over the same scene with all its distinct sights, smells, and feelings. They were well-defined images that she could not get out of her mind.

My memories of the abortion clinic are very vivid. I can even remember the smell of the Women's Center. I also remember the colors on the wall, the expressions on the nurses' faces and what they said to me. I remember putting on a pink paper gown and feeling it crinkle against my body. Every time I think about it I get the chills. The whole thing was horrible.

Gwen also remembered her abortion with uncanny precision.

My memories of the abortion are distinct and clear. You could ask me about every person I talked to in that clinic and I could tell you word-for-word our conversation. You could ask me to tell you everything starting with the day I found out I was pregnant and everything would be accurate.

This kind of abnormally sharp or vivid recall is called *hypermnesia* and is common in many cases of PTSD. Every minuscule detail—sights, sounds, smells, and feelings—can be relived over and over, often through flashbacks.

The opposite of the virtual recall phenomenon is *amnesia*, which is the partial, temporary, or entire forgetting of an event. Partial amnesia is common among women who have had a traumatic reaction to abortion. Diane, for example, was able to remember going to the abortion clinic, but could not recall any of the conversations, the people, or the actual procedure.

I don't remember much of anything except for one scene, lying on a table out in a waiting room—that's it. The whole thing is quite foggy. I can't really describe it. I blocked mostly everything out. And if I try to remember, I tremble—physically shake.

Similarly, Betty was able to recall only a few minor details of the day when she had her abortion:

The abortion is such a blur to me. I remember signing papers, but I couldn't tell you what they were about. I remember cramping afterwards and going to the pharmacy to buy aspirin. If I was in a room with the doctor who did it, I couldn't tell you who he was. That's all I can really remember. I don't remember anything about the procedure. Nothing at all—which is weird because I never had any anesthesia. I remember wanting it though because I didn't want to be awake when they did it.

Diane and Betty experienced *selective amnesia*, a failure to remember some, but not all, of the incidents during a certain period of time. Another type of amnesia is called *localized amnesia*, the inability to recall events during a set period of time following a profoundly disturbing event. Varan's description of her abortion is an example of sharp but limited memories.

I don't even know when I got pregnant. I don't remember any of the discussions that must have taken place between my mother and me. What I do remember is being taken to the finest hospital in the city, rolled into the most sophisticated operating room, and having my baby killed by one of the top GYN doctors available. I also remember waking up and hearing women crying and screaming—including myself. I remember indescribable pain. I remember blood—more blood than I had ever seen. Several days later, I remember being rushed to an emergency room in the middle of the night. I was hemorrhaging and fading in and out of consciousness from a raging fever. Nothing else is there in my memory, it's all gone . . . deleted. My medical records say I was in the hospital for six days, underwent two D&C's, and was rolled back into the O.R. a final time for a complete hysterectomy. I was 16 years old. I have no memory of my life after that. Since those horrible days, this has *never once* been spoken of—by my mother or myself.

Some women cannot recall a single event from the morning of their abortion until several days later. Katie's description of her experience is typical of such localized amnesia.

I remember the morning of my abortion. I remember making my bed, which is weird because I never make my bed. I remember putting on makeup and looking all over for my summer sunglasses. I didn't want anyone to recognize me. Seems stupid now, that I wore sunglasses and a hat. That's all I remember. Everything else is a blank. Kind of like it never happened. I remember being at my sister's afterwards, but I can't tell you anything about that—just that I went there.

Several factors influence whether a traumatic experience is remembered or dissociated (disconnected). For example, if a woman has many opportunities to tell her story and receives sympathy and family support, she is unlikely to develop amnesia about the event. However, a girl who endures a traumatic abortion and is sworn to secrecy by her parents or sexual partner is more likely to have memory impairment from the trauma.

Many women have an acute memory of particular aspects of their abortions, but other portions are shrouded in a mist. In Jennifer's description of her abortion, for example, the "cold steel table" was a strong connector memory. The fear of her memories flooding out of control, however, was enough to keep most of them hidden by a fog, yet at the same time it was a memory that seemed "just like yesterday."

I don't like to think about it. When I do, it's a never-ending nightmare. I remember the pain of the "injection," the cold steel table, the nurse's matter-of-fact demeanor, the pain and the noise of the suction—I just couldn't let it all in. The worst was when I went to have my second abortion. I remember lying on the cold steel table and thinking, "Just get up and get out of here." How many millions of times I have run that back through my mind because I didn't heed that warning.

My memories, except for a few bits and pieces, are very foggy. I remember feeling desperately uncomfortable in the waiting room. My boyfriend was with me. He was supportive of what I was doing, but I look back at that whole thing as nightmarish. It is still a picture suspended in my mind.

After my abortion I was aware of a numbing denial. Looking back, some voice deep inside was crying out, "NO! Don't do this," but it was barely perceptible to me. On the conscious level, I just handled it as if I had undergone any other medical procedure. But I felt so alone.

> I had emotional problems later. I saw a psychologist but never revealed my abortion. Several years later another counselor had a few sessions with me. That was more helpful, but I never divulged my abortions to her either.
>
> It's so odd. Those abortions occurred 20 years ago, yet in some ways it's just like yesterday.

When memories and emotions are repressed, they may come back in vague feelings or perceptions, or they may surface gradually over time as the person becomes more capable of tolerating the threat of the experience. The majority of women I have seen come for counseling at least ten years after the event. At that point they may feel either that they cannot avoid the pain any longer, or that they are in a better, more stable place in their lives and finally feel up to the task of looking at their feelings and working through the problem.

## SPACING OUT — DISSOCIATION

People use terms like "spacing out" and "not being with it" to describe the detached sensations that therapists call "dissociation." For example, a student who is suddenly called upon to answer a question can sometimes experience a flash of "mini-dissociation." Oblivious to time and space, the daydreaming student is abruptly awakened and startled to realize he has no clue about what is going on in the class. This everyday experience of being jarred back into reality demonstrates that the mind has the capacity to leave one's immediate physical surroundings to wander in some imaginary, disconnected, or dissociated state.

When a person is confronted by traumatic, threatening situations, dissociation is a commonly employed defense mechanism that enables the person to survive the event. In many cases, the dissociation will persist long after the traumatic event has passed. Julie Anne's description of her abortion illustrates dissociation before, during, and after her abortion.

> Being faced with an unexpected pregnancy was the most frightening thing I could imagine. The married man with whom I was involved painted a picture so depressing and destructive that I was convinced we only had one choice—to abort. He used every pressure tactic to save his political career, his reputation, and his "family life." He even had me thinking I would lose my job and livelihood. That was when *reality* as I knew it changed forever.
>
> Everything about my abortion was robotic. I remember being in the waiting room, and all of us had blank stares on our faces. After the usual paperwork, I was taken into a small room for the nurses to take blood; I fainted, but no one seemed to think that should deter me from going through with the "procedure" that day. I don't remember much of what was on the papers I signed but probably answered the same way I had felt for the few previous weeks—in a haze—in a dreamy state. I felt like I was watching a movie of someone else's life, that this really was not happening to me. Once I entered the "procedure room," a nurse told me to "hike up my dress" and get on the table; I felt like a

zombie. The "counselor" held my hand and talked throughout the entire ordeal in order to divert my attention from what was taking place on the other end. She said it would be over in a few minutes. I remember starting to cry as the abortionist entered my body with the suction machine. . . . Why couldn't I yell, "Stop, help me," or anything to make them stop? I felt frozen, immobilized, the same way I had been since I learned for sure that I was pregnant and alone.

That same dazed, powerless feeling stayed with me for months as my life took a downward spiral. I was not the woman who had an abortion—the only way I could cope was to bury it.

It is very common for women to undergo abortions in a dissociated state. The reality is so unpleasant that they emotionally exit the scene. Their bodies are there, but their emotional self is not. Consequently, a woman may remember the details of the abortion, but recount them in a numb, apparently unfeeling voice, as if talking about someone else. The emotional memory of the abortion is cut off from the narrative memory of the event.

Sometimes, a woman who is chronically dissociated will engage in self-abusive behaviors just to help herself feel something.

After two abortions I felt very alone, depressed and confused. I never knew what was wrong with me. I would cry and cry. I would cut myself or burn myself on the oven racks. I would punch and bruise myself. I was out of control, and when anyone would ask me, "What's wrong?" I honestly answered, "I don't know." I felt as if I were going insane. Who cries all the time and hurts themselves without knowing why? I was always feeling numb during the times that I would hurt myself. It was like the pain would help wake me up. I hated myself. Years of counseling did not help; anti-depressants did not help; nothing seemed to help. It was all kept pretty much a secret. Only a select few knew of my extreme depression or my abortions.

Though the cutting and burning all began within two months following her first abortion, Michelle never connected her self-abuse to her abortions. The trauma of her first abortion had caused a numbing denial of all her emotions. She used self-torture to try to bring herself back to feelings of reality. When she joined a support group for healing after abortion, Michelle succeeded in getting some insight into her self-abusive behaviors. After completing her grief work, all of Michelle's symptoms were completely eliminated.

## BODY TATTLE

In many cases, hidden memories are reflected through the post-abortive woman's body. Physical symptoms of pain or discomfort may arise when the woman is exposed to events or situations that are connected to her repressed traumatic memories. Women who felt excessive fear and anxiety during their abortions, for example, often feel the same queasiness or terror when reminder incidents arise.

> All I remember during my abortion was a retching nausea in my gut. Through-
> out the whole ordeal I was ready to vomit. Afterwards, I felt that same feeling
> when I was around babies, had sex, or went to the doctor. Anything that
> reminded me of my abortion made me sick to my stomach.

Post-abortive women will frequently experience painful abdominal cramping sensations, upset stomachs, pelvic pain, vaginal numbness, heart palpitations, sweating, or shortness of breath when exposed to some connector to their past abortion. In Tamara's case, the culprit was orange juice.

> I remember taking a sip of orange juice in the recovery room following my
> abortion. I began gagging to the point of vomiting. Afterwards, the same thing
> would happen whenever I saw a glass of orange juice. To this day, I'd get sick
> if I drank the stuff.

Tamara's feelings of nausea at just the sight of orange juice is an example of "psycho-physiological reenactment." This technical term simply means that the mind and the body are both involved in recreating physical sensations that are closely related to the traumatic event. In Tamara's case the sensation was nausea and the connector was orange juice.

In most cases, the association between the connector and the trauma is not understood. The woman's physical reactions are simply discounted, even by her, as strange, or dismissed as a quirk. Even what most would consider to be obvious connectors may not be obvious at all to the woman suffering from this reaction. For example, Jenna had a part-time job doing insurance billing at a local doctor's office.

> I began to feel nausea and cramping abdominal pressure whenever I would
> enter the place where I worked. It was so uncomfortable, I often thought I
> would faint. Each time I returned to his office, I had the same reaction as
> I passed through the entrance where there was hung a poster on fetal
> development. At the time, I thought it was related to something I ate for
> lunch, or something in the air, perhaps an allergic reaction to a deodor-
> izer. For seven months I felt deathly ill every time I entered his office.
> Finally, one day in a heightened panic, I said to the window clerk, "Would
> somebody take that stupid poster down!" She looked at me surprised as
> I blurted out, "It's making me sick!" I was so shocked and embarrassed
> but still did not connect it to my abortion.

For Jena, the link between body and mind remained unconscious. But her repressed feelings found an outlet through her body. In the next chapter, we will look more closely at ways in which traumatic memories can be reenacted in the lives of post-abortive women.

# CHAPTER TEN

# REENACTING TRAUMA

Tina looked up at me as her pale cheeks flushed a deep shade of red. I could tell that her stomach was pitching like a boat being tossed on a wave. She held her hands tightly over her abdomen, as if trying to hold fast to a floundering buoy. Six years earlier, Tina had lost her child through an abortion. The memory was so painful she could barely speak about it. At the time of the abortion, as a 24-year-old graduate student, she had aspired to become an art therapist. But after the abortion, she experienced a depression that was so unmanageable that she had to give up her studies. Tina described her problem:

> I became obsessed with pregnancy after my abortion. I used to go to the maternity section in department stores. I loved to try on maternity clothes. I usually had a towel stuffed into my pantyhose to make it look like I was pregnant. I thought my body looked beautiful and I imagined what it would be like. Other women shoppers would ask me when I was due and stuff like, "Is this your first?"
>
> While shopping I felt so happy and content. But as soon as I'd get in my car I would cry my head off. You have no idea how hard I would bawl. I'd rip the towel out of my belly to dry my tears. I'd tell myself, you're not pregnant . . . this is just a stupid towel. I thought, I am absolutely nuts! If I ever told anyone what I did, they would think I was crazy. I am ashamed of the crazy shopping sprees, but they gave me relief. It was kind of like an addiction.

Tina developed this bizarre ritual as a means to grieve her pregnancy loss and the deprivation of her maternity. This ritual was a form of traumatic reenactment. After a blissful pregnancy fantasy, the baby became the bath towel, violently ripped out of her body and used to dry her tears—the emblem of her pain and regret. The repetitive or addictive aspect of this behavior underscores that it was rooted in a traumatic reaction to her abortion.

## THE MYSTERY, THE DRAMA, THE REENACTMENT OF TRAUMA

In chapter eight we examined how PTSD provides a framework for understanding the interrelationship between the many symptoms of hyperarousal, constriction, and intrusion that may follow an abortion. Of these three categories, intrusion is the most obvious indicator of trauma and the most reliable demonstration that trauma has occurred.[1]

Intrusion includes more than just the arousal of unwanted memories. Perhaps more significantly, it includes behaviors that repeat or reenact elements of the trauma. E.R. Parson, a leading expert on PTSD, has stated the following regarding the importance of repetitive behavior in relation to trauma:

> I have been struck by the utter pervasiveness of survivors' tendency to repeat dimensions of original traumatic experiences in virtually all spheres of their lives. Much of the clinical literature on PTSD . . . tends to focus on dramatic repetitive or reliving tendencies, as in the mental phenomena such as "flashback" (dissociative states), traumatic dreaming, night terror, and other . . . reenactments. What is neither discussed nor appreciated to any extent, it seems, is the multiplicity of non-dramatic ways repetitive phenomena are replayed."[2]

Intrusion can involve more than simply flashbacks or nightmares such as those described in previous chapters. Memories of a trauma may also intrude through behaviors, game play, or even art forms, through which the unconscious mind seeks to express one's horrible experience, but in a veiled form.

Remember, trauma is marked by two opposing emotional needs: the need to deny one's horrible experience and the need to release one's pent-up feelings. This tension between the need to hide a trauma and the need to expose it lies at the heart of many of the psychological symptoms of post-abortion trauma.

*Symbolic reenactment* is one of the ways that the subconscious seeks to simultaneously satisfy both of these needs: the need to expose the trauma and the need to hide it. Reenactment allows the person to expose the trauma with the hope that its exposure will eventually lead to understanding and mastery over the trauma. At the same time, because the trauma is reenacted behind a *symbolic* mask, the essence of the trauma is still concealed and protected. In other words, reenactment allows the person to call for help while disguising the areas that need help. As trauma specialist Judith Lewis Herman, M.D., has observed, when a traumatic experience is wrapped in secrecy and shame, "the traumatic event surfaces not as a verbal narrative but as a symptom."

> The psychological distress symptoms of traumatized people simultaneously call attention to the existence of an unspeakable secret and deflect attention from it. This is most apparent in the way traumatized people alternate between feeling numb and reliving the event. The dialectic of trauma gives rise to complicated, sometimes uncanny alterations of consciousness which George Orwell . . . called "doublethink". . . . It results in the protean, dramatic, and often bizarre symptoms of hysteria. . . .[3]

Because these "bizarre symptoms" are veiled symbols of a prior trauma, one of the most difficult but intriguing parts of a therapist's job is to uncover this mystery, the meaning of the symbol and the trauma of which it speaks. Once the mystery is understood, the therapist can more easily understand his client. As the client sees that she is understood and that the therapist's insights are helping her express her feelings in less veiled forms, she gains confidence that she is free to share more of her feelings. What began as a mystery for both can become the key to freeing the client to tell her whole story. Once it is told, the power of the secret is destroyed, and the trauma victim is free to confront and deal with her past—not alone, but with an ally.

Since sex and abortion are intimately connected, it is not uncommon for both women and men to act out abortion related trauma through real or imagined sexual encounters.

As an example of the latter, Rowena become addicted to "cyber-affairs" on the Internet after a traumatic abortion experience. For Rowena, cyber-sex was "safe," since it did not expose her to another pregnancy and abortion. Moreover, through these chat room driven fantasies, which involved heavy doses of sexual oppression, bondage, and humiliation, she was able to recreate themes that echoed her abortion-related trauma. Rowena's obsession with cyber-sex served as an outlet for unresolved tensions related to her abortion, while providing a "safe" framework for her to revisit and explore her feelings about being manipulated, humiliated, and treated as a sex object.

Men are also vulnerable. Peter was 17 when his girlfriend had an abortion against his will. This experience left him feeling shamed and powerless. When he later married, he kept the abortion a secret from his wife. Although he loved his wife very much, the added burden of keeping his feelings secret created additional tension in his life. In an unconscious effort to act out his feelings of anger, shame, and powerlessness in private, Peter became highly addicted to cyber-sex and obsessed with pornography. A major theme of his fantasies was female domination and abuse; this reflected an unconscious need to explore and master his own sense of shame and impotency.

Peter came for to me for marriage counseling and eventually shared his sad secret with his wife. Together they attended a Rachel's Vineyard retreat for post abortion healing, where he finally allowed her to comfort and support him. Peter's addiction to online pornography was resolved as he went through the process of dismantling his secret and grieving the loss of his aborted child. By sharing this healing journey with his wife, Peter discovered a new intimacy and trust with her which eliminated his dependence on deceit and pornography.

Another way that abortion trauma is sometimes reenacted is through financial problems. For example, one of the major fears surrounding Gail's abortion was the anxiety of how she would pay for it. She was only 17, had no job, no bank account, and was afraid of discussing her problem with her parents. She needed to raise $400 in only a few days, without anyone finding out. To make matters worse, she and her family had just recently moved to another state hundred of miles from the friends and neighbors from whom she might otherwise have secretly borrowed the money. Eventually, her boyfriend sent her a check which she was able to convert to cash. Only a few days after the abortion, however, her mother discovered the transaction and confronted Gail. It was a humiliating experience. The grief Gail had been suffering in the immediate aftermath of her abortion was exacerbated by having her secret so quickly exposed.

After this ordeal, Gail struggled with uncontrollable debt. By recklessly maxing out her credit cards, she recreated a traumatic theme which had accompanied her abortion: "How in the world will I ever pay for this?" In addition, her habit of secret spending and her fear of her parents discovering her debt problem mirrored the feelings of panic, guilt, and helplessness that were so much a part of her abortion. Fortunately, like Peter and Rowena, Gail was freed from her addictive and destructive compulsion after intensive grief work related to her abortion.

## Obsessions

Obsessive-compulsive disorders involve rituals of repetitive behaviors, doing things over and over in a certain perfect order. For example, Vera was a cleaning fanatic. She meticulously polished, vacuumed, and washed each day. When things looked messy or dirty, anxiety and guilt overwhelmed her. The kitchen floor, the toilet, the rugs all became external symbols of something inside her that had to be cleansed. Cleaning provided a way to ritualize her need to make things look "perfect."

Vera did not experience this compulsion to clean until after her abortion. Through this ritual she was able to transfer and hide feelings of anxiety and guilt about her abortion behind more acceptable feelings of anxiety and guilt about orderliness. Looking back, Vera explained:

> It was so important for me to look "perfect." I never wanted anyone to know what I had done—not even myself.

During subsequent pregnancies, a strong connector to her previous abortion, Carrie became obsessed with fears about losing her babies:

> I had tons of anxiety. I constantly obsessed about the chances of having a stillborn. I imagined the cords wrapping around their necks while they were still inside me and having to deliver them dead. During every pregnancy I became so sick . . . but of course, because of my abortion I felt I deserved it. I think I drove my midwife crazy with my obsessions and worry. Every little ache or pain or cramp made me preoccupied with the panic and fear of my baby dying.

In the case of Tiffany, a self-punishing regimen of horseback riding was employed to recreate her traumatic abortion. She would ride her horse for hours without the benefit derived from wearing padded riding pants, which she would deliberately leave at home. She would ride and ride until her vaginal and pubic area bled from the constant battering. The extensive bruising that would result from these marathon rides would leave her hobbled, barely able to walk.

Tiffany had an unconscious need to recreate the wounding to the region of her body most closely associated with her unspeakable trauma. The purpose of this unconscious compulsion was to call attention to the target zone of her violation because she was unable to articulate her feelings in words. When she tried to speak about it, tears and tension would overpower her, blocking out her story. The narrative of her trauma was instead encoded in a vicious pattern of abusive horseback riding through which she recreated the wound, the bleeding, and the excruciating aftermath of her abortion, which left her unable to move forward. Fortunately, through gentle support and encouragement, Tiffany was able to deal with her trauma and grieve the loss of her child. After that, the fixation on creating injury was arrested.

## OBSESSED WITH DEATH

Because abortion involves the issue of death, many women become obsessed with thoughts related to death and the fear of punishment. Many experience a foreshortened sense of the future; they simply cannot imagine that they might live to old age. For one of my clients, Anne, her fear of death and punishment turned into an obsessive fear of contracting AIDS.

Anne was a 33-year-old woman who had been struggling with paranoid fears for nearly a decade. She had straight black hair that was cropped to a sharp angular point, which drove my attention directly to her pointed chin. A vertical line formed a deep furrow between her eyebrows. She was very articulate and utilized an extensive vocabulary. Her words were carefully measured and exact as she recounted her first love affair as if it had happened yesterday.

As a college sophomore, Anne enjoyed many glorious months of falling deeply in love with her new boyfriend. She was enthralled by his charm and romantic manner. He encouraged her dreams of their future together with talk of marriage and assured her she was the only one in his life who mattered. She was soon convinced that he was *the* man with whom she would share her whole life. Before long, Anne had given him everything: her friendship, her heart, and her virginity. But when she told him she was pregnant, he suddenly began to insist they were not ready for marriage. With her trust in her boyfriend shattered,

Anne aborted the pregnancy and kept the event a carefully guarded secret. Soon after the abortion her boyfriend abandoned her for another woman.

The whole experience left Anne feeling doubly stigmatized: first because she had betrayed her child and her own moral beliefs through abortion, and second because she had foolishly believed everything her boyfriend had told her.

All of Anne's disturbed feelings were eventually channeled into the belief that her boyfriend had given her AIDS. She believed he must have lied about how many other sexual partners he had had. If she had contracted the HIV virus from him, it was only a matter of time before her sin became public knowledge.

Anne read articles, books, and journal abstracts about HIV, on topics ranging from AIDS dementia to lists of every support group available in the area. She read testimonies and autobiographies of people who suffered from the dreaded disease and identified with their pain and hopelessness. Anne envisioned how her family would reject her, hate her, and abandon her once they found out about the AIDS. When she would meet men, she would tell them that she believed she had AIDS.

By the time Anne came to me for counseling nine years later, she had a full-blown obsession. She lived as if she had the disease and focused all of her attention on death and dying, with absolutely no hope for the future. She also had survivor guilt; she had survived and her child had not. The AIDS obsession poignantly provided an outlet for her grief and the promise of retribution for what she had done.

For weeks I encouraged her to take a blood test to rule out AIDS. It became clear to me that in Anne's despair and depression she was breaking with reality. She was unable to reason that she might *not* have AIDS, and week after week she would not go to be tested. I watched her personality fragment, and she began to report suicidal urges. Finally, I decided that simply explaining the importance of having the test was not enough. I took her myself to an AIDS intervention clinic for testing.

When we got there, Anne broke down into hysterics and refused to take the test. She could not tolerate hearing the news of her fate. The fact that the test could be negative was not even a possibility to her. After three hours of being gently coaxed, Anne finally consented to having blood drawn.

Her test results were negative, but it took Anne several months to accept this information. Eventually the self-destructive cycle was broken. Anne was grateful that God had given her a second chance at life. But what a painful price she had to pay. For nearly a decade, anxiety and fear had tortured her.

Believing she had this illness was the way Anne punished herself for the abortion. In the framework of traumatic reenactment, her obsession with AIDS recreated all her feelings about the senseless death of her child into the irrational belief that she, too, would be killed. She had made a mistake and she would pay with her life. Her "infection" with the life-draining AIDS virus was a powerful symbol of how she had been infected with shame and guilt that was draining away her life and joy.

Anne's case is an example of the incredible capacity of the human mind to creatively channel unacceptable emotions into other areas of one's life—even into imaginary problems. Her reworking of her grief through an AIDS fantasy was a powerful analogy she used to process her abortion experience. Through her obsession with AIDS she was able to recreate and express the emotions she was suppressing with regard to her abortion: grief, depression, helplessness, fear, anger at her boy-friend, guilt over having had the abortion, and feelings that she needed to pay a penalty for living when her child did not.

## THE ADRENALINE FIX

Helen began a bad habit of shoplifting shortly after her abortion. She did not steal out of need. Instead, stealing was her way of reenacting her feelings of both guilt and relief at "getting away" with her abortion. In addition, the adrenaline rush she experienced when stealing helped to produce a dramatic shift in her emotional state, bulldozing down her emerging grief. Since this did not actually resolve her grief, the pattern of shoplifting sprees became alarmingly addictive.

> Every time I stole something, I would get a rush. My heart would pound, my thoughts would race. I stole all the time—stuff I didn't even need. All the while I had the terror inside me that I might get caught. Walking out the door I envisioned the police arresting me, but I always arrived home safely with my merchandise—with a sense of relief and fatigue. But the guilt always came later, mixed with a sense of superiority that I didn't get caught.

Helen had never stolen before her abortion. But after she aborted, she saw herself as a "bad girl." What was a little stealing compared to killing one's child? Through stealing she reinforced this new self-image. At the same time, her constant stealing invited disaster. Sooner or later, she would be caught and sentenced to prison. Then her guilt and shame would be exposed to her family and friends. Since there was no such penalty attached to her abortion, she recreated that risk through shoplifting. Helen's risk-taking behavior reflected her unconscious need to see herself caught and punished for her crimes.

Another important aspect of Helen's story is that stealing produced an adrenalin rush by which she battled her states of depression. Adrenaline, a chemical released by the endocrine gland, causes the heart to beat faster and provides a boost of energy which pulsates through the body, mind, and emotions. Our bodies always release adrenaline during a state of crisis, so provoking an adrenaline release is one way some depressed people self-medicate their symptoms.

This is actually very typical of people with PTSD, as Joel Brende, M.D., has described:

> [A victim of trauma] feels fragmented, "not together," empty inside, a sense of inner deadness, or deep internal shame. He or she becomes overprotective or easily angered, causing further victimization behavior.
>
> Fragmented victims often become depressed, repetitively self-destructive, isolated, or provoke conflicts during their interactions with others, particularly those within their immediate families. To avoid numbing and depression, they often seek excitement, risky situations, and destructive danger. Not infrequently they become "hooked" on repeating stressful situations and risk taking."[4]

It is not difficult to understand how people may fall into this trap of provoking crisis situations. Trauma victims typically experience symptoms of depression such as lethargy, sadness, exhaustion, and fatigue. During the course of both the little and large crises typical of every life that follow the traumatic event, the resulting adrenaline rush provides them with some relief from their depressive symptoms. They feel momentarily alive and excited again, even if the crisis is an unpleasant one. On a conscious or unconscious level, many trauma victims, like Helen, develop patterns of behavior that provoke crisis situations as a means of obtaining their "adrenaline fix."

This theory is supported by a study of Canadian health care services in which it was found that women with a history of abortion were subsequently more likely to receive treatments in an emergency room for injuries related to accidents.[5] It is most likely that this finding reflects a higher incidence of risk-taking behavior following abortion.

Geraldine recounts her story:

> After my abortion I spent years of reckless wandering. My days and nights were filled with drinking away my anguish. I truly felt like the abortionist had ripped out my heart and my soul. It was a pain so heavy, on more than one occasion I found myself calling the Contact Hotline while contemplating suicide. I overdosed on pills more than once and ended up getting my stomach pumped twice in the hospital.

Because of increased risk-taking behavior and/or suicidal tendencies, women who have had abortions are also two to seven times more likely to die of accident-related injuries.[6] Francine was one of the lucky ones who survived her brushes with death.

> I cracked up my car three times, driving recklessly at extreme speeds. In one wreck, I broke four ribs and punctured my lung. My life became a series of calamities, accidents, and self-destructive benders.

## CRISIS INVENTION

Another common way in which trauma victims subconsciously seek release from their deadened emotional state is by provoking conflicts at work or at home. A depressed person may invite crisis into his or her life on a daily basis, then wonder helplessly, "Why did I do that?" or "Whatever possessed me to allow this to happen?" For the post-abortive woman or man, these questions echo the ones that haunt their abortion experience.

In addition, by provoking crises, the trauma victim is forced to concentrate on solving the crisis at hand. This distracts the individual from the self-examination and grief work necessary for healing. I'm reminded of Roberta, who was caught stealing from the cash register where she worked. She denied her employer's suspicions for six months until they installed a video camera to catch the thief. When confronted with the evidence, Roberta broke down and explained that she felt she deserved the money for all she had been through.

Roberta's traumatic abortion had left her with the feeling that her child had been unjustly taken from her. This is the theme of reenactment that encouraged thoughts of theft. Since her child of inestimable value had been "stolen" from her, she reasoned, why was it wrong for her to steal something of much less value from her employer—after all, she "deserved" compensation for her loss. In a vague way, she felt that other people owed her something to fill the emptiness in her heart.

One obvious way in which people can provoke crisis is by creating conflict in their personal relationships. For example, several years after her abortion, Doris began to avoid her husband even though she insisted she loved him very much. She would call her husband and tell him she was working late and would be home shortly after picking up a bite to eat. Hours would pass before she would return home. Sometimes she would simply spend the time driving around in her car, or going to visit a good friend. Then Doris would secretly sneak into her home, frequently after midnight.

The predictable result was that her husband soon began to experience feelings of mistrust and a deepening rage about her behavior. Soon he began to suspect that she was having an affair. Doris insisted that she was only at work and offered regular alibis with witness testimony. Although she persisted in pledging her love and fidelity to him, her actions continued to provoke his jealousy and feelings of abandonment. Doris was bewildered and grief-stricken when he eventually moved out.

On one level, Doris was recreating the same dynamics that had traumatized her five years earlier at the time of her abortion. In this case, Doris was forcing her husband to go through the same emotions that she had gone through after her abortion when her former boy-friend began to avoid her. Then when her husband did move out, her own feelings of abandonment were reenacted and she experienced a double dose of grief.

> I loved my husband, I really did. He was probably the best thing that ever happened to me. I wanted to have children with him because I thought he would be a good father. Looking back, I suppose I did not feel worthy of his love, and I felt unsure and fearful of children. I sabotaged the relationship . . . it's not like I wanted to set him up to leave me . . . but that was the consequence of my stupid behavior. So many incredible things are linked to the pain of my abortion. I never understood it while I was going through it, but it is crystal clear to me now.

Doris's acting out served to create an emotional distance with her husband. This was an effective way to avoid the pregnancy which she feared. Her routine of coming home late left little room for a romantic sex life. Their time together as a couple was consumed by spats, arguments, and insecurities, thereby killing any possibilities to have a child.

This is just one example of many ways in which people create crises in their lives to distract them from their grief or fears. Jenny's crises, for example, were always work-related.

> After my abortion, I began to fall apart at work. I felt guilty that my performance was not up to standards. I began taking work home, and I stayed up the whole night trying to finish it. They kept giving me more and more work. Out of guilt, I obliged.

Few people I know would expect themselves or others to carry on the tasks of a demanding job right after the loss of someone close to them. Jenny shouldered impossible tasks because they kept her from facing her own pain. Each midnight crisis and encroaching deadline released a surge of adrenaline that enabled her to finish her projects and stave off dealing with her loss. She became a workaholic, which provided a temporary relief from depression.

For many post-abortive women, workaholic tendencies and an obsession with their careers also reflect the fact that they gave up their children for their professions. Since their careers were bought at such a high price, they become obsessed with succeeding in order to prove to themselves that their choice to abort was not a mistake.

The effects of a workaholic lifestyle over time, however, can leave one emotionally and physically depleted. Jenny's career controlled her, rather than giving her a sense of control and balance in her life.

## PSYCHOTIC REACTIONS

> On the day of my abortion, December 9, 1978, my life became part of hell. I had a second abortion close to six months after the first. I remember little

about it. I died on the table after the first one.

I couldn't speak about it to anyone for such a long time, and if I did, they all told me I didn't do anything wrong. Or they told me that abortion was a good thing. So I went where I consider to be underground, emotionally, creating my own little space for the reality of my situation. Hence my psychotic episodes.

I had four trips to the psych ward where doctors could not figure out what was wrong with me. Some of my hospital records state that the only words they could decipher through all the screaming was, "Can you give me back my babies?"

On one visit to the "loony bin," as my husband calls it, I was tied down in leather restraints and when the nurse injected me with Haldol, an anti-psychotic, I screamed, "Stop sucking the life out of me!" No one seemed to know what I was saying since I was already stigmatized as being "nuts" just by being there. A couple of days later, when I was talking to my nurse, he asked me why I had said that. I told him about the abortions, and he said then it made sense. Hurray! Someone finally understood me. I spent the next three years in severe depression, which finally lifted when I went through the Project Rachel post-abortion healing process through my church.

Diana recounted the above experience in a speech she gave in 1997 promoting post-abortion programs. Unfortunately, her experience of psychotic episodes of retreat into her "own little space" is not uncommon. All too often, I have heard women describe how they have writhed in psychiatric wards without anyone understanding the depth or cause of their pain, which is rooted in the unresolved grief and trauma of a past abortion. For example, Anna Mae told me that during her numerous hospitalizations, she only got worse:

I was not capable of dealing with the emotional pain from my abortion. The pain was too intense. In the hospital I was keeping plastic knives from meals to use to cut myself. I would use paper clips that I found lying on the floor. I would use a sharp edge on anything I could find. I would cut myself when I wanted to feel the pain I was no longer able to feel. I would cut myself when I did not want to feel the pain.

I would also cut myself to try to let the pain out. I didn't think I could hold in the pain and thought cutting on myself would free some of it. People could not see the emotional pain I felt, so I could show them some of my pain because it was now all over my hand and arms. I was in and out of the hospital. I continued to abuse and mutilate myself. I just wanted the pain to stop. I did not know what it was all about. It seemed the only way to take the pain away was to die. I could not live in such pain and self-hatred. I hurt so badly. I wanted to go away. I felt like I had caused so much pain and I had to be punished.

In the Elliot Institute survey, 10 percent of the post-abortive women reported having been hospitalized one or more times for psychiatric care, and 20 percent reported experiencing a nervous breakdown after their abortions. According to Jane:

I had horrible nightmares . . . the same dream over and over: I dream I am at the bathroom sink washing my hands–slowly the water turns to blood, then clots of blood, then a child slips out. I would wake up in a cold sweat, afraid to go into my bathroom. Six months following my abortion, I had a breakdown.

> Years later, when my son was born, I remember wanting to throw him out the window of the hospital room. I suffered from post-partum psychosis. I remember thinking . . . who in their right mind would want a boy? At times I imagined that he was a devil, and all I could think was that I needed to get away from him.

In the best record-based study to date of psychiatric admissions following abortion, it was revealed that in the four years following a pregnancy outcome, women who abort are two to four times more likely to be admitted for psychiatric hospitalization than women who carry to term.[7] Furthermore, in another recent study of patients who had been committed to inpatient care in a psychiatric ward for over one year, the authors observed an association between abortion and a greater incidence of psychoactive substance abuse disorder. They also concluded that women with a history of abortion may be at greater risk of rehospitalization than other women.[8]

One compelling example of a woman going through years of repeated admissions for psychiatric care is the story of Brianna. When she became pregnant at age 16, Brianna concealed her pregnancy for six months. When her mother found out, she immediately took Brianna to a hospital, where they performed a second-trimester saline abortion. As a normal part of this procedure, Brianna went into labor and vaginally delivered a dead baby whose skin had been burned by the saline solution. When she saw her baby, she grabbed the dead infant and clutched it against her chest and scrambled off the bed. It took half-a-dozen medical staff to remove the dead baby from her encompassing clutch, as Brianna shrieked with blood-curdling grief.

Brianna named her dead child Billy. She never forgot the event and ritualistically set up memorials to him in one apartment after another as she moved on through her life. By age 44, she had been in and out of mental hospitals and suffered from multiple personality disorder. Several of her alternate personalities were babies; one was named "Billy." Another personality was a sinister commander. Another was a helpless little girl. Like "Billy," these personalities served to recreate aspects of her traumatic abortion.

Not once in all the years of psychotherapy, psychodrama, group and individual treatment did a single therapist pay any attention to Brianna's abortion or recognize it as a trauma worthy of discussion. Her story makes me wonder: Who is more disoriented? Brianna, with all of her personalities, or a medical community that refuses to acknowledge the trauma inflicted on this young girl in the name of "choice?"

# CHAPTER ELEVEN

# REPEAT ABORTIONS

Sharon had the look of a woman who had done some hard living. Her forehead was furrowed deeply with lines carved by decades of stress. Her leathery facial skin was the backdrop for sea-green eyes worn weary and bloodshot from drinking. She was slumped over to one side, resting her head on the side of an overstuffed armchair. In a matter-of-fact tone she stated, "I've had seven, you know."

I let her announcement hang for a moment. This was an admission that needed to be approached gently. I knew Sharon suffered from a lot of anxiety and frequently used alcohol to calm her nerves. I wondered if she was ready to explore her past, as she seemed rather cut off from it. Her collarbone protruded sharply from beneath a checkered halter top. It struck me that her emaciated body was striving to express an anguish and misery that defied words.

"Do you mean seven abortions?" I asked.

"Yeah, seven. That's supposed to be a lucky number, isn't it?" she asked in a childish tone. Twisting long pieces of hair around her middle finger, she looked up at me with a suspicious stare, curious to know if I could help her. She appeared nervous, but also faintly distracted.

"Do you feel lucky?" I asked.

"Lucky to be alive, I guess. There must be some reason why I'm still here," she mused, twisting her hair into a tight knot. "I just haven't figured it out yet."

Sharon began to speak of her life. Her oral history was a desensitized account of abandonment, betrayal, multiple abortions, and abuse. Yet she was starkly detached from her experiences. While divulging her multiple losses, she appeared to be reporting the soapy drama of someone else's life. As a 48-year-old woman with no children or partner, she was isolated and lonely. No sooner did she acknowledge her painful solitude than she would retreat, insisting that none of it really bothered her because she had no reference point for what she was missing. She was numb to both pain and pleasure. She complained that she had little memory of the past twenty years and wondered if it was normal to feel nothing.

"How do you stay so numb and detached from your own life?" I asked with curiosity.

As Sharon drew in a deep breath, the sides of her mouth curled into a grin. "Drinking, I guess . . . but I sure as hell can't do that anymore . . . I've got liver problems now," she said with a droll laugh.

Sharon attended a Rachel's Vineyard weekend retreat to find some peace. She knew that the self-medication provided by alcohol was no longer an option. She attended a weekend with other women who had also undergone the trauma of multiple abortions. This particular group of 12 women had aborted a total of 65 pregnancies. Loretta had twelve, Gianna and Lisa each had nine, and Emily and Roe had eight. There was another woman who had seven . . . Sharon's "lucky number." All of these women suffered from alcoholism. As the group began to reconnect to the past and all their buried feelings, the level of grief was heartbreaking.

Among them was Shelly. After five abortions, Shelly had discovered a way to submerge her menacing grief through severe workaholism. She recalled her powerful desire to become pregnant:

> I wanted more than anything to become pregnant right after the abortion. I wanted to replace what I had lost . . . to continue what I had started. I wanted to prove to God and myself that I had the capabilities of being a good mother.

Hoping to recover her happiness, Shelly quickly became pregnant again within a few months of her first abortion. But since many of the stresses that led to that abortion still existed, she ended up aborting again. Then again, again, and again. Five pregnancies and five abortions.

> After my first abortion, I felt like my life had spun completely out of control. With each abortion, I was crushed. I couldn't believe that things could possibly get any worse. Eventually, I felt like I didn't deserve to ever become a mother, a wife, or anything. I was paralyzed by depression, anxiety . . . fear.

Shelly's cycle of repeat abortions was part of a self-defeating behavior pattern that began after her first abortion. In every area of her life where a new opportunity for a relationship, attachment, or achievement opened up, Shelly slammed the door on her future. For example, nine months before she would have graduated from college, she dropped out. When she subsequently landed a decent job, she worked for only ten weeks before terminating her employment. (Incidentally, her abortion had been at ten weeks of gestation.) In her relationships with men, she would abruptly break off the relationship whenever it reached the point of a possible commitment, and then grieve her lost love. At every turn, she aborted all of her hopes and plans, thereby mirroring the abortion of her children's lives. She was frozen in a longing, dependent state—stuck in the past, reenacting the trauma of her original abortion through the rejection of every opportunity.

Joyce also had five abortions. She reluctantly obtained her first abortion at the urging of an abortion clinic counselor who informed her that since she used medicine for acne, she would probably give birth to a "defective child." Joyce greatly feared such an outcome, so she consented to the procedure rather than take a risk. Likewise, her boyfriend pressured her by saying that he would never be able to raise a "kid with problems."

Joyce felt frightened and helpless over the abortion and became quite depressed. She cried constantly and wished she had known for sure if something was wrong with the baby. Alcohol and drug abuse followed.

When Joyce became pregnant a second time, the fear that she would need another abortion was transformed into anger and hatred. In an effort to master her trauma, she attempted to get out of the victim role by rejecting her feelings of powerlessness and substituting in their place feelings of anger and hatred that triggered a coldness about her abortions.

> So what? I did it before and the father of the baby is a jerk. I don't want to give him a child. He had the chance before and didn't want it.

After the second abortion, Joyce became sexually promiscuous. By the time she was faced with her third abortion, she scornfully laughed at it: "Oh, well, I thought, there goes another one. Time to forget about my white picket fence."

The fourth abortion was a "quickie." By that point Joyce was desensitized to her pain and never paused to consider if she was doing the right thing. Her relationships with men had deteriorated. She hated her original boyfriend and first love, the source of her monumental disillusionment. As time went on, she engaged in ongoing relationships with married men. She also had frequent episodes of promiscuous sex with no special attachment.

The abortions caused a striking change in Joyce's personality. Her first abortion, although agonizing, began a spiraling down into an emotional and moral abyss. She lost the ability to have a meaningful relationship with a man who could truly love her and abandoned the hope of ever having children at her side. She felt helpless to change and tossed aside any aspirations for an ideal life, concluding that such goals were unrealistic and stupid. Her view of the future was truncated, with no sense of use or purpose. Her life was overrun with despair, where only the pleasure of the moment or aimless passions offered any distraction or relief. Joyce became a tragic figure—an underdeveloped reflection of the woman she might have become.

> The loss of my children has caused a bottomless emptiness and unforeseen grief and sadness. The devastation in my life spanned 26 years. I was damaged psychologically, emotionally, and spiritually. I went on the Rachel's Vineyard weekend retreat for healing, and I was finally able to grieve the loss of my children and give them dignity. I was able to come to terms with what had happened. Since making the weekend, I have regained my self-respect and have started living my life instead of just existing.

## REENACTING PREGNANCY AND ABORTION

Sadly, the ways in which Sharon, Shelly and Joyce became trapped in a cycle of repeat abortions are not uncommon. Approximately half of all women who have an abortion have had one or more previous abortions.

Women with a history of more than one abortion are likely to suffer more severe physical and psychological problems from their abortions. Studies of women having repeat abortions show that they are more likely to live in less stable social situations, have nearly twice as many psychological problems, and have twice as much reliance on social support services.[1] They are also more likely to go through a divorce, to be involved in substance abuse, and to rely on public welfare.[2] At the same time, they are also more likely to actively desire pregnancy and to have a low motivation for and irregular use of contraception.

This problem of repeat abortions is not due to callousness or the careless use of birth control. Instead, it is far more likely that women who have multiple abortions are "careless" in their birth control practices precisely because they are caught in a pattern of reenacting their traumatic abortions. For example, Deirdre explained that after four abortions:

> I know I should be using birth control. I don't know why I'm not. I'm not trying to get pregnant or anything. I just don't care if it happens. If it did, I'm not sure what I'd do. Maybe this time someone would want to marry me. That's a joke! Who would want me?

Deirdre's statement reflected her low self-worth and ambivalence regarding pregnancy. She felt powerless to control her future. She did not feel that she had a right to expect anything from life and simply accepted whatever happened. She was stuck. The pattern of pregnancy followed by abortion had become addictive and mesmerizing. Like a ship tossed on a violent sea, Deirdre had no control.

A central aspect of trauma is a sense of helplessness. Reenactment is a means by which individuals like Deirdre revisit their traumas. On some level of their minds, they repeatedly expose themselves to the same traumatic situation in the hope that they will eventually confront, conquer, and triumph over the experience, thus vanquishing the cause of their helplessness.

One way in which women who are traumatized by their abortions seek to reassert power over their lives, and simultaneously to "undo" their abortions, is through replacement pregnancies. Unfortunately, this is a very risky proposition. While some women do carry their subsequent replacement pregnancies to term, others quickly discover that the same pressures that led to their first abortions are still there. As a result, they are likely to have another abortion, which reinforces the trauma of their first. While many forms of reenactment are symbolic, as we have seen, in these cases reenactment of a traumatic abortion can be quite literal, resulting in one, two, three . . . or even a dozen subsequent abortions.

Christine had her first abortion at the age of 18. She was under treatment for mild depression, and her psychiatrist advised the abortion. This was before abortion-on-demand became legal. In order to have the procedure done, they told Christine she would have to sign a paper that stated she would commit suicide if she did not have an abortion. Her mental health care workers orchestrated the entire event. In reality Christine knew she would not kill herself, but she went along as an obliging patient who followed doctor's orders.

At the age of 22, she became pregnant again. Although married this time, she felt anxiety and fear over being a parent. This anxiety was rooted in her first abortion. The message from her psychiatrist that colored her view of herself as a potential mother was that she was not mentally stable enough to have a child and that having a baby would provoke a mental breakdown and even suicidal behavior. Christine's husband was eager and ready to begin a family, yet the thought of having a baby simply terrified her. Because of her fears of inadequacy, she had another abortion and divorced her husband shortly thereafter.

Christine's third pregnancy also ended in a second-trimester abortion. Though she felt tremendous grief and guilt, this pattern continued three more times for a total of six abortions. Each time she had an intense desire to be a mother, but each time she could see no other recourse but abortion, reenacting the first trauma of helplessness to overcome her perceived inadequacy and incompetence.

Riddled with guilt and low self-esteem, Christine had herself surgically sterilized to avoid having to "kill any more babies." Having broken free of reenactment via repeat abortions, her self-destructive impulses were channeled into several subsequent suicide attempts. Her maternal identity shattered, she desperately sought mothering from other women through various attempts at a lesbian lifestyle.

What a different life Christine could have had if her psychiatrist had reinforced her self-esteem and her confidence in her capacity to be a mother. Instead, by encouraging abortion, her therapist imprinted a deadly message deep into her psyche: She was unstable and inadequate to be a mother.

As a therapist, I worked with Christine specifically to bring the meaning of her repeated abortions into her awareness. Soon she began to realize that she had dealt with the original abortion over and over in the same negative way. It caused not only the loss of six children, but also denied Christine an opportunity to give life, love her children, grow as a woman, and experience the joys of motherhood.

Once she became aware of the original conflict, Christine stated that her "whole life finally seemed to make sense." She could finally understand why she had become trapped in such a self-destructive pattern. Although an awareness of these patterns was essential for her healing, it also gave rise to tremendous grief and anger at having lost so many years and so many children. This process, though difficult and bitter, was an important ingredient in helping Christine stop degrading herself. Her episodes of depression subsided, she obtained her first job in 20 years, and she began to ask more for herself in relationships. Instead of viewing herself as an evil person, she saw that her actions had their source in the tremendously painful conflict of an abortion foisted upon her by people she trusted.

Christine's story illustrates one of the many overlooked consequences of abortion. It is the unspoken but accepted message to a woman that she is inadequate. Instead of being offered support, encouragement, and trust in her ability to care for a child, a woman is persuaded to accept a violent solution that invades her physical and psychological integrity. The result, at the very least, is a lack of self-confidence and a diminished sense of self-worth. When traumatized women lose all confidence in their ability to protect and care for others, they are prone to becoming entangled in a pattern of multiple abortions.

Zoe shared her experience between her first and last abortions:

> The one thing that stands out most about that day in 1973 is, oddly enough, not my personal experience—though, don't get me wrong, that had an enormous impact. Yet, I was about to meet the future "me." At the age of 18, I was still very fragile, very frightened . . . and *very* vulnerable and impressionable. Not at all hardened in many ways. The point is, there was still an element of my person that was reachable, teachable, that yearned, that was sensitive and compassionate.
>
> I went into the clinic, went through the paperwork, and sat to await my turn at whatever unknown fate was ahead. Then a young woman came in who did not appear to be much older than me—early 20s at best. She sat near me and had faded blue jeans and shoulder-length brown hair parted in the middle. She was alone yet didn't appear uncomfortable at all. I thought she was really "cool" to be handling this sort of thing with such composure. She smiled at me.
>
> When I asked her if she was having an abortion, she shrugged and stated that it was no big deal—it was her third. I was shocked. She was so young. I was sitting there in anguish at the prospect of having one abortion, and here she was having her third. I could not understand, as horrified as I was, how anyone would go through with this three times? It was like, does she have a learning disability or what?
>
> I found myself blinking and gasping in disbelief. I thought she had to be the dumbest woman I had ever met. She was so hardened to it all—so nonchalant—tough as nails. She was no more concerned about this abortion than having a tooth filled. I promised myself I would never be such a person . . . so hard, so cold, so out of touch. I couldn't understand how this could happen to someone.

I remembered this woman again in 1988 at the time of my fourth abortion. I understood that day what kind of woman would have four abortions. I understood what experience could make a person as tough as nails—so hard, so cold, so out of touch. All those abortions had robbed me of an element of my humanity that is difficult to express in words. Maybe the men who landed in Normandy on D-day understand it. Maybe the members of violent gangs who have seen death and violence again and again. . . .

The taking of a life of another human being has a life-changing impact on a person. I can't give it a name, but I can tell you that it's hard—if not impossible—to recapture it once it is lost.

I struggled for many years with enormous grief and depression because I slaughtered—literally, considering the method of their demise—all of my children, for I have no children today. For many years, I could not even stand to be around children. Even today, you won't see me running to cuddle an infant. I can tolerate 3-year-olds, but infants are still a big problem. So even today, I am still dealing with the aftermath.

## Repeat Abortions as a Result of Coercion

I have heard hundreds of women share stories of how their decisions to have abortions were very much shaped by pressure from people and circumstances. This kind of abortion trauma can keep women imprisoned in destructive patterns of repeat pregnancies, abortion and even abuse. Lexie shares her story:

The first time I got pregnant, I was 19. I was living with a much older man, whom I believed was very much in love with me. Like many couples, we had financial problems, and according to him I was just crazy to even think of having a baby. He said: "Hey, you know you not having it, right? I don't even need to say anything else. I want you to schedule an appointment ASAP." After that he walked out of the door. He was totally determined that I would have an abortion.

He gave me no option to even think about it. I was absolutely on my own if I wanted to have the baby, and I had absolutely nothing, not even family around me to help me to think about what I was doing. All I could think of was, "I can't be a single mother; I am not even married. What am I going to do? Where am I going to live? How am I going to work? I can't leave the baby alone. I have nobody here to help me." Every time I would try to discuss possibilities of having the baby he would just leave me talking by myself, sitting looking at the walls. All I knew was he wanted it done, and done as soon as possible. I was almost 3 months, and every day, every single day, I remember how stressful it was for me to be pregnant. I got really sick every day and was throwing up every time of the day and I felt so depressed and alone on those days . . . like never before.

I started to play this game in the back of my mind. I would pretend that I was just sick, nothing was really happening to me at all. "What baby??? There is no baby. I am just sick and it will all be gone soon."

So the abortion schedule was set. All I cared about was to get it over with. My name was called, the nurse opened my legs, and she told me I was going to sleep in seconds, I didn't even see the doctor's face. I woke up bleeding, some infection medicine was given, the thing was done. I left that place in such emptiness. The whole thing was removed from me, including my soul.

I couldn't forget that suction machine. I was thinking, "Where is my baby now? What are they going to be doing with his body? Where is my baby going to be put? Was it a boy or a girl?" I constantly dreamed about that suction machine—what did they do with my baby? Where is he now? How bad have I hurt him? What kind of person would he be if he had the chance to live?

All that was on my mind after the abortion. Every day got worse. I became self-destructive. I would look in the mirror right into my eyes, I saw a selfish ho, a selfish stupid ho, that's all I could think about myself for so long. I couldn't care for myself at all. Anything that would hurt me—I would go for it, and sex became one of those things. I spent two years trying to tell myself everything was under control: "Come on, it's only a blob of blood—right?"

I got pregnant again, by the same man. This time he totally abandoned me. He wouldn't want the blame for telling me to kill the baby again because we had past terrible discussions blaming each other about the first baby. He totally ignored me again; for almost three months, every time I would think about keeping this baby, he would say something like, "You already know you are on your own! I didn't ask you to get pregnant! You did it to yourself. I didn't ask you for no baby! Plus you going to be a single mother? Is that what you want?"

I remember looking at baby clothes at the store and looking all those pregnant women with their respective husbands, and other kids. All I could feel was, "I am such a ho! Here I am a second time pregnant, 21, all alone, and I have no freaking money, not even to buy popcorn." I tried to think of leaving him and trying to make a living on my own. I asked for help at the school I was going to, all I heard was, "It is very hard, honey, you have no idea what you putting yourself into." Nothing was done or said to help me; all I had was a selfish man, 20 years older than me, telling me I was on my own. He said, "I don't even wanna see your kid; I didn't ask for no babies. You got that, ----?"

The second abortion was performed. I remember waking up in a room, and when I looked straight ahead an abortion was being performed on some girl, right in front of the room I was in, and the curtain was open. I heard the noise of the suction machine, and I saw gloves with blood, and suddenly the nurse saw me staring at that thing and she shut the curtain quickly. Was like a lot of blood I had just seen there. The other woman waking up crying right by my side, crying "Where is my baby at, where is my baby" . . . and I looked at her and I started to cry myself. I could not talk for days.

At this point I had lost my own self a long time ago. All I could feel was hate for allowing this to happen to me. Eventually, of course, the rest of any relationship with my boyfriend went down the drain. He started to drink, do drugs; I started to yell, to hate everything about everything on him and everything that would involve his presence as well. We could not talk with each other for months, otherwise things would fly on the sky and the house would be broken in pieces. Having police at our doors was usual. Bloody noses, kicks, black eyes became our best friends. I had tried to get out of it all so many times, but I had no job, and when I would find one, I would lose it before three months had passed. I just couldn't care about anything. Everything that would bring me pain I would take it.

The third abortion was by some other man. I could not figure out who the father was. I had sex with three guys in a week. Two days, two different guys. Again, I was pregnant for three months and living with the same previous man. This time, at least I was positive this baby was not his—and that somewhat made me feel good. I would make him think it was his and I would hide it from him until he found out I was pregnant. I knew he would tell me to get rid of it. All I could do was have my baby for those three months. I thought, "At least you have three months to live, baby. You know you're going to die . . . just enjoy your three months, ok?

I would talk to the baby and buy baby clothes. The first place I would go in a store was the baby section. I was going insane. But for at least three months I had my baby. No one could take that away from me.

Eventually he found out and I went for my third abortion . . . just like a pro. After all, look at my background: three abortions. It's like, wow, isn't it impressive?

All I know is that since my third abortion, all I can feel and think of is nothing. They took away something special. I had conceived life. But again they had taken the only thing I had that was good and pure in my life.

I have killed my own babies. Do you know what I am saying? What's there left for a person to feel? Tell me.

Lexie's life spiraled out of control after the first abortion. The three months she savored with her baby was a short lived experience of "motherhood" until her pregnancy was discovered and destroyed. Clearly, her mental stability deteriorated quickly as the unrecognized trauma repeated itself—drilling the wound deeper into her psyche—and left her feeling helpless to exert any control over her life. Without intervention and healing, Lexie would have continued this very self-destructive pattern of traumatic reenactments.

## REPEAT ABORTIONS AS A FORM OF MASOCHISM

In many ways, women really do experience their pregnancies and their unborn children as part of themselves. Often, if a woman has masochistic tendencies, abortion may be experienced as a form of self-punishment. When the woman destroys her pregnancy and developing child, she is in some way destroying an extension of herself. The loss and grief she experiences are things she feels she deserves as a punishment for "being bad." Conversely, by depriving herself of the potential pride, joy and sense of accomplishment that come with the birth of a child, she is punishing herself by forbidding the enjoyments of motherhood that she does not deserve. Such masochistic tendencies can be an important factor in many repeat abortions.

Maureen, who had three abortions, said:

I hate myself. I have nothing to be proud of. I have given up everything that means anything to me: school, my children. There is nothing left. I don't deserve anything.

Wendy had five abortions. She was vaguely aware of the fact that she used repeat abortions as a way of reenacting the shame she felt after her first abortion and to inflict punishment upon herself for "bad behavior."

I figured I had done something wicked with my first abortion. I felt like an evil person. After that I figured I didn't deserve to be a mother. I never did have children because I thought I was bad . . . not worthy to be a mother.

Melissa's self-punishing behavior was acted out not only through repeat abortions but also through self-injury and risk-taking.

I've had seven abortions. Each time I felt numb and dissociated . . . like a mental case zombie. Afterwards, I'd feel defeated and frustrated with myself. I have enormous self-disgust and hatred. I punish myself by cutting or banging my hands against a concrete wall until they are swollen and bruised purple. I like to hurt myself. There is a strange pleasure in it. Also, I take a lot of risks where I usually get hurt . . . kind of accident-prone, I guess.

When people like Melissa are afraid to express disturbing feelings outwardly, they may vent these emotions through self-destructive acts. Among the post-abortive women I have seen who engage in self-injury, one commonality is that they have never received permission to grieve the loss of their child. Many self-mutilators brand their anger and pain indelibly into their skin, creating tattoos of scar tissue that mimic their confusion and vexation. Multiple abortions are just another way to act out their pain.

## How Many Is Too Many?

As mentioned earlier, nearly half of all women entering abortion clinics have had one or more previous abortions. Studies have shown that women who abort are highly likely to become pregnant again within one or two years. For example, one study of metropolitan teens who had abortions found that 27 percent were pregnant again within 12 months, and 75 percent were pregnant again within 24 months.[3] More recently, in experimental trials with RU-486 abortions, 25 percent of women who had these chemical abortions were found to have become pregnant again within one year.[4]

When these rapid repeat pregnancies are the result of reenactment of trauma, it is quite likely that the subsequent pregnancy will end in another abortion. When these replacement pregnancies are a reflection of undoing (see chapter six), however, it is more likely that these later pregnancies will be carried to term—*if* the woman is able to resist the pressure to abort which may arise from others.

The problem of repeat abortions is very disturbing to abortion clinic counselors, who spend most of their time counseling women on how to avoid becoming pregnant again. While they embrace a woman's right to choose, many abortion counselors are deeply and rightly disturbed by the pattern of repeat abortions they are seeing. But they are uncertain what, if anything, they can do about it.

At a National Abortion Federation (NAF) meeting, for example, one counselor described a woman who had three second-trimester abortions in a period of less than 18 months. Significantly, each time she would come in for the abortion at 21 weeks, reenacting the late date of her first abortion. Another counselor complained of a patient who had seven abortions because she would deliberately become pregnant every time she "fell in love." Again, the counselor did not recognize how this woman was reenacting her first abortion. An abortion counselor from Connecticut was the closest to understanding this problem when she described a woman who came to their clinic for her 14th abortion, saying, "There was a feeling among some of the counselors that we should not continue to see this patient . . . . A feeling that we were in fact reinforcing this behavior."[5]

That is exactly what they are doing—reinforcing self-destructive behaviors. Unfortunately, since abortion providers are committed to performing abortions on request, they have abdicated their responsibility to understand the reasons why women may choose abortion and to intervene when these reasons are distorted, dysfunctional, or even part of a self-destructive cycle.

There is something quite troubling about "medical care" which responds to the patient without any questioning of the deeper things that may be going on within her. In modern medical practice, patients expect a health care professional to treat the whole person. For example, rather than simply continuing to perform repeated angioplasties on an obese patient suffering from heart disease, a doctor would recommend lifestyle changes to lessen the need for invasive medical procedures. But among abortion providers, a mindless submission to the mantra of "choice" has eviscerated any sense of obligation to ensure that abortion will actually help women rather than hurt them.

One of the counselors at the NAF discussion explained her ability to accept 14 abortions with the comment that perhaps the woman was making the decision "not to contracept. Isn't that valid?" Such an ideological commitment to "choice" without reflection or review of what is behind a choice and what will be its result is a form of blindness. Such counselors, both inside and outside our nation's abortion clinics, have simply blinded themselves to how abortion can be a self-destructive act. Until these counselors confront and overcome their own blindness, they will be unable to truly help women break free from this vicious, self-destructive cycle.

# CHAPTER TWELVE

# SEXUAL ABUSE AND ABORTION

As a child, Heidi was an attractive little girl with a petite stature and a tenacious personality. Her large brown eyes were framed with a long set of auburn braids.

Heidi was only seven when her 15-year-old brother Eric began sexually molesting her. Eric would sneak into her room at night to play "monster." He would sometimes hide under the bed until the lights were out, and then make scary growling sounds, banging from underneath the bed in a pulsating rhythm while Heidi nervously laughed and screamed. Afterwards he would reach around the sides of the mattress to grab her. Heidi would squeal and kick as Eric tackled her, wrestling with her in a rollicking match. One night Eric pulled down her pajama bottoms and began fondling her. Eventually, he began having sexual intercourse with her. This secret ritual was shrouded by a pact of silence. "Don't tell anyone," Eric instructed, "or you'll get in trouble."

Again and again her brother insisted, "See, Heidi, see what you make me do!" Somewhere inside, Heidi felt responsible. Her emotions progressed from fear to submission and helplessness. At times, the sex caused a lot of pain. Sometimes she would endure the abuse by imagining another scene to get her mind refocused on something more pleasant. Other times, she would zoom in on the ticking of the clock, concentrating very hard on each rhythmic tick-tock—counting each beat into what felt like infinity. "It will be over soon," she promised herself. "It will be over soon." When Eric was finished, she always felt an awkward sense of shame . . . like something inside her was too dirty ever to be seen.

As Heidi grew older, Eric continued to sexually abuse her. By the time she was a teenager, Eric's friends were taking turns having sex with her. Heidi mistakenly assumed that this was what *all* boys did. She accepted the mistreatment, thinking it was normal conduct for girls and boys. Added to this embedded concept was the unfortunate message that it was the *girl* who supposedly drove the boy to acts of passion and lust. Heidi began to hear the same message from other boys: "Oh, girl, just look at what you do to me!" Not surprisingly, by age 12 Heidi was overly sensual and carried herself in a provocative manner. The childhood sexual abuse and incest led her directly into a promiscuous teenage lifestyle where she allowed herself to be used by men as an object for their pleasure and perversions.

Heidi was trained from a tender age to believe that her value and acceptance as a female originated from her sexuality. She did not know how to set boundaries with men. They took from her what they liked, and offered nothing in return. Having experienced the violation of her most intimate physical boundaries, Heidi had never learned to set limits when someone desired her body. In addition, she grew up blaming herself for all the things that were done to her.

Heidi had her first abortion when she was only 15. While sitting in the waiting room, Heidi dimly heard the old familiar voice running through her mind: "Don't tell anyone; you'll get in trouble."

Later, while she was lying flat on the abortion table, her feet were placed firmly in stirrups. Heidi felt terror as the abortionist entered the room. "Open your legs," he firmly instructed. Reluctantly, Heidi did as she was told. The doctor moved in quickly, plunging his cold steel instruments in and out of her body . . . destroying the life inside. Another familiar voice began to re-play inside her mind. "Just listen to the clock . . . tick-tock one, tick-tock two," she whispered. "It will all be over soon." Heidi had become skilled at dissociating from bad things as they were happening to her.

Before her twenty-first birthday, Heidi had already undergone five abortions. After that, she stopped counting them. Each procedure left her with more self-loathing and shame. But for Heidi, these feelings seemed normal. She had never been treated with dignity or respect. She was a disposable toy for the boys and men who came into her life. Her body had always been an object dissociated from her real self, which lay shrunken and hiding inside. Why should anything her body created be any less disposable? Why should the tiny life hiding inside her be treated with any more respect than she had ever received?

## ABORTION AND SEXUAL ABUSE

It has been my experience that a high proportion of women suffering post-abortion trauma also have histories of molestation, sexual abuse, or incest. Most other post-abortion counselors with whom I deal have reported a similar observation. In the Elliot Institute survey, 21 percent of the post-abortive women surveyed reported a history of childhood physical abuse and 24 percent reported childhood sexual abuse. In a random sample survey of the general population, Dianne Russell reports that approximately one in three girls is sexually abused before age 18 and one in four is abused by age 14. These alarming statistics have a good deal to do with patterns of abuse and crisis.

Sexual abuse, at any age, can impair one's ability to be healthy in the present. Sexual abuse is even more injurious when it is experienced during the formative years of childhood, since the distortions sexual trauma inflict can be deeper, more stunting, and more ingrained into the child's developing personality.[1] Sexual abuse survivors describe a sense of lost selves, injured inner children, wounded souls, and stolen psyches.

It was not until television talk shows began to open the window on the experiences of those affected by sexual abuse that millions of women received permission to emerge from their closets of shame. Women began to examine the reality and prevalence of sexual abuse and started to discuss openly the wide-ranging detrimental effects it has caused in their lives.

At first glance, the idea that abortion can be an extension of sexual abuse may seem unlikely. However, in my experiences with women traumatized by abortion, common themes reappear within each group. For those with similar painful backgrounds, such as parental alcoholism or sexual abuse, the collective pain reveals a deeper meaning beyond the crisis pregnancy and abortion. So much of human behavior, healthy and unhealthy, can be motivated by conflicts and psychological cravings, unmet needs, and compulsive behaviors that feel normal because they are familiar.

If a history of sexual abuse has existed before an abortion, the woman may experience the abortion itself as simply a further continuation of the violations of self that have gone before. The way in which abortion resembles sexual abuse is striking. In the abortion, the abortionist's hand or instrument penetrates deep into the protective and sacred part of the woman's womb. The abortionist is usually a male, and the entry point is the same as where the woman has been violated by men in her past. The abortion's destruction of the child growing inside her echoes the way sexual abuse destroyed her own innocent childlike nature. In such cases, abortion can take on elements of a symbolic suicide. The death of the innocent "inner child" is a reenactment of the traumatic loss of the abused woman's own self.

The effects of trauma often provide numerous invitations to crisis. Desires, beliefs, longings, past experiences, and fears can be employed by the traumatized person in the form of fantasies, reenactments, or repetitions which are assembled unconsciously around the issues of the trauma. Most experts in the field of trauma and abuse support the idea that victims recreate their abuse or trauma in many ways. It is unfinished business, and the victims will continue to act it out until it is somehow resolved or completed. The reenactment can be a ritualized means through which a woman will intensely grieve and mourn.

The grief of abortion, like the grief of incest, is held in unvoiced cries of secrecy. It is a powerful recreation of the intrusion forced upon the woman during sexual abuse, in which she is once again called upon to lie helpless on her back, silently enduring the invasion of her body. Afterward, just as after episodes of sexual abuse, she must be prepared to hide her shame, guilt, despair, and grief behind a painted mask of normalcy.

## REENACTING ABUSE

Sheila was sexually and physically abused in her childhood. Not surprisingly, she often ended up with abusive partners. She "looked for love in all the wrong places" and repeatedly found herself pregnant with no partner support. She wrote the following about her five abortions:

> There is an enormous hole in my heart, a source of tremendous grief at not having my children. I usually experience deep depression during the holidays, especially at Christmas. Abortion for me has been as inhumane as any abusive relationship I have ever been in. My abortionist took the place of my abusive father and my abusive partner. Neither had any comprehension of my real needs as a little girl or later as a woman. Now I continue to be punished by empty memories of what could have been—what should have been. It's a stark reality that I must live with. The truth of my life is hideous. My abortions, like my childhood, are a pain that will never go away.

Sheila's abortions served as a way to symbolize the damage done to her inner child by mimicking the deprivation of love, childhood, and life that had occurred during her own traumatic childhood. Sheila terminated each pregnancy with tremendous grief and heartache, and saw herself as a victim of her unfortunate circumstances. She felt helpless each time and consented to the procedure as just another casualty. Her road to recurrent trauma was predictable, even habitual. Abortion was a continuation of a pattern begun in childhood and extended into her adult life. It only served to reenact her trauma, while also depriving her of the joy of having children who might have restored meaning and hope in her life.

Maggie had a long and violent history of sexual abuse, which began at the age of four in a child prostitution ring. Years later she described her abortions as her own sentencing and execution.

> I remember walking into the clinic and feeling like I was about to take my rightful place in an electric chair. I knew a part of myself would die. I wanted that baby. I wanted all of them. Yet each time I felt like abortion was something that I just had to do.

Maggie felt compelled to sacrifice her children through abortion because of an abusive history. Her own "inner child" had been sacrificed when she was repeatedly and violently sexually abused as a young girl. For Maggie, the analogy of an electric chair verified abortion as a life-threatening shock, similar to many episodes of abuse she had endured as a child. Her inability or unwillingness to carry a child to term and to take on the responsibilities of being a mother arose from the developmental handicaps she suffered as an abused child. She saw herself as that stunted, abused child and could not see how to make the developmental leap to becoming a responsible, loving parent. She felt emotionally stuck and thus trapped in a pattern of abortion, which recreated the traumatic themes of grief, loss, powerlessness, and violence which had shaped her childhood.

Barbara's history of sexual abuse, followed by six abortions, began with her mother's abortion when she was only seven.

> After her abortion, my mother was never the same. She suffered depression and became a heroin addict. The family split up because of my parent's drug abuse. I was abandoned by my family and spent years in foster homes, where I was sexually violated by my caretakers. I became a prostitute. I sought love and human touch with sex. Many men had me, many times. I remember times when guys sat at a table playing a game of cards over me—I was the winner's prize. They played the same game when it came time to see whose turn it was to take me to the abortion clinic. I was high most of the time, trying with futile effort to drown my pain.

Abortion had become just another tough break in life that Barbara had to accept and endure. It kept her trapped in despair and pain. As a seven-year-old child, she experienced survivor guilt associated with the knowledge that one of her siblings had died in an abortion, while for some unknown reason she had been allowed to survive. As her mother's life deteriorated, so did Barbara's life. Sexual abuse and prostitution led her full circle back to abortion, again and again. She kept returning to the disparaging arena of prostitution because she did not feel worthy of anything more. Her sexual degradation and multiple abortions echoed unresolved issues related to her mother's abortion, and her own survival guilt and childhood sexual abuse.

With counseling and the support of those who understood and accepted what she had endured, Barbara is now free of all the secrets that held her bound. She is now capable of speaking about the unspeakable and connecting private anxieties and fears to their source, instead of acting them out in destructive repetitions. She is married to a patient man who is a stable and loving support in her life and is developing a spiritual life that furnishes her with hope and strength. These are the ingredients that will help her continue to heal as she continues to do extensive grief work related to all these agonizing losses.

Marsha remembered a childhood with habitual molestation from her uncle and his friends. As an adult, she became a topless dancer in a sleazy nightclub. In the nightclub setting, she could reenact the humiliation of being an object of the desires of men, but with an empowering twist. In the nightclub Marsha held the reigns of power. Through the stage manager and bouncers who protected her from the groping hands of the customers, she could excite men, as she had as a child, but control their advances. Also, as an erotic dancer she was paid a great deal of money to do what she once experienced as humiliating. As for many, if not most, erotic dancers, the nightclub was a place where Marsha could attempt to master the traumatic experiences of her abusive childhood. It provided a forum in which she could reenact sexually provocative behavior while exercising some control over the excited men, the type of control she never had enjoyed as a child. She was unable to see, however, that while her erotic dancing provided temporary emotional and financial compensations for her wounded childhood, it was not truly empowering or healing. Her offstage life still lacked a sense of the control and dignity she so deeply craved.

As a result of her promiscuous relationships, Marsha endured eight abortions. For years, she had believed that abortion rights gave her command, authority, and control over her life and the lives of others. It was the type of power she had longed for as a child when she could not make the abuse stop. Yet each abortion only fueled new rounds of dysfunctional relationships, crisis pregnancies, and abortions. Marsha continued to be used and discarded by men who cared nothing for her. It was not until age 51 that she sought help. Her grief over her life and her missing children was profound. However, by dealing with her losses, she began to recognize her inherent worth as a human being, and her desire for real dignity and love.

Certainly not all sexually abused women become prostitutes or erotic dancers, but they are more likely to engage in behaviors that invite despair and humiliation. Even though a sexually abused person can appear on the surface to be quite normal and functioning well, unresolved shame can surface during times of stress. This stress can take its toll in the form of eating disorders, alcohol and drug addiction, extramarital affairs, shoplifting, child abuse, and a host of other behaviors.

## WHEN COMPLEX NEEDS CLASH WITH SIMPLE DESIRES

Like all women, sexually abused women long for real love. The difference is that because their sexual boundaries were violated at an early age, they are more likely to use their bodies in an attempt to obtain that love. Through provocative and promiscuous behavior in the present, they express the sexual abuse and victimization they experienced in the past. In short, women with a history of abuse are seeking a way to satisfy complex needs regarding love, respect, and trauma resolution.

Unfortunately, in this era of sexual freedom, there is a nearly unlimited supply of men who want to satisfy a very simple impulse: their desire for uncommitted sexual release. When sexual abuse victims with complex needs meet predators whose interest in them is limited to their ability to satisfy their sexual desires, the result is predictably disastrous. Rather than finding resolution of their trauma and fulfillment of their need for love and respect, sexually abused women are more likely to encounter additional betrayals of their love, attacks on their dignity, and reenactment of their traumas. Sadly, sexually abused women and abusive males even tend to gravitate toward each other. It is as if these women's heightened vulnerability is a perfect match for these men's dysfunctional need to dominate and humiliate their mates.

When a pregnancy results between a needy woman and an abusive man who does not want the child, the woman is very likely to be subjected to increased levels of verbal or physical abuse, which is intended to compel her to submit to an unwanted abortion.[2] Under these hostile circumstances, many women submit. Their abortions do not free or empower them, however. Instead the abortion experience only strengthens their feelings of self-disgust, shame, and isolation, which serves to reinforce the dynamics that are keeping them locked in abusive relationships. Such was the case of Karen, who had been involved in numerous abusive relationships.

> In my situation, abortion was just another form of sexual abuse. It was just another way of abusing me. He had power over me in demanding that I abort. He was completely "turned off" by me being pregnant. He actually punished me with his anger and rage. I could see that I would have to pay the price. Who cared that we created a life together? His sex with me was just as empty as his heart was. I can't believe I allowed him to control me as much as he did.

Another victim of sexual abuse, Dorinda, commented on the similarity between the horror of incest and the trauma of abortion.

> Nothing that happened to my body mattered. As an incest victim, I had absolutely no volition regarding the integrity of my body—somebody wanted it and they took it, no matter what I wanted. In the case of my abortion, I had no understanding regarding the integrity of my body and spirit—"it" had misbehaved and had to be corrected without thought for how much the act would hurt me.
>
> But who could think that a new life nurtured inside the body as one flesh could be severed from that body and ended without causing lifelong grief and yearning? Only a woman who had no idea that her body, or the spirit that infuses it, or the sexuality that permeates it, were connected or mattered.
>
> I was not alone. The common experience of the women in our post-abortion group was the shock of the devastating feelings surrounding this act that was supposed to have no significance—as if our bodies and what they create have no significance, as if we have no significance. Our experiences were similar. I think it's because there's a common value underlying incest and abortion (and rape and promiscuity and our historic perception of sexuality)—an incredible callousness toward our bodies and others' bodies.

## ABORTION AS ANOTHER RAPE

Nina was raped one night while away on a business trip. To her horror
and shame, she discovered she was pregnant. In an effort to destroy all
reminders of the rape, Nina consented to an abortion.

> The fact that I got pregnant because of the rape was disgusting. I felt like I had
> to get rid of it. Somehow, I figured that because I got pregnant I must have
> enjoyed it. I couldn't tolerate that concept. I was so ashamed. I got my abortion
> out of state so that no one would know.
>
> The rape was nothing compared to the abortion. I developed a raging pelvic
> inflammatory disease (PID) because I never received any antibiotic to prevent
> infection. My gynecologist also informed me that besides the scarring from
> the infection, my cervix is badly damaged from the abortion procedure. I will
> never have children of my own because I am sterile due to the PID.
>
> The rape was bad but I could have gotten over it. The abortion is something
> I will never get over. No one realizes how much that event damaged my life. I
> hate my rapist, but I hate the abortionist too. I can't believe I paid to be raped
> again. This will affect the rest of my life.

Like many rape victims, Nina blamed herself, believing that somewhere along the way she had invited or consented to the rape. Rather
than removing her self-blame, her abortion reaffirmed her sense of
shame and guilt. Now she knew she was culpable; she had even consented to the abortion in writing.

Nina loved children and had always wanted to have a family. The
abortion demolished all her dreams of having children in the future.
No one at the abortion clinic had ever mentioned that possible "side
effect." The child she had lost to abortion was the only child she would
ever conceive. This realization gave rise to intense grief and heartache.
When it was too late, she longed for the aborted baby, even though he
or she was the product of rape. She began to see herself as the guilty
party and her baby as the innocent victim of her violence. The anger
she felt toward the rapist became bitterly directed against herself.
After such a devastating experience, her journey to recovery was long
and difficult.

Nina's experience is not unusual. The largest study ever done of
women who had pregnancies resulting from rape or incest was recently
published in the book *Victims and Victors: Speaking Out About Their Pregnancies, Abortions, and Children Resulting from Sexual Assault*. In this
study of nearly 200 women, 89 percent of those who aborted a pregnancy resulting from sexual assault explicitly stated that they regretted having had their abortions. They often described their abortions as
more traumatic and difficult to deal with than the sexual assault. Over
90 percent stated they would discourage other pregnant sexual assault
victims from opting for abortion. Only seven percent believed that abortion would "usually" be beneficial in cases of sexual assault. Conversely,

among the sexual assault victims who carried to term, in retrospect they *all* believed they made the right decision in giving birth. None regretted not having an abortion.[3]

## FATAL ILLUSIONS

Many in contemporary society are concerned with ending the vicious cycle of abuse, yet they cannot see that the perpetrators of violence are often responding to their own memories of abuse. The theme of the victim becoming the perpetrator permeates the literature and clinical research on family violence. Countless articles and intervention programs have been developed with this aspect of trauma in mind.

The concept of victims becoming perpetrators can also be played out in a broader social context. For example, many of the women who initiated, fought, and are fighting the battle for abortion rights have themselves been badly mistreated, abandoned, and forced to suffer the hardships of life alone, victimized and unloved.[4] For many, the battle for abortion is symbolic of their battle to restore a sense of control and dignity to their own battered lives.[5]

Given the fact that many early advocates of legalized abortion suffered sexual, physical, and emotional abuse, it is not surprising that the language of abortion rights centers on "controlling one's body." For many, the battle over abortion, even on a political level, involves a symbolic reenactment of their struggle to gain mastery over past trauma and abuse.

Unfortunately, those who use abortion as a means of mastering past trauma are doomed to suffer both disappointment and a deepening entanglement in the cycle of self-destructive violence. Mastery over past victimization can never be achieved by depersonalizing or destroying others.

Abortion only offers women who hunger for some resolution of past abuse the illusion of power. Victims of abuse have a deep hunger for respect, love, and justice. Abortion simply cannot fill these needs because it is inherently a destructive, negating act. Abortion does not create; it can only destroy. It cannot fill holes in one's spirit; it can only create new holes. But these truisms are not obvious to those whose needs and yearnings overpower reason. To an uninformed famine victim, for example, a huge mound of cotton candy appears to be a prize worth fighting for. If won, it may even seem sweet for a time. But it will not produce any lasting benefit, because it is not the nature of cotton candy to nourish. In the same way, it is not the nature of abortion to heal broken hearts or to empower the powerless.

Nothing was ever created by abortion. It can only destroy. And like so many other tools of destruction, it can often destroy far more than we intend.

## CHAPTER THIRTEEN

# SOMETHING INSIDE HAS DIED
## Booze, Drugs, Sex, and Suicide

Mary sat in the recovery room, crying almost hysterically. "My God, what have I done?" she moaned. She was doubled over, her arms wrapped tightly around her abdomen as if holding herself together. As tears streamed down her face, she observed other girls reading magazines, as though lined up under dryers at the beauty salon. "How can they be so casual about this?" she marveled.

The tissue box on the table beside her was empty, so she wiped her nose on the sleeve of her denim jacket as she fought the chills which invaded her body. "I have to get a grip!" she told herself. With a determined act of will, she took a deep breath and swallowed back her tears, grief, and heartache.

When she arrived home, her boyfriend greeted her at the door. He had planned a special evening—a steak and lobster dinner with a bottle of champagne—to commend her for her extraordinary bravery on this, the day of her abortion. Needless to say, Mary did not feel pride in her "accomplishment." Instead, the celebration atmosphere made her feel uncomfortable and foolish. When her boyfriend offered her a glass of champagne, she gulped it down. Grateful for its anesthetic effect, she quickly emptied a second glass, then a third and a fourth. It was not long before Mary was so plastered that her boyfriend had to carry her to bed.

The next morning, she woke with cottonmouth and an extreme headache that hung over her memory like an iron blanket, momentarily covering her recollections of the previous day. Mary buried her head under the pillow and asked her boyfriend to lower the shades on the windows. Slowly she became aware of the blood-soaked pad pasted to her underpants—a menacing reminder of the previous day. Her boyfriend, gently rubbing her shoulders, recognized the dim pain surfacing in her eyes. "I'll make you a drink," he offered, eager to assist in an alliance of drowning sorrow.

Mary nodded and shuffled slowly into the shower, aghast at the amount of crimson blood left over from the abortion. When she had finished, her boyfriend handed her a Bloody Mary. "How appropriate!" she mused, choking off a ragged laugh. If she thought too much, she knew, she might burst into a never-ending river of tears. "Bottoms up!" she sighed and swiftly downed the drink. Her boyfriend joined her. Thus was born, in place of her baby, an alcoholic ritual that would dominate Mary's life for nearly ten years.

## INTOXICATED WITH FEELINGS

The human mind has a tremendous capacity to repress undesirable feelings and re-channel them into more tolerable tortures. If we cannot find a way to work through the trauma with our conscious intellect, our unconscious mind will accomplish the task for us. Trying to cope with these shattered phantoms may invite the abuse of alcohol or drugs, and a vicious, unrelenting cycle of self-destruction, heaping insult on top of injury until awareness of the original problem has been annihilated.

I have listened to many women share their sad tales of unacknowledged and unexpressed grief. Drinking and drugs for many becomes an ordinary way of life—like breathing and eating. They become "party people," laughing their way through life to avoid the tears that well up when they are alone and silent. The dreams they once had are choked off by the same self-destructive behaviors they use to drown their grief. Monica shared this all-too-familiar story:

> From the time I was 18 and had my first abortion, the aftermath affected almost every area of my life. I think alcohol and drug abuse were at the top of the list, but also there were nightmares, uncontrollable fear to the point of a panic disorder, and a deep sadness, the source of which I couldn't identify or understand. I frequently thought about killing myself. I had anger and rage, sexual problems, low self-esteem, incredible self-hatred and a depression that came and went like an unexpected wind. But most of all, *grief* that chilled me to the bone. My grief turned on me like a hungry lion waiting to destroy every area of my life. Drinking and drugs were the only way I could cope.

Researchers studying substance abuse identified long ago that women are likely to date the onset of alcohol and drug abuse to a particular stressful event or a "definite life situation."[1] It should not be surprising, then, to find that over a dozen studies have found a strong association between substance abuse and abortion.[2] One found that among women without a prior history of substance abuse, women who aborted their first pregnancy had a 4.5 times higher risk of subsequent substance abuse compared to women who carried their first pregnancy to term.[3] When the most conservative risk estimates from this study are applied to the general population of women, it indicates that at least 150,000 women per year abuse drugs and/or alcohol as a means of dealing with post-abortion stress.[4] One of these women was Jennifer:

> When I look back on my problems with drinking, I never thought it was anything unusual. I grew up in the seventies, and I thought, hey, everybody is drinking and doing drugs. I thought I was normal, just like everyone else. Now I realize that I *never* did any of those things until after my abortion. Sure,

everyone was drinking, but I drank *more* than anyone else. I ended up sleeping around more too. It was a wild and crazy time. I tried to drink away my feelings of grief. I had to keep drinking, because my inner emptiness was always there, and I could not bear the way it made me feel. So I became the party girl . . . the first to arrive, the last to leave. I'd buy drinks for others, hoping they'd keep me company and help me to avoid myself . . . a self I grew to hate. Drinking helped me forget about her—and for however long the buzz lasted, I felt okay.

After Amanda's abortion, she immediately went to the nearest bar to drown her anguish in rum and cola. The sympathetic bartender to whom Amanda related her story assisted her in getting drunk that night out of an authentic pity for her. Thereafter, Amanda reenacted this confession and affirmation scene by getting drunk and confessing her abortion to whomever her bar buddy was that night. Who it was didn't matter—sometimes it would be a complete stranger. With each drunken confession, Amanda experienced the pain and the grief as vividly as she had the night of the abortion. Alcohol provided an altered state of consciousness, unshackled her emotions and exposed a private raw nerve. It also gave her permission to feel and lowered her defenses enough to openly admit her grief. But her relief was limited to her drunken state. Amanda rarely remembered her ritual confessions the next day. When sober, she denied that the abortion had any effect on her, insisting that she was fine with it.

## SPIRALING OUT OF CONTROL

Drugs and alcohol have the power to change a person's emotional center, if only temporarily. In a chemically altered emotional state, one can feel like a different person—separated from one's past. For some women, like Mary, the need to escape from the past through drugs also includes a radical breaking off of relationships.

After the abortion, I cut all contact with my former crowd and made a completely new group of friends. I got into drugs and alcohol. I kept as stoned and drunk as possible so as not to think about it.

Others, like Heidi, cut themselves off from activities they used to enjoy.

I turned to alcohol to forget and ease the pain. I had been a gymnast and had been very health-conscious before the abortion. Afterward, I felt guilty, had no respect for myself and contemplated suicide, and just didn't care about life anymore.

A woman's personality may drastically change after an abortion. Often, she will express this change as having "lost a part of myself" during the abortion. She may go on to live a "half-life," withdrawing from past acquaintances and secretly deadening her pain with alcohol, drugs, promiscuity, and other self-destructive tendencies. The hand-written accounts of the seven women below are sadly typical of these interrelated symptoms.

> I turned to liquor and drugs real heavy as a means of escape. I gave up my job as a bank clerk. I had been a faithful wife, yet now had a succession of affairs. Eventually, I took a deliberate overdose of Valium.

***

> After the abortion, I truly hated myself and became quite self-destructive. I even thought of suicide but was afraid I'd go to hell, so I smoked, drank, did drugs, and had sex.

***

> Immediately after the abortion, I felt like a slut and started to make it a self-fulfilling prophesy. I felt dirty and worthless and became promiscuous because of my low self-esteem. I tried to bury myself in drugs and alcohol but they only made things worse. How many times did I attempt suicide in the next eight years? I couldn't possibly count them all.

***

> The first abortion sent me into heavy drug abuse and sexual promiscuity. I ended up a cocaine addict and a prostitute for drugs.

***

> For years I became depressed on the anniversary of my baby's death. I left my boyfriend and became very promiscuous. Whenever a man committed to me, I ended the relationship. I was lonely and depressed. I turned to cocaine and spent thousands on it.

***

> I became a tramp. I slept with anyone and everyone. Each month, when I wasn't pregnant again, I'd go into a deep depression. My only comfort in those days was alcohol and sleep. I was rebellious. I wanted my parents to see what I had become. I dropped out of college. I tried suicide, but I didn't have the guts to slit my wrists or blow my brains out. I couldn't get my hands on sleeping pills, so I resorted to over-the-counter sleep aids and booze.

***

> I went on a suicide kick. . . . After the abortion, I went to bed with anyone, regularly drank myself into oblivion, and aimed my car at the 100-year-old oak trees that lined the street to my house.

As early as 1972, researchers had observed that young women who abort may develop patterns of promiscuity that did not exist before.[5] In the Elliot Institute Survey, 43 percent of the women surveyed reported post-abortion promiscuity. Statistical analysis of that sample shows that women reporting the onset of promiscuity after an abortion were also significantly more likely to report post-abortion alcohol abuse, drug abuse, suicide attempts, personality changes, and repeat abortions. It is important to note, however, that slightly over half of the women who reported becoming promiscuous also reported a *loss of pleasure* from intercourse. For these women, promiscuous behavior did not satisfy unbridled sexual desires; it served other purposes.

For post-abortive women, promiscuity can be used as a form of degrading self-punishment, or it may be driven by low self-esteem and a desperate need to feel valued by another, if only superficially. Promiscuity can also recreate feelings of shame and guilt related to the traumatic abortion. In such cases, the woman can project her feelings of shame onto her sexual behavior rather than onto the more intimidating issue of her abortion. Nan, for example, shares how her shame following an abortion led her to permit abusive sex:

> After my abortion, I did not care about my body any more. I certainly did not care about what was put into my body. I would only go with partners who were abusive, or those who put things inside me . . . boys who played with sexual toys, fruit, and other objects. I let men experiment and play with me like I was a baby doll.

Nan allowed others to invade her vagina with objects as she lay silent. Having things "put inside" her was a connection to the abortion experience. She described herself as a helpless "baby doll," identifying with her own powerless baby.

Patricia's sexuality was also distorted by feelings of loss, abandonment, death, destruction, and shame. Her approach to sexual relations became sadistic, punishing, and at times masochistic. When she eventually married, Patricia's husband at first thought her sexual preferences were kinky, erotic, and fun. But as time passed, he longed for the gentle intimacy of normal sex. But Patricia was incapable of such intimacy as long as the trauma of her abortion remained braided into her sexual identity.

Similarly, Rita felt trapped by a compulsion to shame and humiliate herself through promiscuous affairs and demeaning episodes with sex. Rita would do just about anything. On one occasion she required hospitalization following sadistic sexual relations. Her only memory of the event was an awareness of self-hatred and pain.

> It didn't matter what anybody did to me. I guess I felt I deserved it. I certainly never got any pleasure out of it. I felt worthless. I had no self-respect. The thought of my abortion disgusted me and made me hate myself.

Conflicted women like Rita, acting out post-abortion trauma through their sexuality, are easy targets for perverted abusers. Rita's self-destructive acts served to reenact the shame, self-hatred, and complete loss of innocence she associated with her traumatic abortion. None of these tendencies emerged until after her abortion. It was only after she had post-abortion counseling that she was able to break free of this pattern.

Promiscuity may also serve the desire, conscious or unconscious, to become pregnant again. Becoming pregnant by an uncommitted male may recreate the rejection of commitment on the part of the baby's father that was implicit in the first abortion. Promiscuity can also serve the purpose of re-experiencing the abortion literally, through multiple abortions, in the subconscious hope that by aborting again she will finally master her trauma. Alternatively, promiscuity can serve as a means of acting out a new vision of self—the carefree party animal, for example.

The relationship between substance abuse and promiscuity is straight-forward. Drugs and alcohol lower sexual inhibitions. Those who are looking for sexual encounters are naturally drawn to bar-hopping and parties where the use of alcohol and drugs is a normal part of the social interactions, or even a necessary prelude to mating rituals. Being intoxi-cated also makes it easier for a woman to settle for a "loser," if it comes to that, just so she won't have to spend the night alone.

As previously discussed, traumatized women will frequently engage in repetitious behaviors as a means of releasing trauma-related tension. Sexual intercourse, alcohol, and drugs are all tension relievers. But coping with an unresolved trauma through such addictive behaviors is like being shackled to a treadmill, running over the same struggles or themes over and over again.

By engaging in these repetitive behaviors, the mind seeks either (1) to finally master the problem by re-experiencing the trauma directly or through symbolic proxies, or (2) to become so accustomed to the behavior that one is no longer bothered by it. By deadening herself to higher aspirations through drugs, alcohol, promiscuity, and repeat abortions, a woman's emotional range can become so restricted that she hardly feels the pain anymore. The price is high, however, since such a woman also loses the ability to feel any lasting joy.

## ABORTION AND SUICIDE

When feelings of joy and hope are no more than dim memories, when depression, despair, or grief weigh upon a soul with the force of a gla-cier grinding a mountain into sand, thoughts of suicide will arise. At some point, the natural fear of death is offset by the longing for death's release from everything in this life. Such was the case for Janet, who was employed as a police officer in a suburban community. Janet shares her memories surrounding her abortion and the despair and inner vio-lence that followed:

> After my abortion they made me lie down for 30 minutes. Finally another nurse

dismissed me. I tried to tell her how much pain I was in. It was as if I was speaking to a brick wall—she said nothing in response. Painfully and slowly, I got dressed and walked into the waiting room. I looked at my boyfriend Mike. He looked deadpan toward me. If I had had a weapon, he and everyone else in that clinic would have died, myself included. We spoke not one word during the long drive back to my home. He finally gave up trying to talk to me. I never saw him again, nor spoke to him, even though we worked in the same place. My feelings for him were far deeper than mere hatred. I fantasized about anni-hilating him (somehow), making him beg for mercy first, as I had in the clinic. Finally, even my hatred drained out of me, leaving only a despairing black-ness. I was at the end of the road, with no salvation. I had finally struck bottom.

With quiet deliberation, I took my handgun from under my pillow, checking to make sure the clip was loaded. I chambered a round, walked into my living room, sat in a chair, put the gun to my head and pulled the trigger. To this day, I cannot think why the gun did not fire. I had always kept it in perfect working order. Still numb, I called my only friend, Susan, and told her what I tried to do. She lived quite a distance from me, but she was there in a flash; under five minutes, I think. She put me on her lap like a child and rocked me for a long time. I don't remember crying, but perhaps I did. After she was sure I was "okay," she took my handgun home with her. I still hadn't told her about the abortion. Bless her. Later that gun went off in her apartment, blowing a hole in her living room wall and scaring her silly. I was so thankful she was not hurt.

Deadened to all joy, my life took an ironic twist. I soon found, without even looking, another job making far more money than my old one. I could easily have supported a child on my new salary. I continued my promiscuous ways out of habit, I think. I no longer knew right from wrong. Gone was even a semblance of joy. There was no sunshine to my days. Oh, how I envied the dead. I used to pray for death, begging a non-existent God to give me an end to my pain. I find it amazing, in retrospect, how we can function so well in front of others, while suffering like that.

The suicide-abortion link is well-known among professionals who counsel suicidal people. Meta Uchtman, director of Suicide Anonymous in Cincinnati, reported that in a 35-month period her group had worked with 4,000 women, and that nearly half had previously had an abor-tion. Of those who had undergone abortions, 1,400 were between the ages of 15 and 24—the age group with the fastest growing suicide rate in the country.[6] According to another study undertaken at the Univer-sity of Minnesota, teenage girls are ten times more likely to attempt suicide if they have had an abortion in the last six months than are teens who have not had an abortion.[7]

In the Elliot Institute Survey, nearly three of every five post-abortive women had subsequent suicidal thoughts. Twenty-eight percent actu-ally attempted suicide, with over half of these making more than one suicide attempt.[8] The higher rates of suicide attempts among post-abortive women are similar to patterns found for suicide in other trau-matized populations. For example, based on interviews nine years after women were the victims of rape, researchers have found that 19 percent of rape victims had made a suicide attempt, significantly more than other victims of crime. Similarly, around 19 percent of combat veterans diagnosed with post-traumatic stress disorder had made suicide attempts, and 15 percent were preoccupied with suicidal thoughts.[9]

The higher rate of suicides among post-abortive women has been definitively demonstrated by two major record-based studies. Researchers in Finland, after examining medical records for all Finnish women of reproductive age over a seven-year period, discovered that women who aborted were seven times more likely to commit suicide in the subsequent year compared to women who carried to term. Aborting women were also four times more likely to die from injuries related to accidents, which may actually have been suicide attempts or at least suicidal risk-taking.[10]

A similar study that examined records for over 150,000 California women eligible for Medicaid found that the aborting women were over 2.5 times more likely than delivering women to commit suicide within eight years of their abortion.[11]

Still another record-based study found that while subsequent suicide attempts increased among aborting women, this could not be explained by prior suicidal behavior.[12] In other words, suicide attempts were not significantly different between groups before their pregnancies, but subsequently increased only among aborting women. These are just a few of many studies identifying the link between abortion and suicide.[13]

By contrast, numerous studies have indicated that pregnancy, even when unplanned, diminishes suicidal impulses. Pregnancy serves a protective role for mentally disturbed or seriously depressed women.[14] Family obligations and the idea that there is someone to "live for" tend to reduce self-destructive inclinations.[15] These findings suggest that for women with prior psychological problems, childbirth is likely to reduce the risk of subsequent suicide attempts, whereas abortion may aggravate that risk.

Despite the overwhelming evidence linking abortion to suicide, abortion providers do not provide the type of psychosocial screening necessary to identify patients who are at higher risk of suicide. Nor do they provide women with information about suicide intervention in the event that they begin to feel suicidal after their abortion. Paulette blamed the abortion clinic's lack of proper screening for her sister's death.

> My sister and I were both victims of incest. My sister had been sexually assaulted by my brothers for a number of years when she got her first abortion at the age of 16. Had she been questioned by anyone as to how a minor like herself had come to be pregnant in the first place, perhaps she could have been saved from any further abuse within the family. This is indeed what should have happened in any agency that claims to be concerned about preventing child abuse. As it turned out, she was given the abortion without my parents' consent or knowledge and then returned to the same environment.

Years later, after having given birth to three children, having had many years of psychotherapy and antidepressant drugs, she became pregnant in a crisis situation. She was advised by friends and self-appointed do-gooders to abort the baby to take care of herself. This caused her a great deal of distress and anxiety. The decision was very difficult for her and in her weakened state she succumbed to the "sensibility" of their arguments and scheduled the abortion.

She was crying when she entered the clinic, she cried throughout the procedure, and was sobbing as she left. But no one at the clinic asked her any questions that might upset her any more. Of course, had anyone asked her they might have recognized that she was not emotionally strong enough to stand the abortion. Had they inquired about her health history, they might have seen her as the high-risk patient she was. But none of this took place.

One week after the abortion she took her life with a gunshot to the chest, striking her heart. Her three children are growing up without their mom because no one wanted to ask questions.

The strong association between suicide and abortion bears witness to how suicidal impulses serve as a means of reenacting a traumatic abortion experience. Thoughts of death mirror the death experience of abortion. Through her abortion, the traumatized woman seeks to solve certain difficulties in her life. When she is later faced with depression, isolation, or an emptiness in her life that cannot be filled by drugs, alcohol, or sex, death again offers a solution. "After all," many reason, "I killed my child. Why not kill myself?"

Eleanor was 16 years old when she had an abortion. When she went to a guidance counselor to discuss her raging emotions, he assured her that she had made a good decision. "Focus on the future," the counselor advised. "Stop looking back." The advice was meaningless. Eleanor needed someone who would acknowledge her pain, not reject it as she had rejected her baby. One of her diary entries, written six years later, explains the struggle which underlay her suicidal thoughts.

I thought about suicide again today. I can't get that thought out of my head. What could God possibly have planned for me in the future? I am really starting to wonder if there is anything planned.

I guess this is because my only dream in life was to be a good mother. Instead, I've become a murderer. I am left wondering what my beautiful child would be doing right now. My life would be filled with joy. Instead it is filled with depression, anxiety and despair.

How could I have ever thought my life would be better without my child? I know that another baby will never replace her in my heart. I don't think I deserve a second chance.

I also wonder how a man on earth could care for or love me after I was able to kill my own daughter. God only knows how anybody could understand how someone who supposedly loves children could choose to destroy her own child.

Will I even be able to chip open a small part of my heart to let someone new in? There is nothing left of my heart to share with another person. I really believe I aborted my heart with my daughter. I have not smiled or felt any joy for six years. I cannot continue this act—this charade of going through the motions when I am so totally dead inside. I had the strength to kill my child—I hope I can find the strength to kill myself. There is nothing left for me here.

Such despair, in Eleanor's case, was the byproduct of years of unresolved grief. Vicky, on the other hand, felt suicidal immediately after her abortion:

> If I had a gun I would have blown my head off. After my abortion I was in such severe pain—death seemed the only solution. It seemed like the only way to be back with my baby. I overdosed on pills and drinks.

The manner in which women recover from suicidal feelings is also instructive. Jill, for example, went on one of my Rachel's Vineyard retreats for post-abortion healing. She described the process of grieving (which she had avoided for so long) as the most liberating feeling of her life. "I feel as though the weight of an entire building has been lifted from me," she said. When I heard her comment, I was struck with the memory of a story she had told me the first night I met her. Jill had described a ritual that she began shortly after her abortion.

> Every morning on my way to work, I walk beneath the porch of a dilapidated building. Each morning, I walk by wishing that the building would crumble and fall on me. I know this sounds sick, but I look forward to walking under that building and hope that this will be the day that it collapses. Sometimes I stand under the structure for a few extra minutes. I examine the bricks which are crumbling and I wonder when God will let it all go . . . and I hope that when it happens, I'm right there. With my luck, though, I wouldn't die— I'd probably be paralyzed.

Beyond a death wish, Jill's decrepit building symbolized her sense of self—a self untended, crumbling, in imminent danger of collapse. Jill was weary of the depression, self-hatred, and guilt that had been her constant companion since the abortion. Just as she waited for the structure of the building to collapse, so she was waiting for her own defense structures to break down. Her preoccupation with being crushed by the falling building was a fantasy brought on by not being able to cope any more. It was about letting go of the pain. Yet she also feared that letting go would somehow be a crippling experience. She was afraid that if she ever faced her real feelings of grief and loss, they would disable her. Death appeared to be the only escape. In the scenario of a crumbling building, God was the one in control. Jill's image of God was punitive—a notion that, for some, perpetuates the abortion experience.

## RISK-TAKING AND OTHER SELF-DESTRUCTIVE TENDENCIES

Fran was another woman who wanted to die at God's hands. To invite this judgment on herself, she went out into the middle of a field and stood in a large puddle during a thunderstorm. She waited for the lightning to strike her dead—an act of God to punish her for the abortion she could no longer put out of her mind. This, of course, appears to be an extraordinary reaction and certainly irrational. But women's feelings about abortion are dramatic and can therefore draw out dramatic expressions of their innermost feelings.

Paige described her abortion experience in terms of having been through a war, and her abortion as a "land mine" she walked on one day. Ever since, she had tried desperately to pick up the pieces of her shattered emotional life. She struggled with chronic episodes of crippling depression and had to be hospitalized for suicidal thoughts and tendencies on the anniversary date of her abortion.

Studies show that post-abortive women are more likely to be involved in accidents[16] —a reflection of risk-taking and suicidal behavior. For example, researchers in Canada found that women who had undergone an abortion in the previous year were treated 25 percent more often for injuries or conditions resulting from violence.[17] Similarly, a study of Medicaid payments in Virginia found that women who had state-funded abortions had 12 percent more claims for treatments related to accidents (resulting in 52 percent higher costs) compared to a case-matched sample of women who had not had a state-funded abortion.[18] Yet another study of women in California found that women who had abortions were 82 percent more likely to die from accident-related injuries than women who had carried to term.[19]

Camille, for example, described how her life was an emotional wreck, which magnetically attracted physical wrecks.

> I was on the verge of a nervous breakdown. I talked to myself a lot, even in public. I had screaming fits when I was home alone. I screamed until every nerve in my body became like an electric wire, vibrating with overwhelming anger and energy. I had about seven serious accidents, too, and one total wreck. I just didn't care any more.

Self-destructive tendencies can also be played out through self-sabotage of opportunities and relationships. Such patterns of self-defeating behavior may persist for years. For example, Laura had an abortion when she was 15. Immediately afterward, she became promiscuous, and by the time she was 18, she was involved with an abusive man.

> Every few years I would go into a downward spiral and fall into a deep black hole. I would go on a binge, doing anything and everything to destroy my life around me. I contemplated suicide, was on anti-depressants and drank heavily.
>
> Then when I was 20 years old I married my best friend. But nobody understood (nor did I) the pain, guilt and trauma I had experienced. We had a child 6 months later—a full-term baby girl—the joy of my life. I was determined to be a good mother, and I was and am.
>
> Even though I had a husband and a life, when my daughter was two years old, I began an affair with a co-worker. I kicked my husband out of the house, and professed that I no longer loved him, because I was so unhappy with myself.
>
> I never could figure out what caused me to act this way. It would last one to

three months and I would be OK. Then four years later, I would do something else to destroy myself or my life. I never inflicted physical pain on myself, just mentally hurting myself and everyone around me and trying to destroy everything in my life. After all, how could I be happy if I killed a child? I didn't deserve to be happy. I needed to be self-destructive so this baby would know that I didn't do it on purpose and I would show it how life was without it. Horrible. Although I had sought counseling several times, and always brought up the abortion (it always came up), the counselor would not address it, just skim over it.

Laura felt that after her abortion, she didn't deserve happiness. Whenever happiness came to her, even through her family, she felt compelled to upset and destroy it, if only to prove to her aborted child that she had not stopped grieving.

## Chapter Fourteen

# Broken Babies

I remember meeting Marita my freshman year in college. She was cute, like a cheerleader, and had the same dynamic, enthusiastic, "rah rah" personality. Marita had boundless energy. She was fun to be around and had a self-assured style. At the same time, she was still very much a little girl. She missed her parents, made frequent phone calls to her siblings, and had a roomful of cherished childhood dolls carefully displayed on her bed pillows and bookshelves.

The first night we met, Marita told me she would remember my name because Theresa was the name of her favorite doll, now a priceless antique. It had been passed down from her great-great-grandmother and was given to Marita when she was a little girl. Marita handed me the doll, a porcelain collector's dream, gussied up in an ivory silk dress and intricate lace pantaloons. Marita and I became friends instantly and used to share library activities like "scoping" for cute guys behind bookshelves.

One night at a drunken fraternity party, Marita found herself having sex with her boyfriend. The details were quite foggy. She didn't remember taking her clothes off, but woke up naked next to the young sophomore. When Marita discovered she was pregnant, she had an abortion immediately and never told a soul, except her boyfriend and her roommate.

When Marita told me about her abortion years later, she explained that her roommate Ruth had taken her to the clinic. Ruth had had an abortion as a senior in high school and told Marita it was no big deal. Abortion was common on campus. Lots of girls had them.

After the abortion, Marita's personality changed. She became irritable and began drinking all the time. She skipped classes on a regular basis, preferring to sleep in and snooze off each hung-over depression. Her attitude was cynical and negative, and she wasn't much fun to be around. At that time, I didn't understand what Marita was going through. But there were signs.

One night we gathered at Marita's dorm for a party. We were drinking beers when Marita's boyfriend jumped up and shouted, "It's time for Baby Soccer!" There was a grand applause, reminiscent of the inauguration of gladiator games. Marita brought out several doll heads that had been decapitated from their torsos, rolling them along with her hockey stick for the grand entrance. Everyone started kicking the baby heads around the room in a frenzy of glee and hysterics. They all cheered while gulping drinks and devouring chips.

As the pastime continued, the aggression toward the baby heads became more severe. One girl picked up a doll head and started gouging out its eyes with a dart. Everyone cackled with delight. Ruth began ripping out shreds of another doll's hair while burning its plastic cheeks with her cigarette. This sparked her boyfriend's imagination. He grabbed another doll from the shelf and put the hot ember of his cigarette between the doll's legs, then ripped them off, leaving only a melted and scarred-looking vagina hole. Ruth threw her doll head on the floor, stamping hard on its skull. They continued to kick the baby heads around the room in a hostile display of rage fused with amusement.

I learned that this had become a favorite game in the dorm. My reaction to this symbolic abuse was a sickening feeling in my stomach. I witnessed this traumatic play, unaware at the time of the psychic release of collective tension this game was providing. Desensitized to the authenticity of the game, I laughed along with the others, silently recalling all the "baby in a blender" jokes that proliferated among my friends.

As I picked up one of the doll heads, I was overcome with a vague sense of familiarity. My heart skipped a beat when I identified the doll as "Theresa," the porcelain antique that had once been Marita's prized possession. Her face was cracked, smashed, and splintered, a jigsaw of fractured pieces—nearly unrecognizable. Where the head had been torn from the body, there were razor-sharp claws of fragmented china.

Suddenly I felt a genuine, aching grief. I feared that at any minute I might burst into tears. What had happened to this doll, "Theresa," passed down through generations of female history within Marita's family? How did this happen? What had happened to my friend?

The trauma was still very much a mystery to me—but I knew that something inside Marita had also been crushed. The desecration was reflected quite clearly in the face of her broken doll. I waited nearly a decade to discover the answer to my questions. Learning that Marita had suffered an abortion made everything crystal clear.

## WHEN THE DOLL BREAKS

Those who study childhood trauma have documented many examples of children working through a traumatic event by recreating aspects of their trauma through games, stories, and art. Child therapists will often observe children playing with puppets and doll houses to get a sense of what is going on in their minds and families. It can be easier to express an emotional conflict by acting it out through a puppet figure than by putting oneself through subjective introspection.

As with my classmates and the game of "Baby Soccer," adults, too, can engage in symbolic reenactment of a trauma under the disguise of games, art, music, humor, and other amusements. This type of play provided an outlet for grief by replacing it with socially acceptable acts of "baby hatred."

Marita's battered doll reflected the abuse of a little girl—ravaged, disfigured, assaulted, and burned. "Baby Soccer" was a sadistic "acting out" of repressed abortion trauma. A baby haunting her unconscious had become the target to be annihilated. Her battered doll's head was a symbol of this conflict.

It is no surprise that this traumatic play so quickly became an amusement for all to enjoy. Like Marita, many of the young women and men drawn into this game had also lost children to abortion. Many others had lost sisters or brothers to abortion. "Baby Soccer" provided a symbolic means to mock, belittle, and display mastery over the babies who were never allowed to be born but who still haunted their memories.

As the group's enthusiasm for this game demonstrated, the acting out of post-abortion trauma can be contagious, as all internalize the hidden message. This is especially the case when so many have had a direct experience with abortion, either through the abortion of their own children or through the abortion of their siblings or potential classmates. One way to deal with the unresolved loss experienced by this "abortion generation" is to belittle what was lost. Sadly, this attempt to belittle and master babies through "Baby Soccer" reinforced and internalized attitudes and behaviors of aggression and hostility against babies.

If the college authorities had seen students beating up and defacing an effigy of a black person or a symbol of Jewish heritage, would they not have felt compelled to intervene against this frightful and shocking behavior? But what is said about the intolerance and contempt displayed for babies? It is unlikely that there will ever be a word uttered.

Collective guilt and trauma have the capacity to disguise massive injustice. The offensiveness of "Baby Soccer" was made socially acceptable because it concealed this display of aggression behind the mask of a "humorously irreverent" diversion, where everyone laughed.

We have all learned to snicker at sick jokes and engage in scapegoating because these things give us momentary relief from the tension of unsettled issues. In this case, we were laughing with the nervous giggle of an entire culture that has been traumatized by the abortion of tens of millions of babies. The sheer magnitude of it all is too much to grasp. So it must be trivialized, reduced to laughter and scorn, or else we will all be crushed by the horror of it all.

That is why the belittling of children is all around us. Themes of abortion-related guilt, rage, and anger are pervasive in modern music, art, and films. "Evil child" movies, like *Alien* and *The Omen*, reflect the demonization of children. The "evil baby" is our worst nightmare—something society must destroy before it destroys us. In the popular TV series *South Park,* the attacks on the child move into the home, where Kenny tries to kill his unborn baby brother. The jokes about abortion slipped by the censors with no reaction. In the story line Kenny tries to abort his mom's baby by making her a Morning After Pill milkshake and using a toilet plunger on her.[1]

These are just a few examples. I believe that many of these images in the arts and popular culture reflect how the memory of aborted children haunts our society. The natural tendency to love and esteem babies has become a painful reminder of the unresolved grief of millions of women and men. To contain and control the unspeakable truth, the natural instinct to nurture and protect children is rejected, and in its place, the "evil baby" is envisioned as an object of mockery and the target of violence.

These are the truths recorded for all to see in the broken face of Marita's cherished doll. It was a shattered face, the mirror image of Marita's own fractured self.

## INTRUSIVE THOUGHTS OF HURTING CHILDREN

For women who have been traumatized by abortion, acts of child abuse are natural symbolic reenactments of unresolved abortion issues. For example, Rhonda was plagued with guilt and shame for having aborted five children. She believed that God wanted her to make up for her past by giving love to children who needed someone to care for them. She tried to meet this obligation by starting a full-time daycare center in her home.

While Rhonda was attempting to master her psychic trauma by giving love to children, the eight children under her care literally exhausted her. By the end of the day she frequently became irritable and anxious. Rhonda reported that she occasionally lost her temper with the toddlers and would find herself hitting or shaking them in a rage of fury and frustration. After these violent outbursts, Rhonda would shrink into a corner and cry, convinced that she was a horrible person.

By placing herself in this stressful situation with young toddlers, Rhonda had recreated her feelings of helplessness and incompetence with children, themes that were dominant in her choices to abort. Her repeated loss of control with the children confirmed her feelings of self-hatred and disgust. The resulting ritual patterns of child abuse, followed by shame, guilt, and grief, mirrored her abortion experiences with complete emotional accuracy.

Dianne, another patient seeking post-abortion counseling, also had a daycare business. She watched infants in her home. Dianne reported disturbing intrusive thoughts about pulling the babies' arms out of their sockets. She felt a compelling desire to grab the infants' little arms and disconnect their limbs. Such thoughts caused excessive anxiety and horrific grief. Each time Dianne was confronted with these traumatic thoughts, she was overcome with horror and sadness. Each intrusive episode confirmed that she was a disgusting person and filled her heart with sickening grief.

Fortunately, on the anniversary date of her abortion, Dianne finally recognized the connection between her abortion and the intrusive thoughts. In a searing moment, the truth of what was happening to her cut through her soul, and she wept with grief over her loss. Fortunately, Dianne sought out help to deal with the long-repressed trauma, and all the unwelcome intrusive thoughts have ceased.

Intrusive thoughts like Dianne's are a common experience for trauma victims. Once an intrusive thought comes, it can be very hard to put it out of one's mind. Some of the more common experiences include thoughts of crashing one's car while driving down the road, going insane, or losing control. Sometimes the notions are ridiculous or unfeasible. Often, they are deeply embarrassing, filling one with such shame that it takes great courage to seek help.

Like dreams and fantasies, intrusive thoughts often contain complex symbols of the trauma. With abortion trauma, intrusive thoughts about harming children may include images that are symbolic of the abortion procedure itself. Kathy related the following story:

> I love my kids. There's nothing I wouldn't do for them. They are everything in the world to me. But I get these horrible thoughts that just mortify me. It's hard to even talk about. I might be standing at the kitchen counter making dinner and I'll think about poisoning their food. I imagine them reacting to the poison and I have to rush them to the hospital. I go crazy with guilt and shame. Then I imagine that the doctors discover I did it on purpose. They call my husband and tell him that I shouldn't have the children . . . that I tried to kill them. These thoughts just jump into my head. They are so crazy . . . I can't believe I think such thoughts. It makes me hate myself.

Kathy, who had first entered counseling for panic attacks, began reporting these types of thoughts each week, with tremendous distress. It was hard for Kathy to talk about them without crying. As we reviewed her life, I was not surprised to learn about a saline abortion in her past. She visibly shook when she talked about it. When I asked her how a saline abortion worked, she described the procedure as a *poisoning* of the fetus.

All of Kathy's symptoms developed after her abortion. Through these intrusive thoughts she continually relived the emotional experience of her abortion. Each episode centered on hurting or killing her living children and the shameful aftermath. Her mourning became complicated and surfaced during these disturbing fantasies.

Kathy is one of the gentlest, most soft-spoken women I have ever met. It was enormously difficult for her to experience such horrendous thoughts. I am happy to say that these impressions, which had plagued her for years, ended after she did grief work related to her abortion.

Emily had a similar case. She had an abortion twelve years before she married. During that time, she refused to allow herself to think about it or grieve her loss. This "stuffing away" of emotions worked fine until she began to have children.

Emily's first flashback to her abortion hit her violently when she had her first ultrasound while pregnant with a "wanted" child. As time went on, she would have frequent intrusive thoughts concerning her abortion when she looked at the faces of her babies. Then Emily began to experience habitual, obsessive, and scary thoughts about hurting her children. She imagined stabbing them with a knife one by one, suffocating them with pillows, and strangling them.

Emily could not figure out why this was happening to her. She was a wonderful and devoted mother, yet she could not escape intrusive thoughts about death and killing that became more elaborate and more real as time passed. She certainly had no intention of ever carrying out such deeds, but she felt appalled that she was capable of such hideous thoughts. Her destructive thoughts were like starving rabid animals, hounding, scratching, and gnawing at her conscience. They left her feeling bewildered, crazy, and ashamed. She desperately yearned to silence these dangerous beasts. Fortunately, all these symptoms were alleviated after Emily had completed the grief work related to her abortion.

In some cases, unfortunately, women fail to restrain their destructive impulses. For example, Renee Nicely of New Jersey experienced a psychotic episode the day after her abortion, which resulted in the beating death of her 3-year-old son, Shawn. She told the court psychiatrist that she "knew that abortion was wrong" and "I should be punished for the abortion." The psychiatrist who was the prosecution's expert witness testified that the killing was clearly related to Renee's psychological reaction to her abortion. Unfortunately, the victim of her rage and self-hatred was her own son.[2]

A similar tragedy occurred just one week after Donna Fleming's second abortion. Depressed and distraught, Donna "heard voices" in her head and tried to kill herself and her two sons by jumping off a bridge in Long Beach, California. Donna and her five-year-old son were rescued; her two-year-old died. Subsequently, Donna claimed she tried to kill herself and her other children in order to reunite her family.[3]

These are only a few of many cases in which a recent abortion was directly linked to women killing their young children. In many other cases, such as that of Susan Smith, who drove her two children into a lake to drown, there is a known history of abortion.[4] But in almost every one of these cases, the connection between the abortion and the killing was never developed in the court record. In a few cases, defense attorneys have explained their unwillingness to explore a post-abortion trauma defense on the grounds that the abortion connection might be construed by the jury as simply more evidence that these women are indeed callous baby killers, rather than women who have been deeply traumatized by their abortions.

Numerous studies have established a strong statistical link between a history of abortion and an increased risk of subsequent child abuse.[5] The clinical experience of many therapists supports the conclusion that this is, at least in many cases, a causal link. Psychiatrist Philip Ney, a clinical professor at the University of British Columbia, has done by far the most research into understanding the link between abortion and subsequent child abuse. Most of his analysis has focused on the role of abortion in disrupting bonding with later children; weakening of maternal instincts; reduced inhibitions against violence, particularly toward children; and heightened levels of anger, rage, and depression. It is probable that all these factors have contributed toward increased levels of child abuse following legalized abortion. Reenactment of abortion trauma through child abuse may be another important factor.

## CHAPTER FIFTEEN

# WHAT'S EATING YOU?
## Abortion And Eating Disorders

A t 23 years of age, Candice was a woman of striking natural beauty. Like the Ivory soap girl, she had a flawless complexion. A tinge of black roots hid beneath the blond ringlets that surrounded her face. Although petite (about 5'4" tall and barely 100 pounds), she was also quite athletic. At first glance, one might wonder what in the world this beautiful young woman could possibly have to complain about. Yet Candice was thoroughly unhappy. Her impeccable appearance concealed a harsh inner demand for perfection. As she spoke to me, she quickly began to express confusion, guilt, and her fear of being hopelessly crazy.

> I'm a miserable bitch. I am never happy. The most miniscule things make me furious. I have absolutely no tolerance or patience. I have no reason to feel this way. I never had any major traumas in my life. It's not like my parents abused me or were divorced or alcoholic or anything.
>
> I do weird things. Food is definitely a problem. It's so disgusting how I am with food. It makes me totally hate myself. I can eat a whole cake or a gallon of ice cream. I get mad at myself and wonder why I am doing it . . . but I can't seem to help myself. Then, when it's over, I feel so gross and so disgusting. I look in the mirror and feel like I want to rip my eyes out of their sockets so I don't have to look at this disgusting person.
>
> I hate myself and I feel so guilty . . . so ashamed. I am uncomfortable in my own skin . . . with my own self. This is so hard to describe. What is wrong with me? I must be crazy. I read a lot of stuff on eating disorders. I wrote a huge paper on binge eating in college. I just don't understand. None of this makes any sense. But I keep doing it. I even leave empty food containers around, half under my bed, and my mom finds them. I get so angry at myself for being so stupid.
>
> Sometimes I think I must want to get caught. But that's crazy . . . of course I don't want to get caught! Who in their right mind would want anyone to see how gross they are!

I've heard this kind of story dozens of times: an eating disorder that becomes the cause of unrelenting shame, guilt, and self-hatred; a pressure, organized around food, that is uncontrollable despite the fact that the person seldom enjoys—and even abhors—the activity. The food and the surrounding rituals become the obsession that torments. The meal is not used for nourishment or to sustain life, but to punish after a brief period of relief.

I asked Candice why she had come to me for counseling. She

responded:

> My mom thought that my abortion might have something to do with my prob-
> lems. I don't know . . . maybe she is right. I never used to be like this. I used to
> be happy.

Her mother was a nurse who had heard me speak at a conference on
pregnancy loss and unresolved grief. What sparked her interest was my
discussion of the correlation between abortion and eating disorders.
Candice had confided in her several years earlier about an abortion she
had undergone as a teenager. At that time, Candice could no longer bear
the weight of the hidden event that had turned her world upside down
with grief and heartache. She had sobbed for hours as she shared her
"terrible secret" with her mother. After that evening, Candice and her
mother never spoke about the abortion again, but her mother noticed
that Candice was still often angry, depressed, and short-tempered. Furthermore, Candice developed bulimia, with episodes of binge eating and
purging followed by radical restrictive fasting.

After hearing my presentation, Candice's mother realized that all of
her daughter's symptoms had taken root following the abortion. When
her mother suggested that the abortion might still bother her, Candice
protested with resentment. "I already dealt with that. It's not a problem anymore," she insisted. But her mother's urging, combined with
Candice's own doubts, had brought her to my office.

I asked Candice when her abortion had occurred, and she began to
tell me her story. Tears surfaced, slowly at first, but within moments she
was grieving so intensely that she quickly depleted the box of tissues on
the small table at her side. I replaced it quietly as she continued to share
her pain and tears.

> When I first found out that I was pregnant, I was shocked. It was hard to
> believe that my body was actually making a baby. Initially, it was mysterious,
> frightening . . . but also exciting.
>
> My boyfriend and I had tickets to an outdoor concert the night we found out.
> I remember lying on the ground watching the stars and feeling so special,
> even though I was afraid. We drank wine out of little cups I brought, left over
> from my aunt's baby shower. While all the fear and joy swirled round in my
> heart like a dizzy merry-go-round, my boyfriend Jim was seeing things differ-
> ently. While I was picking out cute little names, he was using words like our
> "circumstance" and "accident." From my perspective, it was not really an acci-
> dent. We used to talk about having a baby all the time . . . but it was always
> some future event that would happen after we got married. His apprehension
> soon turned to coldness and distance.
>
> It happened all in one night. The next morning, we were on our way to an
> abortion clinic to take care of the problem. Jim did not feel we were ready for
> the emotional and financial commitment of marriage. He wanted to go to law
> school and thought it would be hard enough without a baby to distract him. I
> had to agree. This was the only way that we could secretly rid ourselves of the

crisis at hand, continue our education, and defer marriage until we were ready. I would also spare my parents the embarrassment of an unplanned pregnancy. Jim reminded me how hurt they would be. It was becoming clear that abortion was the logical thing to do.

I allowed Jim to control the situation completely. Although on one level, I felt like he was being supportive of my needs, inside I felt so alone, so utterly alone and abandoned.

Sympathetically I responded, "That must have been difficult." This little acknowledgment was enough to release an eruption of deeply felt shame, anger, and agonizing grief. Candice expressed tremendous relief at finally being able to admit her feelings of loss and to have them validated by someone who did not think she was crazy for feeling that way. She continued her story—like a twig plunging over a waterfall, there was no turning back. As she finished, she said:

I always think I've gotten over the abortion, and then it all comes back as clear as yesterday and I can't bear the pain. I guess this is why I never think about it. It sucks to feel all this crap. It's easier to push it all out of my head.

## POWERFUL SYMBOLS

As I shared at the beginning of this book, my analysis of abortion trauma began while I was working with women who suffered from anorexia and bulimia. At the time, the subject of abortion was so objectionable and anxiety-laden that even my supervisor instructed me to avoid the issue.

In the years that have followed, I have been repeatedly amazed by the intensity of the feelings of grief, anger, rage, and betrayal surrounding clients' abortion experiences. I have also been deeply saddened to see how long women have carried these destructive feelings inside, never to be shared, released, or even recognized. In many cases, these repressed feelings are channeled into eating disorders. In the Elliot Institute survey of women who had been involved in post-abortion counseling programs, 38.6 percent of the women reported having had an eating disorder (bulimia, anorexia, or binge eating) after their abortions.

Food is a powerful symbol. It is central to our human experience. We need it. We crave it. But we will also at times reject it—when it is distasteful or unhealthy, or when we are full, or ill, or dieting, or fasting.

It is no wonder, then, that food and eating are loaded with conscious and unconscious symbolism. For example, the familiar question, *"What's eating you?"* can truly capture the reality of the gnawing distress in the pit of one's emotional gut. Depression and guilt can devour one's life, both figuratively and literally.

From the moment we are born, we are nurtured with food. For the infant, mother's milk and mother's love are inseparable and synonymous. The caress, the taste, the security, the comfort, the nurturing of body and soul—all are tied together in a single experience. Perhaps this is why, even after infancy, we often use food to comfort a crying child. We also use food to comfort ourselves. Depression, or simply boredom, will often lead us to seek out the comfort of food—not to appease any physical hunger, but rather to minister to our emotional hunger, which it never quite fills.

The symbols surrounding food and eating are nearly endless. As children we are often told to swallow our words, and the negative feelings that go with them. Repulsive people or experiences make us want to "puke" or "vomit." When we are angry, we may become "spitting mad."

As described in chapter ten, traumatic reactions are often played out in veiled, symbolic ways. Eating disorders are just another way in which some women recreate emotions (such as shame) or bodily sensations (such as a swollen abdomen) that are connected to their unresolved abortion. In most cases, women will not consciously understand the significance of this physiological reenactment. Compulsive overeating, anorexic tendencies toward starvation, and the bulimic cycle of binging and purging are all usually accompanied by a fixation with food, weight, and body image.

Women generally feel trapped by their eating disorders—continually doing something they despise and detest. For many, this reenacts the experience of feeling trapped into choosing an abortion.

Food often symbolizes the need for love and nurturing. When the desire for love is not satisfied, it is experienced as having painful consequences, and therefore, is something that must be eliminated. Fear of intimacy can become fear of fat—and yet the intense hunger remains, always present, like the predictable rising and setting of the sun.

Despite the changes in women's roles in the modern world, many women lack the skills necessary for self-preservation. Many give themselves up to the goal of satisfying another and accept "powerlessness" as a way to keep the other person from disowning them. Many women are "pleasers," who will go to nearly any extreme to avoid hurting other people's feelings. Some can only express their feelings of rejection and hurt in a symbolic way, through their bodies, emaciated by anorexia or bloated by overeating. For such women, eating disorders are their primary means of communicating the incommunicable. Through appearance or behavior, the woman is crying out, "I'm not okay! I'm in tremendous pain! Can anyone help me?"

On the other hand, some women feel the need to completely hide their pain. Not only do they want to look normal, but they need to look flawless. Bulimia allows such women to engage in the symbolism of binging and purging without the weight gain.

## Vomiting Secrets

Sandra's eating disorder developed shortly after her abortion. It took her nearly two decades to even say the "a" word, which she avoided with fervent commitment. Reflecting on her experience 18 years later, Sandra described her memories:

> I consciously put the abortion out of my mind. It was, without a doubt, the most grievous and shattering event in my life. I was appalled by what I had done, but I could not take it back.
>
> After my abortion, I spent the next three days lurched over a toilet . . . and to be honest, I've been there ever since. I heaved again and again until there was nothing left. I wanted to rid my insides of the disgust, violation, and utter revulsion I felt within me. There are really no words to describe the acute agony and nauseating grief. After that, I completely disconnected from the source of my pain. I buried it deep . . . so deep . . . into an unconscious oblivion.
>
> Yet, I was left with an emptiness that needed to be filled. I tried filling it with food, drugs, alcohol, sex . . . anything that felt good and would take away the pain. But those things only lasted a short time, and the pain would return, worse than before. There was no one who could understand how I felt . . . there was no one to talk to. I had to swallow all of it.

Bulimia is an eating disorder that involves a vicious cycle of binge eating followed by purging to try to get rid of unwanted ingested calories. The duration and frequency of binges will vary from person to person. Sometimes they are carefully planned and executed. For others, the binge is sudden, impulsive, or recklessly driven by anxiety. Purging techniques typically involve induced vomiting and the abuse of laxatives and diuretics. Other methods include excessive exercise, fasting, diet pills, and enemas.

Through bulimic behaviors, food is used to symbolize efforts to ingest and then expel disagreeable feelings. Unresolved emotions, like undigested food, must be rejected from the body. Vomiting can be a way to evacuate anger and rage. In Sandra's case, the compulsion to vomit was closely associated with the days immediately following her abortion, when she lay "lurched over the toilet." In the years that followed, even when she was able to repress thoughts of the abortion, the need to vomit was serving as a connector to her hidden grief.

Some women develop eating disorders after their first sexual experience. When a girl loses her virginity to a man who then carelessly rejects her, the experience can be quite traumatic. Perhaps this is due to the fact that, in their sexual nature, women are receptive. When a young woman allows a man to enter into the deepest personal and most privileged space of her being, it can involve a tremendous gift of faith and trust. In giving herself sexually, she is giving all of herself—her love and affection—in return for being esteemed and special, connected and belonging. When this sexual covenant—the gift of her love, trust, and

virginity—is violated or betrayed, she may internalize profound feelings of rejection and unworthiness. When the broken sexual relationship
also involves an abortion—a violation of her maternal nature in addition to the "theft" of her virginity—this double betrayal is even more
likely to be traumatic. Such was the case for Rickyann:

> My first love left a real bad taste in my mouth. I was certain that I would never
> love again. I felt like I had given up my virginity for nothing. When I got preg-
> nant, it was so easy for my boyfriend to dismiss our relationship when he
> became interested in another girl.
>
> I blamed myself. I was certain that something must be wrong with me. I
> should be prettier, or thinner, or smarter. I desperately wanted his attention. It
> was hard to believe that he could so easily just flush it all down the toilet. My
> eating disorder began after we broke up and I had an abortion.

Rickyann believed that something inside her was bad. She focused
this irrational conviction onto the food she ate and felt a compelling
need to throw up everything she ate. Keeping it inside her made her
feel poisoned and toxic. She had to get rid of it, traumatically recreating the rejected relationship and pregnancy. As Rickyann accurately
recounted, "It was hard to believe he could so easily flush it all down
the toilet." Yet, through her preoccupation with her eating disorder,
Rickyann continued to flush her own life down the toilet. She was certain that intimacy, like food, was toxic to her health. So her obsession
gave her a reason to avoid getting involved with another man.

Rickyann's bulimic ritual, whereby she ingested the nourishing comfort of food and then expelled it with tears of shame and humiliation,
mimicked both her need for intimacy and her sense of violation and
betrayal that followed her own rejection and abortion—both of which
left her grieving and empty.

Joan never thought she would have an abortion. But when faced with
an untimely pregnancy, it seemed her only way out. After the abortion,
she felt an immediate sense of relief. Her problem was behind her. But
in the years that followed, whenever she experienced feelings of anxiety or panic, Joan would calm her terrors by retreating to the kitchen
for a prolonged eating binge. There she would gorge on bowls of ice
cream smothered in chocolate sauce, microwave pizza, potato chips
covered in mounds of gooey onion dip, and chocolate chip cookies
chased with milk. (Joan explained that lots of milk made it easier to
vomit.) She would eat until her stomach was bloated and full, resem-
bling the pregnant state. When she could no longer tolerate the swelling, she would purge herself by vomiting. This ritual became a deeply
ingrained habit. Its persistent repetition was a convincing indicator of
the reenactment of an underlying trauma.

Following these binges, Joan experienced a soothing sense of
relaxation. Endorphins, chemicals released throughout the body after

vomiting, provide a tranquilizing aftermath, calming hostile impulses and soothing agonizing emotions. Endorphins also are a means to medicate depression and provide a temporary relief from sadness and grief.

Joan's initial sense of relief, however, was soon replaced by feelings of self-hatred and disgust. The traumatic secret of her abortion and all her anxious feelings about it were repositioned and concealed in her frenzied bulimia. Every time, she swore she would never do it again, but she knew she was too weak to resist, just as she had been too weak to resist using abortion as her "easy way out." Joan's bulimia provided an outlet for her traumatic tension. Through binging, she continually reenacted the swelling of her pregnancy. Through purging, she reenacted the "quick fix" relief that followed her abortion, which would then subside and be replaced by self-loathing, guilt, and increasing feelings of anxiety.

Brittany, a 42-year-old schoolteacher, also suffered from bulimia. Like Joan, she felt initial relief after the crisis of her pregnancy was over. Yet she admitted feeling a ghastly disgust about the vacuum abortion she had undergone at the age of 20. For many months following the abortion, she suffered from vivid flashbacks and intrusive thoughts of the dismembering and suctioning of her fetus.

> Some of my thoughts were so horrible. I could not live with myself if I continued thinking about it—so I just stuffed it all away. Eventually, I never thought about it anymore and moved on with my life.

Brittany's eating disorder began around the time of her anticipated due date and lasted for the next 22 years. Her repressed grief and disgust became ritualized through bulimia. The feelings she buried would surface again and again. Each retching episode recreated the expulsion of something inside her, something that had once been whole but was now a rejected river of chopped, masticated food, which symbolized her horribly dismembered child.

Brittany's bulimia reduced her to the state of an emotional prisoner. The obsession to binge consumed her relentlessly. Her preoccupation with food interfered with her job and relationships. Above all, her clandestine activity represented a secret she believed would destroy her if it were discovered.

It was easier for Brittany to feel revolted by throwing up than to deal with her disgust stemming from the abortion. She described her abortion as "the sleaziest thing I could ever conceive of," and "my dirty secret." Brittany described her eating disorder in similar words: "loathsome and repugnant." Vomiting after every meal was another "dirty little secret." Brittany went to great lengths to conceal her eating disorder from others, just as she concealed her pregnancy and abortion. She was incapable of asking for support for her emotional pain and spent years tending to an unnamed, festering heartache.

Brittany's emotional trap makes me think of pop singer Fiona Apple shrieking out the lyrics, "I've got my own hell to raise." Since Brittany could not tend to her aborted baby, she created a phantom substitute that demanded her all-consuming attention. In her eating disorder she found a nagging and hungry extension of herself (an unconscious memorial to her unborn child) that needed to be constantly fed.

After finally dealing with the loss of her child, Brittany recovered, too. Her first step in freeing herself from the secrets that imprisoned her was opening up a door for support. By opening the locked chambers of her grief, she was finally able to reconnect her mind to her body.

Often, physical reactions originally associated with a traumatic experience will be precisely and repeatedly mirrored in subsequent physical reactions brought on by obsessive behaviors. This was the case with Carrie, whose eating disorder involved the abuse of laxatives to purge. It was not unusual for Carrie to consume an entire bottle of purgative drugs with the hope, as she put it, of *"getting it all out."* After hearing this, I was not surprised to subsequently hear that Carrie had endured an incomplete abortion. This means that parts of the unborn baby were left inside her during the abortion, causing bleeding and excruciating cramping. She had to return to the abortionist to finish the job and "get it all out."

It was evident to me that the intestinal pain Carrie experienced after her binges and laxative abuse provided a recreation of the cramping she experienced after her abortion. The theme—a desperate need to *"get it all out"*—was a precise echo of her traumatic abortion. The repetition and cramping were evidence of a buried psychic trauma— an expression of body memories which needed a means to reveal themselves. When I made this interpretation to Carrie, she remarked, "You just made my blood curdle."

Often the significance of physiological reenactment does not reach consciousness. For Carrie, her cramping was a veiled narration of her repressed abortion trauma. My connection of her condition to this traumatic event triggered a moment of truth. As a result, she experienced a tremendous amount of relief. In her 11-year battle against her eating disorder, she had been in hospital treatment facilities, support groups and individual therapy. But it was not until she began to deal with her abortion and the feelings of shame, disgust, and hatred of what circumstances "forced" her to do, that she began to experience relief from her obsessive need to use laxatives to eliminate all the food she had eaten.

Interestingly enough, Carrie's food binges were typically in response to the stress of work deadlines. In recovery, she recalled intense pressure to make the decision about her abortion quickly because she was told she was almost past the abortion clinic's deadline for having one.

After that, deadlines became the trigger for an unconscious pattern of trauma-driven reenactment. The pressure of deadlines, filling herself up, purging herself, and cramping all reflected key elements of her unspeakable story.

## ANOREXIA

Karissa suffered from anorexia nervosa. Anorexics typically lose a significant amount of weight due to extreme dieting and a harsh regime of exercise. Although she may become disturbingly thin, an anorexic patient will consider herself fat, no matter what her actual weight is. Even at 80 pounds, a woman suffering from this disorder will perceive herself as overweight and continue dieting—even to her deathbed. An estimated 10 to 20 percent will eventually die from complications related to this illness.[1]

Karissa became emaciated and gaunt within several months following an abortion. Her eating disorder was a disturbing metaphor that symbolized the emptiness she felt inside. After her abortion, Karissa said:

Nothing matters anymore. I feel so empty inside. I regret what I have done and the pain is deeper than anything I could ever imagine.

By cutting off her own life-giving nourishment, Karissa reenacted the withholding of nourishment from her baby. Anorexia became a slow draining-away of life that echoed the life lost because of her abortion. Karissa hid her protruding bones beneath bulky sweaters and baggy sweat pants—repeating the way she had tried to hide her swelling pregnancy and concealing her need for help, love, and protection.

Angela had also battled anorexia since age 16. Before her abortion at age 15, Angela was a well-endowed, curvaceous young lady. But her body had betrayed her by becoming pregnant against her will. Anorexia provided a means to symbolically de-sexualize herself. In Angela's case, starving her body reflected an unconscious effort to get rid of her body: her breasts, her hips, or any part of the body that made her sexually attractive. In the past, her sexuality had only brought forth pain and conflict, so she needed to get rid of it. Her body, admired and taken for the sexual pleasure it offered, had brought forth an unwanted pregnancy, abandonment, and death by abortion. It did not deserve to be fed.

In addition to de-sexualizing herself through her unattractive, skeletal appearance, Angela's anorexia also caused her menstrual cycle to cease. Amenorrhea (the cessation of a woman's menstrual cycle) is common in anorexics and often reflects their need to be little girls again, not yet ready for sexuality. By refusing to eat, Angela was able to revert to a pre-menarchial (pre-menstruation) state of development.

While amenorrhea can be associated with a more childlike, pre-sexual state, it can also be associated with the desire to recover the aborted pregnancy. A woman's missed period is generally the first symptom that calls her attention to her pregnancy. In this regard, some post-abortive women who suffer from anorexia may experience the absence of a period as a reason to fantasize about being pregnant, or conversely, obsess over fears of being pregnant. Either may provoke an obsessive concern over any bulges in her abdomen. The slightest evidence of abdominal swelling symbolizes early pregnancy. This unconscious pre-occupation provides some understanding about the panicky response of post-aborted anorexic patients to the slightest evidence of a tummy and their zealous attempts to starve it away.

Nicole's anorexia was rooted in issues of control. Her parents had made the choice and forced the abortion upon her. Since her abortion represented a complete lack of control over her own future and ability to fight, Nicole took control with food, the only thing in her life she felt she had the right to command. Through her drastic control over her food intake, Nicole was declaring her right to control what went in and what came out of her body.

In the truest sense, Nicole was a survivor of an abuse/death experience. She survived, but her child did not. This traumatic encounter buried the seeds of acute survivor guilt. Her body, emaciated from starvation, signified her hunger to not exist. Through her self-destructive wasting away, she was also punishing her parents: "If I couldn't have my baby, you can't have yours!" In recovery, it was essential that her parents participate in the grief process and validate her loss. Her condition gradually improved only when her family dealt with the trauma and began to reconcile the experience.

## Compulsive Overeating

Compulsive overeating is distinguished by uncontrollable eating and consequent weight gain. Those who engage in chronic overeating usually feel out of control and incapable of monitoring their intake. They feel a disturbing sense of powerlessness, shame, guilt, and incredible failure. They typically exist from diet to diet, struggling with continual stress over the desire to lose weight. Compulsive overeating for many people begins in childhood when eating behaviors are formed. Many never actually learned effective ways to deal with stressful situations and so use food as a way of coping. On the other hand, I have encountered many women who reported that their impulses to gorge on food began only after stressful abortion experiences.

Some women might gain weight after an abortion as a means to insulate themselves from others, particularly men. Overeating is an unconscious attempt to distance oneself from the traditional features and social situations that oblige a woman to be sexually desirable. Carla, an artist with a large advertising agency, gained 55 pounds after her abortion. She explained:

> I used to weigh 120 pounds and I loved to work out. Since my abortion I have gotten into the habit of eating when I am not even hungry. I realize now that getting fat has been a way for me to protect myself. I have been afraid of intimacy. Since my abortion, it has been hard to trust people, especially men. All this extra weight keeps me off the beach and at home on weekends . . . it just seems easier. The abortion changed my personality as well as my eating and exercise habits. I'm not the person I used to be . . . I don't even look like her.

Compulsive overeating may provide momentary comfort and nurturing. People can use eating as a way to calm and soothe anxiety, tension, and emotional pain. It can also become a nervous compulsion that provides a gateway to protective defenses. Overeating may satisfy an unconscious desire to isolate oneself from the source of trauma. After a painful abortion, a woman may try to disconnect from the sexual appeal of a beautiful body. Extra weight can provide a sense of protection from the risk of emotional intimacy.

Barbara became obese following her three abortions. Her hefty weight gain progressed for 12 years until she reached the dire point where she could no longer walk. Eventually, Barbara was fired from her job and ended up on disability. She was also plagued by severe health problems arising from her obesity. Barbara had an unconscious desire to punish herself by becoming as ugly, vile, and defective as she felt inside. Fortunately, Barbara recovered from this insidious expansion once she began to hoist her painful memories and feelings out from under layers of denial, repression, and avoidance.

Laura's boyfriend accused her of allowing pregnancy to occur in order to trap him. She immediately took all the blame and decided it was her job to fix the problem. Certainly she did not want to "force" him to marry her. The pressure to abort was quite subtle. Driven by guilt for a mistake for which she accepted all responsibility, Laura had an abortion. She felt compelled to do this in order to make her boyfriend happy. Conditioned to please, Laura did not want others mad at her. In addition, because her pregnancy was devalued by her boyfriend, she became ashamed of her unique and beautiful capacity to bear children.

Within one year of her abortion Laura had gained 105 pounds. Nothing seemed to fill her emptiness. She described seeing herself in the mirror: ripples of flesh hanging over each other, stretch marks ingrained in deep hues of purple. The sight of her naked body generated intolerable disgust and shame. Laura wrote in her diary:

> I feel so pathetic. I'm tired of fighting. I'm dying inside—weak, misunderstood.

No one understands how much I miss my baby! My soul? Anguished and screaming. I hate it so much. I can't accept myself in this state. I've let people control me and shape me into this horror, this angry person who can only hate those I used to love.

Laura's dramatic weight increase and personality changes were indicative of an attempt to show her internal devastation to the external world. The painful death of her former sense of self reenacted the death of her unborn child. She was trapped in an obese body which she could not escape, heartbroken that her embryonic motherhood had been crushed and pillaged. The grief and disgust she experienced over her body image was a metaphor for a soul entangled in intolerable affliction. Her figure became her symptom—an outward display that invited the criticism, loathing, and rejection of others. Her body had been reshaped to keep people at a distance, even though the resulting isolation and rejection drove her to despair.

## THE ROAD TO RECOVERY

Obviously, not all women who have eating disorders have experienced an abortion. Certainly there is a legion of complex sociological and cultural factors and media influences that may contribute to the development of an eating disorder. However, whenever an eating disorder begins after an abortion, it is essential that the issue of post-abortion trauma be explored. Recovery can be challenging, because using food to devour emotional pain can become an entrenched addiction. Through psychotherapy, however, the woman is helped to talk about these underlying feelings so they can be exposed and understood. In this way, she will begin to develop new coping skills to replace the addictive, repetitive nature of the eating disorder. This is why the treatment for eating disorders is often referred to as "the talking cure."

A pivotal goal in recovery is learning to speak up and find words for the soul to express its pain and release its inner agony. The nature of trauma is that it violently shocks the foundation of our beliefs about safety and shatters our assumptions of trust. A fortress of defenses can skillfully keep a woman from acknowledging her trauma by deflecting all her attention to another arena, where the unwieldy dynamics of something like an eating disorder will demand all her energy and attention.

Whether the pain results from a childhood of abuse and neglect, sexual betrayal, fears of growing up, the death of a loved one, or the loss of one's child because of an abortion, all these injustices, wounds, and violations to a sensitive human heart must filter somewhere. For those who use eating disorders as a means to cope, the chore becomes an arduous task of distraction, calorie counting, obsessing, controlling or forfeiting command, and the vicious, destructive cycle to where all eating disorders eventually end—a prison that assaults its convicts with daily failure, disease, and self-loathing.

What complicates healing for so many women is the difficulty in connecting their eating behavior to their abortion experience. The moral and ideological battles surrounding the abortion issue have led to an almost total blackout in the media, academia, and medical community of any negative repercussions from abortion. This makes it very difficult for women to connect their current emotional or physical symptoms to their experience of abortion, and fosters a disconnection from the body and heart.

And so people turn toward readily available food as the medication to provide control, to inflict punishment, to create indulgence, to vent frustrations, to escape painful feelings, or to recreate a traumatic sense of helplessness. Others strive to find the perfect image in the body that will disguise a deep sense of inadequacy felt in the soul. Eating disorders serve to protect, to defend, to control, and, sometimes, to punish and inflict devastating feelings of failure.

Thankfully, women are not doomed to a lifelong sentence of disordered eating. Recovery begins with the establishment of a sense of personal safety. Feelings and emotions related to one's losses—anger, fear, shame, grief—can then be examined with honesty.

The poet Adrienne Rich once wrote, "I came to explore the wreck. The words are purposes. The words are maps. I came to see the damage that was done and the treasures that prevail."

For those readers who may struggle with food issues, exploring the wreck is more than simply making better food choices and implementing new lifestyle habits. The expedition will entail spending time to get to know yourself better and learning how to communicate feelings, frustrations, isolation, and pain. It will entail digging for subconscious motivations, privately hidden fears, and buried feelings that you have stuffed down with food or camouflaged behind layers of fat. It might mean that you have to assimilate how true physiological hunger feels. If those sensations that you have been connecting and appeasing with food are truly something else, the exploration must become a search for what you are really hungering to satisfy, no matter how uncomfortable or distressing those feelings are.

Indeed, you may need to learn new ways of expressing your emotions. It might mean confronting your fears, anxieties, deeply repressed grief, or churning pockets of anger. At the end of the journey, you just might learn how to trust yourself and how to listen and respond to your "inner voice" and your body's natural cues that intuitively know what is right, good, and nurturing for you.

Much of the focus in counseling attempts to give a person encouragement and permission to explore and experience that which she fears. When a woman experiences and expresses something she had previously tried to avoid, she loses some of her fear and sees that avoidance is not as necessary as she had thought. Healing of the abortion experience itself requires an intense journey of the body, mind, and spirit. Ongoing professional medical treatment and therapy support for the eating disorder are also an important part of recovery.

Confronting the past of any trauma is always a difficult and painful expedition, but only those who embark on this voyage will be able to discover the elusive key to freedom. You will not only survive the expedition, but you can flourish by developing the skills to express and assert your deepest, truest self with respect, confidence, and dignity.

# Chapter Sixteen

# Paradise Lost
## Abortion and Ruined Relationships

Tasha and Steve had been dating for six years. They shared a passion for music. As aspiring song writers and vocalists they were both immersed in the task of building a reputation in the music industry. They had developed a unique style that blended a pop country sound with lyrical and soulful harmonies. Together they performed in local night clubs and did occasional gigs at fairs and outdoor festivals.

They also enjoyed a large circle of friends, many of whom admired and even envied their ideal relationship as lovers and artistic collaborators. As soon as Tasha and Steve saved enough money to buy their dream house, nestled in a river-worn cleavage of the Appalachian mountains, they were going to marry.

It was August when Tasha first discovered she was pregnant. The blistering heat, chronic nausea, fatigue, and dehydration forced her into an air-conditioned emergency room only moments before one of their biggest shows of the summer. The diagnosis of pregnancy actually brought surprising relief for Tasha, who was beginning to suspect she was suffering from some peculiar disease. But on the way home from the hospital, Steve's silence created a deafening rift between them.

"I know you are upset about us missing the concert," Tasha reluctantly commented, as if they had just bungled the opportunity of a lifetime. She waited anxiously for him to acknowledge the pregnancy, but Steve only looked disgusted and continued his silence.

For the first time, Tasha felt disconnected from him. She wondered if he would have offered a more comforting reaction if she *had* been diagnosed with cancer. It wasn't long before Steve's feelings finally burst out. "We have to get rid of it. This whole situation is not in our plan! We can't do this, you know."

They drove almost the rest of the way home in silence, as bile snaked its way up Tasha's throat. She felt determined to have her baby, but she could not imagine being happy without Steve in her life. He was a part of her, too. At that moment a powerful panic gripped her. She could hardly breathe. "I don't want to lose you," she pleaded.

Steve was jarred from his hypnotic stare and broke his silence. "I suppose we could go on and get married," he said flatly.

For a moment, Tasha could breathe again. Even this underwhelming offer to accelerate their marriage plans was enough to give her hope.

But then, he continued emphatically, "But it would be hard to do everything we've been dreaming about. You know, Tash, having a baby is a lot
of work. You can't be out all night singing and then take care of a kid, you
know. Things between us will change. Our love will be different."

The menacing chest pressure on her lungs returned, more forceful
than before. Tasha looked at him with pleading eyes, unable to speak.

"But this is *your* choice," he cautiously reminded her. "I will support
whatever you decide. Remember, you have to make this decision
because you are the one that's pregnant."

Tasha rejected the idea of an abortion. But Steve's lack of support
and intimidating emotional distance began to make an impact. She
might well end up alone and abandoned. Why risk changing what they
already had? Why jeopardize a blossoming career and a passionate
relationship? Why chance alienating Steve with a baby that he really
did not want?

Steve sounded so sure of himself. He was so practical, so clearheaded.
Although he promised to be there for her, Tasha knew he simply wasn't
ready to be a father. What if he resented the baby? What if he were to
carry a grudge about this into their marriage? Clearly, he wanted her to
have an abortion.

Steve's gentle nudging proved more effective than his steely silence
and angry demands. Soon, Tasha began to surrender her hold on her
excitement about the baby in favor of Steve's justification. When Tasha
finally, reluctantly, agreed to have an abortion, Steve put his sheltering
arms around her. With a firm squeeze he pledged his heart and soul to
her forever. "We'll have other kids someday," he promised. "I'm gonna
build you a big old house and you can have all the babies you want."
Tasha clung ferociously to these last words—like a mantra to help her
conquer the overwhelming anxiety and fears of "her choice."

Eight years later, Tasha sat in my office. After the abortion, she said,
her relationship with Steve was never the same. Their nights were no
longer worn comfortably, fitting their bodies like a second skin. Sex
had no sensation; it just reflected the numbness of her heart. Tasha's
consistent indifference toward Steve constantly reminded him of his
failure. He felt a heavy and desperate unspoken guilt for not having
the courage to help her give their baby life. Their baby's death hung
over them like a funeral shroud. Even their music became discordant.
It was as if their creative spirits had been sucked from their souls.

Tasha and Steve tried to part ways after a stormy and somewhat
abusive split. But they kept coming back together in an attempt to mend
the fractured picture of their lives together. Steve found comfort for his
wounded virility in drunken binges, womanizing, and an addiction to
pornography. Tasha sought refuge in the isolation of depression. She
was imprisoned by agoraphobia (fear of public places), which only

reluctantly offered her day passes to see a psychiatrist.

Everything about their relationship echoed the barren landscape their lives had become. Tasha recalled their bleak status:

> There was an eerie stillness to our relationship. A disconnection, a loss of passion, music, and everything else we once shared. It all resounded with the echo of my empty womb where nothing grew, my body where nothing hurt, my life where nothing lived . . . it was the black hole. Our life went on in this vortex . . . with no love. He did his thing to shame himself, and I retreated into my numbness and depression. It was a sentence of eternal abandonment.

## RELATIONSHIPS IN TRAUMA

In trauma theory, it is well recognized that traumatic experiences affect not only the traumatized person, but also the attachments and relationships of that person to loved ones and the community. According to psychiatrist Judith Herman:

> Traumatic events call into question basic human relationships. They breach the attachments of family, friendship, love and community. They shatter the construction of the self that is formed and sustained in relation to others. They undermine the belief systems that give meaning to human experience . . . and cast the victim into a state of existential crisis.[1]

Traumas related to sexual molestation and abortion are particularly damaging to one's ability to trust and engage in relationships. In the case of abortion, some form of relationship, whether casual or committed, was directly involved in the circumstances that led up to the abortion. It is not uncommon, therefore, for relationship issues to become mixed up with unresolved abortion trauma.

After an abortion, some women will become overly fearful, insecure, and dependent in their relationships with men. Others, deeply plagued with self-hatred and guilt, become convinced they don't deserve a devoted relationship. Such individuals will push the loved one away in an unconscious effort to sabotage their relationship. Still others will become stuck in a pattern where they recreate situations of abandonment, helplessness, shame, betrayal, or destruction.

Research shows that abortion is much more likely to damage a couple's relationship than to enhance it.[2] It may also inhibit women's ability to maintain lasting relationships in the future. Evidence of this is seen in studies which show that women with a history of abortion tend to have shorter subsequent relationships with men compared to similar women without a history of abortion.[3] Women with a history of abortion are also significantly more likely to go through subsequent divorces.[4]

There are many reasons why abortion can damage subsequent relationships. In many cases, an abortion will deeply damage women's ability to trust men, including their husbands. This lack of trust can lead to both increased conflict and increased breakups. Lack of trust is seen in the many cases where women will enter into a marriage while keeping their prior abortions a secret from their husbands. The fact that they keep this secret reflects a fundamental fear that their husbands will judge them, reject them, or simply "hold it over their heads."

In other cases, the foundations of a relationship are eroded simply by the failure of the man to help the woman feel healed and forgiven. This is especially true if the woman enters into the relationship with the hope or expectation that it will fill the hole in her life that was left by her abortion. If, for example, a woman tells her fiance about a past abortion but he dismisses it as unimportant, she may experience his lack of concern as a lack of empathy, and even identify it as akin to the cold reaction of the boyfriend who impregnated her and encouraged the abortion. Conversely, if she senses any feeling of aversion or judgment on the part of her fiance, she may carry into their marriage a seed of doubt about the completeness of his trust or the sincerity of his love.

Sharing the secret of a past abortion is not easy. Neither is it easy to respond to such news in a way that acknowledges the other person's feelings without implying either dismissal or condemnation. The latter is especially tricky, since the apprehensive post-abortive woman or man is often inclined to read between the lines and see reactions that are not intended or even truly there. If either or both partners are hesitant to bring the subject up for discussion whenever thoughts or concerns about it arise, this, too, tends to distance them from each other.

However, even if a couple has perfect communication skills and are completely supportive of each other, the reenactment of unresolved abortion traumas will inevitably lead to crises not only for the woman, but also for her partner and children. Similarly, abortion trauma related to substance abuse, sexual dysfunctions, anger, and depression, to name a few, all pose stresses for future relationships.

## PACT OF SILENCE

The passion of youthful love had intensified Elaine's first sexual experience. She was trusting, open, and inquisitive about her sexuality. Her passion led to an abortion, which distorted her views of sexuality and intimacy. Though she and her boyfriend broke up after the abortion, they never truly separated. For two decades, Jeffery continued to call her at least twice a year. But they never once spoke about the abortion. Reflecting on the origin of her trauma, Elaine finally wrote the following letter to her childhood sweetheart:

Dear Jeffrey,

It has been 20 years since we shared our intimate moments. Do you remember? We were in love! We would find a quiet back road where we could feel and touch and show and share love. We'd run off whenever we could. I was always so proud of you. You were popular—remember? You were the best player on your high school soccer team. And I was the one you loved. I knew, because it was me you touched and fondled. And so, by your love, I too was popular.

Remember that day in November? We drove far away to a clinic, so I could find out if I was pregnant. We certainly could not chance being close to home. And then we waited.

I still remember sitting on my parents' bed when I called for the results. Positive. What did it mean? I was pregnant. What did that mean? I was going to be a mother. I'm not even sure what that meant. Did I want to be what my mother was? The more I thought, the more I saw this child . . . smiling, laughing, kicking a soccer ball with you. What a beautiful vision. I started thinking of names—didn't you?

The holidays came, we seemed not to worry about it. Then came January, the cold, empty, lonely time. You came and said to me that you knew where we could go for an abortion and your friend's father—you know, the one who always called me "the Virgin Mary" because I was Catholic—would pay for it. I remember the sadness. I remember getting very drunk the night before the abortion and throwing up on you and all over your mother's car. I think how you deserved it.

Then you took me for the abortion. I was okay. We'd have another baby someday. Because of my love for you I was willing to kill. You would never leave me. But you did. Coldly, in anger, and quickly. And there I stood with my grief.

We killed *our* child. And now forever, we are bonded together as parents of a child without a life. We have nothing in common but all these years later, you still call. We're two marriages, two children and ten states later. You still call me every year. You tell me each time that you love me. Why? Why didn't you love me then?

I think I'll never ever know what love is. Because I loved and it caused me to kill. I know you are still dealing with your grief. I relive it all each time you call. I still hurt, I still ask why.

It took Elaine years to identify the source of her pain. Because of her abortion, she had developed numerous emotional and sexual dysfunctions. Real intimacy was something she had never achieved. For her, sex and love were intermingled with feelings of destructiveness. She reenacted this theme through her actions and fantasies. One way in which this destructiveness was manifested was through repeated promiscuous affairs with married men. She gained great pleasure and satisfaction from watching the affairs destroy marriages in a slow, draining fashion. She achieved a sense of power and control when she was the one who orchestrated the end of a relationship rather than having the separation inflicted upon her. Through custody battles fought for children, she experienced feelings of conquest when the fathers were separated from their children, recreating what had been done to her.

Elaine did not consciously plot and scheme her behavior. Nonetheless, she unconsciously gravitated toward these predictably disastrous relationships because they predictably reenacted themes associated with her traumatic abortion.

Jeffrey, for his part, continued to call Elaine over the years to reassure himself that Elaine was okay. They always spoke of their present concerns—the weather, jobs, kids, and partners. But they never spoke about what bonded them together, the abortion. They shared an understanding to forget the unmentionable, and yet it still connected them. For Jeffrey, the abortion was the source of his sense of obligation to Elaine. His twice-a-year calls were a salve for his own unresolved grief. Through the calls he sought to gain assurance of Elaine's well-being and happiness, to offer her encouragement and comfort whenever needed, and thereby to ease his guilty conscience.

## KEEPING THE MEMORY OF BABY ALIVE

While uncommitted relationships almost always end very quickly after an abortion, more committed couples will often find that the abortion, while damaging their relationship, can also act as a relational glue. Such was the case with Nicky, whose promiscuous lifestyle following her first abortion only ended when she met a "perfect guy." She knew he was the man she would marry, so she wasn't at all upset to learn she had become pregnant.

> I did not want to have an abortion. I told him that I had already had one when I was 18. I was just a kid then. Now I was 25, I had a job, I was an adult, I could actually have this baby. I had health insurance. He just would not hear of it. He said that he would not have a baby now. I could not make him have a baby now. He would not agree, absolutely not. He would not marry anyone because they were pregnant. That was a stupid thing to do. I told him I didn't need to get married. He said no way was a kid of his going to be born without [his parents] being married. That would make him look like a jerk. I begged him for two weeks, cried, argued. Finally, the date had to be set if I wanted to do it. He just refused to discuss it anymore. Period. He would just walk away if I brought it up. "Just do it."
>
> I wrestled with the idea of having the baby anyway. He said he would hate me forever. What would I do without the guy I loved? I would have his baby but not him. In the end I almost called my Mom to tell her I was coming home, but as the phone was ringing I hung up. I made the decision in that instant that I would have the abortion and marry the guy. If I had the baby I might not have the guy I loved.
>
> Anyway, I married the guy about two years later. A year after that I wanted to have a baby. He was never home. Always out doing some team sport. I thought a baby would be good. We had been married a year. He would not hear of it. He said he was too young to have a baby. He was 27, not ready to have kids.
>
> Actually, he was not ready to be married. He had done so many thoughtless things to me during our boyfriend and girlfriend period, people wondered why I would marry him. We fought constantly. He was never treating me the way I wanted to be treated. I wondered for years why the heck didn't I break up

with him. I would meet other guys and have affairs with them, but never just break up and start dating the new guys. Why not? Years later I realized why. Because I had made that deal with myself that I would marry him. I had to marry him. I had had an abortion for him.

As Nicky learned, in some cases abortion can cement a woman to even the most dysfunctional and unsatisfying of relationships. In many cases, women seek to hold onto the memory of their lost pregnancy by maintaining a relationship with their aborted child's father. He is the substitute for their child. Or, in his fertility, he may even be seen as holding the promise of replacing the child that she lost.

Nicky's experience was similar to that of Penny, who came into counseling along with her boyfriend David.

There is so much love in the expectancy of a child. I was so scared, but I was excited too. Wow! Me? A mother? David a daddy?

My excitement soon turned to anxiety when I realized that the baby was not being welcomed with such enthusiasm. David did not feel so thrilled. He said it was a terrible thing to get married just because of a baby and we would resent each other later. I couldn't bear the idea of being resented. I blamed myself for how angry he was. Then I began to resent the child . . . then I had an abortion.

I wasn't prepared for how this affected me. I felt like somebody came in and grabbed a chunk out of my heart. I went home and part of it was missing—the part of my heart that was for that child. Somebody took a piece of my heart. A part of me died.

As time went on, I began to realize how selfish David was. I was filled with rage at him. Everything he did got on my nerves. He played sports a lot, and it seemed that every weekend when I needed him most to get through the depression he couldn't be with me because he had a game. I began to despise those stupid games! They were apparently more important than me! Secretly I hated him . . . but for four years I continued to date him, make love to him, buy things for him, and plan my future with him. In between our time together I would cry. I was with him, but alone. He didn't know me at all! That hurt so much.

As Penny and David discussed their differences, it became apparent that they had very little in common. She felt repulsed by his love of sports, while he existed to play them. She did not like his friends, his style of conversation, or his level of intimacy. David did not like her emotional demands, her neediness, or her relish for "feeling" conversation. Their communication was poor. So the obvious question arose. "What do you enjoy about each other?" I asked. Both sat looking at me, blank-faced. Then they looked at each other. The unanimous answer in a giggled outburst was: "Nothing!"

David and Penny had stayed together as a means to figuratively "keep their baby alive." They were trapped by a form of complicated mourning. They had sacrificed their child so that their relationship could survive without resentment. Since the price they paid for maintaining the relationship was the termination of their pregnancy, their unhappy relationship had to be endured as a memorial to their lost child. In that memorial lay the pain of loss and isolation, re-experienced each day by Penny. Unable to work through her grief and loss, she clung ferociously to their relationship. The thought of giving up David, despite the fact that she knew he would never meet her emotional or intellectual needs, was akin to giving up her baby.

Their relationship served to buy them time. It allowed them to put off their genuine aching grief over the death of their baby until it was more bearable. Their countless relational conflicts became a means of focusing the pain of their loss into something more tolerable. Once Penny became aware of these dynamics, her real grief over the abortion flowed out effortlessly. After that, it was easy for her to say goodbye to David and move on to a future that promised more personal and relational fulfillment.

## POISONED RELATIONSHIPS

As Sasha learned, unresolved grief over a past abortion can poison even the most committed married relationships.

> My marriage ended 12 years later. In hindsight it was a slow death from the very beginning. When the pain of my abortions began to consciously surface more strongly, I went through a grieving process. I began reading a couple of books written by women like me, who had aborted their babies. They allowed me to see that I was not alone. They allowed me to see that I wasn't crazy. I finally could cry. And cry I did. Even as I am writing this, tears are beginning to fall for my babies, my little girls.
>
> But my husband was disgusted by my grief. I felt very rejected, and in turn, I rejected him. All the years we were together I could not stand to have him touch me. Sex became a vile, disgusting thing for me. I always pushed him away. . . . The destruction of a precious sweet child totally destroys the beauty of the sexual union that created it.

Anger and grief obstruct productive communication, prohibiting problem solving and making intimacy, both personal and sexual, a futile effort. When the anger and grief are associated with a past abortion, their effect on a relationship can be even more toxic since discussing the abortion can raise so much anxiety that it is difficult to address in a respectful way.

For many couples, the topic of a past abortion is so threatening that it is simply banished, at the expense of authentic connectedness. Pamela shares how she, too, felt cut off from her husband due to his inability to share her grief.

> Next to the pain of the abortion, the next pain was the fact I couldn't grieve with my husband. He just couldn't (wouldn't) face it. When he would start to consider the horror of it all, he would stop short and "tune out." I personally

think it was too depressing for him to contemplate. I felt completely alone. I grieved alone. I hated him for that. This impacted every area of our marriage. I was repulsed by his touch and felt so much anger it was impossible to be close to him.

An abortion often reveals the weakness or even destructiveness of a relationship. In many cases, however, an abortion may compel women to stay in a flawed relationship because they no longer believe that they deserve anything better. According to Casey:

I felt if I didn't marry my aborted baby's father, no one else would want me because of what I'd done. My sense of unworthiness increased, and my ability to do the "right thing" in raising a child was in question. My husband was abusive, but I felt he was treating me as I deserved. My abortion made me feel like dirt, and I allowed others to walk all over me.

Because of her abortion, Casey lost all sense of personal dignity and self-respect. She didn't believe that she deserved better treatment or a better relationship. This made her more dependent on the relationship she already had, and therefore more tolerant of the abuse that followed. Her need for punishment left her exposed to her husband and others who were continually pricking her painful emotional wounds. By becoming a perpetual victim, Casey recreated the helpless, depressed emotional state that had accompanied her abortion. By the time she entered a program for post-abortion healing, there was nothing of her marriage left to salvage. Only after she was freed from the guilt and shame of her choice was she able to leave her abusive husband.

## WHEN LOVE TURNS TO HATE

A young girl's first experience with romantic love is likely to be idealized and highly charged. The same passionate zeal that is the well-spring of youthful love, however, can also fuel a deep and lasting hatred. This was 15-year-old Kim's experience. She had been involved with an older boy whom she loved with all her heart and soul. After she became pregnant, she felt abandoned and betrayed when her "knight in shining armor" responded with anger and rejection rather than protection or support. Shortly after her abortion, she made the following diary entry about her boyfriend.

I will never be the same!
I refuse to care about you again,
I can't, won't give you my love,
I have tried and failed at the impossible.
I will leave you now and never look back
You hurt me so badly inside
I trusted you, but I was betrayed
I gave you everything I had

> I put you first in my life
> All you did was use and hurt me
> If you knew the pain I felt then
> And only then could you understand
> I guess I just fell too hard for you.
> I'll accept now the truth
> I have opened my eyes and now I see,
> You'll never be there for me.
> I want to kill you, you lying bastard!
> Oh God I want to die! Oh God, how I wish I was dead!
> I hate my life so much, God, how I hate my life.
> I don't even know who I am anymore.
> I am not the girl I was. I want my baby back . . . God I want my baby!

Her boyfriend's rejection and the subsequent abortion corrupted Kim's innocence. Her passion for love had become a passion for hatred. She felt violated, abandoned, and fragmented. She swore she would never trust again. Kim hardened herself to love and life, became angry and defensive, and had frequent thoughts of suicide. She felt like a stranger to herself and found it difficult to have faith in her own judgment. She gave up the flute, an instrument she had previously played with dedication and enjoyment. She experimented with drugs and alcohol, and her grades dropped at school. She knew she would never be the same again. Her dreams shattered, she was left with emptiness, grief, and intense rage.

Abortion can shake the foundation of the psychological and spiritual lives of those who have aborted. The act itself can foster resentment and alienation and, in the case of Judy, an intense anger and desire for revenge:

> I hate myself for what I did. I feel angry at my boyfriend for being such a jerk. I thought he loved me. After promises that I was so incredibly special to him, I had to get an abortion. It was such a slap in the face. I wish he was dead, or got AIDS, or was mutilated in an accident, or had something horrible happen to him. I hope he can never have children. I hate his guts.

In the Elliot Institute survey, 47 percent of the post-abortive women surveyed reported feeling hatred of those involved in their abortion, 35 percent reported hatred specifically of the man who made them pregnant, and 22 percent felt hatred of all men in general.

Heightened levels of anger are even more common than hatred. Eighty-one percent of the post-abortive women surveyed reported that their abortions produced feelings of anger, with 50 percent describing their anger as "rage." Moreover, 59 percent stated that they began to lose their tempers more easily, and 48 percent reported becoming "more violent when angered" after their abortions. Statistical analysis revealed that these higher levels of anger and hatred of others were strongly associated with feelings of self-hatred and unforgiveness of self.

Anger is a protective armor. It tells the rest of the world that a boundary has been violated. Our society would like us to swallow our anger, and many of us do. But swallowed anger can contaminate our thoughts. It can consume our energy and resources. It can lead to still more injustice and violence, and contagiously infect others with anger and hatred.

Anger is also a precursor to grief. When one cannot grieve, one can at least be angry that there is a reason to grieve. If the grief process is blocked, however, and mourning never occurs, anger and outrage can become an ingrained part of one's personality.

Eighteen years after her abortion, Sally described herself as an angry, bitter person. Her bereavement had been stalled in the anger stage for nearly two decades. She was not able to move forward through the stages of grief without professional help.

> Memories of my abortion were triggered by driving past the abortion clinic. Or whenever I saw "stop abortion" bumper stickers. I also got ticked with all my boyfriend's letters of apology. Whenever he sent me a letter, I wanted to shred it in a million pieces and stick it up his ---!

It is not uncommon for traumatized women and men to bury their grief under stockpiles of tremendous rage. Sally's anger, for example, provided an outlet for emotion that kept her from feeling her own pain. It was easier for her to become infuriated with reminders of trauma than to directly feel the pain over her loss.

For some women, the anger that arises from an abortion may fuel activism or even fanaticism into seemingly unrelated, emotionally charged causes, such as human rights, animal rights, or religious issues. By channeling their anger into such activism, they discover ways to act out their anger in a forum that is removed from, but symbolic of, their abortion-related trauma. Micki, for example, developed a deep suspicion of men's motives after her abortion, which drove her to become an outspoken feminist and political activist.

> Because of my abortion, an age of innocence was lost. I became more apt to believe in the innate evil of man instead of goodness. Underneath, I was an angry, bitter person and replaced my sadness and quiet with hatred and animosity. I felt there was nothing to look forward to in my life, that the best years were already behind me and I could never completely trust or be trusted again. In short, my previous life as I knew it was over and instead replaced with an antagonistic life through which I could express rage and hostility. My words were always sharp and cutting. In everything, I was fighting . . . always trying to fight back.

Fighting for the life of her child was something that Micki was unable to do at the time of her abortion. The fighting attitude she adopted for herself afterwards was, in some way, an attempt to avoid and deny the submissive aspect of her younger self, which had led her to such grief. Every project she began or sentiment she offered was done in a defensive, mistrusting fashion. She was certain that everyone was out to take something from her, and continually re-experiencing the emotional threat and fear of losing something valuable to others, just as she had lost her child.

Anger can also arise when women who are prepared to grieve discover that those around them refuse to acknowledge their grief For example, when Grace discovered she was pregnant, her husband badgered her to "get rid of it." When Grace and her husband sought marital counseling after the abortion, their psychologist refused to acknowledge the grief and betrayal she felt about the abortion and told her to "stop acting like a victim." This rejection of her grief compelled Grace to withdraw into an isolated world that no one could penetrate. She remained depressed, anxious, and fearful of future losses.

The marital counseling was a complete failure. Their marriage deteriorated into a contemptuous relationship where both parties taunted and ridiculed each other. Frequently, they engaged in physical violence and outbursts of uncontrollable rage. Grace would often throw china dishes, glassware, and other expensive items at her husband. After the fights, her husband would storm out of the house, leaving Grace alone amid the shattered remains of their valuable possessions. These scenes recreated the traumatic sense of abandonment and destruction associated with her abortion. The shards of glass and ceramic in which she stood mimicked the chaos in her broken heart. As with her mistimed pregnancy, she was left alone to clean up the mess and "get rid of it."

Patterns of anger and violence can also infect later relationships, as is seen in the case of Margie.

> At the time of my abortion, I wanted to please my future husband and my parents so they would continue to love me. I didn't consider the child or myself. I had wanted to get married—we even had the blood test and license—but he came up with the four hundred dollars needed for the abortion.
>
> We got married later. I had a lot of angry feelings toward him but stuffed them most of the time. Toward the end of our marriage, they were coming out all the time. I would lash out verbally and sometimes physically. This trait carried over into my second and third marriage. I continually feel that I am being emotionally violated by not having my feelings considered.

People like Margie may reenact the trauma of violation and abandonment by getting themselves into unstable relationships. These relationships may be sought to satisfy profound needs for protection and nurturing, yet at the same time be plagued by a fear of abandonment or deception that can become self-fulfilling.

For those lucky enough to identify the root of their trauma, however, healing and recovery is possible. But first they must work through their feelings of loss, grief, and anger. Releasing one's anger is a key step on the path to healing, as Sharon discovered.

I felt enraged at my boyfriend for pressuring me. I also felt angry at the people who worked in the clinic. I felt that I had been profoundly cheated. I blamed my boyfriend for my negative feelings about myself. Eventually I realized that I was mostly angry at myself for not listening to my conscience. I wish I had listened to myself. Once I stopped blaming everybody, my grief took total control. It was the most painful experience, but one that unlocked me from the prison of anger and rage. I have forgiven myself and others, and for the first time in a very long time, I have peace.

## COURTNEY'S TANGLED WEB

Courtney's unique story reflects aspects of the three subjects we have just covered: the loss of innocence, keeping the baby alive, and toxic anger. Courtney's struggle with these issues entangled her in behavior and beliefs that blurred the lines between reality and fantasy.

Courtney was 19 at the time of her first abortion. She loved Bob, and when she discovered she was pregnant, she secretly hoped he would want to marry her and raise their baby. Bob made it unmistakably clear that he did not welcome the idea of having a baby. Hurt, rejected, and angry, Courtney decided to abort. Bob took the news with a sigh of relief. Despite her anger and rage with Bob, she continued to date him in an attempt to hold onto the lost pregnancy through the proxy of their relationship. Nine months later, history repeated itself and Courtney became pregnant a second time.

Before the second pregnancy, however, Courtney had also begun to secretly date Justin. He was sensitive, concerned about her feelings, and protective of her. Since she had also been sexually intimate with him, she deceptively told Justin that the baby growing inside her was his child. Then she had a second abortion. She did this because she felt she had a more supportive relationship with Justin, so she believed he would be more willing to listen to her grief and repressed feelings about the loss her abortions entailed. After the abortion, Courtney felt disgusted with herself, extremely depressed, and very anxious. Justin was aware of her pain after the abortion and did his best to comfort her. He encouraged Courtney to get counseling.

As Courtney approached what would have been her due date, she became even more depressed and anxious. She had frequent thoughts of suicide and often fantasized about getting pregnant again. Although Justin was not the father of her aborted baby, Courtney continued to let him believe he was responsible. She felt great satisfaction when he talked of his guilt over what had happened.

Courtney targeted much anger and resentment at Justin as a punishment, while at the same time clinging to him. She was mistrustful and jealous of any contact he had with other women. Justin, out of a sense of guilt and responsibility, remained in the deteriorating relationship with the hope of helping Courtney.

Courtney's possessive accusations finally served the ultimate but unconscious goal of distancing Justin to the point where he rejected her. Immediately after the breakup, however, Courtney informed Justin she was pregnant by him again. Driven to recreate the tragedy, Courtney's lie began to turn into an elaborate fantasy that became very real to her. Through the means of her imagined pregnancy, she blamed Justin for abandoning her, wanting her to have an abortion, and lying to her about his commitment and love. She egged him on by offering another abortion as a possible solution to their problem.

Even though Justin was aware of how much pain the last abortion had caused Courtney, he continued to tell her that it was *her choice* and he would support any decision she made. One night Justin handed her $400 to cover any expenses she might have. This made her even more angry because this again placed all the responsibility for the decision upon her.

What Courtney really wanted to hear was that Justin loved her and would never want her to go through that kind of pain again. She needed him to be there for her in having this baby, the fruit of their love, who really existed only in Courtney's mind.

Her rage at Justin's failure to oppose the abortion compelled her to become even more antagonistic. She informed Justin that even if she kept the baby she would not let him see the child. He begged her not to do that, as he had grown up in a home without a father and had always vowed to be active and involved if he had a child. Courtney began to feel some power and continued in her quest to hurt him. She informed Justin that if their child ever inquired about him she would give the child the $400 and instruct him to go find his father. She would inform her son that this was the money his father had given her in order to kill him as a fetus.

Courtney's attempts to convey the reality of how she experienced abortion were quite desperate. Even though the pregnancy was a fantasy, her psychic trauma drove her to invent a situation in which she could ascribe to Justin all her own rage and grief from the previous abortions—rage and grief that had no outlet and were driving her mad. The line between fantasy and reality became increasingly obscured. Courtney deluded herself into believing that she actually was pregnant and began to act out a repetition of the previous abortions.

Courtney's stress prompted her to make an appointment for a third abortion. She asked Justin to come and be with her. Trying hard to be supportive but in all the wrong ways, he agreed to meet her at the clinic. When Courtney never showed up, he became angry and confused.

They set up another appointment. That time Justin did not attend. Later that night a friend of Courtney's, going along with the traumatic reenactment, called Justin to inform him that the abortion had been botched and Courtney was still pregnant.

Throughout the following months Courtney continued to imagine that she was still pregnant. She often daydreamed about her expanding waistline. She wore large plaid jumpers and tops with big bows, the distinguishing hallmark of expectant maternity. Maintaining the illusion protected her from dealing with the grief born of an empty womb.

Courtney's story is a painful example of complicated mourning. Her fantasies, however bizarre, were quite functional as an attempt to work through her loss. The fictional pregnancy allowed Courtney to once again experience the threat of her loss and to express the unresolved rage, sorrow, grief, panic, and shame that arose from her two prior abortions. The imaginary pregnancy and her "escape" from the abortion also served to reconnect Courtney with her lost children and demonstrate protectiveness, love, and an intense longing for them. As the fantasy-drama progressed, Courtney began to restore her lost maternal identity and even to see herself as a heroine protecting her imaginary child, bravely carrying her baby to term without the man who had rejected her. Through this fantasy she was able to place all of the blame for her pain on Justin and thereby deny, repress, or avoid aspects of the loss, pain, and guilt associated with her past abortions. Her entire fantasy was designed to reconstruct the tragedy and gain mastery over it. It was a reenactment through which she desperately sought to create a happy ending that would erase the pain of her past abortions. In the end, all she wanted was a baby.

Her denial and projection of guilt and rage were quite powerful. Courtney was a sensitive, caring young woman who deeply yearned for someone special to love and cherish her. She had always loved children and her abortions had deeply wounded her maternal nature. Once her denial could no longer sustain itself through this complicated fantasy, her grief overwhelmed her. She cried for hours, curled up in a fetal position, and grieved the loss of her two children and the replacement pregnancy that was only a fantasy. Fortunately, through supportive counseling, Courtney was finally able to face reality and grieve her losses while simultaneously accepting responsibility for everything that had happened.

Several years after this extraordinary soap opera, Courtney came again for counseling. She recalled the acceptance and understanding that had enabled her to understand her crazy behavior, recover from the experience of her abortions, and graduate from nursing school. At this time in her life, she was engaged to a loving man who had weathered her relentless testing of his unconditional love. Courtney recognized quickly that the testing was born of her insecurities and past traumas. With the help of additional counseling, she worked hard to accept responsibility for her feelings and learned how to avoid drag-ging the distrust and pain involved in her past relationships into her future.

## ABORTION AND SEXUAL DYSFUNCTIONS

The destruction of a child conceived in lovemaking can rebound against a woman's sexual identity. For many post-abortive women, the thought of future sexual encounters can become disturbing or even abhorrent. On a conscious or unconscious level, sex can be a connector to unre-solved abortion trauma. For some, even the sexual advances of a man they deeply love can trigger unexplainable feelings of revulsion, anger, grief, insecurity, or betrayal. Ginny shared the difficulties and grief that surfaced after her abortion:

> I remember coming home after the abortion and crying my eyes out. Tears were streaming from my face and staining a white silk coverlet on my bed. I also remember a discharge of white milk coming from both breasts. My feel-ing was that my entire body was crying . . . teardrops of milk seeping from my bosoms.
>
> I wept for days and thought I could no longer bear the agony. I felt like I had defiled my body. I was not using it properly. I vowed right then and there that I would never be with a man again. I did not want anyone to come near me. I reasoned that all men were horrible. I always connected that despicable experience to my physical and sexual self. I was ashamed of my breasts, my body and my sexuality . . . and for a long time I absolutely hated men.
>
> Although years later I did marry, I had major sexual problems. I felt that sex was another shameful duty I had to endure. It was always dreadfully painful. I could not stand sex. Eventually I got divorced and vowed once again to be alone.

Because sex is so closely connected to abortion, some women cope with sex the same way they coped with their abortion, by becoming "numb" or "not present." For example, Tanya's loss of interest in sexual intimacy was a direct result of her traumatic abortion. During her abor-tion, she had dissociated (disconnected) from the experience. Her body was there, but her mind had split off from the emotional experience of the event. After her abortion, Tanya began to react in the same discon-nected way to sex.

> The thought of sex made me sick! I just wanted to get it over with and be left alone. When we did have sex, I felt nothing. There was no pleasure, no any-thing. I was completely numb.

Tanya continued to experience sexual numbing and lack of interest for many years. Her feelings about sex perfectly mirrored her feelings at the time of her abortion, when she anxiously waited to "get it over with and be left alone."

Other women may translate their fears about abortion into a dread of sexual intimacy. This was Janet's experience:

> It was hard for me to separate sex from abortion. Every time I had sex I feared that I would end up having another abortion. I wanted nothing to do with sex and I hated anyone who asked me for it.

Corrie's experience was similar and led to a rejection of her fertility, her sexuality, and eventually her husband.

> After my abortion I never wanted to be pregnant again. I became uninterested in sexual relations with my husband. Eventually we divorced. There was nothing to tie us together: no kids, no sex. I hated both.

Negative attitudes about sexual relations can be carried into a subsequent marriage. If the couple does not quickly identify the source of the frigidity, the anxiety and disappointments that arise can seriously impact their marriage. According to Bernice:

> After my abortion I quit having sex. I wasn't noble or anything . . . I just didn't "like" it anymore. When I got married, my honeymoon night was not what it should have been. I was trying to do my best, or do my job, whatever you want to call it. But it wasn't the joyful exchange of love that it's supposed to be. As you might imagine, if the honeymoon night was like that, the time following didn't exactly get any better. My coolness and lack of interest turned my husband off. Our marriage just went downhill.

For some women, abortion curdles all heterosexual passion. Men who abandon are branded as sexual aggressors, creeps, jerks, no good, lousy and stupid. Some women admittedly develop inclinations toward lesbian lifestyles after such rejection and the subsequent abortions. Through sexual relationships with other women, the danger of repeating the tragedy of abortion is no longer a threat. Kyra explained how her abortion led to her adopting gay practices:

> After my abortions I began to hate men. I came to realize the incredible selfishness and self-centeredness of each of the men I had ever attempted to love. There seemed to be nothing in return for me. I'm sick of not having my needs met. I find women to be more compassionate and caring, more sensitive to my real needs as a woman. I don't think I could ever trust a man in another relationship. Men completely turn me off.

Numerous studies have found that sexual dysfunctions are common following an abortion.[5] In the Elliot Institute survey, 58 percent of the women surveyed reported a loss of pleasure from sexual intercourse following their abortions, and 47 percent reported developing an aversion to sexual intercourse or becoming sexually unresponsive. In addition, a third of the women surveyed reported increased pain during intercourse.

For some, the rejection of their sexuality and reproductive potential is acted out through the self-punishing use of surgical sterilization. In the Elliot Institute survey, one in 12 women reported having themselves sterilized to avoid the risk of undergoing another abortion. This fear can be so great that even very young women will sacrifice their desire for future children just to be spared the risk of having another abortion. Such was the case of Valerie, who was only 19 when she had a tubal ligation.

> I was so afraid of becoming pregnant. I could not risk being in a situation where I might need another abortion. I refused to kill another baby, so I had myself sterilized.

Valerie's pain was so deep that she could not imagine ever being healed from her traumatic abortion experience. Her need to protect herself from another traumatic abortion overwhelmed her long-term desire to be a mother.

As her life went forward, Valerie regretted the impulsiveness of both her decision to abort and her decision to have herself sterilized. Each time she encountered another woman's child who touched her maternal center, her hasty decisions, both born out of irrational fears, came back to haunt her.

> Children are so precious. I would give the world to undo my past. I changed my body forever, for the sake of someone else . . . so he could keep on having sex . . . so that I could avoid another abortion. But my abortion was so traumatic for me. I chose to have my tubes tied rather than ever be in that situation again.

Valerie's decision to have herself sterilized served both to protect herself from another abortion and to punish herself for her abortion. Unfortunately, her doctor was willing to perform a permanent, life-altering sterilization on her without screening for psychological issues that were distorting her decision-making process. This doctor's negligence was even more unconscionable given the fact that Valerie was so young and had no children. By the time she found emotional healing and her true desire to have children was restored, it was too late. In effect, her one abortion ended up costing her all of her children.

## HEALING RELATIONSHIPS

This chapter has examined the impact of traumatic abortion experiences on intimacy, sexuality, and communication in personal relationships. By intimacy, I am not referring to the erotic and sensual familiarity embodied through passion. One of the basic premises for intimacy is authentic and deep communication. It implies the freedom to be who you are in a relationship. Being "who you are" entails the ability to talk frankly about values that are important to you.

People who are authentically intimate in their relationships can take a strong position on where they stand on important emotional issues, desires, hopes, and dreams. They are willing to take risks, communicate their needs, and express their fears. They don't wait for their partners to read their minds or decipher their body language. They are capable of setting boundaries and clarifying what is both acceptable and unacceptable in their relationships. Such partnerships do not permit silence, sacrifice, or betrayal of the self. True intimacy gives a person permission to be vulnerable and dependent as well as capable and responsible.

Couples whose relationships have been damaged by abortion and who both desire to work through the loss can still grow tremendously in their intimacy and love for one another. Our Rachel's Vineyard programs for post-abortion healing are attended not only by individual women and men, but also by couples. Many couples come to grieve abortions they had during courtship or early in their marriage. Some attend as couples even when only one of the partners has been involved in a past abortion. In these cases, the supporting partner is there to better understand and share in the grief and healing process of the other.

The painful but rewarding journey of post-abortion healing can result in many blessings for a marriage, especially when the process is shared. By jointly participating in the process, couples often discover an increase in communication skills and renewed emotional and sexual intimacy. Adrienne and her husband, for example, experienced profound healing on a weekend retreat. After the weekend was over, they wrote:

Through Rachel's Vineyard we had a safe, loving, nurturing environment to share all our guilt, shame, fear, pain and anger. A place to know that we are not alone and to understand and resolve our emotions. A place to find healing for the old infected internal wounds. We left the retreat knowing that God loves us and forgives us for aborting our children. We were able to validate our children's lives and mourn their deaths. Most importantly we left with our marriage intact; finally trusting each other for the first time. I personally promised our children that their lives were not taken in vain. Each and every mother and father of an aborted child needs to know that there is hope, healing, forgiveness and peace for them, too.

Another woman, Melissa, stated that one of the unanticipated results of going through the healing retreat together with her husband was an immediate increase in their sexual passion.

I was shocked at the intense level of erotic desire that Mark and I felt for each other. We were like teenagers in love! Our sex life made a 180-degree turnaround. I found myself feeling an incredible love for him . . . a love I never dreamed possible. It was deep and honest.

It meant so much for me to see Mark bare his soul, his grief, his feelings over what we had gone through. It restored my faith in him as a man to hear him tell me how sorry he was, and recognizing how much this experience had hurt me. I also needed to hear how the abortion affected him. Once he was vulnerable, I felt like I could forgive him. We are rediscovering each other, and there is so much beauty in our marriage. I finally feel like he is not only a friend, but an incredible lover.

For others, the healing of their abortion experience helps them break free of destructive relationship patterns. They are no longer compelled to become involved in promiscuous, abusive, or shallow relationships. Having discovered and healed their inner selves, they are now better prepared to discover and respect another person who will respect and honor them in turn.

Human beings do not survive well as disembodied egos. Abortion creates an acute separation reaction that, on a variety of levels, divides women and men from each other, their aborted children, their families, their community, and God. Post-abortion healing is effective because it restores connections and reconstructs the value of one's traditions and inner beliefs. Through healing, despair gives way to hope, isolation gives way to connectedness, and hatred of others and self gives way to the capacity and desire for authentic, self-giving love.

# CHAPTER SEVENTEEN

# NO CHOICE, HARD CHOICE, WRONG CHOICE

Paula was raised in a loving home with three sisters and two brothers. She always planned to have a big family. When she married and became pregnant, she was ecstatic. After the birth of the baby, she cared for him with love and tenderness. She adored being a mother and longed for the day when she and her husband would have another child.

But Paula's dreams were shattered when she was brutally raped on Halloween night. She was abducted and dragged to a moonlit, muddy construction site. The deep holes in the ground resembled freshly dug graves. The perpetrator, dressed as a ghoul, did everything possible to terrorize, abuse, and destroy his victim. He broke her ribs and nose as he beat her into compliance. Her neck was slashed in several places and bruised with strangulation marks. Rope burns covered her arms and legs. Paula remembered his voice; it had sounded subhuman, like that of a creature from a demonic horror movie. He left her to die. But she survived.

The trauma of the rape precipitated a severe clinical depression and a nervous breakdown. Paula often had psychotic thoughts that she was possessed by the devil, who had raped her on that horrible night. She underwent years of therapy and was repeatedly hospitalized as she tried to recover from this traumatic experience.

One of the many consequences of the trauma was that she was eventually denied custody of her infant son. This came about because after the rape Paula began to self-administer injuries and bruises up and down her arms and around her neck, yet afterwards she had no memory of how the bruises got there. The mental health workers assigned to her case feared she might be inclined to injure the baby in the same way and removed him from her care. This separation was unnecessary. A trauma specialist would have recognized that Paula was engaging in traumatic reenactment—recreating the very same wounds the "ghoul" rapist had left on her body in her struggle with him that Halloween night. This tragic decision to deny her custody of her child resulted in an overwhelming grief that Paula found harder to handle than the rape itself. It was several years before she was finally reunited with her son as his primary caretaker.

Six years after the rape, Paula became pregnant with a second child. The night she discovered her pregnancy, her husband came into the room with mud on his feet. As if a switch had flipped inside her mind, Paula's desires for a large family were suddenly overcome by feelings of panic and anxiety. She angrily told her husband about the pregnancy and said she had to get rid of it. Paula's husband, in an earnest attempt to give her control, told her that whatever she needed to do was fine with him.

Her therapist also agreed, even insisted, that abortion was Paula's only method of coping. She encouraged Paula to have an abortion to escape her role as a "victim" and demanded that she rid herself of any notions of guilt.

Paula's negative reactions to her pregnancy were actually triggered by the mud on her husband's feet, which she associated with the muddy construction site where she had been savagely brutalized. Through this unconscious connector, Paula associated having a baby with the trauma of the violent rape and all of the craziness that followed, which had led to her child being taken away from her. Mud. Rape. Mental breakdowns. The loss of her child. All of these were linked together.

Paula's traumatic reenactment was well underway. She terminated the pregnancy within a week. The abortion took place on a rainy afternoon in mid-October, just two weeks before Halloween.

Shortly after the abortion Paula demanded that her husband have a vasectomy to avoid the possibility of another pregnancy. This finalized the death of her dream for a future with more children.

Paula, the victim, had become the perpetrator. Now she had to deal with her pain and grief alone. There was no one else to blame. She blamed herself for the abortion just as she had blamed herself for being in the wrong place at the wrong time and thereby "allowing" the rape.

Paula cried for weeks after the abortion and entered a terrible state of depression. She became preoccupied once again with obsessive thoughts that she must have been possessed by a devil to have killed her own baby. Over the years that followed she blamed herself, became angry, and hated the woman she had become.

Paula's original trauma had repeated itself like an eerie echo from the past. Abortion provided the means through which she recreated many of the emotions she had endured after the rape. There were coinciding torments: thoughts of being possessed by the devil, the separation from another baby, depression, despair, anger, and an overwhelming sense of helplessness to undo the past.

When I met Paula on a weekend retreat for post-abortion healing, she spoke about the fifteen years of suffering she had endured since the abortion. She never conceived another child and felt guilt and regret that she denied her son a brother because of the abortion. This reenacted the same theme of having lost all those precious years with her living son.

Despite years of counseling, Paula had never once connected her abortion to the trauma of the rape. When I explained how trauma may affect behavior with reenactment, Paula wept with recognition and relief. The association between her rape and the abortion helped Paula grieve her losses and forgive herself.

Paula also saw the abortion as further victimization. It was an act that was contrary to her fundamental moral and maternal beliefs, but it had been performed on her request without any evaluation of whether it was more likely to benefit her or hurt her. She wished her health care providers had recognized the symptoms of trauma repeating itself and helped her avoid making an emotionally charged, ill-informed, and self-destructive choice. Anyone familiar with the risk factors that predict post-abortion trauma would have recognized that an abortion was not in Paula's best interests. But no one screened her for these risk factors. Everyone acted as if Paula's decision—simply because it was her own decision—was a reasonable and appropriate choice to better her life.

## WHEN THE FREEDOM TO CHOOSE ISN'T

Many people mistakenly assume that no woman has an abortion if she does not want one. In fact, while many women believe they *need* an abortion, very few, if any, *want* an abortion. This reality is described in a rather famous line by pro-life feminist Frederica Mathewes-Green, who wrote: "No woman wants an abortion as she wants an ice cream cone or a Porsche. She wants an abortion as an animal caught in a trap wants to gnaw off its own leg."[1] This quote was widely circulated by Planned Parenthood and other advocates of abortion,[2] but the next two sentences from Mathewes-Green's insightful commentary were not included: "Abortion is a tragic attempt to escape a desperate situation by an act of violence and self-loss. Abortion is not a sign that women are free, but a sign that they are desperate."

Many of the problems that follow abortion are not due solely to the traumatic effects of the surgery itself. Often, they are simply a magnification of problems that existed beforehand. In other cases, the problems stem back to the flawed, misinformed, compromising, self-defeating, or simply short-sighted *decision* to have an abortion. For many women, the decision to abort is itself sufficient to provoke feelings of depression, guilt, shame, and more.

To escape the trap of a crisis pregnancy, women who abort must sacrifice some part of themselves. The experience of abortion is an experience of violence. The decision to expose oneself to abortion often entails a betrayal of one's own moral values or maternal instincts, and thereby a loss of some part of oneself. As the psychiatrist and abortionist Dr. Fogel, quoted in chapter two, observed: "This is a part of her own life. When she destroys a pregnancy, she is destroying her-self. . . . I know that as a psychiatrist."[3]

Given this perspective on how abortion is so often the result of desperate and confused choices, how can our society tolerate abortion on request? How can we blithely treat abortion as a matter of "choice," when thousands of women each day are medically maiming themselves through abortions because they are too desperate or misinformed to understand the ramifications of their choice? Wouldn't a truly loving society seek to help them resolve their problem pregnancies in a way that does not require them to hurt themselves or their children in the process?

Any number of factors can drive women to this act of desperation, such as fear of change, self-doubt, or the advice or pressure of other people. In addition, as seen in previous chapters, women may also be driven to choose abortion by psychological compulsions, such as sexual abuse or prior abortions, which incline them to reenact previous losses through abortion.

The notion that women should be "free to choose" abortion without question or hindrance is extremely dangerous. It is based on an ideal of fully informed, emancipated, emotionally stable women that is divorced from reality. In fact, most women are not well informed about the dangers abortion poses to both their psychological and physical health. Furthermore, many women are not truly "emancipated." Instead, many are emotionally dependent on, or easily influenced by, parents, boy-friends, husbands, counselors, employers, or others who may want them to choose abortion far more than they want to choose it for themselves. Finally, many women considering abortion are simply not emotionally stable, and this lack of stability makes them more prone to hasty, ill-considered, or self-destructive decisions.

Even if she does not have a prior psychological illness or trauma to deal with, any woman confronted with an unintended pregnancy will face feelings of shock and fear about how the birth of a child will change her life. The destabilizing effects of a surprise pregnancy are further aggravated by the great hormonal shifts that occur during early preg-nancy. These chemical changes in a woman's body may make her feel more emotional, dependent, exhausted, and physically ill and weak. Any and all of these factors can degrade her ability to make an informed and well-considered decision about abortion.

For most women, abortion is an ambivalent and irresolute choice. Consider the following findings from a survey of 252 women who joined a post-abortion support group:

• Approximately 70 percent had a prior negative moral view of abortion and chose it in violation of their consciences;

- Between 30 and 60 percent had a positive desire to carry the pregnancy to term and keep their babies;
- Over 80 percent said they would have carried to term under better circumstances or with the support of loved ones;
- Fifty-three percent felt "forced" to have the abortion by other people in their lives;
- Sixty-four percent felt "forced by outside circumstances" to have the abortion;
- Approximately 40 percent were still hoping to discover some alternative to abortion when they sat down for counseling at the abortion clinic.[4]

## FLAWED DECISION MAKING

For most women, abortion is more likely to be perceived as an "evil necessity" than a great civil right. Indeed, a major *Los Angeles Times* poll found that 74 percent of women who admitted having had an abortion stated that they believe abortion is morally wrong.[5]

The fact that most women having abortions see them as posing a moral dilemma is itself problematic. Moral dilemmas, by their very nature, involve emotional and intellectual conflict about the options from which one must choose. This conflict produces feelings of ambivalence, tension, and, for many, a powerful sense of crisis in their lives. Many women feel completely overwhelmed by their situation.[6] Under such pressures, many will rush into an abortion without ever examining the full range of their beliefs, needs, and feelings.

Joanna, for example, rushed into an abortion without taking the time to emotionally connect with her own latent maternal desires. Only after the abortion did she realize how much she wanted her baby. Her resulting grief tore her world apart. She dropped out of college for several semesters due to depression and anxiety.

> Everything happened too fast. When I found out I was pregnant I panicked. The woman at the clinic told me I'd better decide quickly. I was afraid to tell my parents. I wanted to spare my father the disappointment I knew he would feel that I had gotten myself into this situation. I was pregnant, unmarried and trying to complete a degree in business.
>
> Abortion seemed pretty logical. But I wasn't prepared for the feelings of loss and unremitting grief which followed. The whole experience was worse than the most horrible nightmare I could ever imagine. This has been a pain I wouldn't wish on anyone.
>
> Abortion is not what I really wanted. But I acted so fast, without thinking. I wanted to have that baby, but I was afraid.

Experts on crisis counseling have found that those who are in a state of crisis are more vulnerable to outside influences than they would be in a non-crisis situation. The state of crisis, especially when it involves moral dilemmas, causes people to have less trust in their own opinions and abilities to make the right decision. This leads them into a state of "heightened psychological accessibility" in which they become more reliant on the opinions of others, especially authority figures. When faced with such a crisis situation, "a relatively minor force, acting for a relatively short time, can switch the whole balance from one side to the other—to the side of mental health or to the side of ill health."[7] In Joanna's case, the abortion clinic counselor's suggestion that she needed to "decide quickly" created emotional pressure to choose abortion immediately, before the opportunity to escape her crisis situation was gone. It is not a coincidence that this same tension-provoking, "choose now" approach is regularly used in marketing programs where consumers are told to "buy now" before a sale price is gone forever.

Persons in crisis "are often less in touch with reality and more vulnerable to change than they are in non-crisis situations."[8] They often experience feelings of tiredness, lethargy, hopelessness, inadequacy, confusion, anxiety and disorganization. Thus, they are more likely to stand back and let other people make their decisions for them, instead of protecting themselves from decisions that may not be in their best interests.

A person who is upset and trapped in a crisis, like Joanna, wants to reestablish stability, and is therefore very susceptible to any influence from those who claim to be able to solve the crisis, especially those who have status or authority.[9] Thus, with minimal effort on the part of a mental health professional, family member, minister, or male partner, an enormous amount of leverage may be exerted upon a woman whose life has been destabilized by a crisis pregnancy.

Uta Landy, an abortion counselor and former executive director of the National Abortion Federation, an association for abortion providers, has admitted that the decision-making processes of women seeking abortion can be temporarily impaired by feelings of crisis related to their pregnancy. Landy defines four types of defective decision-making styles that she has observed in abortion clinics.[10] She calls the first defective process the "spontaneous approach," wherein the decision is made too quickly, without taking sufficient time to resolve internal conflicts or explore options.

The second defective decision-making process is the "rational-analytical approach," which focuses on the practical reasons to terminate the pregnancy (financial problems, single parenthood, etc.) without consideration of emotional needs (attachment to the pregnancy, maternal desires, etc.).

The third defective process is the "denying-procrastinating" approach, which is typical of women who have delayed making a decision precisely because they have a conflicting desire to keep their babies. When such a "denying-procrastinator" finally agrees to an abortion, it is likely that she has still not resolved her internal conflicts, but is submitting to the abortion only because she has "run out of time."

Fourth, there is the "no-decision making approach," wherein a woman refuses to make her own decision but allows others, such as her male partner, parents, counselors, or physician, to make the decision for her. Landy encourages counselors to be aware of the fact that

> Some women's feelings about their pregnancy are not simply ambivalent but deeply confused. This confusion is not necessarily expressed in a straight-forward manner, but can hide behind such outward behavior as: 1) being uncommunicative, 2) being extremely self-assured, 3) being impatient (how long is this going to take, I have other important things to do), or 4) being hostile (this is an awful place; you are an awful doctor, counselor, nurse; I hate being here).[11]

Despite her recognition of the fact that many women are making ill-considered decisions, however, Landy does not recognize any obligation of abortion providers to refuse to perform an abortion on such women, who are at higher risk of severe emotional problems later.

## COERCION

Coercion to choose abortion can be subtle or overt. In Mary's case, there was no subtlety at all.

> The night I told him I was pregnant, he destroyed our apartment. He was screaming at me, telling me I was a whore, slut, pig, you name it. He told me that the kid would be retarded, abnormal, and to get rid of it. NOW! The whole time he cornered me in the bedroom, throwing things and killing me with his words. I'm surprised he didn't come right up and punch me right in the stomach. I wonder what stopped him that time?
>
> For several months he wouldn't look at me or talk to me. He was so mean. Even after the abortion he was the same. His eyes were so black with anger. He never came to the hospital to see me or ever once asked how I was feeling. What a coward!
>
> The abortion ripped my world apart. Any strength I had to leave the abuse was torn away from me.

While some abusive males are happy about a pregnancy and may reduce their abusive behavior for fear of hurting their child,[12] research indicates that being pregnant places women at higher risk of being physically attacked.[13] These findings suggest that abusive men are more likely to reject their partner's pregnancy than to accept it. In such cases, especially if the woman resists the suggestion to abort, verbal and physical abuse is likely to escalate as part of an effort to compel the partner into submitting to an unwanted abortion.[14] According to one study of battered women, the target of battery during their pregnancies shifted from their faces and breasts to their pregnant abdomens,[15] which suggests hostility toward the woman's fertility. Indeed, the leading cause of death among pregnant women is murder.[16] In many of these murder cases, it is known that these women were killed solely because their killers wanted to stop them from giving birth to their children.[17]

While violence against pregnant women is frighteningly common, it is far more common for a pregnant woman's parents or boyfriend to threaten to withdraw love, approval, housing or economic support unless she "does the best thing for everyone" and submits to an abortion. In other cases, rather than resorting to threats, the coercing party may employ the "guilt trip" game: "If you loved me, you wouldn't be doing this to me."

This was the type of emotional blackmail employed by Cindy's boyfriend. He told her that her plans to give birth would ruin his life. When she refused to abort, she began to receive phone calls late into the night from his friends, mother, and other family members, who advised her, pressured her, and begged her to have an abortion. Finally, her boyfriend began to threaten that he would kill himself if she did not have an abortion.

Six months into her pregnancy, worn out from the battle, the nighttime phone calls, and her general state of confusion and sense of isolation, Cindy finally agreed. She reluctantly went to a city teaching hospital and was immediately scheduled for an abortion without any interview process or inquiry about why she had waited so long. Nothing was done to identify her as a high-risk patient who was submitting to an abortion solely to please others, at the expense of her own maternal desires and moral beliefs.

After her abortion, Cindy developed the chronic and clinical depression anyone familiar with this field would expect. There were many days when she was unable to get out of bed. She would retreat for weeks at a time and not bathe or comb her hair. She reverted to a near vegetative state. Her paralysis echoed her failure to do something against the pressures that eventually culminated in her abortion. Cindy's immobility reflected catastrophic grief and a mutilated spirit, shamed and humiliated by her powerlessness.

Often it is a girl's parents who are pushing for the abortion. In these cases, a young girl will often hear in the parental push for abortion an unspoken message that undermines her own sense of worth. "Is parenting that bad? Would they have chosen to abort me in these circumstances?" These concerns can become quite painful, as in Maureen's case.

> When I got pregnant, my mom came to my side trying to be supportive. But she was rather insistent that I have an abortion because she didn't want me to ruin my life by having a baby.

I know that my mom and dad got married because she was pregnant with my older brother. I was shocked when she wanted me to abort. It was almost like she was telling me that having us had ruined her life and that she wanted to spare me from her fate. It was such a rejection!

At the time of my own crisis I looked to her for advice and counsel. I had the abortion. . . but as I look back on it, the whole situation really screwed me up. I developed the notion that kids would ruin my life. I had to hold onto that thought and live it because it was the only way I could make sense of my abortion. I never did have kids. I blame my mom for giving me that message. Because of her "mistake" she has us. Because of my mistakes, I have no one.

## REJECTING MOTHER

A woman's mental picture of "mother" is determined first of all by her own mother. Both her positive and negative attitudes and her perceptions of her mother will attach meanings to her own sense of herself as a maternal person. In many cases, the choice to abort is subconsciously driven by a need to act out mother-daughter conflicts. Often, it reflects the choice to reject the identity of being a mother, a role that is saturated with the feelings of dislike she harbors toward her own mother.

Sharon, for example, made no bones about her hatred of her mother. She often told herself and others, "I never want to become like my mother. She makes me completely sick." She recalled her mother as an angry, depressed, unhappy woman who frequently complained of imaginary illnesses. During one of their many fights, her mother had chopped through Sharon's bedroom door with an axe to make her go to school.

One of the saddest parts of family abuse is how it repeats itself through cycles. A woman who has had violent conflicts with her own mother may be more likely to turn on her own children. In Sharon's case, rejection of her mother and her own motherhood was acted out through multiple late-term abortions, six months into her pregnancy.

Each time, Sharon experienced overwhelming and sickening grief after the abortion. She admitted she was seeking pity and compassion, someone to understand a pain so great as to drive her to these desperate acts. Instead, her choices, made so late in her pregnancies, were met with disgust and condemnation. The rejection sentenced her to reenact her painful past again.

The psychological dynamics of Sharon's case reinforce the view that abortion can involve several complex levels of attempted conflict resolution. In Sharon's case, there was (1) the continuation of violence passed on through generations, (2) acts of symbolic suicide through which Sharon grieved the loss of her baby as well as of her own "inner child" that had died from rejection and abuse, (3) an attempt to gain control of her fear of becoming like her mother, and (4) an effort to awaken others to her pain by means of arousing their shock and repulsion.

Another client, Bridget, remembered her mother as extremely unhappy and depressed, a chronic complainer. Her mother had often expressed frustration that having children had prevented her from finishing school. She complained that she had never experienced a fulfilling job or made anything of herself because she had to "waste" all her energies on caring for kids. The message ingrained in Bridget and her sisters was that they were responsible for their mother's misery and to blame for all her failures.

Bridget grew up with this concept of children deeply embedded in her view of herself and mothering. Seeing herself as a burden on her mother, Bridget suffered from depression. She constantly doubted her value as a person, and struggled with feelings of grief and guilt over her mother's ambivalence and rejection of her and her sisters. While determined to please her mother, Bridget was also determined not to become as miserable as her mother. When she became pregnant, Bridget immediately assumed that abortion was the only way to avoid being trapped in misery. What she never anticipated was the depression and guilt she would suffer from the abortion.

Motherhood requires a woman to be the caregiver, responsible for the nurture, support, and love of a baby. A woman who experienced poor or absent mothering during childhood may find it difficult to accept a maternal identity when she is stuck with an image of herself as a rejected or abused child who needs nurture and love herself. If she has never experienced being mothered, she wonders, how is she to mother another? If she never felt emotionally bonded to her mother, how is she to bond with her own child? These issues can be quite complex, especially for an adolescent girl who is struggling to find her own identity. For such women, abortion appears to offer a simple solution. In fact, it only creates new questions and reinforces negative feelings.

Melissa's choice to abort was also driven by her feelings of rejection as a child. Unfortunately, the abortion only confirmed her impression that she must really be a horrible little girl.

> All my life my mother and grandmother told me I was a bad girl. My abortion proved they were right. I did not want others to see me that way, so I never told anyone in my life about the abortion. I was raised with a life theme of "What will people think?" or "How would it look?"
>
> When I became pregnant, I knew it would prove to my mother that I was a bad girl. I could not give her that satisfaction. My sister was five years younger. She became pregnant when she was a freshman in college. She ran away and married her boyfriend and kept the baby. At least my sister has her baby. All I have are bad feelings inside.

Pamela's relationship with her mother was permeated with rage, frustration, hostility, guilt, and hatred. Like Melissa, Pamela saw herself as "bad." When she became pregnant, she had frightening daydreams about the baby inside her. She began to project all her negative feelings about the "bad child" she had been upon her own child. In her intrusive fantasies, she imagined her baby as an atrocious monster she had to eliminate. Abortion was a means to eliminate the "bad child" inside her. But as Pamela regretfully learned, in the end abortion simply amplified her negative self-image.

Amanda took great pride in the fact that she was "childless by choice." The slogan gave her a sense of control, and she committed her life to helping other women achieve the same freedom. Amanda worked in an abortion clinic and believed that she truly empowered other women. What she did not realize at the time was that her own conflicted relationship with her mother motivated her ideology, politics, and career.

> I hated my mother. The last thing I ever wanted was to become like her. She was critical and judgmental. She let everybody walk all over her. It took me years to realize that for me to have a baby and become a mother was a way to identify with her. This was something I would not allow myself to do. Finally, at the age of 40, I had my first child. After the birth of my son, my attitude toward my own mother changed . . . and so did my attitude toward abortion.

After her baby was born, Amanda remembered driving to the abortion clinic where she had worked for a baby shower. As her former co-workers congratulated her and gave gifts to celebrate the occasion, Amanda had a sick feeling in her stomach as she wondered, "How can they be celebrating here with me when other babies are being destroyed in the next room?" Amanda found it difficult to reconcile the two events, happening at the same time, separated only by one plaster wall.

Amanda was fortunate enough to move through her fears and enter the next developmental phase of womanhood. The experience gave her broader insight and vision into what had motivated some of her own conflicts and ideology. It also gave her a different perspective on the act of mothering, thereby leading her to a deeper appreciation and understanding of her own mother. Some women never make that transition.

## COMMUNICATION ERRORS

Sadly, many abortions are the tragic result of couples failing to communicate with each other in a meaningful way. An example of such a mistake occurred between Barbara and her fiancé, Jim.

> I went to the doctor to have a pregnancy test. The doctor came in and told me I was pregnant. In the next breath he told me that he could perform an abortion at eight o'clock the next morning. He asked me if I would like to come to the hospital to have it done. I shrugged my shoulders and thought that would be okay.
> I never talked about it with my fiancé. When I called him later that day, I

remember saying, "I'm pregnant, but it's okay, honey. I'm having an abortion in the morning." The problem wasn't really a problem. We just got rid of it. We never had time to question if it even was a problem.

I can't believe I just did it. I never got to think about what abortion even meant. I was happy about being pregnant. It's so weird. My initial response was happiness . . . but in the next moment I decided to end the pregnancy. When I look at my own children now, 17 years later, I feel so much pain about that child I should have had. My kids are everything to me. I love them so much. I can't believe I killed one of them . . . just like that. Just because a doctor suggested it as a reasonable thing to do . . . as the first thing I should do.

We discovered in our counseling sessions, 17 years later, that the emotional trigger for conflict and antagonizing fights was when Barbara did something—*anything*—without asking for Jim's opinion. This trigger was rooted in the pain he experienced over the loss of his first child to an abortion over which he had no say. For years, the couple had become embroiled in bitter battles because they were unable to name the pain and betrayal that lay beneath the surface of their love. Before they came for counseling, Barbara's abortion had surfaced briefly when she began to have "wanted" children. The same doctor who aborted her child delivered her living children. Barbara remembered desperately wanting to change doctors, but was unable to do so because of shame.

When I was pregnant again, I really wanted a doctor who respected life, but I couldn't bear the thought of telling a new baby doctor about having had an abortion, so I stayed with the same one who aborted my first child. I hated him. I always hated him. Every time I went in for a pre-natal checkup I had panic attacks. It makes me angry that I stayed with him.

Barbara continued to bury her grief beneath a passive anger. It took many years before Barbara and Jim had the courage to deal with this tragic loss and express their true feelings about what had happened. Until that point, Barbara and Jim both recreated a sense of conflict and powerlessness over many everyday issues. But finally, they wept together over the loss of their first child. Barbara grieved that she never consulted Jim about the abortion and recognized the destructive impact this had on their relationship.

Barbara and Jim may have been spared the loss of their child, and 17 years of marital conflict, if only Barbara's doctor had not casually suggested abortion as the "obvious" thing to do. Unfortunately, the doctor's cavalier attitude led Barbara to treat abortion as a casual decision. The doctor never suggested, nor did it ever occur to Barbara, that she should take time to reflect on it or discuss it with Jim.

In less committed relationships, the communication channels between couples are likely to be less well developed. In many cases, this is because the couple is still getting to know each other and may still be hesitant to completely reveal their thoughts, feelings, and beliefs. In other cases, the relationship has not matured precisely because the couple has never developed a deeper level of communication. This failure can be due to many causes: poor social and communication skills, the lack of a desire to commit, self-centeredness, emotional problems, unwillingness to commit to the other person, a fear of exposing one's inner self, or any number of other factors.

It is not uncommon for couples who have poor communication skills to remain in relationships for a long period of time. In many cases they are held together by little more than sex and inertia—the hesitancy to leave "a" relationship until they find "the" relationship they truly desire. Such was the case for Andrea.

> My baby's father and I had an on-again, off-again relationship for most of the four years. When I found out I was pregnant, it brought out all the bad aspects of the relationship.
>
> Our inability to communicate effectively led us to fight constantly over what to do about our child. I was not able to express my desire to keep the baby. I did not expect or want to marry him. I knew that we had too many problems, that a marriage would never work. I knew we would both feel trapped and that wouldn't be a positive atmosphere in which to raise a child. But I did feel that we had a strong enough friendship to raise a child together.
>
> Our failure to communicate well, which was always a problem between us, was one of the reasons we got into this situation. We didn't communicate our thoughts about a possible pregnancy before we started sleeping together. We tended to just let our relationship coast along as if we were afraid to upset it by having real communication over the things that mattered.
>
> This changed after the abortion. He couldn't take the day off work to go with me for the abortion, and that really hurt. After I got home, he called to make sure I went through with the procedure. It seemed like that was all he was concerned about. That one call told me I didn't want to have anything more to do with him. He never asked how I was or if I needed anything. I knew then that he wouldn't be in my life any more. That was the end.

For those like Andrea who are ambivalent about commitment and have simply been coasting along in a relationship, pregnancy can actually be an intentional crisis that provides a door of hope for change or commitment, or an impetus to push the relationship beyond its stagnant state. When a woman's needs are not being fully satisfied, pregnancy will force the desired communication about the issues that have not been openly addressed. Many couples may discover in a painful moment of truth that they don't really have any love, just the convenience of sex and companionship.

In one study, researchers interviewed women seeking abortions and found evidence in 35 percent of the cases "suggesting that the women had an underlying conflictual wish to become pregnant."[18] In many cases, an emotional need to be pregnant was exhibited in the women's sporadic contraceptive use, feelings of isolation, depression, and similar factors. The author concluded that pregnancies that lead to abortion often arise from "an underlying unresolved conflict which is being acted out through the pregnancy."

Many women simply expose themselves to pregnancy because of an underlying need for a change in their lives. Some want to break away from parental control. Some want to test their partner's commitment. Some who are lonely or depressed are toying with the idea of changing their lives by building new attachments. Such women are more likely to be ambivalent about the pregnancy and are therefore at higher risk of subsequent ambivalence and regret about their decision to abort.

## "A Gift to My Dead Mother"

Sometimes a prior emotional conflict can be acted out in incredible ways. When Karen became pregnant at the age of nineteen, she enjoyed tender affection from her family and a showering of gifts. Initially, she was ecstatic about being pregnant. She and her boyfriend had been talking about getting married. The pregnancy would simply push things along. Her boyfriend and his family were pro-life. They had shown her models of the developing baby and had all rejoiced at the new, growing life.

Despite the apparent support and the public knowledge of her pregnancy, Karen had an abortion. She lied to her boyfriend, telling him she had experienced a miscarriage. Within days of the abortion, she became suicidal. She could not comprehend why she had done such a thing. She hated herself for lying about a miscarriage but believed her boyfriend would despise her if he ever found out the truth. Afraid of abandonment, she clung desperately to her secret.

As we talked about Karen's life, I learned that her mother had died when Karen was seventeen. At the grave site, she remembered throwing herself on top of the coffin, screaming, "I want my mommy, I want my mommy!" as the crowd looked on in fright. She had lost her best friend. The grief had become unmanageable. Shortly thereafter, Karen was admitted to a psychiatric hospital for suicidal ideation. She was still depressed and processing the traumatic death of her mother when she entered another death event with an abortion.

If pre-abortion screening to identify high-risk patients had been performed, Karen's profile would have set off blaring sirens and flashing red lights. Karen's decision to abort a child she loved was actually a disturbed attempt to resolve a deeper conflict. By separating herself from her own child, Karen was recreating the loss she felt at the way her mother had been separated from her. Even more significantly, ever since her mother's death she had been trying to send a part of herself to be with her dead mother. Since her first attempts at suicide had failed, she sent the next best thing . . . her own baby, whom she loved, and who was an intrinsic part of herself.

When I made this interpretation, Karen told me an interesting story. The nickname her mother had always used for her was *"my little baby angel."* Through her abortion, she had attempted to send a "little baby angel" to be with her mother.

After the abortion, Karen remembered feeling additional grief when she was told by a Planned Parenthood counselor that her aborted baby was only a piece of tissue. This added to Karen's grief, as she imagined her mother sitting in heaven with only a bit of lumpy tissue on her lap. Since the "uterine tissue" wasn't good enough for her mother, Karen reverted to more thoughts of suicide, believing death would reunite her to both her mother and her aborted baby.

## "MEDICALLY INDICATED" ABORTION

Even under the best of circumstances, the state of pregnancy tends to make even an emotionally strong woman feel more vulnerable and dependent. When health problems lead doctors to recommend abortion, the pressure to abort, even against one's conscience, can be immense.

Lee's doctors recommended a "medically indicated ('therapeutic')" abortion because of medications that her doctor feared could cause fetal anomalies. Even with the medical reasons her doctors offered as to why she had "no choice" but to abort, Lee still experienced trauma. It was 13 years before she recovered.

> There I was, middle-aged, receiving the shock of my life when the nurse said, "Congratulations, the pregnancy test is positive." It felt as if someone had thrown a bucket of ice-cold water in my face.
>
> I remember beginning to cry as she ushered me into the doctor's office for privacy. When he came in, he said, "Lee, you do know this just cannot be allowed to happen, don't you? You're on several heart medications, all of which aren't conducive to a fetus. We need to get this fetus aborted as soon as possible."
>
> Everything within me was yelling, "No! No! No!" But they all advised strongly against my having the child. So I allowed them to control the situation . . . and me.
>
> As the thumping of gurney tires pounded in my ears, inside my head my voice was screaming, "Please do not do this!" I'd been lightly sedated to keep me calm before the procedure was started. The doctors and nurses tried to console me, saying this was "therapeutic" because of my heart disease and quadruple bypass surgery only months before. "It truly was the only way," they told me.
>
> But how did they know for sure, I wondered. Who did they think they were—God? "Oh, forgive me," I cried, reaching up from the blanket to wipe my tears. "There, there, it's going to be all right," one of the nurses whispered, as she

smiled and handed me a tissue.

My mind shrieked, "How dare you utter those words! Do any of you realize we are committing murder? This child was conceived in love between my husband and me, and even though my health isn't the greatest, I believe God wouldn't have allowed it to happen, if He didn't know best."

Glaring lights in the ceiling were blocked out as the anesthesiologist bent over me saying, "Okay, Lee, we're going to have you sleep now, and when you wake up, this will all be over!" Little did he realize how untrue those words were.

This scene is as fresh as if it just happened, yet it was thirteen years ago and I had a second marriage later. For almost all those thirteen years, I have lived with intense guilt. My life has gone on, but I must say, I wasn't really living, just existing—going through the motions.

I tearfully shared the news of my "therapeutic" abortion with my immediate family. They attempted to console me, saying, "Lee, you really didn't have any choice," but somehow that didn't give me the peace or validation I so desperately needed. It was MURDER, plain, pure, and simple, and I would have to answer for it eventually before my Creator. For many years fear and guilt ravaged my soul and spirit. I continued to shove it further down. Severe health problems plagued me during this time, convincing me of the reality that "guilt and anger" were detrimental to my health.

Thankfully, I felt a release from the guilt and shame I had carried for years because of a religious conversion experience.

I've been asked whether or not I would do it again. My answer is emphatically no! I suffered years of excruciating grief because I weakened and allowed others to control my choices and my life. I allowed them to be both judge and jury, deciding the fate of my unborn daughter. All the women who have undergone this tragedy have shed enough tears to fill a river.

Research has shown that nearly 80 percent of women who have abortions because of suspected fetal malformations are very likely to suffer severe grief reactions.[19] In another study of 13 families who had abortions due to suspected genetic defects, 92 percent of the women and 82 percent of the men suffered from subsequent depression.[20] It was also learned that in many cases the abortion threatened marital stability. Four of the 13 couples subsequently separated.

Abortions for indications of fetal anomaly or because of the woman's physical health problems are likely to involve increased psychological risks for women and their families, including the siblings of the aborted child.[21] Part of the increased risk of trauma for women is related to an increased sense of helplessness they feel in these circumstances. Rather than feeling that abortion is *their* choice, they are likely to feel they have *no* choice. Furthermore, abortions for fetal anomaly are more likely to occur in the second or third trimester, after women have already felt their babies move. A later-term abortion also means that women have had more time to bond with their children.

Another reason for greater emotional strain following a "therapeutic" abortion is that in most such cases the couple is aborting a *wanted* pregnancy. The initial decision to carry the child to term has been reversed solely because of a diagnosis of potential fetal handicaps. The twists and turns that such news can produce in the hearts and minds of parents cannot easily be resolved. The news that a child is not perfectly healthy is shocking. It involves a loss, the loss of higher hopes and expectations, and this loss requires time for grief. Abortion does not resolve this grief. Instead, it simply adds the loss of a life to the loss of high hopes.

The label "therapeutic abortion" is actually a misnomer, a kindly intended disguise of the truth. Abortion in such cases does not cure the unborn child. Nor does it cure a woman of any preexisting illness. Instead, "therapeutic abortions" merely trade the burdens of raising a handicapped child (or suffering through a difficult pregnancy) for the burden of impacted grief and post-abortion trauma.

Margaret's abortion, for example, was undertaken after an amniocentesis test revealed a possible birth defect. When she heard the results of the prenatal screening, Margaret felt frightened and wondered how she would ever cope with the special needs of a disabled child. Although she felt overwhelmed and anxious, initially she had no intention of aborting. She already had one child, and could not imagine aborting a baby that was growing within her. However, her husband Rick, a successful business investor, took the test results as a clear sign to abort. When Margaret showed reservations, Rick replied in an impatient tone, "Why do you think you had the test done? You can't handle a situation like this!"

Margaret would hold her hand over her protruding belly and rock back and forth as she rubbed the baby. She wondered if abortion was something she could do. After all, she had no guarantee that the child definitely had any defects. Margaret had heard many stories about women who were told their babies would be born without brains or severely retarded, and yet the women had delivered perfectly normal and beautiful children. On the other hand, what if the doctors were right? What if she was not capable of handling the day-to-day realities of living with a child who had special needs? (Ironically, Margaret had a master's degree in special education and had spent 14 years working with handicapped and mentally retarded children.) Sad, but feeling abortion was her only choice, Margaret acceded to her husband's wishes and had the abortion.

Afterward, Margaret avoided asking the doctors her most burning question: "Was anything wrong with the baby?" She could never have handled it if their answer was "No."

Her initial reaction after the abortion was one of relief. It was finished. There was no more need to struggle with the decision. Within days, however, her relief crumbled and she was relentlessly plagued with regrets. Several of her friends were pregnant at the same time. As their rounding bellies took shape and began to protrude, Margaret ached for her lost pregnancy.

As the due date of her aborted pregnancy approached, she entered a state of severe clinical depression. During this time she did some "crazy" things. She wrote numerous checks to charities, gave her best friend a loan of $10,000 to renovate a dilapidated house, and transferred money from her own account into her sister's account. Her outraged husband considered Margaret's actions completely insane and had her committed to a mental hospital. The hospitalization occurred in the week of her due date.

Doctors diagnosed Margaret with manic depressive disorder. Themes of maternal abandonment permeated her counseling sessions. The psychiatrist was convinced that Margaret's mother must have had similar traits and symptoms. His treatment regimen focused on anti-depressants, lithium, and tranquilizers. Never once did he explore Margaret's abortion as a contributing factor to her depressive illness.

At the time of her abortion, Margaret's husband had promised her they would try again to have another baby. But after her spending spree and hospitalization, he punished her with anger and the stigma of "mental illness." He insisted they would never have another child because she was "nuts."

An analysis of Margaret's bizarre behavior reveals some interesting metaphors. Margaret's husband had pressed her to give up the most important thing in her life—her own child—and afterwards she felt compelled to give away something that meant so much to her husband, their money. Her insecurities were also further aggravated by the fact that her husband had wanted the abortion because of the possibility of a birth defect. Now that she was "defective," Margaret figured he would want to get rid of her, too.

Post-abortion recovery can be especially difficult for couples who have had "therapeutic" abortions because their abortion decisions are seldom entirely their own. In these cases, the choice to abort was strongly encouraged and sanctioned by physicians and other authority figures. The opinions of all these experts that they "did the right thing" may make the couple's subsequent grief appear to be wrongheaded.

In a culture such as ours, where physical and mental abilities are idealized, the pursuit of perfection results in a corresponding decrease in tolerance for the physically and mentally disabled. This cultural phenomena is systematically reinforced through genetic screening programs, which directly or indirectly communicate to young couples the idea that handicapped children (1) are an unmanageable burden for most families, and (2) should not be "forced" to live a life of "suffering" as "inferior" persons because of their possible handicaps.

As discussed earlier, the study of crisis behavior suggests that people faced with a crisis are more likely to be influenced by persons seen as authority figures and to adopt the attitudes of these authority figures. In the case of prenatal genetics counseling, a negative prognosis creates feelings of crisis in a setting where the authority figure is already there to lead and guide. The eugenic and elitist philosophy that underlies genetic screening ("search and destroy") programs is seldom closely examined. One recent evaluation of genetic counseling concluded that many couples were given "grossly inadequate" or "frankly misleading" information that exaggerated the effects of genetic disorders.[22] Eugenic-minded healthcare workers often lead young couples one step at a time into accepting their expert guidance. Each little yes to each diagnostic test inches couples closer to accepting the final "solution."

Since all pregnancies involve change in women's lives, and change is associated with uncertainty, fear, and dependence on experts, it is remarkably easy to lead pregnant couples to accept all the rational arguments for aborting a child who, just hours before, was a welcome addition to their families. Unfortunately, their hearts rarely adjust to abortion as easily as their heads. A good example of this is illustrated by Lucinda, who had aborted a child due to a diagnosis of Down's Syndrome.

Lucinda was suffering all the classic signs and symptoms of post-abortion trauma. But because her abortion had been "medically indicated," she refused to acknowledge that she felt loss concerning her abortion. It was only after Lucinda's unreasonable and angry refusal to attend her sister's baby shower that her family members finally convinced her to attend a Rachel's Vineyard retreat to confront her pregnancy loss.

As the weekend retreat progressed, Lucinda made no progress. Instead, she only became more and more angry and defensive. She was resistant to many of the exercises and became disgusted with the grief expressed by the other women. They had freely chosen to abort their babies, she insisted, while she would never have aborted a "normal" child.

Lucinda was insensitive and judgmental in her remarks. Her attitude gave the impression that she was looking down on the other women for their abortion decisions while simultaneously defending the rightness of her own abortion. Although each person on the retreat was going out of her way to tolerate her behavior and accept Lucinda where she was at, Lucinda was projecting her own feelings of guilt and shame onto those around her and was convinced that the other women were in turn judging and condemning her.

By the final day, all the women and men had made tremendous strides in confronting and purging their grief, loss, anger, and shame. As the retreat drew to a close, they had begun to share their joy and sense of accomplishment. All but Lucinda, who became increasingly enraged because everyone knew that she still had not dealt with her loss. This only added to her sense of being different and judged by the others. Suddenly, in a tearful outburst, Lucinda lambasted the group:

> I am so annoyed and irritated by all of you! You think everything is so wonderful and peachy! Can't you just accept me the way that I am? Don't you realize the world is not perfect?

In these few angry words, Lucinda's unconscious revealed the barrier she could not face. After allowing her emotions to abate with a few minutes of calming conversation, I turned to Lucinda and told her how well she had articulated the conflict she must have been struggling with throughout the entire weekend. Perhaps the conflict and pain she was experiencing, I suggested, were an echo of what she was afraid her own child was asking of her, "Can't you just accept me the way that I am? Don't you realize the world is not perfect?"

My repetition of her words instantly gripped her. The crux of her secret self-blame had been exposed. Her denial was broken. Her icy defenses collapsed. Her grief flowed out in an intense torrent of tears.

Lucinda had been projecting all the conflicts she was having with her own grief onto the group. Her projections enabled her to avoid her own perfectionism, the pain of having rejected her imperfect child, and the bitter sadness, guilt, and loss that followed, but could not be confronted. To distract herself from these feelings, she had accused those around her of the very things over which she was feeling guilt. Moreover, the same defenses she used to deny her own grief had also made her incapable of being sympathetic toward the other parents who were also suffering the loss of their children. But by a fortunate turn of phrase, Lucinda had revealed both the lock that barred her way to healing, and the key. Once these were revealed, she was finally able to confront her grief and complete the weekend having made great progress in finding self-forgiveness and peace.

## THE FAILED PROMISE

Abortion is chosen for many reasons. Only a minority of women choose abortion simply because they do not want to have a baby. Most abort out of a fear that carrying their unplanned pregnancy to term will deprive them of a wanted relationship, the approval of others, their education, a career, or some other desired goal.

While women often hope that having an abortion will help them to achieve these other goals, there is no research that shows that it generally does. Clearly, abortion does not make poor women wealthy. Nor does it generally improve relationships; indeed, the evidence indicates that abortion is more likely to harm relationships. Nor does abortion ensure one's social standing or a sense of approval from one's parents or peers. Finally, there are no studies showing that aborting women achieve higher educational levels or better careers than women who carry unintended pregnancies to term. Instead, studies comparing aborting women to women who carry unplanned pregnancies to term reveal that aborting women are more likely to have higher levels of subsequent depression, anxiety, and alcohol abuse.[23]

Even if abortion helps women to achieve some desired goal, many women discover that the goal they have achieved has been drained of meaning. This is how Katrina described her experience:

> I had my abortion because we were poor. I was raised poor and I didn't want my kids to grow up in poverty. It's awful because now we have a great income and plenty of money. I can't enjoy any of it. Money was the reason I had the abortion. . . . Now I have money and I hate it. Nothing I buy makes me happy and I miss the child who should be with me now.

Similarly, Millie's goal was simply to complete her education. Thoughts of her missing child, however, left her unable to enjoy the fruit of her accomplishments.

> I had my abortion because I wanted to finish college. The day of my graduation I felt absolutely no joy or accomplishment. I am always thinking about what my child would have been like. He or she would have been five years old now. I wonder what my life would have been like. I wonder if I would have met someone nice and gotten married. When I see mothers with young children I feel so sad. Sometimes, I feel angry.

Janice simply wanted her life to unfold in a controlled pattern. She wanted the security and peace of mind that would come from knowing she was prepared to be the best mother she could be.

> I know I made the decision for a reason, and I know that my life will continue to be "convenient" for the next few years as I prepare for motherhood properly. I also know that a baby is too important a thing to happen by accident.
>
> But all this knowledge and understanding and reasoning does nothing to heal the raw wound of death that I have chosen to inflict upon myself. And that is the worst part of all of this: the fact that I chose to kill my own child. How do you ever forgive yourself for something like that? What kind of mother could I be if I could do something like that to a life that I helped create?
>
> All the normal fears run through my mind constantly: What if I never get a second chance? What if I have a baby and there is something wrong with it? What if I never feel life again?
>
> Will I ever forget the devastation on the faces of the women who went through abortions on the same day that I did? Their voices and their eyes and their stories live with me like ghosts. The very word "pregnancy" fills me with intense pain, and I don't know how to escape this jail of madness I am locked in. I am just dead, dead, dead inside!

While Janice had hoped to gain more control over her life through her abortion, Roxanne was tired of control. Roxanne wanted simply to be free to enjoy her youth.

> I was not ready for parenthood. I felt like I was still under the control of my parents. I wanted to experience freedom before I tied myself down with a baby. I never anticipated the grief and misery I felt after my abortion. I had my freedom, but I hated it. There was nothing I could enjoy. I lost interest in everything and became a bit of a recluse. I thought a baby would stop me from having fun . . . but all I could do was think about the abortion. Believe me, after the abortion there wasn't any fun.

Susie simply wanted to please her boyfriend and hang onto their wonderful love life. Like so many women before her, she belatedly learned that her abortion ended up destroying the relationship she had hoped to save.

> I assumed that if I did what he wanted, he would love me. Sex overpowered the rational observations I had about my partner. It was the "all in all" of our relationship. The abortion ruined our sex. When that died, there wasn't anything left.

For many women, the choice to abort seems clear and easy. They know what they want, and when they want it, and at least at that time in their lives, a baby is not at the top of their list. But abortion doesn't just turn back the clock. It does not undo what has been done. Once a woman becomes pregnant, something happens deep inside her that no one can touch or fully explain. Because of this emotional, maternal, spiritual change, abortion cuts away not only a human fetus, but also a part of her new, changed, emerging self.

For Brittany, abortion appeared to offer a safe harbor, a means to buy time, regroup, rest, and prepare to launch the next phase of her life. She never suspected that abortion could be a trap.

> I felt like a fly caught in sticky paper. Eventually I pulled off but I left parts of myself behind, like an insect leaving its wings stuck in the glue. Since the abortion I have felt crippled, like a part of myself had to be disconnected to gain freedom from my problem.

Perhaps abortion helps some women to achieve their dreams. But clearly such women have no need to come to me for counseling. So it should be no surprise that in my experience, Brittany's experience seems typical. Abortion is like a well designed lure. Even when abortion appears to be the right choice, only after the lure has been swallowed does the fish discover that it was the wrong choice.

The risks and costs of having an abortion can never be fully anticipated. Even after the fact, it is impossible to measure all the effects it has had on women, their partners, and their families.

In many cases, abortion is clearly devastating women's lives. Is it also saving women's lives? This is highly doubtful. But even if it *seems* to offer more benefit than harm to some women, is it worth the harm it inflicts on other women? Is it worth the harm inflicted on these women's relationships, families and other children who have been deprived of stable mothers?

When abortion is emotionally crippling women (whether just a few, many, or most), how can we call unrestricted abortion a victory for women's rights? When unwanted abortions are so frequently pushed on women by their boyfriends, husbands, parents, or doctors, how can we call this a matter of reproductive rights? When abortion is embraced without a full understanding of its general failure to fulfill the promises made on its behalf, how can we call unregulated access to abortion a matter of free choice?

According to Marlene:

> I never thought of abortion as killing till I got older . . . and wiser . . . and realized the foolishness of my choices. Not just for myself, but for my daughter and how she has been deprived of the joy of a sister or brother.
>
> People always told me there's nothing like family when things get rough. I watch my grandmother, 87 years old. She lives with her sister. The two of them help each other out and give each other company since their husbands are dead. I aborted two pregnancies and I always regret it. My daughter could have had a sister or a brother, but never will because of what I've done. It's not just my own losses I grieve now, but the loss this was to my family.
>
> When I first started having these thoughts, I kept trying to put them out of my mind. I told myself that I was being ridiculous, even crazy. Facing the truth is the hardest thing I have ever done—but it has been worth it. Now I finally understand my anger and pain.
>
> Although it has been difficult to continue talking about this experience, even with other women who have been to the same place I am currently in, I think it is an important part of the healing process. The wounds must be understood if the scars are going to teach us anything.

## Chapter Eighteen

# The Labor of Grief and Birth of Freedom

L ike so many other women and men, Michelle had come to believe that she could never be free from the emotional pain of her abortion. At best, she thought, she might be able to cope with it, from day to day. But to truly be free of its burden? That, she thought, was impossible.

After two abortions I felt very alone, depressed and confused. I never knew what was wrong with me. I would cry and cry, I was out of control, and when anyone would ask me, "What's wrong?" I honestly answered, "I don't know." I felt as if I were going insane. Who cries all the time and hurts themselves without knowing why? I hated myself. Years of counseling did not help, antidepressants did not help, nothing seemed to help. It was all kept pretty much a secret. Only a select few knew of my extreme depression, hurting myself, and of my abortions.

Finally, after years of this torture, I told my dad everything. I told him of the abortions, sleeping around, drugs I had been doing to get me through, and of the abuse inflicted on me by myself and the others. He shocked me by being there for me. He understood why I did what I did. He sat with me as I told my mother and she also shocked me when, instead of being mad at me, she hugged me and cried and said that she wished she could have been there for me. These are reactions I never expected.

But the depression and self-abuse did not stop. My father, who is a counselor himself, tried everything he could to figure out what was wrong with me. He sent me to more counseling, which did not seem to help. My father wanted more than anything to figure out how to help me. Finally, at a seminar he attended, he met a woman named Theresa Burke. She was teaching about abortion trauma and talking about other people who suffered with many of the same symptoms I had, and they also could not figure out what was wrong with them.

My father learned that they would be holding a Rachel's Vineyard retreat for people who had abortions. The retreat would be a way of letting go of guilt and maybe feeling better. When my father told me about the retreat, I have to admit, I just thought, 'what the hell, I'll try it,' but that it would not change anything, just as nothing else had. I felt this way straight up to when I arrived for the weekend retreat. It was nice, but I still felt it was not going to change my depression.

I cannot describe what happened over the course of that one weekend. Through the exercises and sharing we did, I was drawn gently into God's love and forgiveness. That night, I knew God existed and that I am not a terrible person, and that I have already been forgiven by God and my children. It was overwhelming. Never had anything like this happened before in my life. I cannot begin to describe on paper the wonderful sense of peace and love I felt that night. Nothing like that has ever happened to me before.

The profound healing that Michelle experienced was new to her, but not to me. I have been privileged to witness literally thousands of such transforming moments, when the labor of grief ends in the birth of a new, restored woman. It is as though an emotional key turns, simultaneously releasing all the muck and grime and weight of past abortions while opening a door to a fresh new future. These are truly miraculous moments. One can actually feel God touching souls to make them whole. Tears of sorrow are mixed with tears of joy as women and men experience their first taste of freedom after years of cruel bondage.

No post-abortion counselor who has witnessed the journey through "forbidden grief" into the peace and acceptance of healing can doubt the existence of a God who truly cares, truly forgives, and truly heals. One simply cannot help but feel humbled and privileged to be a witness to such restoration and healing.

But such healing can only happen when the isolation and secrecy are dismantled, and one's story is revealed to others who do not seek to judge or condemn. Only then is it finally possible, with the support of a small community of others who compassionately affirm the loss and respect the grief, to grieve one's losses to their fullness. The importance of social support to the grief process reflects an important aspect of our human nature: Though we are individuals, we are inescapably social beings. The lack of social support will degrade or destroy our well-being. Conversely, the experience of social support, in even a single relationship, can strengthen our well-being.

For most of us, it is only when we have the support of others who will not judge or condemn us that we feel safe from social rejection. This support makes it easier for us to confront and explore the deepest part of our souls. With it, one learns how to accept forgiveness from God and one's aborted child. With it, one learns how to extend forgiveness to oneself and others. And with it, one discovers how the most difficult, soul-breaking experiences imaginable can be used as the foundation for building a richer, deeper, and more meaningful existence.

My motivation in writing this book (over the course of several years) has been to encourage two sets of people—(1) women and men troubled by past abortions, and (2) counselors and others in a position to help them—to learn more about post-abortion problems and to set their feet on the path toward healing. Obviously, however, this book is not a "how to" manual for obtaining healing after an abortion. That's a subject that could fill another book. Instead, the goal of this book is to lift the veil from the forbidden grief of abortion, which is so misunderstood, or ignored, in our culture. Before our society will ever expend much effort in helping people heal from their past abortions, it must first recognize that healing is even needed. If you have read this far, you are no doubt convinced of that.

On the other hand, while this book is not intended as a "how-to" guide to healing, I would like to outline at least some fundamental issues. If you have had an abortion, however, I want to emphasize that what I'm presenting here is not enough to help you complete your journey. Just as you would not contemplate going on a hike through the Amazon jungle with a map torn out of an encyclopedia, neither should you consider this or any book as a sufficient map for finding healing. Sticking with the Amazon tour analogy, I discourage you from trying to blaze your own way even with a very detailed map. Instead, it would be much wiser to find an experienced jungle guide to accompany you on the trip. In the same way, while books and articles on post-abortion healing will be very helpful to you on your healing journey, they can never be adequate substitutes for an experienced counselor who knows where all the stumbling blocks lie—and there are plenty of them, many of which you won't see because you are simply too close to them.

Furthermore, you should remember that post-abortion healing is a specialty unto itself. The average psychiatrist, psychologist, social worker, or counselor of any other academic stripe who does not understand post-abortion issues can often inflict more harm than good on the unsuspecting woman. Many may believe they have enough insight to help, but unless they have had additional training, they often don't. Certainly, if your thoughts and feelings become so overwhelming that you feel you can no longer cope, seek professional assistance immediately. But generally, I encourage you to take the time to find one of the growing number of professional therapists and experienced lay counselors who have received special training in post-abortion healing. A list of recovery resources is included at the end of this book.

## MAKE A COMMITMENT TO RESIST YOUR FEARS

In chapter six, I discussed the approach-avoidance conflict, which is at the heart of the struggle to find healing. On one hand, you desire to be completely free of your past abortion. On the other hand, you fear the tears, the grief, the opening up of old wounds. Perhaps, like some women, you even fear being healed because you "don't deserve to be happy." This fear of being healed resembles the ironic condition of prisoners who become so accustomed to their prison cells that they begin to fear freedom.

Fear is your greatest enemy. Perhaps you are afraid of losing control, going crazy, or opening up a wound that is so excruciating it can never be healed. Remember, however, that your fears are just an expression of unresolved emotions arising from your trauma. Fear is normal. But if you keep your eyes fixed on your goal, you will do fine, just as Hanna did:

> I was terrified to take that first step forward and participate in Rachel's Vineyard. It seemed safer to remain hiding in the darkness, keeping the pain locked up deep inside rather than to risk exposing my shame to another soul. Now I'm grateful to have experienced God's healing and forgiveness with other women in an atmosphere of complete acceptance and trust. Rachel's Vineyard has been a blessing to me.

You need to make a thoughtful, determined commitment to go through the healing process and finally put this part of your life to rest. Keep reminding yourself that hundreds of thousands of women and men have gone before you. They are on your side, encouraging you, and promising you that your efforts will be well rewarded. According to Deanna:

> I was scared to death to attend the Rachel's Vineyard retreat. I was so leery about it that I made my friend drop me off and take my car so that I wouldn't be able to leave if I wanted to. What I experienced that weekend is hard to put into words. I went through so many different feelings in three short days but I did not go through anything alone. There was always someone there with a hug or the words I needed to hear. This experience took a great weight off of me and opened the door to forgiving myself. This allowed a space in my heart for hope to grow.

Many people are afraid to grieve because they have never fully understood the grief process. In fact, grieving is a multifaceted process that we must learn how to do.[1] With the help of others, you, too, can learn how to work through your grief.

Healing involves naming, claiming, and taming an unspeakable wound so that you can move out of the silence and beyond the secret. To grieve means to open up and release the toxic feelings and emotions that are robbing your life of joy and peace. Recovery can't begin until you peel away festering layers of guilt and anger. This will expose the underlying wound of loss, which can then be treated through the grief process. Will there still be a scar? Yes. But the infection will be gone. You can and will be whole again.

There is no alternative. Healing is never found by hiding from the truth. Healing is discovered by meeting the truth with an honest and humble courage. Beyond acknowledging the death of your child, it is also necessary to understand the depth and breadth of what has happened. This includes recognizing the host of situational and personal factors that fed your desperation. Confronting the truth means facing and better understanding yourself, not for the purpose of condemning yourself, but for the purpose of learning to become the person you want to be.

Grieving normally involves a social context, a connection to other people. This is why we hold funerals as a means of helping each other through the grief process. Grieving an abortion loss is also best accomplished with the support of others. If you feel isolated, your fears may be exacerbated, along with feelings of shame, guilt, and depression. The thought of breaking out from your seclusion may create intense feelings of anxiety. As Julie recalled:

> I thought my abortion was something "put away" in my memory bank until my husband and I sought marriage counseling (after 22 years together!). Suddenly the abortion was coming up as an issue. I am finding this to be very tough, and part of me doesn't want to continue as I get physically ill from it all. Part of me doesn't want to think that my abortion can really have something to do with my life "now," but then another part of me says that I have never been "me" since the abortion. It's because of this that I find myself "fighting" myself inside—one part holds me back so much, the other part wants to be "free" again. Yet I am simply terrified to allow myself to "go there."

Many women report being petrified by the prospect that others will learn about their painful secret. The anxiety attached to revealing hidden emotions about an abortion can be overwhelming and may even include physical symptoms such as nausea, dizziness, and shortness of breath. Even when one knows that there is healing on the other side of counseling, the struggle against feelings of shame can be difficult, as Helen explained:

> I kept thinking up excuses as to why this wasn't the best time for me to go through the weekend retreat. But finally, I had to face that there would never be a better time than now, because I was so tired of carrying the heavy burden of depression, guilt, and anger. I was vacillating between wanting to deal with my feelings, and incredible panic. When I approached the retreat center, I was so anxious! I had a deep fear of being judged and condemned.

This fear of judgment may be especially intense if you have encountered judgmental attitudes in the past, or if those who already know about your abortion have shown a lack of appreciation for the intensity of your grief. These past experiences of being judged or dismissed may make it harder for you to seek support again. When you have been "burned" in the past, it's natural to fear getting burned again. Susan offers a description of her struggle:

> I "knew" right when I was on the table that abortion was wrong—I felt it inside, yet went ahead with it anyway. I got sick afterwards and ended up in the emergency room for a D&C. It was then that my parents were notified. Nothing was said by them except to later use this "weapon" against me. No one asked me how I was or how I felt. So it's been extremely difficult to discuss. I am afraid of being condemned by others or having my past used against me.

Fear of condemnation or rejection is the opposite of feeling accepted and loved. To battle these fears, remind yourself constantly that the people involved in post-abortion ministries already understand your pain and your fears. Many have been through the same experiences you have. They are here to help you, not condemn you. The fact that so many are volunteers—or poorly paid staff members—is evidence that they are motivated by concern and love for you. You will never find a better audience with whom you can share your thoughts, your fears, your hopes.

Many of the fears you may have about sharing your feelings "out in the world" are well-grounded. But in the safe environment of a post-abortion ministry, the same fears don't apply. They are only a hindrance. Joanna describes her experience on the first night of a Rachel's Vineyard retreat:

> I was so frightened walking up to the front door, but the warm greetings and friendliness of others in our group made me feel welcome and lowered my anxiety. I was terrified of more rejection in my life. There was no rejection—only love, support, and encouragement. By the end of the retreat, I felt relief and hope! Release from the terrible feelings of unworthiness and hopelessness. It was incredible to see that so many others felt the same way and gathered their courage to come on the retreat.

We have all heard the isolating rhetoric: "Abortion is a personal and private decision." But the fundamental fact is that we are human beings—social creatures who need and rely on our connections to others. Abortion severs the connection between a mother and her child, but it doesn't necessarily stop there. Abortion can break relationships between lovers, spouses, and family members. It encourages isolation and secrecy. It can even create a disconnection from self.

The healing process, then, must build connections. One of the best ways to do this is through group counseling sessions with other post-abortive women or men in a supportive framework, with the assistance of knowledgeable professionals and lay counselors. In this safe, understanding environment, you will not only experience how others connect to you, but you will be able to connect with and help other women with your empathy and words of encouragement.

## GIVE YOURSELF PERMISSION TO GRIEVE

> Someone told me I should grieve to get over this loss, but I feel guilty when I do. How can I grieve for something that I ended? How can I grieve for someone I never even knew? What right do I have to grieve for someone I didn't want? When I chose to have the abortion, didn't I give up the right to grieve?

Jillian's self-doubts are common. Her feelings of guilt were blocking her expression of grief. Since the abortion was something she freely chose, she reasoned, she didn't deserve the luxury of tears. Tears bring relief. But she wasn't a mother who lost her child to an auto accident. She aborted her child. What right did she have to cry for her lost child in the same way as women whose children are taken from them? What right did she have to seek the relief of tears?

For many women and men like Jillian, guilt immediately rears its ugly head whenever they begin to think about their loss. But guilt is precisely the feeling the subconscious most wants to avoid. So guilt drives them away from examining the multitude of feelings hidden beneath that guilt.

If you have been trying to cut yourself off from feelings of loss, anger, or sadness, it is likely that you are obstructing your grief. By justifying, rationalizing, and making excuses that defend and protect your abortion decision, you may be sidestepping a very real grief that will haunt you until it is recognized.

In order for you to work through your grief, you have to allow yourself to experience it as an acceptable emotion. You will not be able to grieve if you keep telling yourself that you have to be "strong," or that you "just won't think about it," or that you "have nothing to feel bad about." All these excuses are forms of denial by which women and men seek to hide their sense of loss. But abortion invariably involves a loss.

Abortion is a death experience. Whether you want to call it "losing a pregnancy," losing a "potential person," or the death of your baby, it is still a loss. This loss extends to relationships, maternal attachments, and a sense of lost innocence. It also involves the loss of all the "could have been" scenarios which may invade your reasoning. The loss may assume even deeper levels of grief as the future becomes the present, and some of the reasons the loss was endured in the first place (the hope of saving a relationship or career, for example) are now seen to be false hopes.

It is difficult or impossible to grieve a death without recognizing the spiritual aspects of the human heart. All faith perspectives utilize a spiritual foundation when dealing with issues of death. Our rituals, rites, and ceremonial customs play an important role in providing closure, respect, and dignity for both the one who has died and those who mourn the death.

Giving permission to grieve means facing the painful reality of what was lost and how it was lost. Yet denial usually takes time to eliminate and often breaks down into stages. The first stage is *recognition;* this entails admitting the problem. The second phase of breaking denial is *acceptance.* During this phase the problem is addressed, but often with conditions and a continued reluctance to fully face the true nature and seriousness of the problem. In the final phase of working through denial there must be a *surrender.* Here, there is a complete resignation to the reality of the situation and a willingness to address its true nature and meaning. Once this phase is reached, the work of feeling one's grief and letting it go can begin.

## BE PERSISTENT TO THE END

A common saying about grief work is that "the only way out—is through." Going through your grief means accepting it for what it is and being willing to experience it fully. In that process, do not be surprised if you discover feelings you did not expect to have, or which surface in the form of fantasies. Regardless, if you give yourself permission to feel whatever is there, you can break through to the other side.

Initially, your grief work may feel unbearable. You must make a commitment to yourself and your loved ones to work at it for as long as the process takes. Don't expect to resolve everything in just a few short days or weeks. Although taking breaks from the work of grief can be helpful, you must continually go back until all your feelings have been dealt with. Avoid the temptation to run away because the work is difficult. Also, make a commitment to avoid numbing yourself with alcohol or drugs. You will need all your resources and faculties to carry out the important work of grief.

In addition, since abortion in many cases can be a symptom of deeper losses and pain, to fully grieve you must be prepared to accept and examine other feelings, such as rejection, ambivalence, abuse, abandonment, desperation, and all the other conscious and unconscious fears and circumstances that may have made you vulnerable to abortion. Feelings of loss and grief can be intensified, especially if you have experienced rejection as a child yourself. In this and many other cases, such as in experiences of rape, sexual abuse, or abandonment, your abortion may have become a storage place for other grief issues that you have not yet addressed.

The support of others is especially important if your abortion is connected to other grief issues. It is not always possible, or even desirable, to limit the grief issues that you need to address. Dealing with an unresolved grief in one area is likely to trigger other areas where painful memories or feelings have been tucked away. Again, this is not a journey to make alone. One should be accompanied by those experienced in helping women and men after abortion. But remember that while the grief process is never easy, even with the help of others, it is always freeing.

## RECOGNIZE THAT YOUR GRIEF IS UNIQUE

Despite the fact that you may share many symptoms with others who have suffered from abortion, your grief is distinct to you alone. Some women struggle for years to overcome their heartache. Others may appear to have an instantaneous cure. Still others have strong religious convictions that may help them move more graciously through the pain of their loss.

*Every person is different!*

Do not make the mistake of comparing yourself with someone else. Your needs will vary, as will the range of intensity of your emotions. Likewise, your history and previous experiences with grief will shape the way you go though this process. Do not allow the judgments of others to influence the way you feel. The extent of your grief and what you need to do about it can only be understood in the context of what it means to you.

There is no single, correct way to grieve. There are many different ways to reach the same destination. You need to choose the path. You must find the path that is best for you, with the one proviso that you must be constantly alert to any tricks of your subconscious to lead you off the path and back into denial. This is why an experienced guide is helpful. And if you don't feel you are making progress with your first guide, don't be afraid to find another.

## BE REALISTIC IN YOUR EXPECTATIONS

Grief takes time. There are no easy, quick cures for post-abortion trauma. I say this even though I frequently see what others might consider to be instantaneous breakthroughs. But these breakthroughs resulting in a complete release of tension are not truly instantaneous. Before they occurred, there was always a lot of hard work done by the woman (alone, or in counseling) in confronting her loss and recognizing its effects on her life.

You may experience breakthroughs, followed by periods of steady progress or periods of no progress at all, and then discover you have yet another new hill to climb. Sometimes, after you have begun to feel you are making progress, you may suddenly feel like you're going backwards. This, too, is normal, especially if your grief work exposes you to other losses and feelings.

Grieving any major loss will always cause old issues, unfinished business, and unresolved conflicts to resurface. The experience of loss can stir up conflicts related to the past—parent-child attachments, dependency, feelings of inadequacy, unwantedness, insecurity, and a lack of control.[2]

When these losses are coupled with past trauma, and traumas you face in the future, you may feel overwhelmed for a time by this release of your toxic emotions. You might also feel as if you are carrying your grief to extremes. Eventually, however, when you have given yourself permission to pass through these feelings, you will no longer feel overwhelmed. When grief has been exhausted, you will feel tired and depleted, but the inner tension will be gone. You will begin to feel relief. In addition, the energy you have been using to push away these emotions will be accessible to you, freed up for more meaningful uses.

Be gentle with yourself. Focus not on the distant future, but on taking it one day at a time. Soon you will begin to see a better future opening up than you previously imagined.

Eventually, you can expect to achieve a certain level of healing and peace over what has happened. But do not be surprised if some later event triggers additional feelings of grief that you thought you had already conquered. This is very normal. In many cases, this later event has simply struck an unrecognized connector, which has lain buried in your subconscious like an abandoned land mine. If this happens to you, take time again to honor those feelings and understand the connection that aroused them. Set some time aside to work them through and defuse that connection.

It is unrealistic to think you will ever completely forget your aborted child. However, you can move beyond the intense feelings of loss, guilt, and grief that you may be experiencing now. Fr. Michael Mannion, a Catholic priest who has written extensively about abortion and healing, states: "When a mother is giving birth to a child, the mother is the child's physical lifeline into the world. When an abortion has occurred, the child can become the mother's spiritual lifeline to God." This faith can be the spiritual element that allows us to make sense out of misery and suffering—and give us hope. Faith gives us an object to transcend our losses. You can learn to find meaning in what has happened and look forward to being reunited with your child in Heaven.

## TAKE CARE OF YOURSELF

Grieving requires a vast amount of energy. Many women mistakenly think that grieving entails sackcloth and ashes, fasting and sleepless nights. This is a foolish and unsuccessful way to proceed.

Grieving is not an exercise in masochism. Don't expect to be able to tolerate your grief if you don't eat or sleep. Don't attempt to confront your grief if you are not taking optimal care of your health. Part of your commitment to recovery involves a commitment to your own health.

In the past, you may have neglected your own personal needs because you felt you deserved to suffer. Now you must get plenty of rest. Embrace a heathy, nutritious diet, and exercise. Physical activity will decrease depression, help you sleep, and release endorphins that will enable you to relax.

Allow your journey toward healing to be a time of inner transformation. It is a time to be good to yourself and treat yourself with gentleness.

No matter what has happened in your life, you are created in the image and likeness of God. He created you for a great good, and He will help to restore you when you feel broken and worn down.

You can use your gifts, talents, and experiences—including even your most painful experiences—for the good of yourself and others. When you have finished all your grief work, you will have a depth of understanding and compassion that will make you more effective in helping others.

It is true that much good can come out of a bad experience. It is your job now to take care of yourself so that you can find that goodness and begin sharing it with those you love.

## BUILD CONNECTIONS OF SUPPORT

It is well documented that when mourners are socially isolated, they have greater difficulty resolving their grief. The support of others, especially those who understand your trauma and will validate your feelings, will help you recover more quickly. Knowing that others care about you will also help you restore your sense of dignity and worth.

One way to find this social support is through post-abortion ministries, which I'll discuss more below. But you should also look around at the people in your life who already know and love you. Are there any people who can listen to your heartache without judging you? Are they a resource of understanding, compassion, concern?

If you are not confident of someone's ability to understand and support you through this grief process, you may want to educate that person a bit *before* you share your own story and feelings with them. Ask your friend or loved one to read about the way abortion has affected other women. You can recommend this book,  or share a testimony from www.rachelsvineyard.org or www.afterabortion.org. The Elliot Institute publishes a 12-page newspaper-like primer on post-abortion issues called *Hope and Healing*.[3] This is a good resource for helping those who haven't had abortions understand what women and men can go through and how they can help create a more healing environment for loved ones hurt by a past abortion. Just hand one of these resources to your friend and say: "I need you to read this. Then we can talk about it, okay?"

If a loved one refuses to talk about it, this may be your cue that he or she has unresolved issues about abortion—either yours, his or her own, or someone else's—and just isn't ready to deal with it. Move on and find another support person.

When you do find a loved one you can talk to, make it clear that it is not their responsibility to "fix" the problem. Don't be hesitant to say, "I don't need you to fix this, but just to try to understand me. I'm about to start on a journey to work through a big, unresolved grief issue, and I just need to know you're behind me in case I need someone to cry with."

Don't be afraid to tell others what you need. Most of your loved ones will be glad to give you the kind of emotional support you need if they know exactly what it is you need from them. Accepting their support now will help make you stronger in the future.

Don't make the mistake of thinking that you have to do this all on your own. When trying to heal, it is important to learn how to reach out to others whom you can trust—those who will not desert or abandon you. For many, this reaching out may itself be an important part of the recovery process. Sadly, many women have gone through the experience of an abortion completely alone. Reaching out now will help you grow in your ability to become interconnected with other people.

Asking for help does not mean that you are dependent or immature. It means you are human, a social being. Nor are you asking others to do the grief work for you. What you are doing is allowing them to comfort and reassure you at a time when you are experiencing a very heavy loss. Wouldn't you want to do the same for your loved ones? If so, give them the chance to do this for you, now, when you need support.

## TELL YOUR STORY

As with any trauma, processing what has happened and being able to tell your story helps to diminish its damaging effects. If you are not ready to talk about it with someone else, or if there is no one you feel you can talk to about it, you may experience some relief simply by sitting down and writing it all out. Let everything you want to say flow out onto the paper.

Reviewing the situation surrounding your abortion, its significance in your life, and the grief you feel over the loss—whether verbally or in writing—will help you understand how and why the abortion occurred. From there, you will be able to put it in perspective and integrate the story into the account of your life. You will be able to find some meaning and sense out of what has happened.

Remember that each time you tell your story, it will get easier. Telling your story is like a slow detoxification process; you can expect that the first few times you tell it, you may experience nervous jitters and monumental anxiety. Yet each time you experience the feelings associated with your memories, you will get more of a grip on what has happened. You will begin to feel more control over your painful emotions, and the anxiety and trembling will diminish a little more. Eventually, the pain will not control you anymore.

## Avoid the Guilt Trap

Many women cannot imagine ever finding healing, simply because they can never imagine being free from their guilt. Although they may have an intellectual awareness of God's willingness to forgive them, they cannot imagine ever being able to forgive themselves. Such was the case with Bianca:

> I couldn't begin to count all the nights I have cried to God. I know He forgives me. But I still have a void in my heart. The hardest part is forgiving myself. Is it *really* possible to get my guilt to go away? To not live in fear of others judging me? I feel that if I could believe that I am forgiven completely, that my whole life will change dramatically! It is this hope that keeps me searching.

Like so many others, Bianca was stuck in the guilt trap. It wasn't God or religion that was keeping her there, it was herself. No amount of preaching, platitudes, or theology is likely to relieve you of a guilty verdict you have imposed on yourself.

It is important to be aware of the trap of using guilt as a way of memorializing your aborted child. Many women are afraid to give up their guilt because they think that without it they will lose the memory of their babies. Those who delve further find that under the guilt is a profound and aching grief. The trick of the mind is to believe that it is easier to grapple with guilt or anger than to be confronted by an abyss of agonizing grief. Yet the possibility for recovery exists only when we give our souls the freedom to grieve our losses so we can move beyond the pain. By acknowledging your grief, you can honor the memory of an aborted baby in a healthier way, one that does not require that you continually sacrifice your own chances for happiness.

Guilt is a universal reaction for any parent who has suffered the death of a child. This is even more true after an abortion, when parents torment themselves by groping for reasons to justify their actions, or proposing the "if only I had" solutions to all the problems that overwhelmed them at the time of the crisis. Furthermore, individuals who perceive themselves as murderers rather than victims are struggling with a double tragedy. Although some women feel victimized if they were forced to abort against their wills, there are others who struggle with the guilt that they willingly chose to participate in the destruction of their children's lives. Both situations involve complicated levels of guilt that can block healthy grieving.

Many women and men incorporate their guilt into the mourning process, and they seem incapable of separating the two. This is why the most effective post-abortion healing programs include a spiritual component that helps those who struggle with the inability to forgive themselves. After all, guilt is a spiritual issue. I have never seen a woman recover from post-abortion trauma without addressing the issue of guilt. To resolve grief, it is essential to confront and move past guilt, as Rebecca describes:

> As the weekend unfolded, I was able to reach the grief that was buried so deeply within me. I had dug through all my defenses, and there was nothing left to protect me from the profound sorrow I felt over the loss of my baby. I never knew how to separate the feelings of shame from feelings of grief, but now I was finally there. The experience of grieving my loss was indescribably painful, but it was the key for me to release the guilt and shame.

By confronting guilt, shame, and the fear of disclosure, you will free yourself to accomplish the real work of grief. It is there that you will discover reserves of strength and courage that you never knew you had. According to Cathy:

> I am truly grateful for the opportunity to experience this journey with others in the same situation. I don't feel alone or unworthy anymore. I found sharing our stories and also meditating on our feelings was a beautiful way of releasing my guilt and sadness. I feel that I have let go of so much anger.

## JOIN A POST-ABORTION SUPPORT GROUP

I have discovered in my own work in developing a post-abortion healing program that working through the grief process in an ordered and specific way is the most reliable way of providing the necessary support and control needed on this very difficult journey. The process is broken down into stages so that the mourner can identify and confront each potential issue before moving forward. This is why I encourage you to participate in a well organized post-abortion program with experienced leaders. Moving through a specific process, with support, will help prevent a host of potential complications in dealing with your grief.

Support groups allow people to share emotions and pain in a non-threatening environment. While the group does not take the place of private therapy for specific problems, it can serve the function of helping women and men know that their reactions and emotions are not unique, to witness how others overcome their problems, and to reach outside of themselves to help others experience understanding and relief. Whenever there are several people who share the painful experience of having undergone an abortion, their feelings of loss and grief will be quickly validated. Dottie comments on how the group helped her move on:

> It was a wonderful experience of release and sharing. Once I realized that everyone was struggling in different ways, but just like me, I felt very safe in sharing my feelings and emotions over my abortions. We shared our stories—we dug into the pain, the skeletons in our past—without being judged. Many of the stories touched me personally, and we began to feel close to

each other in our shared pain and struggle. The years of silent suffering and isolation had ended, and I could make room for the forgiveness and healing that would follow.

Although you may be feeling shame and guilt about exposing your problems, sharing with others who are struggling with the same issues can be a wonderful way to end your isolation and journey together to triumph over grief and find new meaning and purpose.

Personally, I prefer to help those suffering from post-abortion difficulties within the context of a support group or weekend retreat. I have found that group work quickly ends the isolation that many post-abortive women and men struggle with. Furthermore, the experience of being with others is very cathartic for your own emotional release. An individual in your group may be able to articulate thoughts and feelings that you share but have difficulty verbalizing.

The group process will challenge you on many levels. But because people in a group will undoubtedly be at different levels of recovery, the group will also offer the necessary hope that you can and will get better. As with war veterans, there is an unspoken bond among those who have suffered deeply because of abortion. There is acceptance and compassion and, more importantly, a strong desire to see others move beyond their pain. This desire eventually will be extended to you.

## ATTEND A WEEKEND RETREAT

The program I have developed for healing is called Rachel's Vineyard, a very gentle but emotionally intensive therapeutic process that combines both psychological and spiritual elements. This curriculum is used by many post-abortion ministries throughout the United States. We offer a support group program that spans a 13-week period. In addition, we offer the program in the format of a condensed weekend retreat, usually from Friday evening through Sunday afternoon.

Rachel's Vineyard offers women and men an opportunity to examine their abortion experience, identify the ways that the loss affected them, and acknowledge whatever pain is there. The program helps them deal with repressed grief, guilt, anger, feelings of abandonment, pressure, and ambivalent attachments to their aborted children.

These issues must be dealt with and validated before an individual is ready to reconcile the experience within herself and move toward healing. It bears repeating that until anger or grief is validated and released, there will be little room in one's heart for hope.

Here is how Connie described her weekend experience:

No words can explain the healing that I experienced on this weekend retreat. It was conducted with love and gentleness in an area of my life that was war-torn, raw, and bleeding. God's mercy and love were behind this retreat, and He can make all things possible—hope, love, faith, life—where there was searing grief, pain, and desolation. Although this retreat was full of love, the conductors did not back away from reaching into the painful areas of our lives and beings. It was so important for us to dig deep and release the pain and the skeletons of the past. I believe this made room for God, who then filled that room with genuine love for lost children, family, friends, and especially our-selves.

Rachel's Vineyard has a number of powerful rituals that help par-ticipants connect with and release their grief and sorrow. These unique exercises help connect the participants to their inner voice, to each other, and to the love and compassion of the Divine Creator. Participants also learn how to internalize forgiveness for themselves and others. Through a memorial service at the end of the weekend, participants have the opportunity to honor and give dignity to their aborted babies in a fash-ion that reconnects their memories and emotions regarding their lost children in a positive and healthy way.

There is also an opportunity to examine one's entire life. Frequently, abortion can be a symptom of other losses and hurt. Painful relation-ships with parents, a history of sexual abuse, and numerous other factors can all influence life's patterns and crises. The retreat allows partici-pants a chance to examine these areas, look at the larger picture of their lives, and gain a different perspective.

Whether one participates in the 13-week support group or the week-end retreat, one can expect a lot of work. But those who are willing to journey through their grief will experience the power of resurrection in their own lives. They will find meaning in what has happened and allow God to transform their experience into something that gives hope, liberation, and peace. Following are the comments of four women.

> Rachel's Vineyard went far beyond anything I could imagine. It was an incred-ible journey from grief to joy. The exercises brought depth and meaning to our experiences. I felt like God was very much in our midst. Rachel's Vineyard was a long-awaited answer to years of immense suffering.

* * *

> I was terrified to take that first step forward and participate in Rachel's Vine-yard. It seemed safer to remain hiding in the darkness, keeping the pain locked up deep inside rather than to risk exposing my shame to another soul. Now I'm grateful to have experienced God's healing and forgiveness with other women in an atmosphere of complete acceptance and trust. Rachel's Vine-yard has been a blessing to me.

* * *

> At the end of the retreat, I felt relief and hope! Release from the feelings of terrible unworthiness and hopelessness, and learning that so many others felt the same way and gathered their courage to come on the retreat. I found love and understanding from the many dear women of all ages who made up the

body of retreat attendees, as well as help and interest shown by the volunteers who conducted the retreat.

* * *

This has been one of the most memorable and wonderful personal events of my life. Had I not been here and participated, I would still be a wandering soul without purpose. Now I am on my new journey to peace and being filled with the Holy Spirit. I found it most meaningful that God is truly forgiving; therefore, I can forgive myself. Also, all of our babies are God's creation and are happy in their eternal life in Heaven waiting to be re-united with their mothers.

I invite you to come to Rachel's Vineyard. You will be greeted and treated with compassion and respect. You will be helped and guided by myself or one of the many experienced counselors whom I have helped train.

In the vineyard you will experience the support and friendship of others as you move through the levels of your grief. Once your own pain has been emptied out there will be room for God's love. This is why the retreat is psychologically effective and spiritually renewing. It is not theology, or a lecture, or anyone telling you what you should feel. It is an experience. An experience of deep release and mercy, felt within the wounds of the suffering community of which you have become a part.

While this experience is not limited to Christians, and can benefit people of all faiths or no faith, the exercises do draw on familiar biblical images and events. Christians will discover a weekend that is reminiscent of Christ's journey to Calvary, walking with Him through His passion and death. But by Sunday you will also share in His resurrection to new life.

The retreat is an enormous amount of work. But if you are willing to do it, with the help and support of myself and others, you will find incredible healing and peace.

## Rediscover the Real You

If the emotional and spiritual wounds of abortion have been sapping faith, virtue, and joy from your life, you can be certain that once you enter a spiritual process for healing, your life will change. There can be fear at accepting this change, because the pain of bearing that burden is very familiar. To move beyond that familiar pain entails the risk of discovering a new you.

Who would you be without the heartache and grief? If your identity has been wrapped up in shame and guilt, self-loathing, or despair, the thought of living without the weight of these chains may seem strange or even frightening. Don't let this fear paralyze you.

There is a saying that came out of Alcoholics Anonymous: *"Religion is for people who are afraid of going to hell—but spirituality is for people who have been there."* This saying explains why the quest for healing of the deepest emotional wounds frequently becomes a spiritual journey.

Perhaps, like many others, you have experienced a deep sense of alienation from God. In that case, you may be afraid that healing will involve allowing God into your life, and you are uncertain what that may mean. Will He demand something of you? If you are healed, will He change your life more than you want it to change?

The spiritual part of our being, which shares a spark of the Divine through our capacity to create life, suffers a terrible shock during an abortion. Annie's faith was lost the moment she stepped out of the abortion clinic.

> As soon as I stepped out into the sunlight, I knew that God could not exist. I figured that if there was a just God in the world, He would have struck me down dead. Since I was still there, I knew there can't be a God.

Other women live in constant fear of God's impending judgment, meted out to them through an early death or the deaths of loved ones. Others simply drift away from the faith they once had because they no longer feel worthy to have a relationship with God. Just as you can be filled with anxiety about approaching a loved one again after a major fight, so it is natural to feel nervous about how you will ever be able to restore your spiritual relationship with God. The amazing thing is, God wants to restore His relationship with you even more than you want to restore it with Him. There is no need to be afraid. Even at this moment, as you read these words, He is reaching out to you, encouraging you, offering you the peace of reconciliation. Working through your loved ones, your post-abortion counselor or group, or through a pastor, priest, rabbi, or mullah, He is reaching out to draw you back to Himself.

Kathleen made that journey, and in doing so discovered a new depth in herself and others, as she described in her very moving poem:

### There Is a Place

> There is a place within a woman
> no man has ever known.
> A place touched only by God,
> tucked somewhere behind
> memories of the heart.
> It is the place where
> babies come from,
> where dreams are stored
> of things to come,
> and children yet to be . . .

There is a place within a woman
no man has ever known.
A God-less place
her soul inhabits
that only God can heal.
Abandoned by man
she abandons God
sacrificing her unborn child
and herself . . .
In the abortionist's room.

There is a place within a woman
no man has ever known.
A place touched only by God
and a few who do his will.
"Remember," says the priest,
"He does not make mistakes;
Before you were conceived,
God thought of you and loved you.
He has cried real tears for you.
Let Him heal you . . ."

There is a place within a woman
No man has ever known.
A place touched only by God
and a few brave souls
with healing hands
and prayerful hearts
who dare to journey with her.
They weep with her
and rock her gently
leading her back to herself . . .

There is a place within a woman
No man has ever known.
A place touched only by God
where memories are born
from memories
and forgiveness is carried
on the voice of a child.

Few ears can hear,
Few hearts will know
Except for Him and me
And, now, maybe, you . . .

The spiritual process of grief work and reconciliation with self, God, and one's aborted child can truly result in the birth of a new you—still connected to the old you, but more whole, balanced, complete, and free. The result of this reconciliation process is a softening of the heart, a deeper compassion for yourself, and a reclaiming of the aspects of yourself that you treasured before your trauma. It is also a process that will give you a new appreciation of your strength and ability to learn and grow from every event that has and will occur in your life, even the tragic events.

By integrating all of these components, you will create a new self, a self liberated from the repetitions of trauma and the sense of hopelessness. You will have the potential to revisit abandoned goals and dreams, articulate your truest and deepest desires, and dare to live life fully. Consider Michelle's description of her journey:

> I was a participant in the Rachel's Vineyard weekend. It was a wonderful experience. Of course, when I first arrived, I was filled with great anxiety and very little desire to actually be there, but I knew it was time to face what I dreaded so much.
>
> Although the retreat was exhausting on an emotional level, I now feel renewed and revitalized. I feel reborn and find myself sensitive to my surroundings. It is difficult to explain, but I have a sense of softness about me. I have to turn down the volume on my radio because my ears are sensitive to noise. My skin is sensitive to touch, and my taste is more acute. For the first time in my life, taking a shower is a wonderful experience because I actually feel clean.
>
> I know I was healed at the retreat, and I feel such an infusion of God's spirit in me. It is truly awesome. I felt like I was dead before, numb and senseless. My senses have returned. I feel alive, and like I am truly embracing my life now, with joy and hope.

I would like to close this chapter with the reflections of Josie, who also traveled the path into her grief and discovered an unexpected rebirth.

> As I look out upon God's creations, I am struck with awe by His love and mercy for us.
>
> Life is so resilient. Even after destruction and seemingly total decimation, life is there. The seed for rebirth is there, waiting; waiting to be watered and nurtured, and with just a little tender care, a shoot will sprout from what was once a wasteland.
>
> In nature God has shown us what we are capable of; He has given us examples of the power of life. A whole forest is laid bare by fire, and yet, out of the ashes comes growth. It is said that there are certain seeds which remain dormant until there is a fire and then, and only then, when they have gone through fire, do they sprout new life.
>
> I feel inside of me that seed. That seed has lain dormant for so many years, protected by an outer shell. Now I feel that I have walked through the fire of my fears, faced the agony and pain and grief; I have been ripped asunder, but all this was necessary, for only in facing what I fear, by facing the pain, can I grow and feel the sprout inside of me grow. It is being nurtured and tended to by God's Holy Spirit. I feel a warmth fill me and a light reaching into the darkest recesses of my soul. Everywhere I look, there is life and growth, beauty and joy.
>
> The irony is that it has always been there; it was I who could not see, for I was blinded by my own fear, by pain over something that was over long ago. But God has been so patient, so kind, so gentle. He has provided me what I needed when I needed it, even when I was totally ignorant of my needs. I look back over my life and see the stepping stones—the people who have been there doing the Lord's work, and some not even aware of the impact they had

on my life. God has lovingly protected me and gently guided each step of my journey. I praise God for his infinite wisdom, mercy, and love. I rejoice, for I have been washed clean, and this day is a new beginning on a journey which began long ago. Now there is new life within me, joy, and comfort.

Although I grieve the death of my children, I rejoice, for they are with the Lord. I rejoice, for I have been blessed and given the privilege to know that their souls live with the Creator. I have also been given the promise and the hope that we shall be reunited when my journey here on earth is completed.

Be not afraid. Go forward and find the same.

# Appendix A

# The Politics of Trauma

Our society has a love-hate relationship with victims. Or perhaps it would be more accurate to say we have an empathize-despise relationship.

On one hand, we naturally tend to empathize with people who have suffered from some abuse or adversity. We want to help them and protect them. On the other hand, we also tend to be *suspicious* of people or individuals who seek our empathy or special privileges by claims of how they have been victimized. Do they really deserve our sympathy? Our help? Our protection? Are they really victims, or are they just fakers?

Another factor that contributes to the dismissing of victims' claims is that as a society we also want people to be strong and independent. When the victim of a tragedy does not pull his life together fast enough, some people have a tendency to despise him for "wallowing in the pit" of his hurts and needs. This impatience is reflected in the advice of self-help gurus who insist: "Stop being a victim. Get over it. Take responsibility for your own life." In this same vein, those who are politically motivated to dismiss the claims of victims will often argue that victims' problems are of their own making. If they had been stronger, wiser, or more resilient, they wouldn't have suffered their misfortune, or at least they could have recovered on their own.

The study of psychological trauma has repeatedly been hampered by this combination of suspicion and impatience with victims. In part, this is because many causes of trauma arise from the failures of society to protect its members. Looking at the causes of trauma forces us to look at the flaws of our society, which we are often loathe to do. In addition, when the strong traumatize the weak, the strong will naturally deny their victims' stories, accuse them of lying or exaggeration, and insist that their problems arise from their own deeply flawed personalities.

These dynamics make the study of trauma intensely political. It is a mistake to believe that psychology is a pure science. It is not subject to the precise mathematical measure, definition, and proofs that apply to physics or chemistry. The definition of mental disorders is subject to investigation, negotiation, and in many cases, social fashion or personal agendas.[1]

The political nature of psychology is especially evident in the study of trauma. In the case of abortion, there are many different reasons why proponents of abortion are inclined to dismiss the claim that women can be traumatized by abortion. Those who financially profit from abortion, for example, are not inclined to believe that abortion is bad medicine. Similarly, those who see abortion as a means to control the quantity and "quality" of people born into the world want to preserve the reputation of this important tool of population control. Then there are those who have participated in coercing women into unwanted abortions, who want to avoid their own personal responsibility for these women and their children. Certainly, those who coerce in the name of "love" or what is "best for everyone" do not want to acknowledge how severely they have hurt women through abortion. Then there are the physicians, psychologists, politicians, and other public figures who are politically and emotionally invested in their decision to support abortion. To retreat from that position, or even to admit that abortion *sometimes* hurts women, involves an embarrassing loss of authority. It may even impute culpability to them for allowing so many women to suffer from the consequences of traumatic abortion through their failure to support enough research and safeguards to protect women. Any and all of these reasons may explain why so many people experience an irrational, knee-jerk opposition to the claim that abortion is emotionally harmful for at least some women.

The present situation is strikingly similar to what has gone before. The modern history of trauma research is marked by advances and then retreats into denial. These retreats are only overcome by political changes, through which marginalized victims finally obtain enough power to demand recognition. In this appendix, we will take a quick look at how this pattern has played out in the past and how it has been repeated in the present controversy over abortion trauma.

## The Politics of PTSD

In an intriguing chapter on the history of trauma research in her book *Trauma and Recovery,* Dr. Judith Lewis Herman has observed that the study of trauma has been marked by society's fear of acknowledging the causes of trauma. The following is a brief summary of her review.

In the late 1800s, thousands of women suffering from "hysteria" were incarcerated in insane asylums. French intellectuals, led by neurologist Jean-Martin Charcot, had begun to promote the idea that hysteria was a psychological disease linked to religious superstition. They offered demonstrations of hysteric symptoms to the public as scientific evidence of the dangers of religion. Conversely, they argued, claims of miraculous cures, apparitions, religious ecstasy, and stigmata could be scientifically explained as manifestations of hysteria. These views were widely held and encouraged by leaders of the French Enlightenment who sought to undermine the authority of the Catholic Church.

By the mid-1890s, Charcot's followers were anxious to expand and elaborate on his work. To this end, Pierre Janet and Sigmund Freud independently sought to document the causes of hysteria. In a departure from past psychiatric practices, they conducted prolonged interviews with women over long periods of time. Both Janet and Freud quickly discovered that the symptoms of hysteria appeared to be linked to intensely disturbing memories, in many cases to a history of sexual abuse. In 1896, Freud put forth the hypothesis that "at the bottom of every case of hysteria there are one or more occurrences of premature sexual experience, occurrences which belong to the earliest years of childhood." His theory was coldly received, however, and within a year Freud had recoiled from the implications of his own explanation.

> Hysteria was so common among women that if his patients' stories were true, and if his theory was correct, he would be forced to conclude that what he called "perverted acts against children" were endemic, not only among the proletariat of Paris . . . but also among the respectable bourgeois families of Vienna, where he had established his practice. This idea was simply unacceptable . . . Freud's discovery could not gain acceptance in the absence of a political and social context that would support the investigation of hysteria wherever it might lead.[2]

Soon after this, Freud began to question his patients' stories of abuse and to explore the idea that these stories were invented as erotic fantasies. "Out of the ruins of the traumatic theory of hysteria," Herman writes, "Freud created psychoanalysis.[3]

Unable to confront the unspeakable problems of incest, rape, and sexual exploitation, psychiatrists and society preferred to think that the fundamental problem lay in the fragile nature of women themselves. The link between hysteria and sexual assault was not seriously explored again until the 1970s, when the feminist movement prompted an explosion of interest in the problem of sexual assault. It was only in the 1980s, when social and political support existed for investigations of the psychological effects of rape and incest, that the traumatic nature of sexual assault and the resulting symptoms of PTSD were universally accepted.

It is interesting to note that the term "hysteria" (from the Greek word for womb, *hystera*) reflected the belief of the ancient Greeks that this psychological disorder particular to women was rooted in the uterus. Perhaps this ancient belief reflected an insight into how the violation of a woman's sexuality could result in long-term psychological problems. Obviously, rape, incest, and abortion were not unknown to the ancient world. It is not unlikely that the ancient Greeks observed that women with hysteria were particularly likely to become agitated regarding any physical examinations related to their abdomen or genitalia, which may have then given rise to the name hysteria.

Herman notes that a similar pattern of discovery, rejected findings, and rediscovered findings is seen in regard to the traumatic nature of war.

> One of the many casualties of the [First World War]'s devastation was the illusion of manly honor and glory in battle. Under conditions of unremitting exposure to the horrors of trench warfare, men began breaking down in shocking numbers. Confined and rendered helpless, subjected to constant threat of annihilation, and forced to witness the mutilation and death of their comrades without any hope of reprieve, many soldiers began to act like hysterical women. They screamed and wept uncontrollably. They froze and could not move. They became mute and unresponsive. They lost their memory and their capacity to feel. . . . According to one estimate, mental breakdowns represented 40 percent of British battle casualties. Military authorities attempted to suppress reports of psychiatric casualties because of their demoralizing effect on the public.[4]

At first, psychologists attributed these breakdowns to the physical concussion of explosive "shell shock." Eventually, however, military psychiatrists began to conclude that prolonged exposure to death and the threat of death could produce symptoms in men that resembled the condition of hysteria in women. This connection, in turn, quickly led to the view that men who were susceptible to the "hysteria of women" had defects in their masculinity. Military traditionalists insisted that true men, noble men, would never succumb to terror but would instead find glory in the challenges and hardships of war. A proponent of this view, psychiatrist Lewis Yealland, advocated treatments based on exhorting men for their laziness and cowardice, threats, punishment, and electric shock therapy.

Dr. Robert Graves, on the other hand, held the view that even men of great bravery could collapse under severely stressful conditions. His approach to treatment was to respect the soldier, encourage his sense of self-respect, and motivate him to return to battle by appeals of duty to his fellow soldiers or hatred of the enemy. It was this theory that was adapted by American military doctors in World War II. American psychiatrists believed that *any* man would eventually break down under prolonged stress. They concluded that the best antidote was to develop strong emotional dependency between soldiers in small fighting groups. Treatments for emotional collapse were not oriented toward full recovery, but rather for rapid reinsertion with their unit, to whom they owed the duty of allegiance. After the Second World War, as after the first, little attention was subsequently paid to how these traumatized war veterans subsequently lived their lives.

Interest in the long-term effects of battle trauma did not take root until the 1970s, when returning soldiers organized the group Vietnam

Veterans Against the War. Embraced by the antiwar movement, these soldiers began organizing peer "rap groups" in which they exchanged their stories of trauma and grief. Through this means, the veterans found a way to validate the reality of their trauma and developed the confidence and strength necessary to resist efforts to discredit their bravery. These veterans refused to be ignored and eventually found the support of therapists who held the view that war could cause psychological injuries. By the end of the 1970s, political pressure from the veterans led the Veterans' Administration to develop Operation Outreach to provide peer-counseling programs by veterans for veterans. It was during this time that psychiatrists treating veterans began to develop the definition of post-traumatic stress disorder (PTSD) that we have today.

These histories of hysteria and shell shock demonstrate the powerful social and political issues involved in identifying and acknowledging the victims of trauma. In both cases, society at large, and psychiatrists in particular, were reluctant to acknowledge the reality of trauma that challenged their worldview and demanded compassion for "moral misfits, malingerers, and cowards." According to Herman:

> The study of psychological trauma must constantly contend with the tendency to discredit the victim or to render her invisible. . . . It is not only the patients but also the investigators of post-traumatic conditions whose credibility is repeatedly challenged. Clinicians who listen too long and too carefully to traumatized patients often become suspect among their colleagues, as though contaminated by contact. Investigators who pursue the field too far beyond the bounds of conventional belief are often subjected to a kind of professional isolation.[5]

The same dynamic has and continues to be played out in regard to abortion-related trauma.

## THE POLITICS OF ABORTION TRAUMA

Prior to the 1960s, investigations of the psychological effects of abortion "concluded almost without exception that abortion inevitably causes trauma, posing a severe threat to psychological health."[6] By the late 1950s, however, population control advocates had set their sights on overturning state laws regulating birth control and abortion. Major population control donors, like the Rockefeller Foundation, made new research dollars available to prove the benign nature of abortion. In retrospect, the subsequent shift in social, political, and scientific thinking was perfectly coordinated. By the late 1960s, when the fear of the population explosion was at its peak, and "free love" and feminism were on the rise, the American Medical Association, the American Psychiatric Association, and the American Psychological Association reversed their prior positions in opposition to abortion. Citing the new body of research that purported to prove that abortion was safe, the AMA and both APAs actively supported the repeal of anti-abortion laws.

Since the *Roe v. Wade* decision in 1973, the commitment of these professional health organizations to abortion has not wavered. They have individually and collectively lobbied and litigated against laws that would regulate abortion clinics. In this regard, they have consistently argued that abortion is so safe that clinic regulation and parental notice requirements are unnecessary or even dangerous to the well-being of women.

In the late 1970s however, a few women who had experienced emotional or physical problems after abortion banned together under the name Women Exploited. This effort did not have a national impact until 1982, however, when Nancyjo Mann started a group called Women Exploited By Abortion (WEBA), which offered group and peer counseling programs.

Mann had been severely traumatized by a second-trimester saline abortion in 1974, during which she delivered her perfectly-formed daughter into her own hands. After four years of substance abuse, sleep disorders, sexual dysfunctions, broken relationships, risk-taking and suicidal behavior, she found a measure of peace in a religious conversion. After another four years, she felt drawn to reach out to other women whom she believed were suffering as she had. She began public speaking, and within a year, WEBA had thousands of members with chapters in all fifty states. In the following decade, WEBA became fragmented and was replaced by dozens of separate ministries. Many of the post-abortion ministries in the United States today were founded by former WEBA members.

The formation of WEBA marked the start of the social movement of women who had experienced traumatic abortions to minister to each other. Since women involved in post-abortion programs typically report that it takes an average of eight to ten years before they begin to confront and deal with their post-abortion problems, it is perhaps not coincidental that this movement emerged almost exactly ten years after *Roe v. Wade*.

At approximately the same time, a small number of psychologists had begun to recognize that women they were treating who had a history of abortion had clusters of symptoms that fit into the newly published criteria for PTSD. In 1981, family psychotherapist Vincent Rue was the first to attempt a systematic definition of post-abortion syndrome (PAS) as a variant of PTSD.[7] He was almost immediately threatened with legal action by the general counsel of the American Psychiatric Association if any notes he published making reference to the PTSD diagnosis for abortion did not include a specific disclaimer stating that the APA denies that there is "any clinical evidence for the basis of the diagnosis of 'post-abortion syndrome.'"[8]

Another significant milestone in the early post-abortion movement occurred with the publication of psychologist Susan Stanford's auto-biographical *Will I Cry Tomorrow?* in 1986. After a difficult recovery from her own traumatic abortion, Stanford began recognizing traumatic symptoms in her own post-abortive clients. To assist them in their recovery, she began to develop a treatment model using visualization techniques. Variations on these techniques are now widely used by post-abortion counselors. Through her book, Stanford helped thousands of women find validation of their own grief experiences and provided them with encouragement to seek professional help. (As a side note, Rue and Stanford met each other in 1986 when they crossed paths in their efforts to promote awareness of post-abortion trauma. They were married in 1988 and shortly thereafter co-founded the Institute for Pregnancy Loss in Stratham, New Hampshire.)

A fourth significant event in the early 1980s was the formation of Project Rachel, a post-abortion ministry in the Catholic Archdiocese of Milwaukee. This ministry was founded in 1984 by Vicki Thorn as a result of her observations of the traumatic effects of abortion on a close friend. It was Thorn's hope that Project Rachel would provide a means by which the Catholic Church could offer both psychological counseling and pastoral care to women and men who had undergone abortions. This step provided the blessing of a significant institution on this growing effort to understand and aid those who have suffered from abortion. Project Rachel was subsequently adopted as the official post-abortion ministry and outreach program of the Catholic Church by hundreds of dioceses in the United States and in many countries around the world.

These initial steps toward broader recognition of post-abortion trauma, however, were quickly opposed by abortion supporters. On the public relations front, the testimonies of women such as Nancyjo Mann were dismissed as "guilt tripping by a small minority of women." Even if a few women regretted their abortions, it was argued, at least they "had a choice," and their regrets should not threaten the welfare of the vast majority of women.

At the same time, the academic world quickly closed ranks. While even poorly designed studies "proving" that abortion was safe readily found their way into publication, papers by Rue and other therapists and researchers reporting negative psychological effects of abortion were, and continue to be, hostilely received and rejected. In a few cases, these articles have been refused publication with the frank admission of editors that their findings and viewpoints are simply too controversial. It was not until 1992 that Rue's description of PAS was finally accepted for publication in an official journal of the American

Psychological Association, *The Journal of Social Issues.*[9] In this instance, Rue's paper was invited by the editors of the journal to "bring balance to the special issue," though all of the eight other published papers in that issue were written by pro-abortion authors who disagreed with Rue.

During the 1980s, researchers supporting abortion produced a new round of studies showing that the majority of women do not report "significant" psychological problems in the first few months following abortion. None of these studies, however, directly addressed the trauma-related symptoms proposed by Rue. In many respects, it appeared as if these studies, done in collaboration with abortion providers, were designed to avoid looking too deeply or too long at how women's lives were changed after an abortion.

During this time, a new line of reasoning emerged in defense of abortion. To explain the fact that a significant minority of women report negative reactions no matter how a study is designed, researchers began to suggest that the negatively affected women were those who were most psychologically fragile before their abortions, and therefore would have been worse off if they had carried to term. In other words, the same "blame the victim" approach that had been used in the case of hysteria and shell shock was being applied to abortion patients. Only defective, weak women had any adjustment problems. But even then, researchers insisted, these women would probably have had more problems if they had carried to term. There was also the implication that if these "defective" women had not had abortions, they would have been defective mothers raising more defective children.

By the early eighties, however, pro-life organizations were providing a platform for post-abortive women and counselors to speak publicly about the emotional aftermath of abortion. The term "post-abortion syndrome" or PAS, first presented in Congressional hearings in 1981 by Rue, slowly began to be used in pro-life circles to describe any negative reactions to abortion, and is now even used in the public media. Interest in this issue was boosted in 1987 when President Ronald Reagan, prompted by a pro-life aide, asked Surgeon General C. Everett Koop to prepare a report on the physical and psychological effects of abortion. Koop asked the president to excuse him from this politically contentious request, but his request was denied. In the end, Koop delivered a letter to the president stating that all of the research in the field was so methodologically flawed that he could not offer any firm conclusions either for or against the safety of abortion. Koop's lack of any official findings was held up by abortion defenders as proof that pro-life groups were simply trying to intimidate and scare women away from safe abortions.

Perhaps the culmination of specious denials was the publication in

1992 of a commentary in the prestigious *Journal of the American Medical Association,* entitled "The Myth of Abortion Trauma Syndrome," which emphatically declared that post-abortion trauma "does not exist" and that "there is no evidence of an abortion trauma syndrome."[10] In making this proclamation, the commentator avoided any direct reference to the published works of Rue or others advocating the PTSD diagnosis. Even the few citations presented to support the "doesn't exist" theory were self-contradictory and misrepresented (see appendix B).

Shortly thereafter, the American Psychiatric Association attempted to close the door on continued efforts to gain recognition for the existence of post-abortion trauma. In previous issues of the APA diagnostic manual (DSM), abortion had been listed as a type of psychosocial stressor. Psychosocial stressors, according to the DSM III-R, were capable of causing PTSD.[11] In the fourth revision of their manual, the DSM-IV, published in 1994, the APA pointedly removed any reference to abortion, though "death of a family member" continues to be listed as a type of psychosocial problem.[12]

Despite this opposition, evidence about the traumatic nature of abortion continues to accumulate. More and more therapists are seeking and receiving training in the treatment of this "nonexistent" disorder. The number of women and men receiving counseling for post-abortion trauma or grief is increasing at a rapid rate, a trend that is also fueling a new political activism by post-abortive women in the form of organizations like Women at Risk and Feminists for Life.

As in the case of hysteria and shell shock, the effort to gain recognition for the traumatic nature of abortion has only been sustained because (1) post-abortive women have banded together in peer support groups, (2) a social and political movement exists in which the post-abortion movement has at least received acknowledgment, and (3) there have been consistent minority voices in the professional mental health communities asserting these various and serious post-abortion injuries.

It should be noted, however, that the post-abortion movement is unique and separate from the pro-life movement. While pro-life groups have promoted awareness of post-abortion syndrome as another argument against abortion, they have typically treated it as simply a secondary argument against abortion. Most significantly, major pro-life groups have generally declined to give financial assistance for either post-abortion research or counseling programs. Some pro-life leaders have even insisted that concerns about the effects of abortion on women are a distraction to pursuing the goal of protecting the right to life of unborn babies. Koop even went so far as to write: "The pro-life movement had always focused—rightly, I thought—on the impact of abortion on the fetus. They lost their bearings when they approached the issue on the grounds of the health effects on the mother."[13] Legislative proposals brought forth by the post-abortion movement that are focused on protecting women have generally been ignored by established pro-life groups, and in some cases actively blocked.

While there is collaboration between pro-life groups and post-abortion ministries, and many shared values, it would be a mistake to see the latter as simply a subset of the former. As a matter of necessity, post-abortion ministries, advocacy groups, and researchers continue to chart their own course.

# APPENDIX B

# THE COMPLEXITY AND DISTORTIONS OF POST-ABORTION RESEARCH

E fforts to scientifically measure psychological problems after abortion are very difficult, highly politicized, and frequently distorted in reports to both individual patients and to the media. In fact, while there have been many studies regarding the emotional aftermath of abortion, very little has been firmly established. This is because the very nature of abortion is such that it would be extremely difficult, if not impossible, to complete a study that would be generally conclusive and above reproach.

Researchers are faced with four major obstacles:

First, in longitudinal and retrospective studies, approximately 50 to 60 percent of women who have had an abortion will conceal their abortion(s) from interviewers.[1] Even in short-term follow-up studies, there are high dropout rates, typically in the range of 20 to 60 percent. Demographic comparisons of those who initially consent to participate in a follow-up study and then subsequently refuse to be interviewed indicate that those who exclude themselves from the final sample are more likely to match the profiles of women who report the greatest post-abortion distress.[2]

Second, women can experience a wide variety of psychological reactions related to a previous abortion, not all of which are always covered in a given study or easily categorized. As is evident from the case studies described throughout this book, in my own practice I have treated women with symptoms of depression, anger, impacted grief, chronic guilt, anxiety, intrusive memories, self-destructive behaviors, eating disorders, substance abuse, sexual maladjustment, and personality disorders, to name only a few. Some abortion reactions may fit into the model of complicated bereavement or pathological grief.[3] In other cases, women exhibit symptoms that fall within the diagnostic criteria for post-traumatic stress disorder (PTSD).[4] Still other women report symptoms that are not placed in any existing category for mental disease.

In addition, researchers who support abortion may have an entirely different definition of what symptoms are considered significant than do researchers who are anti-abortion. As a result, it is practically impossible for researchers to examine the entire range of every possible post-abortion reaction in a single study. While hundreds of studies have been done, all of them provide only a limited look at a small, specific group of reactions.

Third, reactions to abortion vary over time. Women who are initially filled with grief and self-reproach may subsequently find emotional healing, whereas women who were initially coping well may subsequently find themselves emotionally shattered. In one study of 260 women who reported negative post-abortion reactions, between 63 and 76 percent claimed there was a period of time during which they would have denied any negative feelings connected to their abortions. The average period of denial reported by the survey population was 63 months.[5]

This can have an impact on both short and long-term studies. A woman facing a delayed reaction may score "normal" on some scale three weeks after her abortion and be a wreck three years later. Ten years later, the same woman may score "normal" again because she has worked through her negative feelings in the intervening years. If she is surveyed at this time and if the researcher fails to ask how the abortion affected her previously, she will be tallied as "normal" and unaffected by her abortion. Without a properly designed research instrument, the researcher would have no way of knowing that the abortion previously led to problems like substance abuse or a nervous breakdown.

Fourth, standardized questionnaires have been shown to be inadequate for uncovering deeply repressed feelings related to abortion.[6] One psychiatrist has reported that in the course of psychotherapy for 50 women, none of whom had originally sought treatment for abortion-related problems, deep feelings of pain and bereavement about a prior abortion emerged while the patients were receiving therapy for seemingly unrelated problems.[7] In subsequent research with women who were not in psychotherapy, he found that an initial reaction of emotional numbness could distort questionnaire-based studies. He concluded that an underlying sense of loss and pain can only be reliably identified in a clinical setting.[8]

In summary, drawing conclusions from research regarding the emotional aftereffects of abortion is exceptionally difficult because (1) the cooperation of the study population is inconsistent and unreliable, (2) the variety of negative reactions reported by women is so broad that it may be impossible to examine every claimed dysfunction in a single study, (3) the intensity of reactions appears to vary over time, with many women reporting delayed reactions, and (4) the use of questionnaires and other standardized survey instruments may be inadequate for uncovering deep-seated reactions.

Given such complexities, it is understandable that Surgeon General C. Everett Koop concluded, in 1987, that the research in this field is entirely inadequate for drawing any general conclusions about either the efficacy or the dangers of induced abortion.[9] With the exception of the recent record-based studies that were discussed in chapter two under "Approaching the Truth," the same criticism holds true to this day.

## THE DISTORTIONS OF SCIENTIFIC RESEARCH

Nonetheless, abortion proponents are often quick to make sweeping statements regarding the safety of abortion. For example, on Feb. 10, 1988, a front-page story in *USA Today* reported that a study by Brenda Major of 600 women found that "most women who choose abortion don't suffer physical or emotional distress." A more careful reading revealed that "only" 15 percent of the women (a rather significant minority) did report depressive symptoms.

It is only in reading the actual study that one discovers other important qualifying facts. First, the researchers were only looking for signs of depression. Second, this evaluation took place just *30 minutes* after the abortion, with a second follow-up evaluation three weeks after the abortion. Third, six percent of the patients refused to participate in the 30-minute follow-up, and a full *60 percent* dropped out at the three-week follow-up. Finally, in comparing patients who did exhibit depression with those who did not, Major identified six predictive risk factors for depression in the short term, each of which encompassed 33 to 52 percent of the patients studied.[10]

As a therapist who has found that most of my clients suffering from post-abortion problems had long periods of denial during which they coped well, I would interpret a 15-percent depression rate (with a 60-percent study dropout rate) as being very worrisomely high. While it is true that 15 percent is less than 50 percent, to characterize this study as evidence that "most" women never experience emotional distress after an abortion is a gross exaggeration.

Another example is a study published by Nancy Felipe Russo in 1992, and again in 1997.[11] Russo, who is the director of the women's studies program at Arizona State University, used data from the National Longitudinal Study of Youth (NLSY), which is funded by the U.S. Department of Labor. NLSY has tracked the education and employment patterns of several thousand people yearly over the last two decades. At various intervals, NLSY researchers have asked women about their reproductive histories. On two occasions, in 1980 and 1987, women also answered ten questions from the Rosenberg Self-Esteem Scale. Analyzing this subset of data, Russo found that on average women reporting a single abortion did not have lower Rosenberg Self-Esteem scores than women who did not report a history of abortion. Major newspaper articles quoted Russo as claiming that her study "proves" that abortion does not have any psychological risk. She insisted that talk about post-abortion syndrome was a "dangerous myth," and she used her findings to attack informed consent laws requiring that women be told about the physical and mental health risks of abortion.[12]

The numerous flaws and deceptions in Russo's study have been documented at length.[13] I will review only a few of the most glaring problems.

First, Russo went to great lengths to represent her findings as being applicable to the general population of women having abortions. After all, the NLSY data set included 5,300 women. What she failed to tell the media, or even to mention in her paper, is that the Alan Guttmacher Institute (Planned Parenthood's research arm) had previously looked at the NLSY data set and concluded that with only 773 of those women reporting a history of abortion, more than 60 percent of the women had lied to researchers to conceal their past abortions.[14] In other words, the women who were most ashamed of their abortions were not included in Russo's sample of women who had abortions. It is well known that those who conceal their abortions are more likely demographically to match those women who are most likely to complain of post-abortion maladjustments.[15]

Second, Russo found that women with a history of multiple abortions had lower self-esteem scores than both those women who did not report a history of abortion and those who reported only one abortion. But oddly, although this finding is noted in the data, it is almost completely ignored in Russo's discussion of the findings and was *never* mentioned in her press releases or interviews. Since approximately half of women having abortions have had a previous abortion, this is a very disturbing finding.

Third, even when Russo's data is confined to women admitting a history of a single abortion, the self-esteem scores are clearly skewed from the "normal" sample. While the average score is about the same, women with a history of abortion were more likely to score at the extreme ends of the scale, either very low or very high. What she fails to note is that extremely high scores may be as indicative of poor adjustment as extremely low scores. Some women will attempt to compensate for an injured psyche by projecting a grandiose or inflated sense of their self-worth. Attempting to boost their image in their own eyes and in the eyes of others, they would naturally answer Rosenberg Self-Esteem questions such as, "I am a person of great worth," at the highest end of the scale. Indeed, one in-depth study of women three to five years after their abortions found that 68 percent exhibited significant histrionic characteristics and 33 percent had narcissistic characteristics.[16] Either of these personality disorders could inflate Rosenberg

Self-Esteem scores in such a way that a high score could actually be an indicator not of "well-being," as Russo asserts, but of ill-health.

Fourth, the Rosenberg Self-esteem Scale used in the NLSY provides only a "snapshot" of a woman's self-esteem (as defined by the limitations of that scale) at any given moment in time. A woman who scores high self-esteem at one moment might score much lower if she is first asked about any number of stressful issues, such as abortion, divorce, or her relationship with her parents. Nor can it distinguish between women who were devastated by their abortions for several years but are now recovered and those who are still in denial but will have a nervous breakdown next year. Russo's wholesale dismissal of "post-abortion syndrome" based on this "snapshot" measure of self-esteem is like taking the temperatures of AIDS patients and declaring, based on a finding that the average temperature is normal, that there is no such thing as AIDS.

Finally, self-esteem is simply not a very sensitive measure of post-abortion reactions. Research has shown that self-esteem measures may remain relatively steady even though women are experiencing more depression or other negative reactions to abortion.[17] These results suggest that a self-esteem score is more closely related to a personality trait than to emotional reactions and therefore may be a poor measure of environmental stressors. One would expect anxiety or depression scores to be more sensitive measures of women's emotional reactions to abortion. In fact, Russo's analysis failed to include an examination of the NLSY's assessment of depression. This 20-question scale, administered in 1992, reveals that women reporting a history of abortion have significantly more depression than women who do not report a history of abortion. Even after controlling for age, total family income, and an evaluation of their mental health at least one year prior to their pregnancies, aborting women were 41 percent more likely than non-aborting women to score in the high-risk range for clinical depression. They were also 73 percent more likely to complain of "depression, excessive worry, or nervous trouble of any kind" an average of 17 years after their abortions.[18] Due to the high concealment rate of abortion in the NLSY, these findings would clearly tend to under-represent the actual risk of more depression among aborting women.

In short, neither the NLSY data set nor the Rosenberg Self-Esteem Scale were ever designed to examine post-abortion problems. They are of limited value. Examining this data set may certainly produce some insights to guide future research, as was done with the evaluation of depression scores. But Russo's presentation of the self-esteem scores alone as proof that abortion has no mental health risks is an example of either sloppy thinking or dishonest reporting.

## So Maybe It's Not a Myth, After All

A final example of how the medical discussion of abortion risks has been deeply politicized can be seen in a commentary published in the prestigious *Journal of the American Medical Association,* entitled "The Myth of Abortion Trauma Syndrome," by Dr. Nada Stotland. Stotland begins and ends her piece with the emphatic pronouncement that post-abortion trauma "does not exist" and that "there is no evidence of an abortion trauma syndrome."[19] Ironically, however, her broad declarations of absolute certainty were inconsistent with the evidence she herself presented to bolster her argument.

For example, Stotland cites a study by Bryan Lask finding that 11 percent of the women in the study reported adverse psychological effects six months after their abortions.[20] Rather than expressing concern about these women's post-abortion problems, or worrying that this short-term study may have revealed just the tip of the iceberg, Stotland insists that this minority (less than 50 percent) reaction supports her conclusion that psychiatric illness after abortion is "rare."

In fact, Stotland only reported part of Lask's findings. Lask actually found that 32 percent of those studied had an "unfavorable" outcome to their abortion. This 32 percent included not only patients who had suffered post-abortion mental illness, but also patients who regretted having the abortion and those who had moderate to severe feelings of guilt, loss, or self-reproach that were not classified as mental illness at the time of the six-month follow-up.

Another example of Stotland's selective reading of the literature occurred in her summary of a study by Elizabeth Belsey. Stotland cited this study to prove that the majority of women having abortions feel relief and regain their pre-abortion mental health status. But once again, a reading of the study's complete findings reveals a different picture.[21]

Belsey's main finding is that 49 percent of the group (still a minority!) had experienced one or more maladjustments within three months after the abortion. Most importantly, Belsey found that the women most at risk of experiencing negative reactions could be identified during pre-abortion screening. Belsey broadly summarized these high-risk screening criteria as: (1) a history of psycho-social instability, (2) a poor or unstable relationship with her male partner, (3) few friends, (4) a poor work pattern, and (5) failure to take contraceptive precautions. Using these factors, Belsey found that 64 percent of the abortion patients she studied should have been referred for more extensive counseling. Of this high-risk group, 72 percent actually did develop negative post-abortion reactions, compared to the low-risk group, among whom 28 percent experienced one or more negative reactions.

It is notable that in 1998 Stotland published a case study that would indicate a retreat from her previously unequivocal view that "abortion does not cause emotional problems or mental illness."[22] In this case study, Stotland describes a patient whose miscarriage precipitated an unexpected release of grief over a prior abortion that shook both the patient and Stotland.[23] Her experience with this patient inspired Stotland to question her own preconceived views about how abortion does not involve any psychological risks. In this later, less circulated article, she attempts to call attention to "the psychological complexities of induced abortion." She observes that no matter what a woman's political perspective may be, "an abortion is experienced by that woman as both the mastery of a difficult life situation and as the loss of a potential life. There is the danger that the political, sociological context can overshadow a woman's authentic, multilayered emotional experience." The failure to address this loss, Stotland writes, "leaves the person vulnerable to reminders and reenactments, to difficulties that may surface in life and in subsequent psychotherapy."

## Is Abortion Better Than Having an "Unwanted" Child?

As abortion proponents have been forced to retreat from the position that abortion does not have psychological risks, they are beginning to move to the argument that "even if abortion causes emotional problems, giving birth to an unwanted child is worse." For example, after publishing her case study acknowledging her treatment of a woman with post-abortion psychological problems, Nada Stotland has now taken the position that "women who are at high risk [of psychological problems] after abortion are at equally high or higher risk if they continue their pregnancies."[24] She has refused, however, to identify any research that substantiates this assertion.[25] Nor has she been willing to clarify precisely what emotional problems, in her view, women who carry to term are at "higher risk" of suffering.

No matter how many medical degrees an abortion proponent like Stotland may have, it is important to recognize that this presumption that abortion is beneficial to women, or is in any measurable way better for women than carrying to term, is no more than that—an unsubstantiated presumption. Not only do abortion proponents lack any studies to support this conclusion, but all the existing research clearly contradicts their position.

Studies comparing women who carry an unintended pregnancy to term (without any known history of abortion) to women who abort reveal that the aborting women have more subsequent depression[26] and anxiety.[27] In addition, aborting women are more likely to have difficulty providing a nurturing environment for their subsequent children, and their children are more likely to have behavioral problems.[28] The best available evidence, therefore, contradicts the claim that women who carry an unintended pregnancy to term will suffer as much or more than women who abort. Aborting women, and their subsequent children, are more negatively affected.

## THE OBLIGATION OF PHYSICIANS

Clearly, both childbirth and abortion will forever change a woman's life. The question before us, however, is how to measure in some meaningful way how these two experiences affect the psychological and physical health of women. Obviously, there are some risks that are unique to abortion. Certainly, even Stotland would not claim that women who carry to term are at "equally high or higher risk" of experiencing the particular symptoms of guilt, shame, or remorse uniquely associated with abortion.

In fact, regarding more general psychological problems, several studies have been done comparing women who abort to women who carry to term. In many, but not all, of these studies, the comparison has been to women who carry an unplanned pregnancy to term. An exhaustive review of these studies clearly shows that women who carry to term are less likely than those who abort to attempt suicide,[29] experience depression,[30] require subsequent psychiatric care,[31] experience sexual dysfunctions,[32] and engage in alcohol abuse, drug abuse, or smoking.[33]

In addition, while there is a long list of factors that reliably predict greater risk of experiencing psychological or physical problems after an abortion, there is simply no corresponding list of characteristics that predict any benefit of abortion compared to childbirth. It is actually rather shocking to discover that abortion providers have not published any research that identifies situations or characteristics wherein abortion is most likely to improve a woman's life or well-being, much less any research that has quantified such improvements.

Even in such cases where women may not be hurt physically or emotionally by an abortion, there is no logical basis for assuming that lack of harm correlates to positive benefit. Human beings are extremely adaptable. Research has shown that women who have been denied abortion will frequently claim in retrospect that they never really wanted an abortion in the first place and that they are happy that their children were born.[34]

It was for this very reason that Aleck Bourne (whose trial for an illegal abortion in 1938 sparked the trend toward the liberalization of abortion laws in Britain, if not the world) expressed his opposition to legalized abortion in a 1967 interview, saying that granting general access to abortion would be a "calamity" for women: "I've had so many women come to my surgery and pleading with me [sic] to end their pregnancies and being very upset when I have refused. But I have never known a woman who, when the baby was born, was not overjoyed that I had not killed it."[35] A similar sentiment is frequently reported by crisis pregnancy counselors and physicians who have successfully encouraged abortion-minded clients to choose birth.

It should never be presumed, then, that abortion automatically confers some benefit upon women. It certainly changes the courses of their lives, as does childbirth, but it has never been scientifically established when, if ever, an abortion is likely to be beneficial. Therefore, just as it is impossible to accurately estimate how many women are adversely affected by abortion, it is also impossible to estimate how many women benefit from abortion. The only difference is that while there are well-established risk factors that predict post-abortion sequelae, there is not a similar body of identified factors that are helpful for predicting when abortion is likely to benefit women.

Since abortion is sought for a wide variety of reasons, it would seem essential to know in which cases abortion best fulfills the hopes and expectations of patients. Are women who seek abortions because of relationship problems likely to report that their relationships were improved? Or were their relationships hindered? Or did the abortion not make a difference? Are women who abort to protect their educational or career plans more likely to finish school or advance in their careers than women who carry to term and resume their education or career at a later date? Do women who abort in order to avoid embarrassing themselves or their families achieve higher levels of emotional security or family harmony?

In the absence of any research demonstrating when abortion is beneficial, it is difficult to understand how physicians can fulfill their obligation to give women considering abortions sound *medical* advice. Just as the risks of abortion vary by the characteristics of the individual, it is likely that research into any benefits that may be attributable to abortion would also indicate that these benefits are most likely to be attained in certain situations or by women meeting certain physical and psycho-social criteria. Until this research is done, proper screening for known and suspected risk factors is even more important to safeguard patients' health.

This challenge to abortion proponents has been well articulated by Philip Ney:

> We should remember that in the science of medicine, the onus of proof lies with those who perform or support any medical or surgical procedure to show beyond reasonable doubt that the procedure is both safe and therapeutic. There are no proven psychiatric indications for abortion. The best evidence

shows abortion is contraindicated in major psychiatric illness. There is no good evidence that abortion is therapeutic for any medical conditions with possible rare exceptions. In fact, there are no proven medical, psychological, or social benefits. . . . If abortion was a drug or any other surgical procedure about which so many doubts have been raised regarding its safety and therapeutic effectiveness, it would have been taken off the market long ago.[36]

## APPENDIX C

# THE ELLIOT INSTITUTE SURVEY
## Psychological Reactions Reported After Abortion

This survey instrument was distributed to women who had contact with one of three post-abortion ministries: WEBA, Victims of Choice, or Last Harvest Ministries. The latter two organizations used it as an intake form for women inquiring about post-abortion counseling or crisis pregnancy counseling. Compared to women who received the questionnaire from these latter two sources, the 111 participants from the WEBA distribution were significantly more likely to have already participated in post-abortion healing programs, and were significantly more likely to report feeling "reconciled with" their abortion "today" (56.1 percent vs. 13.9 percent).

Using chi-square tests for significance, women who had at least one abortion as a teen were significantly more likely to report nightmares; flashbacks to the abortion; hysterical outbreaks; unforgiveness of those involved; feelings of guilt; fear of punishment from God; fear of harm coming upon their other children; a worsening of negative feelings on the anniversary date of the abortion, during a later pregnancy, or when exposed to pro-choice propaganda; preoccupation with thoughts of the child they could have had; excessive interest in pregnant women; excessive interest in babies; experiencing false pregnancies; a dramatic personality change for the worse; a waking or sleeping "visitation" from the aborted child; and having talked to the aborted child prior to the abortion.

Women who aborted as teens were significantly less likely to report a history of professional counseling prior to their abortion; that the memory of the abortion had faded with time, having undergone surgical sterilization to avoid the risk of another abortion; being more in touch with their feelings after the abortion; and feelings of hatred toward all men.

Women who reported having had more than one abortion were significantly more likely to report a history of being physically abused as a child; a period of strong feelings of relief after the abortion; being pro-choice after the abortion; hatred of the men who had made them pregnant; ending the relationship with their partner after the abortion; difficulty in maintaining and developing personal relationships; becoming promiscuous; being self-destructive; beginning to use or increasing the use of drugs after the abortion; feelings of anxiety; fear of God; fear of another pregnancy; fear of needing another abortion; fear for unknown reasons; frequently experiencing heavy bleeding after the abortion; emotional aftereffects of the abortion which were so severe that there was a period during which they could not function normally at home, at work, or in personal relationships; and having experienced a nervous breakdown at some time after the abortion.

Women with a history of multiple abortions were significantly less likely to report that the memory of their abortion was vividly clear, and a worsening of abortion-related feelings on the anniversary date of the abortion or the due date of the pregnancy.

The following are the summary statistics to all questions, for all respondents.

## SURVEY OF REACTIONS TO ABORTION

A total of 260 women participated in this survey. Most questions are answered on a Likert scale between 1 and 5, indicating the range of the subject's agreement or disagreement with a statement regarding a particular reaction to her abortion.

Since some women skipped questions that they felt were not applicable to them or that they did not want to answer, or answered in a form that could not be coded, each item is accompanied by a number in parenthesis (N), which indicates the number of women who responded to that question. The percentages given correspond to this (N).

## Section 1

**Present age:** (N = 259); Avg: 32.0 yrs

| <u><20</u> | <u>20-24</u> | <u>25-29</u> | <u>30-34</u> | <u>35-39</u> | <u>>39</u> |
|------|-------|-------|-------|-------|-----|
| 2.7% | 11.2% | 27.0% | 24.3% | 23.9% | 10.8% |

**Race or ethnic origin:** (N = 255)

| <u>White</u> | <u>Non-White</u> |
|-------|-----------|
| 92.3% | 7.7% |

**State of residence:** Respondents from 35 states

**Highest grade completed:** (N = 254); Avg: 13.6 yrs

| <u><12</u> | <u>12</u> | <u>13</u> | <u>14</u> | <u>15</u> | <u>16</u> | <u>17</u> | <u>>17</u> |
|------|------|------|------|------|------|------|------|
| 7.5% | 40.2% | 12.2% | 17.7% | 1.6% | 16.9% | 1.2% | 2.8% |

**How old were you at the time of your abortion?** (N = 257); Avg: 21.5 yrs

| <u><15</u> | <u>15-19</u> | <u>20-24</u> | <u>25-29</u> | <u>30-34</u> | <u>>35</u> |
|------|-------|-------|-------|-------|-----|
| 1.9% | 40.1% | 36.2% | 15.6% | 4.3% | 1.9% |

**Time since abortion, in years (a calculated field):** (N = 257) Avg: 10.6 yrs

| <u><6</u> | <u>6-10</u> | <u>11-15</u> | <u>16-20</u> | <u>>20</u> |
|------|------|-------|-------|-----|
| 19.8% | 33.1% | 31.1% | 12.1% | 3.9% |

**Was your abortion . . .** (N = 251)

| LEGAL? | ILLEGAL? | (Indicated one of each) |
|--------|----------|-------------------------|
| 92.1% | 7.1% | .8% |

**How many abortions have you had?** (N = 258)

| One | Two | Three | Four or more |
|-----|-----|-------|--------------|
| 73.6% | 17.8% | 5% | 3.5% |

**Marital status at that time:** (N = 254)

| Single | Married | Engaged | Separated/Divorced |
|--------|---------|---------|--------------------|
| 64.6% | 15.4% | 7.1% | 13.0% |

**How many weeks pregnant were you at that time?** (N = 247) Avg: 9.6 wks

| <5 | 5-6 | 7-8 | 9-10 | 11-12 | 13-16 | 16-20 | >20 |
|-----|-----|-----|------|-------|-------|-------|-----|
| 7.7% | 11.7% | 28.3% | 16.2% | 21.1% | 10.9% | 2.4% | 1.6% |

**How many children did you have at that time?** (N = 260)

| Zero | One | Two | Three | Over Three |
|------|-----|-----|-------|------------|
| 74.2% | 13.8% | 8.5% | 2.7% | 0% |

**What type of abortion procedure was used?** (N = 245)

| Suction | D & C | Saline/Prostaglandin | Other |
|---------|-------|----------------------|-------|
| 80.0% | 13.5% | 3.7% | 2.9% |

**Were you awake during the procedure?** (N = 255)

| Yes | No | Unsure |
|-----|-----|--------|
| 79.6% | 18.8% | 1.6% |

**Were you given pain killers or anesthetics prior to the operation?** (N = 256)

| Yes | No | Unsure |
|-----|-----|--------|
| 54.7% | 32.0% | 13.3% |

## Section 2

The questions in the following section require an answer on a scale ranging from 5 to 1. Answer by circling number 5 if you **strongly agree** with the statement, 4 if you **agree**, and 3 if you are **uncertain**. If you **disagree** with the statement, circle number 2, and if you **strongly disagree** with the statement or if the opposite was true in your case, circle number 1. If you believe the question does not apply to you, leave it blank.

| | (N) | Strongly Disagree | | | | Strongly Agree |
|---|-----|-------------------|---|---|---|----------------|
| 1. Prior to my abortion, I believed that abortion was a moral choice. | (252) | 15.1% | 9.1% | 36.9% | 22.2% | 16.7% |

| | (N) | Strongly Disagree | | | | Strongly Agree |
|---|---|---|---|---|---|---|
| 2. I believed abortion should be a legal option for all women. | (257) | 29.2% | 10.1% | 24.9% | 19.5% | 16.3% |
| 3. My choice to abort was consistent with my prior beliefs about abortion. | (254) | 36.2% | 17.3% | 18.5% | 16.1% | 11.8% |
| 4. My choice was inconsistent with my prior beliefs. I felt my decision was a betrayal of my own ideals. | (248) | 12.9% | 11.3% | 15.3% | 14.9% | 45.6% |
| 5. My decision to have an abortion was an agonizing one. | (256) | 8.4% | 11.6% | 7.2% | 18.5% | 54.2% |
| 6. Prior to my abortion I was a religious person. | (259) | 16.6% | 19.7% | 17.0% | 26.3% | 20.5% |
| 7. There was a time prior to my abortion when I received professional counseling for emotional or psychiatric difficulties. | (248) | 59.7% | 12.9% | 4.0% | 10.1% | 13.3% |
| 8. The memory of my abortion has faded with time. | (256) | 52.0% | 22.3% | 6.6% | 10.2% | 9.0% |
| 9. The memory of my abortion is vividly clear. | (255) | 8.2% | 10.2% | 9.8% | 25.1% | 46.7% |
| 10. The abortion procedure was painful. | (257) | 10.9% | 8.2% | 12.1% | 22.2% | 46.7% |

## Section 3

The following is a checklist of possible post-abortion reactions. Answers again range from 1, **strongly disagree**, to 5, **strongly agree**. In general, answer 2 for **no**, 3 for **uncertain**, and 4 for **yes**. Only if you experienced a **severe reaction**, should you answer with number 5. If you experienced a strong reaction **opposite** to the one questioned, answer by circling number 1. If the question is not applicable to your case, leave the question blank.

**After my abortion, I experienced feelings of:**

| | (N) | Strongly Disagree | | | | Strongly Agree |
|---|---|---|---|---|---|---|
| 1. Guilt | (256) | 0.4% | 2.3% | 4.7% | 31.3% | 61.3% |
| 2. Depression | (255) | 0.4% | 3.9% | 7.5% | 35.7% | 52.5% |
| 3. Anger | (255) | 1.2% | 9.0% | 9.0% | 35.7% | 45.1% |
| 4. Sorrow | (255) | 0.4% | 2.4% | 5.5% | 36.5% | 55.3% |
| 5. Happiness | (241) | 62.2% | 22.4% | 7.9% | 5.4% | 2.1% |
| 6. Grief | (255) | 0.8% | 5.5% | 9.0% | 40.8% | 43.9% |
| 7. Bitterness | (251) | 3.2% | 8.8% | 13.5% | 34.7% | 39.8% |
| 8. Regret | (257) | 1.9% | 3.5% | 9.7% | 32.7% | 52.1% |
| 9. Rage | (245) | 9.4% | 20.0% | 20.4% | 21.2% | 29.0% |
| 10. Anguish | (245) | 02.0% | 07.8% | 14.3% | 37.1% | 38.8% |
| 11. Remorse | (254) | 1.6% | 5.9% | 6.3% | 41.3% | 44.9% |
| 12. Power | (237) | 58.6% | 23.2% | 12.2% | 3.8% | 2.1% |
| 13. Despair | (245) | 2.4% | 9.8% | 13.9% | 35.5% | 38.4% |
| 14. Shame | (254) | 0.4% | 2.8% | 5.9% | 39.0% | 52.0% |
| 15. Horror | (241) | 4.6% | 13.3% | 23.2% | 29.0% | 29.9% |
| 16. Unworthiness | (254) | 1.6% | 3.9% | 8.7% | 33.5% | 52.4% |
| 17. Loneliness | (250) | 2.0% | 6.8% | 7.6% | 38.4% | 45.2% |
| 18. Hopelessness | (247) | 2.0% | 11.3% | 13.4% | 32.0% | 41.3% |
| 19. Helplessness | (248) | 2.0% | 14.1% | 11.7% | 31.5% | 40.7% |
| 20. Self-condemnation | (251) | 1.2% | 2.4% | 5.6% | 33.9% | 57.0% |
| 21. Liberation | (234) | 44.4% | 25.2% | 16.7% | 11.5% | 2.1% |
| 22. Rejection | (238) | 4.6% | 10.1% | 24.8% | 31.1% | 29.4% |
| 23. Confusion | (250) | 1.2% | 6.4% | 11.6% | 44.4% | 36.4% |
| 24. Anxiety | (248) | 1.6% | 6.5% | 10.5% | 43.5% | 37.9% |
| 25. Constant stress | (246) | 2.0% | 14.2% | 19.5% | 33.3% | 30.9% |
| 26. Withdrawal | (245) | 2.9% | 15.5% | 16.7% | 33.1% | 31.8% |

## After my abortion, I experienced:

| | (N) | *Strongly Disagree* | | | | *Strongly Agree* |
|---|---|---|---|---|---|---|
| 27. Isolation | (241) | 3.3% | 17.4% | 17.4% | 31.5% | 30.3% |
| 28. Sexual freedom | (235) | 40.0% | 25.5% | 19.1% | 11.1% | 4.3% |
| 29. Self-hatred | (250) | 2.8% | 6.8% | 13.6% | 33.2% | 43.6% |
| 30. Alienation from others | (238) | 3.4% | 20.6% | 18.5% | 31.9% | 25.6% |
| 31. Inner peace | (237) | 63.7% | 25.7% | 5.5% | 2.1% | 3.0% |
| 32. Unforgiveness of self | (258) | 1.9% | 5.8% | 6.6% | 31.4% | 54.3% |
| 33. Unforgiveness of those involved | (252) | 5.6% | 15.5% | 14.7% | 34.9% | 29.4% |
| 34. Having become degraded or debased | (243) | 2.1% | 12.8% | 17.7% | 37.4% | 30.0% |
| 35. Having been exploited by others | (243) | 2.9% | 15.2% | 19.3% | 30.9% | 31.7% |
| 36. Hatred of those involved | (240) | 7.9% | 22.5% | 22.9% | 22.9% | 23.8% |
| 37. Hatred of man who made me pregnant | (249) | 15.3% | 29.7% | 20.1% | 16.9% | 18.1% |
| 38. Hatred of all men | (243) | 23.0% | 33.7% | 19.8% | 15.2% | 8.2% |
| 39. Fear of punishment from God | (249) | 4.4% | 12.0% | 13.3% | 34.9% | 35.3% |
| 40. Fear of harm to my other children | (218) | 17.0% | 21.6% | 12.8% | 25.2% | 23.4% |
| 41. Fear of another pregnancy | (245) | 13.5% | 23.7% | 13.9% | 25.3% | 23.7% |
| 42. Fear of needing another abortion | (244) | 24.2% | 28.7% | 12.3% | 15.2% | 19.7% |
| 43. Fear of touching babies | (246) | 24.8% | 37.0% | 13.0% | 13.8% | 11.4% |
| 44. Fear of others learning of abortion | (255) | 5.5% | 9.4% | 8.2% | 42.0% | 34.9% |
| 45. Fear of making decisions | (245) | 6.9% | 21.6% | 23.3% | 28.2% | 20.0% |

**After my abortion, I experienced:**

| | (N) | Strongly Disagree | | | | Strongly Agree |
|---|---|---|---|---|---|---|
| 1. Nightmares | (241) | 16.2% | 22.4% | 14.9% | 28.6% | 17.8% |
| 2. Insomnia | (243) | 15.2% | 25.5% | 14.4% | 25.5% | 19.3% |
| 3. Flashbacks to the abortion | (249) | 8.0% | 18.1% | 10.4% | 35.3% | 28.1% |
| 4. Hysterical outbreaks | (244) | 11.1% | 25.4% | 12.7% | 22.5% | 28.3% |
| 5. Uncontrollable weeping | (242) | 5.8% | 14.5% | 9.9% | 35.5% | 34.3% |
| 6. Suicidal feelings | (244) | 12.3% | 22.5% | 9.4% | 24.2% | 31.6% |
| 7. Greater closeness toward my lover | (242) | 51.7% | 29.8% | 9.1% | 7.0% | 2.5% |
| 8. A loss of self-confidence | (249) | 2.4% | 9.2% | 12.9% | 38.2% | 37.3% |
| 9. A loss of self-esteem | (254) | 1.2% | 5.9% | 10.6% | 38.2% | 44.1% |
| 10. A loss of dignity | (251) | 1.2% | 8.0% | 10.4% | 42.2% | 38.2% |
| 11. A general sense of loss | (253) | 1.6% | 4.3% | 7.9% | 42.3% | 43.9% |
| 12. Greater self-awareness | (237) | 36.3% | 27.8% | 19.0% | 11.8% | 5.1% |
| 13. Hallucinations related to abortion | (233) | 30.0% | 41.6% | 13.7% | 6.9% | 7.7% |
| 14. Eating disorders such as bulimia, anorexia, or binge eating. | (241) | 22.4% | 31.5% | 7.5% | 20.3% | 18.3% |
| 15. A general sense of emptiness | (248) | 1.6% | 7.7% | 7.3% | 42.7% | 40.7% |
| 16. A loss of sympathy for others | (242) | 16.5% | 22.7% | 21.5% | 22.7% | 16.5% |
| 17. A compulsion to be a perfect mother | (231) | 10.0% | 19.0% | 21.2% | 24.7% | 25.1% |
| 18. An inability to keep jobs | (232) | 27.6% | 33.6% | 14.2% | 15.9% | 8.6% |
| 19. A loss of concentration | (236) | 8.9% | 22.5% | 21.2% | 29.2% | 18.2% |
| 20. Difficulty in maintaining and developing personal relationships | (246) | 9.3% | 19.5% | 14.2% | 30.1% | 26.8% |

**After my abortion, I became:**

| | (N) | *Strongly Disagree* | | | | *Strongly Agree* |
|---|---|---|---|---|---|---|
| 1. Preoccupied with thoughts of death. | (243) | 14.4% | 29.6% | 13.2% | 20.6% | 22.2% |
| 2. Preoccupied with thoughts of the child I could have had. | (252) | 5.6% | 12.7% | 10.3% | 34.9% | 36.5% |
| 3. Excessively interested in pregnant women. | (243) | 21.0% | 33.7% | 15.2% | 17.7% | 12.3% |
| 4. Excessively interested in babies. | (244) | 18.9% | 28.3% | 15.2% | 19.3% | 18.4% |

**Negative feelings about my abortion became worse:**

| | (N) | *Strongly Disagree* | | | | *Strongly Agree* |
|---|---|---|---|---|---|---|
| 1. On the due date of pregnancy. | (238) | 10.9% | 25.6% | 20.6% | 21.8% | 21.0% |
| 2. On the anniversary of the abortion. | (235) | 11.5% | 17.4% | 19.6% | 26.4% | 25.1% |
| 3. During a later pregnancy. | (199) | 16.1% | 18.1% | 11.1% | 28.6% | 26.1% |
| 4. At the birth of a later child. | (200) | 19.5% | 21.0% | 10.5% | 23.0% | 26.0% |
| 5. At the time of a later miscarriage. | (151) | 33.8% | 28.5% | 10.6% | 11.3% | 15.9% |
| 6. When I later tried to get pregnant. | (181) | 24.3% | 24.3% | 11.0% | 19.9% | 20.4% |
| 7. When exposed to pro-life propaganda. | (242) | 8.3% | 9.9% | 5.0% | 38.8% | 38.0% |
| 8. When exposed to pro-choice propaganda | (227) | 10.6% | 15.0% | 9.3% | 31.3% | 33.9% |
| 9. When exposed to information in the mass media about fetal development | (239) | 7.1% | 8.4% | 7.9% | 34.3% | 42.3% |

**After my abortion:**

| | (N) | Strongly Disagree | | | | Strongly Agree |
|---|---|---|---|---|---|---|
| 1. I felt more in touch with my emotions | (247) | 37.7% | 36.4% | 14.2% | 6.1% | 5.7% |
| 2. I felt a need to block out and stifle my feelings | (250) | 3.2% | 6.8% | 10.8% | 35.2% | 44.0% |
| 3. I needed to "force" myself to be happy | (250) | 2.0% | 10.8% | 17.6% | 38.8% | 30.8% |
| 4. I felt unable to grieve | (248) | 8.5% | 17.7% | 13.7% | 35.1% | 25.0% |
| 5. My attitude toward life became more calloused or hardened | (245) | 5.3% | 11.4% | 17.6% | 35.5% | 30.2% |
| 6. I felt more in control of my life | (244) | 41.8% | 41.4% | 9.4% | 3.7% | 3.7% |
| 7. I started losing my temper more easily | (245) | 5.3% | 14.3% | 21.2% | 35.1% | 24.1% |
| 8. I became more violent when angered | (246) | 10.6% | 26.4% | 15.4% | 26.8% | 20.7% |
| 9. I began to drink more heavily | (244) | 27.0% | 27.5% | 9.0% | 19.3% | 17.2% |

| | (N) | Yes | No | Unsure |
|---|---|---|---|---|
| If so, would you describe yourself as having become an alocholic? | (107) | 27.1% | 50.5% | 22.4% |

| | (N) | Strongly Disagree | | | | Strongly Agree |
|---|---|---|---|---|---|---|
| 10. I began to use, or increased my use of drugs | (234) | 33.8% | 20.5% | 5.1% | 21.4% | 19.2% |

| | (N) | Yes | No | Unsure |
|---|---|---|---|---|
| If so, would you describe yourself as having become addicted? | (106) | 25.5% | 61.3% | 13.2% |

|  | (N) | Strongly Disagree |  |  |  | Strongly Agree |
|---|---|---|---|---|---|---|
| 11. I underwent a dramatic personality change. | (240) | 6.7% | 15.4% | 26.7% | 26.7% | 24.6% |
| If so, the change was for the better. (1 - worse, 5 - better) | (155) | 61.3% | 18.1% | 12.9% | 4.5% | 3.2% |
| 12. I experienced a radical change in my ideals and moral beliefs. | (237) | 8.4% | 17.7% | 29.5% | 21.5% | 22.8% |

## Section 4

Answer the following questions by checking the appropriate box or filling in the blank space as required.

|  | (N) | Yes | No | Unsure |
|---|---|---|---|---|
| 1. Was there a time after your abortion when you would have considered yourself pro-choice? | (250) | 46.0% | 36.8% | 17.2% |
| 2. Was there a time after your abortion when you would have encouraged or supported a woman in similar circumstances to consider abortion? | (252) | 31.7% | 54.0% | 14.3% |
| 3. Have you ever regretted having had the abortion? | (251) | 94.0% | 3.2% | 2.8% |
| 4. Have you ever had a waking or sleeping visitation from the aborted child? | (248) | 17.7% | 73.0% | 9.3% |

|  | (N) | vengeful | or | forgiving |
|---|---|---|---|---|
| If so, was the mood of the visitaton . . . | (46) | 23.9% |  | 74.1% |

|  | (N) | Yes | No | Unsure |
|---|---|---|---|---|
| 5. Did you ever talk to the aborted child prior to the abortion? | (249) | 32.1% | 61.8% | 6.0% |
| 6. Did you ever talk to the aborted child after the abortion? | (248) | 48.8% | 45.6% | 5.6% |

| | | Yes | No | Unsure |
|---|---|---|---|---|
| 7. Did your relationship with your sexual partner come to an end after the abortion? | (248) | 66.1% | 31.0% | 2.8% |

| | | within 1 month | within 6 months | a year or more |
|---|---|---|---|---|
| If so, how soon after the abortion? | (166) | 55.4% | 22.9% | 21.7% |

| | | Yes | No | Unsure |
|---|---|---|---|---|
| 8. Did you experience greater irregularity of menstrual periods after your abortion? | (249) | 33.7% | 55.8% | 10.4% |
| 9. Did you frequently experience heavy bleeding after your abortion? | (250) | 41.2% | 50.4% | 8.4% |
| 10. Did you experience pain in the cervix or abdomen? | (249) | 58.2% | 31.3% | 10.4% |
| 11. Did you experience an increased sense of pain during intercourse? | (247) | 33.2% | 49.0% | 17.8% |
| 12. Did you experience a loss of pleasure from intercourse? | (248) | 58.5% | 28.2% | 13.3% |
| 13. Did you develop an aversion to sexual intercourse or become sexually unresponsive? | (247) | 46.6% | 38.5% | 15.0% |
| 14. Did you become promiscuous after your abortion? | (246) | 42.7% | 51.6% | 5.7% |
| 15. Did you experience greater fear of becoming pregnant when waiting for each period to begin? | (246) | 48.8% | 45.5% | 5.7% |
| 16. Did you have your self surgically sterilized in order to avoid the risk of needing another abortion? | (250) | 8.8% | 90.4% | 0.8% |
| 17. Did you ever experience any false pregnancies after your abortion? | (247) | 24.7% | 68.4% | 6.9% |
| 18. Did you attempt to atone for your abortion by conceiving a "replacement pregnancy?" | (245) | 28.6% | 62.9% | 8.6% |

| | 1-6 months | 7-12 months | 13-24 months | 25-36 months | >36 months |
|---|---|---|---|---|---|
| If so, how long after your abortion did you become pregnant again? (N=76) | 15.8% | 28.9% | 15.7% | 11.8% | 27.6% |

|                                                                           | (N)   | Yes    | No     | Unsure |
|---------------------------------------------------------------------------|-------|--------|--------|--------|
| 19. Did you ever attempt suicide?                                         | (248) | 28.2%  | 70.2%  | 1.6%   |

|                        | One   | Two    | Three  | Four  | >Four  |
|------------------------|-------|--------|--------|-------|--------|
| If so, how many times? | 46.8% | 30.6%  | 16.1%  | 0%    | 6.5%   |

|                                                                                  | (N)   | Yes    | No     | Unsure |
|----------------------------------------------------------------------------------|-------|--------|--------|--------|
| 20. Were you ever physically abused as a child?                                  | (248) | 20.6%  | 71.4%  | 8.1%   |
| 21. Were you ever sexually abused as a child?                                    | (247) | 24.3%  | 65.6%  | 10.1%  |
| 22. Did you ever abuse your children before your abortion?                       | (193) | 2.1%   | 96.9%  | 1.0%   |
| 23. Did you ever emotionally abuse your children before your abortion?           | (190) | 4.2%   | 92.6%  | 3.2%   |
| 24. After your abortion, did you experience a strong feeling of relief?          | (248) | 37.9%  | 49.6%  | 12.5%  |

|                      | (N)   | weeks  | months | or years? |
|----------------------|-------|--------|--------|-----------|
| If so, did it last . . . | (95)  | 60.0%  | 12.6%  | 25.3%     |

|                                                                                            | (N)   | Yes    | No     | Unsure |
|--------------------------------------------------------------------------------------------|-------|--------|--------|--------|
| 25. After your abortion, did you experience any negative reactions or ambivalent feelings? | (253) | 89.3%  | 2.0%   | 8.7%   |

|                                                                                                              | (N)   | Immediately | Within 6 months | After a year or more |
|--------------------------------------------------------------------------------------------------------------|-------|-------------|-----------------|----------------------|
| If so, when did you experience the first of your negative or ambivalent feelings?                            | (228) | 64.5%       | 18.9%           | 16.7%                |
| If so, when did you experience the majority (or worst) of your negative feelings?                            | (222) | 21.2%       | 18.5%           | 60.4%                |

|                                                                                  | (N)   | Yes    | No     | Unsure |
|----------------------------------------------------------------------------------|-------|--------|--------|--------|
| 26. Do you feel fully reconciled with your abortion experience today?            | (251) | 31.9%  | 51.0%  | 17.1%  |
| 27. Knowing where your life is today, did your abortion improve your life?       | (253) | 5.9%   | 71.9%  | 22.1%  |

## Section 5

If you have never experienced any negative or uncertain feelings about your abortion, you may stop here. THANK YOU for your valuable participation.

| | (N) | *Mild* | *Moderate* | *Severe* | *Very Severe* |
|---|---|---|---|---|---|
| 1. Overall, how severe were the emotional aftereffects of your abortion? | (246) | 5.3% | 23.6% | 41.5% | 29.7% |

| | (N) | *Yes* | *No* | *Unsure* |
|---|---|---|---|---|
| 2. Was there any time during which your reactions were so severe that you were unable to function normally at home, work, or in personal relationships? | (244) | 55.3% | 34.8% | 9.8% |

| | *1-6 months* | *7-12 months* | *13-24 months* | *25-36 months* | *>36 months* |
|---|---|---|---|---|---|
| If so, how long did this disability last? | 41.5% | 7.6% | 12.2% | 12.2% | 26.4% |

| | (N) | *Yes* | *No* | *Unsure* |
|---|---|---|---|---|
| 3. Would you describe yourself as self-destructive? | (245) | 36.7% | 50.6% | 12.7% |
| 4. Did you undergo a nervous breakdown at some time after your abortion? | (241) | 20.3% | 63.1% | 16.6% |
| 5. Were you ever hospitalized for psychological treatment because of the abortion? | (244) | 10.2% | 89.8% | --- |
| 6. Was there a period of time during which you denied the existence of any doubts or negative feelings about your abortion? | (245) | 62.9% | 24.1% | 13.1% |

| | *1-6 months* | *7-12 months* | *13-24 months* | *25-36 months* | *>36 months* |
|---|---|---|---|---|---|
| If so, for how long? Avg: 63.1 mos. (N = 124) | 24.2% | 9.7% | 8.0% | 8.0 | 50.0% |

| | (N) | *Yes* | *No* | *Unsure* |
|---|---|---|---|---|
| 7. Despite your negative feelings, do you still believe the choice to have an abortion was the right thing to do? | (247) | 2.8% | 86.6% | 10.5% |
| If not, was there a time after recognizing your negative feelings during which you would have still insisted that you had done the right thing? | (214) | 19.2% | 61.2% | 19.6% |

|  | 1 year | 2 years | 3 years | 4 years | 5 years | >5 years |
|---|---|---|---|---|---|---|
| If so, for how long?<br>Avg: 4.6 yrs. (N = 37) | 32.4% | 16.2% | 8.1% | 5.4% | 18.9% | 18.9% |

|  | <1 year | 1-2 years | 3-5 years | 6-10 years | >10 years |
|---|---|---|---|---|---|
| 8. How long did it take for you to begin to reconcile yourself to your abortion experience? Avg: 7.5 yrs. (N = 184) | 6.5% | 11.4% | 25.6 | 35.3 | 21.2% |

|  | (N) | Yes | No | Unsure |
|---|---|---|---|---|
| 9. Do you feel fully reconciled with your abortion experience today? | (241) | 31.9% | 48.5% | 20.3% |
| 10. Has abortion made your life worse? | (238) | 60.9% | 16.4% | 22.7% |

11.  Place a check mark next to whichever of the following persons you went to for help in coping with your negative feelings, and check whether or not they were helpful.

| (N) | Talked with: | Was Helpful | Not Helpful | Uncertain |
|---|---|---|---|---|
| (86) | psychologist/psychiatrist | 38.5% | 58.1% | 3.5% |
| (63) | social worker/counselor | 41.3% | 57.7% | 1.6% |
| (92) | clergy | 68.5% | 31.5% | 0.0% |
| (69) | parent(s) | 36.2% | 62.3% | 1.4% |
| (145) | husband/boyfriend(s) | 46.9% | 49.0% | 4.0% |
| (144) | friends | 60.4% | 38.2% | 1.4% |
| (88) | post-abortion counseling group | 90.9% | 8.0% | 1.1% |
| (45) | other : _____ | 80.0% | 17.8% | 2.2% |

Among the most frequent listed "other" were religious references to God, Jesus, the Bible, and prayer (39%). Also listed were sister, aunt, and bartender, nurse, and pro-life person.

Originally appeared in *The Post-Abortion Review*, 2(3):4-8, Fall 1994. © 1994, Elliot Institute.

# Appendix D

# Resources

Below is a partial list of the many organizations worldwide that offer support and counseling to those struggling with a past abortion. Many offer phone or online counseling or referral to a counselor or support group in your area.

If you are seeking post-abortion counseling, be sure to ask lots of questions to find an organization with which you are comfortable. If you would like a professional counselor or therapist (especially if you have a history of psychological problems or other trauma), ask the group for a referral if they don't have a professional on staff.

The services offered by these groups are confidential and, in many cases, free. While an effort has been made to verify the credentials and work of each organization, inclusion in this list should not be taken as an endorsement of a particular group's programs or philosophy.

## Organizations for Healing After Abortion

*Rachel's Vineyard Ministries*
Theresa Karminski Burke, Ph.D., and J. Kevin Burke MSS/LSW, Directors
PO Box 195
Bridgeport, PA   19405-0195
1-877-HOPE-4-ME (1-877-467-3463)
www.rachelsvineyard.org

Offers post-abortion weekend retreats and support groups at many sites across the U.S. and abroad. Provides leadership and clinical training seminars, conferences, publications and resources for other healing ministries that wish to offer the retreats. Current retreat dates and locations are listed on the web site.

*Hope Alive*
Dr. Philip Ney and Dr. Marie Peeters Ney
International Institute for Pregnancy Loss & Child Abuse Research & Recovery
PO Box 27103, Colwood Corners
Victoria, BC   V9B 5S4
CANADA
(250) 642-1848
www.messengers2.com
Email: iiplcarr@islandnet.com

Provides research and training for people in group counseling, as well as support for those affected by child abuse or abortion. Research and support for survivors of attempted abortion and those who have lost a sibling to abortion. Also runs a small training college. Hope Alive programs are available in 22 countries. For a referral outside the US or Canada, contact Fr. Seamus O'Connell at IIPLCARR's International Office via email at iiplcarr@btinternet.com.

*Hope Alive USA*
Sonja Kvale
52 Waleny Dr.
Bella Vista, AR 72715
(479) 855-0072
www.HopeAliveUSA.org
Email: HopeAliveUSA@aol.com

Hope Alive group treatment program for those deeply damaged by child abuse, neglect and pregnancy loss. Helps set up training, resources and supervision for those desiring to become Hope Alive counselors. Provides referrals to trained counselors for those desiring the 30-week treatment program.

*The National Office of Post Abortion Reconciliation and Healing*
Vicki Thorn, Director
PO Box 07477
Milwaukee, WI 53207-0477
(414) 483-4141
1-800-5WE-CARE (national referral number)
www.marquette.edu/rachel

National office of Project Rachel, a ministry of the Catholic Church composed of a network of specially trained clergy, spiritual directors and therapists who provide compassionate care to those who are struggling with the aftermath of abortion. Provides confidential help to women and men of all faiths. For referrals to support groups and outreaches of various denominations, contact the national referral number.

*P.A.C.E. (Post Abortion Counseling and Education)*
CareNet
109 Carpenter Drive, Suite 100
Sterling, VA 20164
800- 395-HELP

Provides referrals for individual or group post abortion peer counseling services throughout the country.

*Ramah International*
Synda Masse, Director
1776 Hudson Street
Englewood, Florida
(941) 473-2188
www.ramahinternational.org

Seeks to bring post-abortive individuals to Christ's healing, and supports post-abortion ministry through training programs, resources, research and promoting awareness of post-abortion issues around the world.

## ON-LINE POST-ABORTION MINISTRIES

### *After Abortion*
www.afterabortion.com

Provides neutral, non-judgmental, non-religious, non-political on-line support, information, help and healing for women who have had an abortion. Provides "peer support" from other post-abortive women (does not offer professional counseling), volunteer helpers, communication and online information. Also offers support for partners and family members of post-abortive women. Seeks to have post-abortion syndrome recognized as a medical issue for women, not a political or religious one.

### *Flames of Fire*
Cynthia Kretschmar, Director
www.flamesoffire.com

Seeks to help individuals overcome behavior patterns that negatively affect your emotional, relational, or spiritual development which may have been damaged by abortion.

### *Healing Hearts*
www.web-light.com/heart

Provides confidential one to one e-mail and support group counseling to anyone suffering from the effects of an abortion.

### *Last Harvest Ministries Inc.*
Ken Freeman, Director
www.lastharvest.org.
Email:   minister@lastharvest.org

Provides Christian-based on-line recovery support to men and women suffering from the aftermath of abortion and related life-dominating issues.

## POST-ABORTION SUPPORT FOR MEN

*NOTE: Groups previously listed may also offer support or counseling for men.*

### *Fathers and Brothers Ministries*
350 Broadway, Suite 40
Boulder, CO 80303
(303) 494-3282

Provides support, counseling and information for men who have lost children to abortion.

## Support for Former Abortion Providers/Workers

*The Centurions*
Joan Appleton, R.N., Director
PO Box 75368
ST. Paul, MN 55175\0368
(651) 771-1500
www.plam.org
Email: joan@plam.org

Ministers to former abortion workers and those attempting to leave the abortion industry, providing guidance, long-term support, fellowship and a path to reconciliation and healing.

## Periodicals Which Focus on Abortion's Impact

*The Post Abortion Review*
The Elliot Institute
Dr. David Reardon, Director
PO Box 7348
Springfield, IL 62791-7348
(217) 525-8202
www.afterabortion.info

A quarterly publication that focuses on the impact of abortion on women, men, families and society. Includes summaries of the latest research findings and other relevant information. The recommended donation is $20 per year, but can be received for a smaller donation. Also publishes brochures and books on post-abortion issues.

*Research Bulletin*
Thomas W. Strahan, Editor
The Association for Interdisciplinary Research in Values and Social Change
419 7th Street NW., Suite 500
Washington, DC   20004
(202) 626-8800

A scholarly review of research on post-abortion issues, published six times yearly.

## Resources for Women in Crisis Pregnancies

*Bethany Christian Services*
901 Eastern Ave. NE
Grand Rapids, MI 49503-1295
1-800-238-4269
www.bethany.org

Provides pregnancy counseling, temporary foster care, alternative living arrangements for pregnant women, and national and international adoption services. Also offers family and marital counseling and services for refugees, runaways and homeless youth.

*Birthright*
1-800-550-4900

Provides free and confidential pregnancy testing, support for pregnant women, maternity and baby clothes, parenting classes, adoption services, medical care, family counseling and referrals for legal assistance.

*Carenet*
109 Carpenter Dr., Suite 100
Sterling, VA 20164
1-800-395-HELP (1-800-395-4357)
Email: carenet@juno.com

A national network of crisis pregnancy centers that help women in need with free pregnancy tests, maternity clothes, medical and professional services, and special care for single mothers. Also offers post-abortion counseling.

*Feminists for Life*
Serrin Foster, President
733 15th Street, NW, Suite 1100
Washington, DC 20005
(202) 737-3352
www.feministsforlife.org

A non-sectarian, non-profit organization proudly following in the footsteps of our early pro-life feminist foremothers. Efforts focus on education, outreach and advocacy, as well as facilitating practical resources and support for women in need.

*Heartbeat International*
Peggy Hartshorn, President
7870 Olentangy River Rd., Suite 304
Columbus, OH 43235-1319
(614) 885-7577
Email: heartbeat@qn.net

Offers pregnancy services, maternity homes for expectant mothers and adoption counseling. Also serves as a major support organization for crisis pregnancy centers.

*International Life Services*
(213) 382-2156
www.life-services.org

Provides counseling and support for women facing unintended pregnancies, and offers referrals to local support centers.

*The Nurturing Network*
Mary Cunningham Agee, Director
1-800-866-4666
www.nurturingnetwork.org

A network of 30,000 volunteer member resources nationwide that provide individually-tailored, practical support to college and working women with unplanned pregnancies. Offers counseling and medical, residential, educational, employment and financial resources.

# BIBLIOGRAPHY

*Aborted Women, Silent No More*
David C. Reardon (Springfield, IL : Acorn Books, 1987)

*Abortion and Healing: A Cry to be Whole*
Michael Mannion (Kansas City, MO: Sheed and Ward, 1992)

*Abortion's Second Victim*
Pam Koerbel (Wheaton, IL: Victor Books, 1986)

*After Abortion: Stories of Healing*
Pat King (Ligouri: MO: Ligouri Publications, 1992)

*A Path to Hope: For Parents of Aborted Children and Those Who Minister to Them*
John J. Dillon (Minela, NY: Resurrection Press, 1991)

*A Season to Heal: Help and Hope for Those Working Through Post-Abortion Stress*
Luci Freed and Penny Yvonne Salazar (Nashville: Thomas Nelson Publishers, 1993)

*Blessed Are the Barren: The Social Policy of Planned Parenthood*
Robert Marshall and Charles Donovan (San Francisco: Ignatius Press, 1991)

*Deeply Damaged*
Philip G. Ney, MD. (Victoria, British Columbia: Pioneer Publishing, 1997)

*Detrimental Effects of Abortion: An Annotated Bibliography With Commentary*
Thomas W. Strahan (Springfield, IL: Acorn Books, 2001)

*Disenfranchised Grief: Recognizing Hidden Sorrow*
Kenneth J. Doka (New York: Lexington Books, 1989)

*From Heartache to Healing: Coping with the Effects of Abortion,*
Linda Bartlett (St. Louis, MO: Concordia Publishing House, 1992)

*Giving Sorrow Words*
Melinda Tankard Reist (Sydney, Australia: Duffy & Snellgrove, 2000)

*Healing Post-Abortion Trauma: Help for Women Hurt by Abortion*
Holly Trimble (American Life League, P.O. Box 1350, Stafford, VA 22555; 703-659-4171)

*Healing Relationships with Miscarried, Aborted and Stillborn Babies*
Sheila Fabricant, Matthew Linn and Dennis Linn, S.J. (Kansas City, MO: Sheed and Ward, 1985)

*Help for the Post-Abortion Woman*
Teri Reisser, M.S., and Paul Reisser, M.D. (Grand Rapids, MI: Zondervan Publishing House, 1989)

*Helping Women Recover from Abortion*
Nancy Michels (Minneapolis, MN: Bethany House Publishers)

*Her Choice to Heal*
Synda Masse and Joan Phillips (Colorado Springs, CO: Chariot Victor Publishing, 1998)

*Hope Alive: Post Abortion and Abuse Treatment* (therapist's training manual)
Dr. Phillip Ney and Dr. Marie Peeters (IIPLCARR, PO Box 27103, Colwood Corners, Victoria, British Columbia, V9B 5S4; 604-391-1840) 1993

*Identifying and Overcoming Postabortion Syndrome*
Teri K. Reisser, M.S. and Paul C. Reisser, M.D. (Focus on the Family, 1605 Explorer Dr., Colorado Springs, CO   80995) 1992

*The Jericho Plan: Breaking Down the Walls Which Prevent Post-Abortion Healing*
David C. Reardon (Springfield, IL: Acorn Books, 1996)

*LIME 5* (documents abortion injuries and deaths)
Mark Crutcher (Life Dynamics, Inc., P.O. Box 2226, Denton, TX 76202;   817-380-8800) 1996

*Making Abortion Rare: A Healing Strategy for a Divided Nation*
David C. Reardon (Springfield, IL:  Acorn Books, 1996)

*Men and Abortion*
Arthur Schostak and Gary McClouth (New York: Praeger Publishers, 1984)

*The Mourning After: Help for Post-Abortion Syndrome*
Terry L. Selby, MSW (Grand Rapids, MI: Baker Book House, 1990)

*Parental Loss of a Child*
Therese A. Rando, editor (Champaign: IL, Research Press Company,  1986)

*Post Abortion Trauma — 9 Steps to Recovery*
Jeanette Vought (Grand Rapids, MI: Zondervan Publishing House, 1991)

*Psycho-Social Stress Following Abortion*
Anne Speckhard, Ph.D. (Kansas City, MO: Sheed and Ward, 1987)

*Real Choices*
Frederica Mathewes Green (Ben Lomond, CA: Conciliar Press, 1997)

*The Scarlet Lady: Confessions of a Successful Abortionist*
Carol Everett (Brentwood, TN:  Wolgemuth and Hyatt Publishers, Inc., 1991)

*Soul Crisis: One Woman's Journey Through Abortion to Renewal*
Sue Nathanson, Ph.D. (Markham, Ontario: New American Library/Penguin Books)

*The Tentative Pregnancy: Prenatal Diagnosis and the Future of Motherhood*
Barbara Kay Rothman (New York: Viking Press, 1986)

*Victims and Victors: Speaking Out About Their Pregnancies, Abortions, and Children Resulting from Sexual Assault*
David C. Reardon, Julie Makimaa and Amy Sobie, editors (Springfield, IL: Acorn Books, 2000)

*Will I Cry Tomorrow?*
Susan Stanford-Rue, Ph.D. (Old Tappan, NJ: Revell Publishing Co., 1987)

*Women Exploited: The Other Victim of Abortion*
Paula Ervin (Thaxton, VA: Sun Life Books, 1984)

# NOTES

## INTRODUCTION

1. Mary K. Zimmerman, *Passage Through Abortion* (New York: Praeger Publishers, 1977); H.J. Osofsky & J.D. Osofsky, eds., *The Abortion Experience* (New York: Harper & Row, 1973); David C. Reardon, *Aborted Women, Silent No More* (Chicago: Loyola University Press, 1987).
2. *Los Angeles Times* Poll, March 19, 1989, question 76.

## CHAPTER ONE: GINA'S STORY

1. Reardon, *Aborted Women, Silent No More*, op. cit. (introduction, no. 1) 333.

## CHAPTER TWO: HIDING THE TRUTH

1. Letter from an aborted mother, "An Apology to a Little Boy I Won't Ever See," *Evening Bulletin*, Providence, Rhode Island, April 23, 1980.
2. Arthur Lazarus, "Psychiatric Sequelae of Legalized Elective First Trimester Abortion," *J. Pscyhosomatic Obstet. Gynec.* 4:141-150 (1985). Many women reported both negative and positive reactions at the same time. In interviews conducted with women immediately after their abortions, Lazarus observed that "denial and rationalization seemed to play a major role in assuaging negative effect for many women." These findings support the view that abortion is a complex experience.
3. Colman McCarthy, "A Psychological View of Abortion," *Washington Post*, March 7, 1971. Dr. Fogel, who did 20,000 abortions over the subsequent decades, reiterated the same view in a second interview with McCarthy in 1989: "The Real Anguish of Abortions," *The Washington Post*, Feb. 5, 1989.
4. Reardon, *Aborted Women, Silent No More*, op. cit. (introduction, no. 1) 15-19.
5. For discussions of heightened psychological accessibility of persons in crisis, see Gerald Caplan, *Principles of Preventive Psychiatry* (New York: Basic Books, 1964) and Howard W. Stone, *Crisis Counseling* (Minneapolis: Fortress Press, 1976).
6. Zimmerman, *Passage Through Abortion*, op. cit. (introduction, no. 1) 139.
7. Zeckman and Warrick, "Abortion Profiteers," Special Reprint, *Chicago Sun-Times*, 1978.
8. Reardon, *Aborted Women, Silent No More*, op. cit. (introduction, no. 1) 215-243.
9. Ibid, 256.
10. David C. Reardon, *Making Abortion Rare: A Healing Strategy for a Divided Nation* (Springfield, IL: Acorn Books, 1996) 77-79.
11. Vincent M. Rue, *Examining Postabortion Trauma: Controversy, Diagnosis & Defense* (Denton, TX: Life Dynamics, 1994); citing Magyari, et. al. (1987).
12. Patricia King and Melinda Beck, "Persuasion, Not Blame: Now, a 'kinder,

gentler' pro-life movement," *Newsweek*, March 25, 1996, 61.

13. William West, M.D., "Honesty at issue," *The Dallas Morning News*, Feb. 12, 1995, 3J:1.

14. Cecily Barnes, "Pregnant Silence," *Metro*, Feb. 18-24, 1999.

15. Paul Marx, *The Death Peddlers: War on the Unborn* (Collegeville, MN: St. John's University Press, 1971) 18-21, citing transcripts from a national conference for abortion providers.

16. B. Major, P. Mueller, and K.Hildebrandt, "Attributions, Expectations, and Coping With Abortion," *J. Personality and Social Psychology*, 48(3):585-599.

17. Wanda Franz and David Reardon, "Differential Impact of Abortion on Adolescents and Adults," *Adolescence*, 27(105):161-172 (1992). See also Vaughan, *Canonical Variates of Post Abortion Syndrome* (Portsmouth, NH: Institute for Pregnancy Loss, 1990); and Steinberg, "Abortion Counseling: To Benefit Maternal Health," *American Journal of Law & Medicine* 15(4):483-517 (1989).

18. Surgeon General C. Everett Koop, Department of Health and Human Services, Letter to President Ronald Reagan, Jan. 9, 1989.

19. Gloria Feldt, "AntiChoice Spinmaster," *The Wall Street Journal*, letters section, circa Aug. 31, 1996; responding to Candace C. Crandall, "Legal but Not Safe," *The Wall Street Journal*, guest editorial, July 1996.

20. John Whitehead and Michael Patrick, "Exclusive Interview: U.S. Surgeon General C. Everett Koop," *The Rutherford Institute*, Spring 1989, 31. In a letter to David Reardon of Oct. 14, 1998, Dr. Koop agreed that Gloria Feldt, like others, had misrepresented the position he reported to President Reagan. Unfortunately, it is impossible for Dr. Koop's corrections to keep up with all the distortions.

21. E.F. Jones and J.D. Forrest,"Underreporting of Abortion in Surveys of U.S. Women: 1976 to 1988," *Demography*, 29(1):113-126 (1992).

22. Nancy Adler,"Sample Attrition in Studies of Psychosocial Sequelae of Abortion: How Great A Problem?" *J. Applied Soc. Psych.*, 6(3):240-259 (1976).

23. Mika Gissler, Elina Hemminki, Jouko Lonnqvist, "Suicides after pregnancy in Finland: 1987-94: register linkage study," *British Medical Journal*, 313:1431-4 (1996).

24. D.C. Reardon, P.G. Ney, F.L Scheuren, J.R. Cougle and P.K. Coleman, "Suicide deaths associated with pregnancy outcome: a record linkage study of 173,279 low income American women." *Archives of Womens's Mental Health*, 3(4) Suppl. 2:104 (2001). See also Reardon et. al., "Deaths Associatied with Pregnancy Outcome: A Record Linkage Study of Low-Income Women," *Southern Medical Journal*, 2002. In press.

25. Henry P. David, "Postabortion and post-partum psychiatric hospitalization," *Abortion: Medical Progress and Social Implications* (Pitman, London: Ciba Foundation Symposium 115, 1985) 150-164.

26. J.R. Cougle, D.C. Reardon, V.M. Rue, M.W. Shuping, P.K. Coleman, and P.G. Ney, "Psychiatric admissions following abortion and childbirth: a record-based study of low-income women," *Archives of Women's Mental Health* 3(4) Suppl. 2:47 (2001).

27. George Skelton, "Many in Survey Who Had Abortion Cite Guilt Feelings," *Los Angeles Times*, March 19, 1989, 28.

28. H. Söderberg, C. Andersson, L. Janzon, N.O. Sjöberg, "Selection bias in a study on how women experienced induced abortion," *Eur. J. Obstet. Gynecol. Reprod. Biol.*, 77(1):67-70 (1998); Adler,"Sample Attrition in Studies of Psychosocial Sequelae of Abortion?" op. cit. (ch. 2 no. 22).

## CHAPTER THREE: FORBIDDING THE GRIEF

1. James Davison Hunter, *Before the Shooting Begins: Searching for Democracy in America's Cultural War* (New York: The Free Press, 1994) 93.
2. J.R. Ashton, "The Psychosocial Outcome of Induced Abortion," *British Journal of Ob&Gyn.*, 87:1115-1122 (1980); C.A. Barnard, *The Long-Term Psychosocial Effects of Abortion* (Portsmouth, NH: Institute for Pregnancy Loss, 1990); E.M. Belsey et al., "Predictive Factors in Emotional Response to Abortion: King's Termination Study - IV," *Soc. Sci. & Med.*, 11:71-82 (1977); B. Lask, "Short-term Psychiatric Sequelae to Therapeutic Termination of Pregnancy," *Br. J. Psychiatry*, 126:173-177 (1975); A. Lazarus, "Psychiatric Sequelae of Legalized Elective First Trimester Abortion," *Journal of Psychosomatic Ob&Gyn.*, 4:141-150 (1985); W.B. Miller, "An Empirical Study of the Psychological Antecedents and Consequences of Induced Abortion," *Journal of Social Issues*, 48(3):67-93 (1992); P.G. Ney and A.R. Wickett, "Mental Health and Abortion: Review and Analysis," *Psychiatr. J. Univ. Ottawa*, 14(4):506-16 (1989).

## CHAPTER FIVE: MATERNAL CONFUSION

1. 1. Philip G. Ney, T. Fung, and A.R. Wickett, "Relationship Between Induced Abortion and Child Abuse and Neglect: Four Studies," *Pre- and Perinatal Psychology Journal*, 8(1):43-64 (1993); M. Benedict, R. White, and P. Cornely, "Maternal Perinatal Risk Factors and Child Abuse," *Child Abuse and Neglect*, 9:217-224 (1985).

## CHAPTER SIX: MIND GAMES

1. K. Franco et.al., "Anniversary Reactions and Due Date Responses Following Abortion" *Psychother Psychosom* 52:151-154 (1989).
2. Philip Ney, "The Effects of Pregnancy Loss on Women's Health," *Soc. Sci. Med.* 48(9):1193-1200 (1994).

## CHAPTER SEVEN: CONNECTIONS TO THE PAST

1. K. Franco et. al., "Anniversary Reactions and Due Date Responses Following Abortion," op. cit. (ch. 6 no. 1).
2. L.H. Roht et. al., "Increase Reporting of Menstrual Symptoms Among Women Who Used Induced Abortion," *Am. J. Obstetrics Gynecology*, 127:356 (1977).
3. Cindy Hendrickson, "Consequences," *The Post-Abortion Review*, 5(2):8 (Spring 1997). www.afterabortion.info.

## CHAPTER EIGHT: ABORTION AS A TRAUMATIC EXPERIENCE

1. For a more complete information on the Bobbitt case see a series of articles in *The. Post-Abortion Review*, 4(2):1-15 (Spring-Summer 1996). These articles are also posted on the Internet at www.afterabortion.info.

2. Theodor Reik, "Men, Women, and the Unborn Child," *Psychoanalysis* 2:8 (Fall 1953).

3. Victor Calef, "The Hostility of Parents to Children: Some Notes on Infertility, Child Abuse, and Abortion," *Intl. J Psychoanalytic Psychotherapy* 1(1):76 (Feb. 1972).

4. *Diagnostic and Statistical Manual of Mental Disorders, 4th Edition* (Washington, DC: American Psychiatric Association Press, 1994).

5. Judith Lewis Herman, M.D., *Trauma and Recovery* (New York: Basic Books, (1992) 34.

6. Ibid, 35.

7. J.P. Wilson, *Trauma, Transformation and Healing: An Integrative Approach to Theory, Research, and Post-Traumatic Therapy* (New York: Brunner-Mazel, 1989).

8. David C. Reardon, Julie Makimaa and Amy Sobie, *Victims and Victors: Speaking Out About Their Pregnancies, Abortions, and Children Resulting from Sexual Assault* (Springfield, IL: Acorn Books, 2000).

9. Linda Bird Francke, *The Ambivalence of Abortion* (New York: Random House, 1978) 84-95, 167; Reardon, *Aborted Women, Silent No More*, op. cit. (introduction, no. 1) 51, 126.

10. D.E.H. Russell, *Sexual Exploitation: Rape, Child Sexual Abuse, and Sexual Harassment* (Beverly Hills, CA: Sage, 1984).

11. Sallie Tisdale, "We Do Abortions Here," *Harper's Magazine*, Oct. 7, 1987.

12. Herman, *Trauma and Recovery*, op. cit. (ch. 8, no. 5) 54.

13. Zimmerman, *Passage Through Abortion*, op. cit. (introduction, no. 1) 69. In Zimmerman's study, only 15 percent explicitly denied that the fetus was a person or a human life (194-195). In a national poll, 74 percent of women with a history of abortion agreed with a statement that abortion is morally wrong. (*Los Angeles Times* Poll, March 19, 1989.) See also Hunter, *Before the Shooting Begins*, op. cit. (ch. 3, no. 1) 93, regarding views of the general population regarding the fact that abortion causes the death of a human life.

14. Zimmerman, *Passage Through Abortion,* op. cit. (introduction, no. 1) 194-195; Miller, "An Empirical Study of the Psychological Antecedents and Consequences of Induced Abortion," op. cit. (ch. 3, no. 2); also Reardon, *Aborted Women, Silent No More*, op. cit. (introduction, no. 1).

15. Zimmerman, *Passages Through Abortion*, 139; also Reardon, *Aborted Women, Silent No More*, 16-18. Both op. cit. (introduction, no. 1).

16. Even the prominent abortion defender Daniel Callahan, director of the Hastings Center, writes: "That men have long coerced women into unwanted abortion when it suits their purposes is well-known but rarely mentioned. Data reported by the Alan Guttmacher Institute indicate that some 30 percent of women have an abortion because someone else, not the woman, wants it." Daniel

Callahan, "An Ethical Challenge to Prochoice Advocates," *Commonweal*, Nov. 23, 1990, 684. Similarly, a survey of women who subsequently regretted their abortions found that 55 percent reported feeling "forced" into their abortion by other people, with 61 percent saying they felt their lives at that time were being controlled by others (Reardon, *Aborted Women, Silent No More*, op. cit. (introduction, no. 1) 11. Similar findings are reported in Zimmerman, *Passages Through Abortion*, op. cit. (introduction, no. 1) 110-112, 122; and Miller, "An Empirical Study of the Psychological Antecedents and Consequences of Induced Abortion," op. cit. (ch. 3, no. 2).

17. Magda Denes, *In Necessity and Sorrow: Life and Death in an Abortion Hospital* (New York: Basic Books, Inc., 1976) 57.

18. Frederica Mathewes-Green, *Real Choices* (Sisters, OR: Multnomah, 1994) 19.

19. Jane Doe, "There Just Wasn't Room in Our Lives Now for Another Baby," *New York Times*, May 14, 1976.

20. Colman McCarthy, "A Psychological View of Abortion," op. cit. (ch. 2, no. 3).

21. Catherine Barnard, *The Long-Term Psychological Effects of Abortion*," op. cit. (ch. 3, no. 2).

22. Adler, "Sample Attrition in Studies of Psycho-social Sequelae of Abortion," op. cit. (ch. 2, no. 22).

23. Rachel L. Anderson et.al., "Methodological Considerations in Empirical Research on Abortion, in *Post-Abortion Syndrome: Its Wide Ramifications*, ed. Peter Doherty (Cambridge, Great Britain: Cambridge University Press, 1995) 103-115.

## CHAPTER NINE: MEMORIES UNLEASHED

1. Vincent M. Rue, Ph.D., *Post Abortion Trauma: Controversy, Diagnosis & Defense* (Lewisville, TX: Life Dynamics, 1994), 40.

2. Lenore Terr, *Too Scared to Cry* (New York: Basic Books, 1990). See especially chapter 13 concerning examples of post-traumatic reenactment.

3. Reardon, *Aborted Women, Silent No More*, op. cit. (introduction, no. 1) 81.

## CHAPTER TEN: REENACTING TRAUMA

1. Terr, *Too Scared to Cry*, op. cit. (ch. 9, no. 2). See especially ch. 13.

2. E.R. Parson, "Post-Traumatic Self Disorders: Theoretical and Practical Considerations in Psychotherapy of Vietnam War Veterans," in *Human Adaption to Extreme Stress*, eds. J.P. Wilson et. al. (New York: Plenum Press, 1988).

3. Herman, M.D., *Trauma and Recovery*, op. cit. (ch. 8, no. 5) 1-2.

4. Joel Osler Brende, M.D., FAPA, "Post-Trauma Sequelae Following Abortion and Other Traumatic Events" *Association for Interdisciplinary Research in Values and Social Change*, 7(1):1-8 (July-Aug. 1994).

5. R.F. Badgley et. al., *Report of the Committee on the Abortion Law* (Ottawa: Supply and Services, 1977) 313-319.

6. Mika Gissler et. al., "Pregnancy-associated deaths in Finland 1987-1994—definition problems and benefits of record linkage," *Acta Obstet. Gynecol. Scand.*,

76:651-657 (1997); D.C. Reardon et. al., "Suicide deaths associated with pregnancy outcome," op. cit. (ch. 2, no. 24).

7. Cougle et. al., "Psychiatric admissions following abortion and childbirth," op. cit. (ch. 2, no. 26).

8. T. Thomas, C.D. Tori, J.R. Wile, and S.D. Scheidt, "Psychosocial Characteristics of Psychiatric Inpatients with Reproductive Losses," *Journal of Health Care for the Poor and Underserved* 7(1):15-23 (1996).

## CHAPTER ELEVEN: REPEAT ABORTIONS

1. M. Tornbom et.al., "Repeat Abortion: A Comparative Study," *Journal of Psychosomatic Obstetrics and Gynecology,* 17:208-214 (1996); M. Bracken et.al.,"First and Repeat Abortions: A Study of Decision Making and Delay," *Journal of Biosocial Science,* 7:473-491 (1975).

2. M. Shepard and M. Bracken, "Contraceptive Practice and Repeat Abortion: An Epidemiological Investigation," *Journal of Biosocial Science,* 11:289-302 (1979); Kuzma and Kissinger, "Patterns of Alcohol and Cigarette Use in Pregnancy," *Neurobehavoral Tocicology and Tertology,* 3:211-221 (1981).

3. M.A. Koenig and M Zelnik, "Repeat Pregnancies Among Metropolitan Area Teenagers, 1971-1979," *Family Planning Perspectives* 14(6):341 (Nov.-Dec. 1982). See also M. Jacoby et. al., "Rapid Repeat Pregnancy and Experiences of Interpersonal Violence Among Low-Income Adolescents," *Am. Journal Prev. Med.* 16(4):318-321, 1999.

4. M.D. Creinin, "Conception rates after abortion with methotrexate and misoprostol," *Int'l. Journal Gynaecol. Obstet.* 65:183-188 (1999).

5. Diane M. Gianelli, "Abortion Providers Share Inner Conflicts," *American Medical News,* 3 (July 12, 1993).

## CHAPTER TWELVE: SEXUAL ABUSE AND ABORTION

1. Richard J. Gelles, *Intimate Violence in Families,* 2nd Edition, Family Studies Text Services, vol. 2 (Sage, 1990)

2. R. M. Tolman, "Protecting the children of battered women," *J. Interpersonal Violence,* 3(4):476-483 (1988).

3. Reardon, Makimaa and Sobie, *Victims and Victors,* op. cit. (ch. 8, no. 8), 20-21.

4. Gloria Steinem, *The Revolution From Within: A Book of Self-Esteem* (New York: Little Brown & Company, 1992); Patricia Ireland, *What Women Want* (New York: Penguin Books 1996).

5. Amy R. Sobie and David Reardon, "The Benediction of Kate Michelman: A Case Study on Coping with Post-Abortion Trauma," *The Post Abortion Review,* 7(1):3-4 (Jan.-March 1999). www.afterabortion.info.

## CHAPTER THIRTEEN: SOMETHING INSIDE HAS DIED

1. J. Wall, "A Study of Alcoholism in Women," *American Journal of Psychiatry*

93:943, 1937; G. Lolli, "Alcoholism in Women," *Connecticut Rev. Alcoholism* 5:9-11, 1953.

2. E. Morrissey and M. Schuckit,"Stressful life events and alcohol problems among women seen at a detoxication center," *J. Studies Alcohol* 39(9):1559-1576 (1978); R.W. Wilsnack, S.C. Wilsnack and A.D. Klassen, "Women's drinking and drinking problems: Patterns from a 1981 national survey," *Am. J. Public Health* 74:1231-1238 (1984); A. Klassen and S. Wilsnack, "Sexual experience and drinking among women in a U.S. national survey," *Arch. Sex. Behav.* 15(5):363 (1986); Thomas et. al., "Psychosocial characteristics of psychiatric inpatients with reproductive losses," op. cit. (ch. 10, no. 8); S.J. Drower and E.S. Nash, "Therapeutic abortion on psychiatric grounds. Part I. A local study," *S. African Medical J.* 54(15):604-608 (Oct. 7, 1978); L.G. Keith et. al., "Substance abuse in pregnant women: recent experience at the Perinatal Center for Chemical Dependence of Northwestern Memorial Hospital," *Obstet. Gynecol.* 73(5, Pt. 1):715-720 (May 1989); K. Yamaguchi, "Drug use and its social covariates from the period of adolescence to young adulthood. Some implications from longitudinal studies,"*Recent Dev. Alcohol* 8:125-143 (1990); H. Amaro et. al., "Drug use among adolescent mothers: profile of risk," *Pediatrics* 84(1):144-151 (July 1989); A.S. Oro and S.D. Dixon, "Prenatal cocaine and methamphetamine exposure: maternal and neo-natal correlates," *Pediatrics* 111(4):571-578 (1987); D.A. Frank et. al., "Cocaine use during pregnancy, prevalence and correlates," *Pediatrics* 82(6):888-895 (Dec. 1988).

3. David C. Reardon and Philip G. Ney, "Abortion and subsequent substance abuse," *Am. J. Drug Alcohol Abuse* 26(1):61-75 (2000).

4. Ibid.

5. Wallerstein, Kurtz, and Bar-Din, "Psychological Sequelae of Therapeutic Abortion in Young Unmarried Women," *Arch. Gen. Psychiatry* 27:828 (1972).

6. David C. Reardon, "The Abortion/Suicide Connection," *The Post Abortion Review* 1(2):1-2 (Summer 1993).

7. B. Garfinkle et. al, *Stress, Depression and Suicide: A Study of Adolescents in Minnesota* (Minneapolis: University of Minnesota Extension Service, 1986).

8. See Appendix C.

9. Herman, *Trauma and Recovery*, op. cit. (ch. 8, no. 5) 50.

10. Gissler et. al., "Suicides after pregnancy in Finland," op. cit. (ch. 2, no. 23).

11. David C. Reardon, et al., "Deaths Associated with Pregnancy Outcome," op. cit. (ch. 2, no. 24).

12. Christopher L. Morgan, et. al., "Mental health may deteriorate as a direct effect of induced abortion," letters section, BMJ 314:902, 22 March, 1997.

13. See also Carl Tischler, "Adolescent Suicide Attempts Following Elective Abortion," *Pediatrics* 68(5):670 (1981); E. Joanne Angelo, "Psychiatric Sequelae of Abortion: The Many Faces of Post-Abortion Grief," *Linacre Quarterly* 59:69-80 (May 1992); David Grimes, "Second-Trimester Abortions in the United States, Family Planning Perspectives 16(6):260; Myre Sim and Robert Neisser, "Post-Abortive Psychoses," in *The Psychological Aspects of Abortion*, ed. D. Mall and W.F. Watts, (Washington D.C.: University Publications of America, 1979); H. Houston and L. Jacobson, "Overdose and termination of pregnancy: an important association?" *Br. J. Gen Pract.* 46(413):737-738, Dec. 1996.

14. L. Appleby, "Suicide during pregnancy and in the first postnatal year," *British Medical Journal* 302:137-140 (1991); B. Jansson, "Mental disorders after abortion," *Acta Psychiatr Scand.* 41(1):87-110 (1965); G. Hoyer and E. Lund, "Suicide among women related to number of children in marriage," *Arch. Gen. Psychiatry* 50(2):134-137 (Feb. 1993).

15. M.M. Linehan, J.L. Goodstein, S.L. Nielsen, and J.A. Chiles, "Reasons for staying alive when you are thinking about killing yourself: The reasons for living inventory," *J. Counseling Clinical Psychology* 51(2):276-286 (1983).

16. Tischler, "Adolescent Suicide Attempts Following Elective Abortion"; and Angelo, "Psychiatric Sequelae of Abortion." Both op. cit. (ch. 13, no. 13).

17. R.F. Badgley, D.F. Caron and M.G. Powell, *Report of the Committee on the Operation of the Abortion Law* (Ottawa: Supply and Services, Ottawa, 1977) 313-321.

18. J. Nelson, "Data request from Delegate Marshall, Interagency Memorandum," Virginia Department of Medical Assistance Services, Mar. 21, 1997.

19. Reardon et al., "Deaths associated with pregnancy outcome," op. cit. (ch. 2, no. 24).

## CHAPTER FOURTEEN: BROKEN BABIES

1. Snead, Elizabeth, "'Park': Pedophilia, abortion, uncensored," *USA Today.* This news report was posted online at www.usatoday.com/life/enter/tv6/25/00.

2. Reardon, *Aborted Women, Silent No More*, op. cit. (introduction, no. 1) 129-130.

3. A. McFadden, "The Link Between Abortion and Child Abuse," *Family Resources Center News*, Jan. 1998, 20.

4. Charles M. Sennott, "S.C. Tragedy Has Its Roots in Troubled Life," *Boston Sunday Globe*, Nov. 6, 1994, 1.

5. P. Ney, T. Fung, and A.R. Wickett,"Relationship Between Induced Abortion and Child Abuse and Neglect: Four Studies," *Pre- and Perinatal Psychology Journal*, 8(1):43-63 (Fall 1993); M. Benedict, R. White, and P. Cornely,"Maternal Perinatal Risk Factors and Child Abuse," *Child Abuse and Neglect*, 9:217-224 (1985); E. Lewis,"Two Hidden Predisposing Factors in Child Abuse," *Child Abuse and Neglect*, 3:327-330 (1979); P. Ney,"Relationship Between Abortion and Child Abuse," *Canadian J. Psychiatry*, 24:610-620 (1979).

## CHAPTER FIFTEEN: WHAT'S EATING YOU?

1. Michelle Siegel, Judith Brisman and Margot Weinshel, *Surviving an Eating Disorder: Perspectives and Strategies for Family and Friends* (New York: Harper & Row) 1988.

## CHAPTER SIXTEEN: PARADISE LOST

1. Herman, *Trauma and Recovery*, op. cit. (ch. 8, no. 5) 51.

2. Belsey et al., "Predictive Factors in Emotional Response to Abortion," op. cit. (ch. 3, no. 2).

3. Bracken and Kasl, "First and Repeat Abortions," op. cit. (ch. 11, no. 1).

4. J.R. Cougle, D.C. Reardon and P.K. Coleman, "Depression associated with abortion and childbirth: A long-term analysis of the NLSY cohort," *Arch. Women's Mental Health* 3(4) Suppl. 2:105 (2001).

5. Belsey, op. cit. (ch. 16, no. 2) 71-82; David H. Sherman et al, "The Abortion Experience in Private Practice," in *Women and Loss: Psychobiological Perspectives,* eds. William F. Finn et. al., The Foundation of Thanatology Series, vol. 3 (New York: Praeger Publishers, 1985) 98-107; Anne Speckhard, *Psycho-Social Stress Following Abortion* (Kansas City, MO: Sheed & Ward, 1987); Dennis A. Bagarozzi, "Post-Traumatic Stress Disorders in Women Following Abortion: Some Considerations and Implications for Marital/Couple Therapy," *International Journal of Family and Marriage* 1:51-68 (1993); Janet Mattinson, "The Effects of Abortion on Marriage," in *Abortion: Medical Progress and Social Implications* (Ciba Foundation Symposium, 1995) 165-177; Victor Calef, "The Hostility of Parents to Children," op. cit. (ch. 8, no. 3).

## CHAPTER SEVENTEEN: NO CHOICE, HARD CHOICE, WRONG CHOICE

1. Frederica Mathewes-Green, "Unplanned Parenthood," *Policy Review,* Summer 1991.

2. This quote was reprinted as "Quote of the Week" in the *Planned Parenthood Federation of America Public Affairs Action Letter,* Sept. 25, 1992; and as "Quote of the Month," in *The Pro-Choice Network Newsletter*, May 1993; and reprinted in a commentary column by Ellen Goodman, "Not 'Choice,' but 'Better Choices,'" *The Baltimore Sun,* Sept. 18, 1992.

3. McCarthy, "A Psychological View of Abortion," op. cit. (ch. 2, no. 3).

4. Reardon, *Aborted Women, Silent No More,*" op. cit. (introduction, no. 1) 11-21. See also Zimmerman, *Passage Through Abortion,* op. cit. (introduction, no. 1) 62-70; and Miller, "An Empirical Study of the Psychological Antecedents and Consequences of Induced Abortion," op. cit. (ch. 3, no. 2).

5. *Los Angeles Times* poll, March 19, 1989, question 76.

6. Vincent M. Rue and Anne C. Speckhard, "Informed Consent and Abortion: Issues in Medicine and Counseling," *Med. & Mind* 6(1):75-94 (1992).

7. Gerald Caplan, *Principals of Preventive Psychiatry* (New York: Basic Books, 1964).

8. Howard W. Stone, *Crisis Counseling* (Fortress Press, 1976).

9. Wilbur E. Morely, "Theory of Crisis Intervention," *Pastoral Psychology* 21(203):16 (April 1970).

10. Uta Landy, "Abortion Counseling: A New Component of Medical Care," *Clinics in Obs/Gyn.* 13(1):33-41 (1986).

11. Ibid.

12. P.J. Hillard, "Physical abuse in pregnancy," *Obstet. Gynecol.* 66(2):185-190

(1995).

13. R. Gelles, "Violence and Pregnancy: Are pregnant women at greater risk for abuse?" *Journal of Marriage and the Family* 50:841-847 (1988); J. A. Gazmararian et al., "The Relationship between pregnancy intendedness and physical violence in mothers of newborns," *Obstetrics and Gynecology,* 85:1031-1038 (1995); H. Amaro, et. al, "Violence during pregnancy and substance use," *Am. J. Public Health* 80(5):575-579 (1990).

14. Tolman, "Protecting the children of battered women," op. cit. (ch. 12, no. 2).

15. E. Hilberman and K. Munson, "Sixty battered women," *Victimology* 2:460-470 (1977-1978).

16. Isabelle L. Horon and Diana Cheng, "Enhanced Surveillance for Pregnancy-Associated Mortality Maryland, 1993-1998," *JAMA* 285:1455-1459 (2001).

17. "The Many Faces of Coercion," *The Post-Abortion Review*, 8(1):4-5 (2000). www.afterabortion.info.

18. Michael Blumenfield, "Psychological Factors Involved in Request for Elective Abortion," *J. Clinical Psychiatry* 978:17-25 (Jan. 1978).

19. J. Lloyd and K.M. Laurence, "Sequelae and Support After Termination of Pregnancy for Fetal Malformation," *British Medical Journal* 290:907-909 (March 1985).

20. B.D. Blumberg, M.S. Globus and K.H. Hanson, "The psychological sequelae of abortion performed for a genetic indication," *Am.J. Obstet. Gynecol.* 122(7):799 (Aug. 1, 1975).

21. R. Furlong and R. Black "Pregnancy Termination for Genetic Indications: The Impact on Families," *Social Work in Health Care* 10(1):17 (Fall 1984).

22. Lenore Abramsky, et al., "What parents are told after prenatal diagnosis of a sex chromosome abnormality: interview and questionnaire study," *British Medical Journal* 322:463-466 (2001).

23. David C. Reardon and Jesse R. Cougle, "Depression and Unintended Pregnancy in the National Longitudinal Survey of Youth: A Cohort Study," *British Medical Journal*, 324:151-152 (2002).

## Chapter Eighteen: The Labor of Grief and Birth of Freedom

1. Therese A. Rando explains the six "R" processes of mourning in *The Treatment of Complicated Mourning* (Champaign, IL: Research Press, 1993). According to Rando, there are six processes which mourners must complete to successfully deal with their grief. These include: (1) recognizing the loss, (2) reacting to the separation, (3) recollecting and re-experiencing, (4) relinquishing attachments, (5) readjusting and (6) reinvesting. Rando provides a thorough framework for dealing with loss and grief.

2. Therese Rando, *How To Go On Living When Someone You Love Dies* (Lexington Books, New York) 17.

3. You can get a free copy of *Hope and Healing* by writing to the Elliot Institute, PO Box 7348, Springfield, IL 62791. A donation to support this service is welcome.

## APPENDIX A: THE POLITICS OF TRAUMA

1. See Herman, *Trauma and Recovery*, op. cit. (ch. 8, no. 5) 117-118, for an interesting inside look at the negotiations and public relations effort involved in battling the proposed diagnosis of "masochistic personality disorder."

2. Ibid, 14, 18.

3. Ibid, 14.

4. Ibid, 20.

5. Ibid, 8-9.

6. Mary K. Zimmerman, "Psychosocial and Emotional Consequences of Elective Abortion: A Literature Review," in ed. Paul Sachdev, *Abortion: Readings and Research* (Toronto: Butterworths, 1981) 66.

7. Vincent Rue, "Abortion and Family Relations," Testimony before the Subcommittee on the Constitution of the US Senate Judiciary Committee, U.S. Senate, 97th Congress, Washington, DC (1981).

8. "We request that you immediately cease using any reference to the American Psychiatric Association or the DSM III with respect to materials concerning 'post abortion syndrome'." Letter from J. Klein, general counsel to the American Psychiatric Association, Sept. 11, 1990.

9. Anne Speckhard and Vincent Rue, "Postabortion Syndrome: An Emerging Public Health Concern," *Journal of Social Issues*, 48:95-120 (1992).

10. Nada L. Stotland, "The Myth of Abortion Trauma Syndrome," *JAMA*, 268(15):2078-2079 (Oct. 21, 1992).

11. DSM-III-R, American Psychological Association, *Diagnostic and Statistical Manual of Mental Disorders* (Washington, D.C.: APA, 1987) 20.

12. DSM-IV, American Psychiatric Association, *Diagnostic and Statistical Manual of Mental Disorders* (Washington, D.C.: APA, 1994), 427-429.

13. C. Everett Koop, *Koop: Memoirs of America's Family Doctor* (New York: Random House, 1991), 275.

## APPENDIX B: THE COMPLEXITIES AND DISTORTIONS OF POST-ABORTION RESEARCH

1. E.F. Jones, and J.D. Forrest, "Under reporting of Abortion in Surveys of U.S. Women: 1976 to 1988," *Demography*, 29(1):113-126 (1992).

2. Söderberg et. al., "Selection bias in a study on how women experienced induced abortion," op. cit. (ch. 2, no. 28); and Adler, "Sample Attrition in Studies of Psychosocial Sequelae of Abortion," op. cit. (ch. 2, no. 22).

3. Angelo, "Psychiatric Sequelae of Abortion," op. cit. (ch. 13, no. 13); D. Brown, T.E. Elkins, and D.B. Lardson, "Prolonged Grieving After Abortion," *J. Clinical Ethics* 4(2):118-123 (1993).

4. Speckhard and Rue, "Postabortion Syndrome:," op. cit. (appendix A, no. 9); Barnard, *The Long-Term Psycho social Effects of Abortion*, op. cit. (ch. 3, no. 2).

5. David Reardon,"Psychological Reactions Reported After Abortion," *The Post-Abortion Review*, 2(3):4-8 (1994). See www.afterabortion.info.

6. A. Lazarus and R. Stern, "Psychiatric Aspects of Pregnancy Termination," *Clin. Obstet. Gynaecol.*, 13:125-134 (1986).

7. I. Kent et. al., "Emotional Sequelae of elective Abortion," *BC Med. J.* 20:118-119 (1978).

8. I. Kent, and W. Nicholls, "Bereavement in Post-Abortion Women: A Clinical Report," *World J. Psychosyn.* 13:14-17 (1981).

9. C.E. Koop, Letter to President Reagan, Jan. 9, 1989.

10. Brenda Major, Pallas Mueller and Katherine Hildebrandt, "Attributions, Expectations, and Coping With Abortion," *J. Personality and Social Psychology,* 48(3):585-599 (1985).

11. N.F. Russo and K.L. Zierk, "Abortion, Childbearing, and Women's Well-Being," *Professional Psychology,* 23(4):296-280 (1992); N.F. Russo and A.J. Dabul,"The Relationship of Abortion to Well-Being: Do Race and Religion Make A Difference?" *Professional Psychology* 28(1) (1997).

12. Kathy Nixon, "Study refutes claim that abortion threatens mental health," *Mesa Tribune,* Oct 4, 1992, I-1; Jane E. Brody, "Study Disputes Abortion Trauma," *New York Times,* Feb. 12, 1997, B12; Karl Bland, "Is Politics Tainting Research? Post-abortion syndrome disputed by ASU professor," *The Phoenix Gazette,* Oct. 6, 1992, B1.

13. David C. Reardon, "A Study of Deception: Feminist Researcher 'Proves' Abortion Increases Self-Esteem," *The Post-Abortion Review,* 3(4):4-7 (1995). See www.afterabortion.info.

14. Jones and Forrest, "Under reporting of Abortion in Surveys of U.S. Women," op. cit. (ch. 2, no. 21).

15. Söderberg et. al, "Selection Bias in a Study on How Women Experienced Induced Abortion,"op. cit. (ch. 2, no. 28); Adler, "Sample Attrition in Studies of Psycho social Sequelae of Abortion," op. cit. (ch. 2, no. 22). See also B. Major and R.H. Gramzow, "Abortion as Stigma: Cognitive and Emotional Implications of Concealment," *J. Pers. Soc. Psychol.,* 77(4):735-745 (1999), which shows that shame and secrecy regarding one's abortion is correlated to greater distress.

16. Barnard, "The Long Term Psychological Effects of Abortion," op. cit. (ch. 3, no. 2).

17. W.B. Miller, D.J. Pasta, and C.L. Dean, "Testing a Model of the Psychological Consequences of Abortion," in *The New Civil War: The Psychology, Culture, and Politics of Abortion,* eds. L. J. Beckman and S. M. Harvey (Washington, DC: American Psychological Association, 1998); see also B. Major, C. Cozzarelli, M.L. Cooper, J. Zubek, C. Richards, M. Wilhite, and R.H. Gramzow, "Psychological Responses of Women after First-trimester Abortion," *Arch. Gen. Psychiatry,* 57(8): 777-84 (Aug. 2000).

18. J.R. Cougle, D.C. Reardon and P.K. Coleman, "Depression associated with abortion and childbirth," op. cit. (ch. 16, no. 4).

19. Nada L. Stotland, "The Myth of Abortion Trauma Syndrome," *JAMA,* 268(15):2078-2079 (Oct. 21, 1992).

20. Lask, "Short-term psychiatric sequelae to therapeutic termination of pregnancy," op. cit. (ch. 3, no. 2).

21. Greer and Belsey, et. al., "Psycho social Consequences of Therapeutic Abortion:

Kings Therapeutic Study III," *Br. J. Psychiatry*, 128:74-79 (1976); and Belsey et. al., "Predictive Factors in Emotional Response to Abortion," op. cit. (ch. 3, no. 2).

22. Nada L. Stotland, *Abortion: Facts and Feelings* (Washington, DC: American Psychiatric Press, 1998) 106.

23. Nada L. Stotland, "Abortion: Social Context, Psychodynamic Implications," *Am. J. Psychiatry*, 155(7):964-967 (1998).

24. Nada L. Stotland, letter to David C. Reardon, Ph.D., Feb. 16, 1999. www.afterabortion.info.

25. "Give and Take: Notes on the Public and Personal Exchange of Views on the Psychological Effects of Abortion Between Nada Stotland and David Reardon." See www.afterabortion.info\research\StotlandRisk.htm.

26. Reardon and Cougle, "Depression and Unintended Pregnancy in the National Longitudinal Survey of Youth," op. cit. (ch. 17, no. 23).

27. D.C. Reardon and J.R. Cougle, "Pregnancy Outcome Related to Subsequent Anxiety in the National Survey of Family Growth." In preparation.

28. P.K. Coleman, D.C. Reardon, and J.R. Cougle, "Child Developmental Outcomes Associated with Maternal History of Abortion Using the NLSY Data," *Archives of Women's Mental Health* 3(4) Suppl. 2:104 (2001).

29. Reardon et. al., "Suicide deaths associated with pregnancy outcome," op. cit. (ch. 2, no. 24); Gissler, et. al. "Suicides After Pregnancy in Finland," op. cit. (ch. 2, no. 23).

30. Reardon et. al., "Depression and Unintended Pregnancy," op. cit. (ch. 17, no. 23); and Cougle et. al., "Depression associated with abortion and childbirth," op. cit. (ch. 16, no. 4).

31. See the following review article that examines 23 studies comparing women who carried to term to women who aborted. Thomas W. Strahan, "Childbirth as Protective of the Health of Women in Contrast to Induced Abortion-III: Mental Health and Well-Being," *Research Bulletin*, 12(4):1-8 (May/June 1998).

32. Thomas W. Strahan, "Sexual Dysfunction Related to Induced Abortion," *Research Bulletin*, 11(4):1-8, (Sept./Oct. 1997).

33. See the following review article that examines 25 studies comparing women who carried to term to women who aborted. Thomas W. Strahan, "Childbirth as Protective of the Health of Women in Contrast to Induced Abortion-II: Smoking, Alcohol and Drug Use," *Research Bulletin*, 12(3):1-7 (March/April 1998).

34. See H. David, et. al., *Born Unwanted: Developmental Effects of Denied Abortion* (New York: Springer, 1988).

35. Valentine Low, "The Rape that Really Changed Our Minds about Abortion," interview with Aleck Bourne, *Evening Standard*, Feb. 28, 1992, 20. The original interview was published in the *London Daily Express*, Jan. 15, 1967.

36. P.G. Ney, "Some Real Issues Surrounding Abortion, or, the Current Practice of Abortion is Unscientific," *The Journal of Clinical Ethics*, 4(2):179-180 (1993).

# INDEX

abortion as surgical rape  113–115
abortion counseling  35–38, 38–44, 154–155
abortion decision making  223–243
  role of males  227–229, 231–234
abortion, for medical reasons  235–240
accidents, after abortion  46, 140, 174, 177–178
Alan Guttmacher Institute  280
alcohol abuse *See* substance abuse
American Medical Association  271–272
American Psychiatric Association  271–272, 275
American Psychological Association  271–272, 273
amnesia  128–130
anniversary reactions  97–99, 110
anorexia *See* eating disorders
anxiety  41–44, 72–77, 241, 247–250, 287
approach-avoidance conflict  82–83
  avoidance behavior  118

Belsey, Elizabeth  313
Bobbitt, John Wayne  106–108
Bobbitt, Lorena  106–108
Bourne, Aleck  284
broken relationships, as a result of abortion  201–220 *See also* divorce
bulimia *See* eating disorders

Charcot, Jean-Martin  268, 269
child abuse, and abortion  162, 182–185
coerced abortion  227–229
connectors, to a past abortion  93–104, 122–123, 132
constriction *See* post-traumatic stress disorder (PTSD): symptoms
conversion *See* defense mechanisms

crisis, provoked by post-abortive women  141–142

defense mechanisms  81–92, 130
  conversion  90
  denial  25, 35, 52, 83, 91–92, 109, 117–118, 278, 279
  displacement  89–90
  dissociation  130–131
  introjection  87
  projection  88–89, 91
  provocative behavior  89
  reaction formation  87, 91
  regression  90
  repression  85–86, 91
  suppression  84–85, 91
  undoing  88
  withdrawal  90, 110
denial *See* defense mechanisms
depression, after abortion  32, 76, 97, 110, 111, 126, 185, 241, 281, 283, 284
displacement *See* defense mechanisms
dissociation *See* defense mechanisms
divorce, after abortion  47, 148, 203, 216, 217, 289
dreams *See* nightmares
drug abuse *See* substance abuse
DSM (APA diagnostic manual)  275

eating disorders, and abortion  15–17, 82, 92, 187–200
  anorexia  195–196
  bulimia  191–195
  compulsive overeating  196–198
Elliot Institute survey  287–288
"evil child" movies  182

fantasies  126, 159, 252, 269 *See also* hallucinations
Feldt, Gloria  44
flashbacks, to the abortion  110, 111, 122–123, 128, 134, 287

Fleming, Donna  184
Fogel, Julius  33, 118
Freud, Sigmund  269

Graves, Robert  270
grief, and the grieving process  49–62
guilt, after abortion  38, 42, 47, 48,
    51, 72, 88, 181, 273, 287

hallucinations  126–127, 287
Herman, Judith Lewis  115, 134,
    203, 268–271
Hope and Healing  255
hyperarousal *See* post-traumatic
    stress disorder (PTSD): symptoms

incest and abortion *See* sexual abuse
Institute for Pregnancy Loss  273
introjection *See* defense mechanisms
intrusion *See* post-traumatic stress
    disorder (PTSD): symptoms
intrusive thoughts, about the abortion
    57, 110, 123, 182–185

*Journal of Social Issues, The*  274
*Journal of the American Medical
    Association (JAMA)*  275, 282

Koop, C. Everett  44–45, 274, 275,
    278
Kriefels, Sheila  40

Lask, Bryan  282
Last Harvest Ministries  287
*Los Angeles Times*  20, 47

Major, Brenda  42, 279
Mann, Nancyjo  272, 273
masochism, and repeat abortion
    153–154
monthly reactions, after abortion  99–
    100
"Myth of Abortion Trauma Syndrome,
    The"  282

National Longitudinal Study of Youth
    (NLSY)  279–281
nervous breakdown, after abortion
    62, 143, 288

Ney, Philip  185, 285
Nicely, Renee  184
nightmares, after abortion  97, 101,
    110, 111, 123–126, 134, 287

obsession with death or punishment,
    after abortion  137
obsessive-compulsive disorder, and
    abortion  110, 136–137

Parson, E.R.  134
personality disorders, and abortion
    47, 144, 280
Planned Parenthood  40, 44, 57, 280
post-abortion counseling  40, 52,
    118, 258–261, 287
post-abortion syndrome, as a form of
    PTSD  272–276, 280, 281
post-abortion trauma  39, 101, 110–
    120, 133–144, 181, 185, 271–
    276, 282–283
post-partum psychosis, after abortion
    47, 76, 127, 144
post-traumatic stress disorder (PTSD)
    106, 108–120, 121–132, 133–
    144, 174, 268–276, 277
  causes of PTSD  111–113
  symptoms
    constriction  109–111, 119,
      121, 133
    hyperarousal  109–111, 119,
      121, 133
    intrusion  110–111, 114, 119,
      121, 133–136
Project Rachel  143, 273
projection *See* defense mechanisms
promiscuity, after abortion  163, 170–
    172
provocative behavior *See* defense
    mechanisms
psychiatric treatment, after abortion
    46–47, 143–144, 284
psychosomatic illness, after abortion
    131–132
psychotic reactions, after abortion
    47, 127, 142–144

Rachel's Vineyard  219, 259–261

rage, after abortion 180–185
rape and abortion *See* sexual abuse
reaction formation *See* defense
    mechanisms
regression *See* defense mechanisms
religious beliefs, and abortion 96
repeat abortions 110, 145–155, 160–
    162, 170–172, 288
replacement pregnancies 72–75,
    88, 110, 148–151
repression *See* defense mechanisms
research on post-abortion trauma
    271–276, 277–286
risk factors, for post-abortion trauma
    69, 279, 285
*Roe v. Wade* 272
Rosenberg Self-Esteem Scale 279–281
Rue, Susan Stanford 273
Rue, Vincent 272–276
Russo, Nancy Felipe 280–281

self-blame, after abortion 89, 115–
    117, 164
self-destructive behavior, after
    abortion 110, 114, 140, 165,
    168–178, 287
sexual abuse, and abortion 16, 100,
    114, 157–165, 260, 269–270
    incest 157–165, 269–270
    rape 114, 164–165, 173–174,
    269–270
sexual dysfunction, after abortion
    204, 205, 216–218, 284
"shell shock" 270–271
shoplifting
    after abortion 139
    and reenactment of trauma 162
sleep disorders, after abortion 125
Smith, Susan 185
smoking, and abortion 284
Stanford, Susan *See* Rue, Susan
    Stanford
Steinem, Gloria 31
sterilization, surgical 217–218, 287
Stotland, Nada 283, 284
substance abuse, after abortion
    92, 144, 148, 168–171, 172,
    204

alcohol abuse 82, 90, 110, 162,
    168–171, 172, 241, 284
drug abuse 82, 90, 110, 162,
    168–171, 172, 284, 287
suicide, and abortion 82, 92, 97,
    110, 140, 170, 172–178, 284
Suicide Anonymous 173
suppression *See* defense mechanisms
survivor guilt, after abortion
    111, 113, 138, 161, 196
symbolic reenactment, of trauma
    134–136, 165, 181–182

Taft, Charlotte 40
Thorn, Vicki 273
traumatic reenactment, and abortion
    92, 133–144, 148–151

Uchtman, Meta 173
undoing *See* defense mechanisms
*USA Today* 279

*Victims and Victors* 164
Victims of Choice 287
Vietnam Veterans Against the War
    270
violation of conscience or maternal
    desires 20, 42, 87, 116 *See also*
    abortion decision making
violation of physical integrity 113–
    115
violence, abortion as an experience of
    113–115
violence, against pregnant women
    227–228
violence, resulting from abortion
    177, 185, 212

*Wall Street Journal, The* 44
West, William 40
*Will I Cry Tomorrow?* 273
withdrawal *See* defense mechanisms
Women Exploited By Abortion 272,
    287

Yealland, Lewis 270

# ADDITIONAL RESOURCES ON POST-ABORTION ISSUES

**Finally, something new to say about abortion.**

# Making Abortion Rare

*A Healing Strategy for
a Divided Nation*

Making
Abortion
Rare

*A Healing Strategy
for a Divided Nation*

David C. Reardon

Is it possible for abortion to become rare even though it remains legal? Yes! This book shows readers a clear and practical strategy for making abortion not simply illegal, but unthinkable.

*Making Abortion Rare* reveals a comprehensive and compassionate program of pastoral, political, and educational reform  that will reduce antagonism, create a healing environment for those who have been wounded by abortion, and draw Americans together through their common concern for women.

Here's what the reviewers are saying:

> *"Practical and realistic, yet free of moral compromise . . .* Making Abortion Rare *will accomplish what its title claims—and much more . . . Brilliant."*
>
> —Rev. Paul Marx, Founder, Human Life International

> *"This is exactly what women who have had abortions have been wanting to hear . . . I pray that this book will be widely read. It provides us with the road map to a kinder and gentler pro-life movement, one which will achieve far more, far more quickly, than we have ever achieved in the past."*
>
> —Nancyjo Mann, Founder, Women Exploited by Abortion

> *"David Reardon has shown a rare grasp of the current dynamics of the abortion controversy as it is today. His analysis and suggested pro-life strategy  are right on the mark."*
>
> —Dr. Jack Willke, President, International Right to Life

> *"Under the old rules of the abortion debate, where the rights of women and the unborn were in opposition, there was no room for agreement. But Reardon has changed the rules . . . From this point on, the abortion debate will never be the same."*
>
> —Mark Crutcher, Author, *Lime 5*

**How can you help others—or yourself—find emotional and spiritual healing after abortion?**

**Read this book!**

# The Jericho Plan
*Breaking Down the Walls*
*Which Prevent*
*Post-Abortion Healing*

"The Jericho Plan *arrived just this morning and I have already read it from cover to cover . . . once again, you have been instrumental in another miracle!"* —*Connie Nykiel, Author,* Nobody Told Me I Could Cry

*The Jericho Plan* shows how women and men struggling with past abortions feel trapped, unable to express their pain or seek comfort from their loved ones. On the one hand, they fear that those who are pro-life will condemn and reject them. On the other hand, they fear that those who are pro-choice will deny their need to grieve their loss.

Prepared with the help of experienced post-abortion counselors and clergy, *The Jericho Plan* teaches readers how to break through these and many other obstacles which prevent post-abortion healing. You will find comfort and direction for your church, your loved ones, and perhaps even yourself.

- Learn seven steps to post-abortion healing.
- Become a "stealth healer" and give hope to women and men plagued by post-abortion grief—even if their abortions are still secret!
- Create a healing environment in your church and community by offering dynamic examples of God's mercy and grace.
- And much more . . .

While useful for anyone interested in post-abortion healing, *The Jericho Plan* is especially directed toward ministers and clergy. Through background information on post-abortion issues, compelling testimonies, sample sermons, and an extensive directory of resources, it shows them how to preach on abortion in a compassionate and unifying way.

**List Price: $8.95 / Quantity Discounts Available**
**Available through Acorn Books at 1-888-412-2676**

## Does abortion truly help pregnant rape and incest victims?

Learn the truth about abortion in the "hard cases."

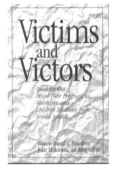

# Victims and Victors
### Speaking Out About Their Pregnancies, Abortions and Children Resulting From Sexual Assault

In this compelling book, 192 women reveal the seldom heard truth: most pregnant sexual assault victims don't want abortions! Among those who do abort, abortion has only aggravated their suffering.

This is the largest, most comprehensive study ever published on this issue. These women deserve to be heard.

"After my daughter was born, it was love at first sight . . . I know I made the right decision in having her."  —Nancy "Cole"

"Often I cry. Cry because I could not stop the attacks. Cry because my daughter is dead. And I cry because it still hurts."  —Edith Young

"They say abortion is the easy way out, the best thing for everyone, but they are wrong. It has been over 15 years, and I still suffer."  —"Rebecca Morris"

"Abortion does not help or solve a problem—it only compounds and creates another trauma for the already grieving victim by taking  away the one thing that can bring joy."  —Helene Evans

"The effects of the abortion are much more far-reaching than the effects of the rape in my life."  —"Patricia Ryan"

"I thank God for the strength He gave me to go through the bad times and for all of the joy in the good times. I will never regret that I chose to give life to my daughter."  —Mary Murray

**List Price: $11.95 / Quantity Discounts Available**
**Available through Acorn Books at 1-888-412-2676**

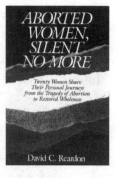

## The Essential Reference Guide to the Risks of Induced Abortion

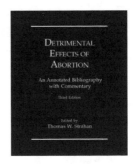

# Detrimental Effects of Abortion
## *An Annotated Bibliography with Commentary*

*Detrimental Effects of Abortion* is an indispensable reference guide to studies on the most hotly contested social, moral and political topic of our day.

*This is the only publication to list, all in one place, all the major statistically significant studies on abortion.*

This newly revised third edition of *Detrimental Effects of Abortion* has been updated with listings for recent studies, additional commentary by the editor and a newly revised table of contents.

### More than 1200 Entries

Edited by attorney and medical/legal expert Thomas W. Strahan, this bibliography includes citations to more than 1200 studies—with summaries of the research findings for each entry—that have been organized into more than 40 categories and subcategories. Major topic categories include:

- Abortion Decision Making
- Standard of Care for Abortion
- Psychological Effects of Abortion
- Social Effects and Implications of Abortion
- Physical Effects of Abortion
- Abortion and Maternal Mortality
- Adolescents and Abortion

*Detrimental Effects of Abortion* is an invaluable resource for researchers, therapists, counselors, medical professionals, students, political activists and others interested in abortion as a social issue. This is a reference guide you will want to have on your bookshelf!

**List Price: $34.95 / Quantity Discounts Available**
**Available through Acorn Books at 1-888-412-2676**

# The Post-Abortion Review

*"Your newsletter is TOP-NOTCH. God bless you for your hard work."*

*"Incredibly powerful. If only more people would read it, abortion would end."*

*"I'm so excited about your publication. I've gone through an abortion myself, just two years ago. This is a much-needed area of research."*

*"Once in a while I read something that really makes me feel great, and this just happened to me. The whole newsletter is terrific. Keep up the great work!"*

Our readers love *The Post-Abortion Review*, and so will you. This quarterly journal focuses on the impact of abortion on women, men, families and society.

*The Post-Abortion Review* is edited by Dr. David Reardon, a leading expert on post-abortion issues. It includes summaries of the latest research, critiques of pro-abortion propaganda, personal testimonies, book reviews, pro-life news and views, and more. No pro-lifer should be without it!

Past topics covered include:

- The Abortion/Suicide Connection
- Forgotten Fathers: Men and Abortion
- Abortion and the Feminization of Poverty
- Abortion and Domestic Violence
- The Wounded Generation: Survivors of Abortion
- The Hidden Agenda of Population Control Zealots
- Abortion Trauma and Child Abuse

The recommended donation for a one-year subscription (four issues) is $20 per year. To subscribe, send your check or money order payable to the Elliot Institute to: Post-Abortion Review, PO Box 7348, Springfield, IL 62791-7348.

**Special Offer! Save $15!** For a donation of $30 or more, you will receive a one-year subscription to *The Post-Abortion Review*, plus one copy each of Dr. Reardon's books *The Jericho Plan* and *Making Abortion Rare*. If, after reading these books, you aren't satisfied for any reason, simply return the books for a full refund—no questions asked! To receive this offer, simply send a check with a note reading "Special Offer" to the address above.